Milwaukee Wisconsin

Charter of the City of Milwaukee

Being Chapter 184, Laws of 1874...

Milwaukee Wisconsin

Charter of the City of Milwaukee
Being Chapter 184, Laws of 1874...

ISBN/EAN: 9783744721660

Printed in Europe, USA, Canada, Australia, Japan

Cover: Foto ©Suzi / pixelio.de

More available books at **www.hansebooks.com**

THE

CHARTER

OF THE

CITY OF MILWAUKEE

BEING CHAPTER 184, LAWS OF 1874,

As amended by subsequeut acts of the Legislature to and including the acts of 1891, and General Laws operating as amendments thereto, up to and including those passed by the Legislature of 1895.

Compiled and annotated under instructions of the Common Council

BY

CHARLES H. HAMILTON,

CITY ATTORNEY.

MILWAUKEE;
Edward Keogh, Printer, 586 and 588 Broadway.
1895.

NOTE.

The resolution instructing the City Attorney to revise the Charter further instructs him to insert annotations of Supreme Court decisions which construe or refer to Charter provisions. It is believed no case of this nature has been omitted. There has been no attempt to make a general digest of all decisions of our Supreme Court involving questions of municipal law, but notes of some decisions construing charters of other cities having charter provisions similar to ours, and some decisions upon matters of general interest which may assist city officers in the performance of their municipal duties, have also been inserted.

The notes have further been made with special reference to construction of the Charter provision under consideration rather than to the general questions of law involved. All citations of Wisconsin decisions are to the top paging in the reports.

I have not attempted to go back of the work performed by City Attorney Elliott in 1889. Its accuracy has been proved by six years of daily use, and numerous conflicts in the courts.

Contents.

[EDITION 1895.]

CHARTER OF THE CITY OF MILWAUKEE.

Chapter 184, Laws of 1874,

As amended by Acts of the Legislature to and including
Laws of 1891, and General Laws operating
as amendments thereto, up to and
including those passed by the
Legislature of 1895.

AN ACT to revise, consolidate and amend the charter of the city
of Milwaukee, approved February 20, 1852, and the several acts
amendatory thereof.

*The people of the State of Wisconsin, represented in senate
and assembly, do enact as follows:*

CHAPTER I.

CITY AND WARD BOUNDARIES.

SECTION 1. All the district of country in the county
of Milwaukee contained within the limits and boundaries
hereinafter described, shall be a city by the name of Milwaukee; and the people now inhabiting, and those who
shall hereafter inhabit, within the district of country so
described, shall be a municipal corporation by the name
of the "City of Milwaukee," and shall have the general
powers possessed by municipal corporations at common
law; and, in addition thereto, shall possess the powers
hereinafter specifically granted; and the authorities thereof
shall have perpetual succession, shall be capable of contracting and being contracted with, of sueing and being

*The city of Mil-
waukee.*

Powers conferred.

sued, of pleading and being impleaded, in all courts of law and equity; and shall have a common seal, and may change and alter the same at pleasure.

City charters are public acts of which courts are bound to take judicial notice.

> Janesville vs. M. & M. R. R. Co., 7 Wis., 410.
> Terry vs. Milwaukee, 15 Wis., 543.
> Alexander vs. Milwaukee, 16 Wis., 264.
> State ex rel Cothren vs. Lean, 9 Wis., 254.

A municipal corporation cannot be made liable as garnishee.

> Burnham vs. Fond du Lac, 15 Wis., 193.
> Buftham vs. Racine, 26 Wis., 449.
> Merrell vs. Campbell, 49 Wis., 535.

The corporate authorities of Milwaukee were authorized to contract for the construction of a breakwater designed to protect certain streets in the city from destruction by the waters of Lake Michigan, by virtue of the general powers possessed by municipal corporations at common law.

> Miller vs. Milwaukee, 14 Wis., 699.

A municipal corporation, under its general common law powers, has no authority to employ counsel to aid in criminal prosecutions instituted on behalf of the State against persons, formerly officers of the city, for crimes committed under color of the discharge of their official duties.

> Butler vs. Milwaukee, 15 Wis., 546.

Boundaries of the city of Milwaukee. SECTION 2. The territory included within the following boundaries and limits shall constitute the city of Milwaukee, to-wit: Beginning on the shore of Lake Michigan where it is intersected by the quarter section line in section ten of township seven north, range twenty-two east, in said county of Milwaukee, running thence west along the said quarter section line to the northwest corner of the southeast one-fourth of section twelve, of township seven north, range twenty-one east, thence south along the north and south quarter section line through said section twelve, and the continuation thereof to the southwest corner of the southeast one-fourth of section twenty-five, of township seven north, range twenty-one east, thence east along the south line of said southeast one-fourth section twenty-five to the southeast corner thereof, thence south along the west line of section thirty-one, of township seven north, range twenty-two east and the continuation thereof, to the southwest corner of the northwest one-fourth of section seven, of township six north, range twenty-two east, thence east on the quarter section line running east and west through said section seven, and the continuation thereof to the one-eighth section line running north and south through the southwest one-fourth of section nine in township six north, range twenty-two east, thence south along said one-eighth section line to the south line of said section nine, thence east along the south line of sections nine and ten to the east boundary of said county of Milwaukee, thence north to a point due east of the place or point of beginning, thence west to said place or point of beginning.

As amended by Chapter 449, Laws of 1891. Former amendments to Charter of 1874, are as follows:

Chapter 272, Laws of 1883. Chapter 116, Laws of 1885. Chapter 37, Laws of 1887. Chapters 56, 450 and 437, Laws of 1889.

SECTION 3. The said city shall be divided in (eighteen) wards, numbered and bounded as follows: **Number of wards.**

Chapter 388, Laws of 1885. Chapters 36, 37, 38 and 416, Laws of 1887. Chapter 449, Laws of 1891.

The First ward shall embrace all that part of said district which lies east of the center of the Milwaukee river, north of the center line of Juneau avenue, south of the center line of Brady street, produced east, to its intersection with the center line of Prospect avenue, thence northeasterly with the center line of Prospect avenue to a point where it would be intersected by the northerly line of lot twenty, in block one hundred and ninety-nine, in Rogers' addition, produced west, thence along the northerly line of said lot to Lake Michigan, thence east to the east boundary of the city. **First ward boundaries.**

The Second ward shall embrace all that part of said district which lies west of the center of the Milwaukee river, south of the center line of Vliet street, north of the center line of Cedar street, and east of the center line of Thirteenth street. **Second ward boundaries.**

The Third ward shall embrace all that part of said district which lies east and north of the center line of the Milwaukee river and of the straight cut harbor, and south of the center line of Wisconsin street and a line east from the point where the center line of Wisconsin street intersects the shore of Lake Michigan. **Third ward boundaries.**

Fourth ward boundaries.

The Fourth ward shall embrace all that part of said district which lies west of the center line of Milwaukee river, south of the center line of Cedar street, east of the center line of Thirteenth street and of Muskego avenue, to the south boundary line of section thirty and north of the south boundary line of sections twenty-nine and thirty, in township seven north, range twenty-two east.

Fifth ward boundaries.

The Fifth ward shall embrace all that part of said district which lies east of the center line of First avenue, south of the south boundary lines of the Fourth and Third wards, hereinbefore described, and north of the center line of Greenfield avenue and its continuation east, to the east boundary of the city.

Sixth ward boundaries.

The Sixth ward shall embrace all that part of said district which lies west of the center of the Milwaukee river, north of the center line of Vliet street, east of the center line of Seventh street, and south of the center line of North avenue.

Seventh ward boundaries.

The Seventh ward shall embrace all that part of said district which lies east of the center of the Milwaukee river, north of the center of Wisconsin street and a line due east from the point where the center line of Wisconsin street intersects the shore of Lake Michigan, and south of the center line of Juneau avenue.

Eighth ward boundaries.

The Eighth ward shall embrace all that part of said district which lies south of the north boundary lines of sections thirty-one and thirty-two, in township seven north, range twenty-two east, west of the center line of First avenue, and north of the center line of Greenfield avenue.

Ninth ward boundaries.

The Ninth ward shall embrace all that part of said district which lies west of the center line of Seventh street, north of the center of Vliet street, and south of the center line of Walnut street to its intersection with Fond du Lac avenue, and south of the center line of Fond du Lac avenue to the west boundary line of the city.

Tenth ward boundaries.

The Tenth ward shall embrace all that part of said district, which lies west of the center line of Seventh street, between the center lines of Walnut and Burleigh streets, and west of the center line of Louis avenue and its continuation from the center line of Burleigh street to the north boundary line of the city, north of the center line of Walnut street from the center line of Seventh street, to where it intersects the center line of Fond du Lac avenue, and north of the center line of Fond du Lac avenue, to the west boundary of the city, and south of the center line of Burleigh street, from the center of Seventh street to the center of Louis avenue, and south of the north boundary line of the city from the center of Louis avenue, to the west boundary line of said city.

The Eleventh ward shall embrace all that part of said district which lies south of the center line of Greenfield avenue, west of the center line of First avenue between the center lines of Greenfield avenue and Maple street and west of the center line of Eighth avenue between the center lines of Maple and Burnham streets and north of the center line of Maple street, between the center lines of First and Eighth avenues, and north of the center line of Burnham street from the center line of Eighth avenue to the intersection with the center line of Forest Home avenue, and north of the center line of Forest Home avenue from the center line of Burnham street to the west boundary line of the city. *Eleventh ward boundaries.*

The Twelfth ward shall embrace the northeast one-fourth of section eight in township six north, range twenty-two east, and all that part of said district which lies east of the center line of First avenue, and south of the center line of Greenfield avenue and its continuation to the east boundary of said city, and north of the center line of Lincoln avenue and its continuation east, to the east boundary of said city. *Twelfth ward boundaries.*

The Thirteenth ward shall embrace all that part of said district which lies west of the center line of Milwaukee river, north of the center line of North avenue from the center line of Milwaukee river to the center line of Seventh street, and north of the center line of Burleigh street from the center line of Seventh street to the center line of Louis avenue, and east of the center line of Seventh street from the center line of North avenue to the center line of Burleigh street, and east of the center line of Louis avenue and its continuation north to the north boundary of said city, from the center line of Burleigh street to the north boundary of said city. *Thirteenth ward boundaries.*

The Fourteenth ward shall embrace all that part of said district which lies west of the center line of First *Fourteenth ward boundaries.*

avenue and south of the center line of Maple street between the center lines of First and Eighth avenues, and south of the center line of Burnham street, from the center line of Eighth avenue to the intersection with the center line of Forest Home avenue, and south of the center line of Forest Home avenue from the center line of Burnham street to the west boundary line of the city.

Fifteenth ward boundaries.   The Fifteenth ward shall embrace all that part of said district which lies west of the center line of Thirteenth street, south of the center line of Vliet street, and north of the center line of Cedar street.

Sixteenth ward boundaries.   The Sixteenth ward shall embrace all that part of said district which lies west of the center line of Thirteenth street and Muskego avenue to the south boundary line of section thirty, south of the center line of Cedar street and north of the center line of Canal street.

Seventeenth ward boundaries.   The Seventeenth ward shall embrace all that part of said district which lies east of the east line of section eight, in township six north, range twenty-two east, and south of the center line of Lincoln avenue and its continuation east to the east boundary of said city.

Eighteenth ward boundaries.   The Eighteenth ward shall embrace all that part of said district which lies east of the center line of Milwaukee river, from the north boundary line of said city to a point where the center of Milwaukee river would be intersected by the center line of Brady street produced west, and which lies north of the center line of Brady street from said Milwaukee river to the intersection of the center line of Brady street with the center line of Prospect avenue, thence northeasterly along the center line of Prospect avenue to a point where it would be intersected by the northerly line of lot twenty, in block one hundred and ninety-nine, in Rogers' addition, produced west, thence along the northerly line of said lot, easterly to Lake Michigan, thence easterly to the east boundary line of said city of Milwaukee.

Not to repeal or modify charter, or rights of any cemetery association thereunder.   SECTION (3) 4.   Nothing in this act shall be considered or construed as repealing or modifying the charter or any existing law pertaining to, or in any way affecting the powers, rights, interests, property, exemptions or privileges, of any corporation, society or association, now owning or using for cemetery or burial purposes any lands within the limits described in section one of this act; and any provisions of the charter or ordinances of the city of Milwaukee, and acts amendatory thereof, and any general statutes of the state, prohibiting the location or use of lands for cemetery or burial purposes within the limits of the city of Milwaukee, or relating to the taking of lands for any public use, or to the opening, vacation or improvement of streets, alleys or highways, or to any other public work or improvements by said city, shall not have reference or application to such corporation, society or association, or any of the lands owned and used by them for cemetery or burial purposes; provided, however, any such corporation, society or association, if it request the same, shall be furnished by said city, upon such terms and regulations as may be just, connections with its water and sewerage systems, and the service of its police and fire departments.

Water and sewer connections may be made.

Chapter 449, Laws of 1891.

CHAPTER 309, LAWS OF 1895.

SECTION 1. The common council of all cities of the first class, and of all cities organized under special charter, containing a population of forty thousand and upwards, is hereby authorized by a two-thirds vote, on or before the first day of December after each state and national census, to redistrict, readjust and change the boundaries of wards within such city, so that the wards shall be as nearly equal in population as may be, and for accomplishing the purposes of this act, such common council may create new wards and consolidate old ones, but no ward shall be created having a population less than eight thousand nor exceeding twenty thousand. In the redistricting of the city, as herein provided, the original numbers of the wards and the geographical outline shall as far as possible be retained, and the wards so created and the old ones the boundaries of which are changed shall be in as compact form as practicable.

Common Council to change ward boundaries, when.

CHAPTER 166, LAWS OF 1893.

SECTION 1. Section 18, of chapter 392, of the laws of Wisconsin for the year 1856, is hereby amended by striking out all of said section after the word and figures "section 18," and inserting in lieu thereof the following: In case of an extension of the corporate limits of the city of Milwaukee beyond such points and places where toll gates are erected, in such cases toll gates are to be removed beyond the limits of the city of Milwaukee, the distance of one-half of one mile, and in case said company fails

Amends Sec. 18, Ch. 392, Laws of 1856.

Toll gates, when to be removed.

and neglects to remove such toll gates, such toll gates shall be thrown open upon complaint by any person being made in writing, in manner provided by sections 19 and 20, of this chapter, and remain open until such removal.

CHAPTER 245, LAWS OF 1895.

Adjacent territory, how annexed.

SECTION 1. Section 18, of sub-chapter 4, of Chapter 326, Laws of 1889, is hereby amended, so as to read as follows: Section 18. Three-fourths of the electors and the owners of at least one-third of the taxable property, according to the last tax roll, in territory adjacent to such city, may present a petition to the common council of such city asking for annexation thereto; provided, that if no electors reside therein, such petition must be signed by the owners of at least three-fourths of the taxable property desired to be annexed before the common council shall have power to act thereon; provided further, that the common council of such city, may upon the petition of one-half of the resident electors and by the owners of one-half of the real estate within the limits of the territory proposed to be annexed, pass an ordinance annexing such proposed territory when the proposition to annex has been submitted to a vote of the electors of the district to be annexed and a majority of the resident electors have voted in favor therefor.

SECTION 2. Whenever a proposition to annex territory has been submitted and not adopted the same or substantially the same proposition shall not be again submitted within two years thereafter.

SECTION 3. Chapter 214, Laws of 1893, is hereby repealed.

SECTION 21, OF CHAPTER 326, LAWS OF 1889, AS AMENDED BY SECTION 15, CHAPTER 316, LAWS OF 1895.

Adoption of ordinance, to operate as annexation.

SECTION 21. The adoption of said ordinance shall operate to annex such territory to said city and of the ward or wards designated therein, ninety days after the same is passed and published. The validity of the proceedings annexing such territory shall not be called in question collaterally in any of the courts of this state; nor shall the validity of any such proceeding be called in question in any other manner in the courts of this state, unless the action or proceedings therefor be commenced within ninety days after such ordinance is adopted. The sufficiency of all pending proceedings wherein the full time of ninety days has not elapsed, shall be determined by the provisions of this enactment except in cases where some action or proceeding has been commenced in court.

Property belonging to a town does not become the property of the city upon the annexation to the city of the territory embracing such property.

Town of Milwaukee vs. City, 12 Wis., 103.

CHAPTER II.

OFFICERS AND ELECTIONS.

SECTION 1. The officers of said city shall be a mayor, City officers. two aldermen from each ward, constituting a common council, a city treasurer, a city comptroller, a city attorney, a city clerk, a board of public works, a city engineer, a school board, a tax commissioner, ward assessors, a board of commissioners of the public debt, a board of health, justices of the peace, a chief of police, one chief engineer of the fire department, one or more harbor masters, three inspectors of election for each ward or election precinct, and as many bridgetenders, firemen, constables, policemen, and such other officers and agents as may be provided for by this act, or as the common council may from time to time direct.

Chapter 205, Laws of 1887.

The general powers of the city government are vested in the common council, with special delegations of power to particular subordinate officers and subordinate agencies or bodies, for the better and more convenient administration of city affairs.

Koch vs. Milwaukee, 89 Wis., 220.

SECTION 2. The annual municipal election in said Annual municipal city shall be held on the first Tuesday in April of each elections. year, at such place or places in each election precinct as the common council shall designate, at which time there shall be elected by the qualified voters of said city, in the manner herein provided, all officers required to be elected at a general municipal election. The polls of such election shall be opened and closed at the same hours which are or may be prescribed by law for the opening and closing of the polls at general elections in the State of Wisconsin. Ten days previous public notice of the time and place of such election, and of the officers to be elected, shall be given by the city clerk, by publication in one or more newspapers published in said city.

SECTION 3. The mayor, treasurer, comptroller, attor- Elected by the peo- ney, aldermen, justices of the peace and constables shall ple at large. be elected by the people. The mayor, treasurer, comptroller and attorney shall be elected on the first Tuesday of April, A. D. 1874, being the first municipal election under this act, biennially thereafter. The officers so elected shall enter upon the duties of their respective offices on the third Tuesday of April in the year of their election, and shall hold their respective offices for the term of two years, and until their successor shall be elected and qualified. The term of office of the city attorney shall be four years. All constables elected in the city of Milwaukee, at and after the municipal election of 1890, shall hold their office for the term of two years, and until their successors are elected and qualified.

As amended by Chapter 35, Laws of 1889.

See Chapter 144, 1875. Repealed by Chapter 104, Laws of 1878. See also Chapter 332, Laws of 1875. Repealed by Chapter 191, Laws of 1876.

The provisions of Chapter 35, Laws of 1889, changed the term of office of the city attorney from two years to four years, and continued the term of office of the then incumbent for the extended term. *Held*, such attempted extension was an appointment to office by legislative enactment, and void under Section 9, Article XIII, Const.

State ex rel. Hamilton vs. Krez, 88 Wis., 135.

Two aldermen for each ward. SECTION 4. Each of the several wards of the city of Milwaukee shall hereafter be represented in the common council by two aldermen. The aldermen elected at the municipal election in the city of Milwaukee, in April 1889, shall hold their office for the term of three years. The aldermen elected at the municipal election in 1890, shall hold their office for two years, and thereafter all aldermen for the city of Milwaukee shall be elected for the term of two years.

As amended by Chapter 205, Laws of 1887 and Chapter 35, Laws of 1889.

Vacancies, how filled, etc. SECTION 5. If any alderman shall remove from the ward represented by him, or shall engage or continue in any service, business, or employment, causing a continuous absence from the city for more than four months, his office shall thereby become vacant; the mayor of the city of Milwaukee, shall appoint, within thirty days after the occurrence of such vacancy a suitable person to fill any vacancy that shall hereafter take place in the office of alderman in said city, for the unexpired term thereof. The aldermen of the city of Milwaukee, shall after the third Tuesday of April, 1889, each receive an annual salary of four hundred dollars, which shall be paid as are the salaries of other city officers of said city. For non-attendance at a regularly called standing committee meeting, or of a special council committee meeting, a fine of two dollars and fifty cents shall be imposed upon any member so absenting himself. For non-attendance at a regular council meeting a fine of five dollars will be imposed. The council may remit such fine upon the presentation of satisfactory excuses. Fines shall be deducted from such salaries.

As amended by Chapter 318, Laws of 1889, and Chapter 159, Laws of 1889.

SECTION 6. *Sec. 1.* The city of Milwaukee is hereby divided into eleven districts, for the purpose of electing justices of the peace and constables, as hereinafter mentioned. — City to be divided into districts for election of justices and constables.

Section 2. The First, Seventh and Eighteenth wards in said city, shall constitute the First district; the Second and Fifteenth wards shall constitute the Second district; the Third ward shall constitute the Third district; the Fourth and Sixteenth wards shall constitute the Fourth district; the Fifth ward shall constitute the Fifth district; the Sixth and Thirteenth wards shall constitute the Sixth district; the Eighth ward shall constitute the Seventh district; the Ninth ward shall constitute the Eighth district; the Tenth ward shall constitute the Ninth district; the Eleventh, Twelfth and Fourteenth wards shall constitute the Tenth district; the Seventeenth ward shall constitute the Eleventh district. — District boundaries.

See Section 2, Chapter 191, Laws of 1876. Section 3, Chapter 416, Laws of 1887. Section 3, Chapter 36, Laws of 1887. Section 3, Chapter 388, Laws of 1887. Section 3, Chapter 38, Laws of 1887, and Section 9, Chapter 37, Laws of 1887.

Sec. 3. The votes given for justice of the peace and constables in each of the said districts shall be canvassed and returned by the inspectors of election in each ward comprising said districts, in the same manner now provided by law for city officers in said city of Milwaukee. Justices of the peace now in office in said city of Milwaukee shall hold their offices for and during the term for which they have been elected and until their successors have qualified according to law. Justices of the peace now in office in the said city of Milwaukee shall at the expiration of his term of office and after his successor in office shall have qualified according to law, deliver to — Election of justices of the peace and constables.

him all books and records in his possession connected with his said office. Justices of the peace and constables elected under the provisions of this act shall give bond and take the oath of office as required by law.

As amended by Sections 4, 5, 6, 7, Chapter 191, Laws of 1876.
See also Chapter 35, Laws of 1889.

Other officers. SECTION 7. All other officers necessary for the proper management of the affairs of said city shall be appointed by the common council, or by the mayor, or in such manner as the common council may direct, except when otherwise directed in this act. The city clerk, the commissioner of public works, city engineer, superintendent of schools, secretary of the school board, tax commissioner, commissioner of health, chief of police, and chief engineer of the fire department, shall respectively hold their offices for the terms for which they are respectively elected or appointed.

As amended by Section 1, Chapter 324, Laws of 1882.

Elections. SECTION 8. All elections by the people shall be by ballot, and a plurality of votes shall constitute an election. **Qualifications of electors.** All persons entitled to vote for county or state officers, and who shall have resided in the city for one year next preceding the election, and for ten days in the ward where they offer to vote, shall be entitled to vote for any officer to be elected under this act, and to hold any office hereby created.

As amended by Section 3, Chapter 144, Laws of 1875.

Election precincts. SECTION 9. The common council may at their discretion, by ordinance, divide the several wards of the city into election precincts by geographical divisions and boundaries as they may deem proper, so that there shall not be more than three polls in each ward; and each voter shall deposit his vote at the poll in the election precinct within which he shall reside.

See amendments by Chapter 21, Laws of 1889, in foot note.
NOTE—The restriction to three polls for each ward is virtually repealed by Subd. 3, Sec. 2, Ch. 288, Laws of 1893, and the city was re-districted under the authority of that Chapter, by ordinance No. 156, passed Nov. 27, 1893.

Inspectors and clerks of election. SECTION 10. (The aldermen shall be inspectors of election for the precinct in which they may respectively reside. The mayor shall annually appoint two clerks of election, and also additional inspectors of election for each election precinct, if required, to make the whole number of inspectors, three in each such precinct, including such aldermen there resident. Each inspector and clerk of election shall be an elector and resident of such precinct, and shall hold his office for one year from the time of his appointment, and until his successor shall be appointed by the mayor; and the mayor, by appointment, shall fill any vacancy; *provided, however*, that in case of a failure to appoint, or in case of a failure of any such inspector or clerk to appear at the opening of the polls at any election, the electors then present may proceed to fill the vacancy, as provided by the laws of this state regarding elections; but no member of the common council or other person, being a candidate for any office at any election shall be inspector at such election. Said inspectors and clerks shall, before entering upon their duties, and within ten days after their said appointment, respectively take and file with the city clerk the usual oath of office.)

Vacancies, how filled.

Candidates shall not be inspectors.

Amended by Chapter 389, Laws of 1885, and Chapter 442, Laws of 1889, which see in foot note hereto.

SECTION 11.   If either of the inspectors shall suspect that any person offering a vote does not possess the qualifications of an elector, or if any vote be challenged by an elector, the inspectors, before receiving the vote of such person, shall require him to take the following oath, which either of said inspectors is hereby authorized to administer: " You do solemnly swear (or affirm as the case may be) that you are twenty-one years of age, that you are a citizen of the United States (or have declared your intentions to become a citizen conformably to the laws of the United States on the subject of naturalization), that you have resided within this city one year and within this ward ten days next preceding this election; that you now reside within this election precinct, and that you have made no bet or wager, and have not become directly or indirectly interested in any bet or wager depending upon the result of this election."

Challenging votes.

Oath of elector.

And if the person so offering to vote shall take such oath, his vote shall be received.   If such person shall take such oath falsely, he shall be deemed guilty of wilful end corrupt perjury, and upon conviction thereof, upon

Penalty for false swearing and fraudulent voting.

indictment or information, shall suffer the punishment provided by law for persons guilty of perjury. If any person who is not a qualified voter shall vote at any election, or if any person qualified shall vote in any other precinct than the one in which he resides, or shall vote more than once at any one election, he shall be liable to a criminal prosecution by indictment or information; and on conviction thereof, shall forfeit and pay a sum not exceeding one hundred dollars, nor less than twenty-five dollars. It shall be the duty of the inspectors to keep a list of the names of all persons whose votes may be challenged as aforesaid, and who shall swear in their votes; and if **Penalty for knowingly receiving and tallying fraudulent votes.** any inspector shall knowingly and corruptly receive the vote of any person not authorized to vote, or shall make out false returns for an election; or if any clerk shall not write down the name of every voter as he votes, or shall wilfully make untrue and incorrect count and tallies of votes, each and every such inspector and clerk shall be liable to be prosecuted therefor by indictment or information, and on conviction thereof, shall forfeit and pay a sum not exceeding five hundred dollars for each offense. All such indictments and informations shall be tried in the county of Milwaukee.

Amended by Section 4, Chapter 144, Laws of 1875.

Inspectors shall make returns. SECTION 12. As soon as the poll of the election shall be closed, the inspectors shall proceed immediately to canvass the votes given at such election, and continue without adjournment until completed. The canvass of votes shall be made publicly in the presence of any person desiring to attend the same, and when the number of votes for each candidate or person voted for shall be counted and ascertained, the said inspectors shall make returns thereof, stating therein the number of votes cast for each person, for each and every office; and shall deliver or cause to be delivered, such returns to the clerk of the common council, with the ballots cast at such election. **Council shall canvass returns.** Within one week after any election the common council shall meet and canvass said returns, and declare the result as it appears from the same, and the clerk shall forthwith give notice of his election to each officer elected.

As amended by Section 5, Chapter 144, Laws of 1875.

SECTION 13. In case of a tie vote, or a failure in making an election of any officer, or in case of the dismissal of any officer, or when any officer elected or appointed for the city shall remove his residence without the limits of the city, or when any officer elected or appointed in and for any ward or division of the city, shall remove his residence without the limits of such ward or division, or when any such officer shall refuse or neglect for ten days after notice of his election or appointment, to qualify and enter upon the discharge of the duties of his office, the office shall be deemed vacant; and whenever a vacancy shall occur in such manner, or in any other manner, in any office to be filled by an election by the people, except in the office of mayor or alderman, the common council shall order a special election upon a public notice of five days, to be given in like manner as notice is given of the general municipal election, for the election of a person to fill such vacancy. And whenever the vacancy shall occur in any office to be filled by a vote of the common council, the same proceedings shall be had for an election to fill such vacancy as are required for the election of any officer by the common council.

Tie vote, failure to elect, or other cause of vacancy.

Special elections.

Amended by Section 6, Chapter 144, Laws of 1875.

SECTION 14. Special elections by the people to fill vacancies, or for any other purpose, shall be held and conducted by the inspectors and clerks of elections of the several election precincts, in the same manner, and the returns thereof shall be made in the same form and manner as of general annual municipal elections, and within such time as may be prescribed by ordinance.

How conducted.

SECTION 15. Every person elected or appointed to fill a vacancy, shall hold his office and discharge the duties thereof for the unexpired term, with the same rights, and subject to the same liabilities as the person whose office he may be elected or appointed to fill.

Rights and liabilities of persons appointed to fill vacancies.

SECTION 16. All the elective city and ward officers now in office, shall hold their respective offices until the expiration of the terms for which they were respectively elected and until their successors shall be elected and qualify under this act.

Mayor—vacancy how filled.

SECTION 17. When any vacancy shall happen, by death, resignation, removal or otherwise, in the office of mayor, such vacancy shall be filled by a new election, and the common council shall order a new election within ten days after the happening of such vacancy, provided more than six months of the term shall then remain unexpired, and if less then six months of such term shall remain unexpired, the common council may, in their discretion, order a new election to fill such vacancy.

As amended by Section 7, Chapter 144, Laws of 1875.

NOTE.—Elections are held under the provisions of Chapter 288, Laws of 1893. It is deemed inadvisable to insert it here.

CHAPTER 313, LAWS OF 1895.

Mayor to appoint board of city service commissioners.

SECTION 1. The mayor of each city in this state of the first class, or of the second class, as defined by section 1, of chapter 312, of the general laws of Wisconsin, enacted in 1893, whether such city be incorporated by special act of the Legislature or under the general laws of the state, shall, before the fifteenth day of June, A. D. 1895, or the fifteenth day of June in the year next following the first state or national census, showing such city to belong to either said first or said second class, appoint four persons, citizens and residents of said city, who shall constitute and be known as the board of city service commissioners of such city, and shall designate one of the persons so appointed to serve for a term of four years, one for a term of three years, one for a term of two years, and one for a term of one year, from the first Monday of July in the year of their appointment and until their respective successors are appointed and qualified; and in each and every year after such first appointment, the mayor shall in like manner, in the month of June, appoint one person as the successor of the commissioner whose term shall expire in that year, to serve as such commissioner for four years from the first Monday of July then next ensuing and until his successor is appointed and qualified. Three commissioners shall constitute a quorum necessary for the transaction of business. Any vacancy in the office of commissioner occurring during the term shall be filled for the unexpired term by appointment by the mayor, and all appointments, both original and to fill vacancies, shall be so made that not more than two commissioners shall at the time of any appointment be members of the same political party. Said commissioners shall hold no lucrative office or employment under the United States, the state of Wisconsin, or any municipal corporation or political division thereof, and each commissioner shall, before entering upon the discharge [of the duties] of his office and within ten days after receiving notice of his appointment, take and subscribe the oath of office prescribed by the constitution of this state, and file the same, duly certified by the officer administering it, with the clerk of his city, and no salary or other compensation for his services shall be paid to any such commissioner.

Vacancy in office of commissioner, how filled.

SECTION 2. The said commissioners shall make rules adapted to carry out the purposes of the act and not inconsistent with its provisions, for the examination and selection of persons to fill offices and positions in the service of their respective cities, which are required to be filled by appointment, and for the selection of persons to be employed in the service of such city. All rules so made shall be subject to the approval of the mayor of the city, and they may with like approval be from time to time altered or rescinded by said commissioners. The said commissioners shall supervise the administration of the rules so established, and they shall, on or before the fifteenth day of March in every year, report to the mayor their doings during the preceding year, including any rules adopted under the provisions of this section.

Commissioners to make rules for examination and selection of applicants.

SECTION 3. The rules mentioned in section 2, of this act may be made from time to time:

1st. For open, competitive and other examinations by which to test applicants for office or for employment as to their practical fitness to discharge the duties of the positions which they desire to fill, which examinations shall be public and free to all citizens of the United States, with proper limitations as to residence, age, health, sex, habits and moral character.

Rules may be made, for what.

2nd. For the filling of vacancies in offices and places of employment in accordance with the results, of such examinations, and for the selection of persons for public employment in accordance with such results, or otherwise, as may seem most desirable to carry out the provisions of this act.

3rd. For promotions in office or positions on the basis of ascertained merit and seniority in service and examination as may seem desirable.

4th. For a period of probation before an appointment or employment is made permanent.

All rules made as provided in this act and all changes therein shall forthwith be printed for distribution by said board.

SECTION 4. From and after the adoption of such rules, all appointments to subordinate offices, positions and employments in the several departments of the service of such city which are subject to such rules, shall be made by the respective heads of such departments under and in conformity with the provisions of such rules, and such heads of departments shall respectively have power to remove or discharge at pleasure any person holding any subordinate office, position or employment in their respective departments.

Appointments to be made in conformity with rules.

SECTION 5. All applicants for offices, places or employments in the civil service of such city, except those mentioned in section 6, shall be subject to examination under and in accordance with the rules so made by said commissioners. Such examinations shall be practical in their character and shall relate to those matters which will fairly test the relative capacity and fitness of the persons examined to discharge the duties of the particular service to which they seek to be appointed, and shall include tests of physical qualifications and health, and, when appropriate, of manual skill. No question in any examination shall relate to

Applicants for offices to be subject to examination.

political or religious opinions or affiliations, and no appointment or selection to an office or for employment within the scope of the rules established as aforesaid, shall be in any manner affected or influenced by such opinions or affiliations.

Officers, what exempt from rules.

SECTION 6. Officers who are elected by the people, or who by statute are required to be elected by the city council, inspectors and clerks of election, members of any board of education, the superintendents and teachers of schools, heads of any principal department of the city, all members of the law, fire and police departments, officers and clerks for the faithful discharge of whose duties a superior officer is required to give bond, one private secretary of the mayor, and any other officers, clerks or employes in the service of the city whose positions, in the judgment of the said city service commissioners cannot, for the time being, be subjected, with advantage to the public service, to the general rules prepared under this act, shall not be affected as to their election, selection or appointment, by such rules made by said commissioners.

Facts to be stated by applicants.

SECTION 7. Every application; in order to entitle the applicant to appear for examination or to be examined, must state the facts under oath on the following subjects: (1) full name, residence and postoffice address; (2) citizenship; (3) age; (4) place of birth; (5) health and physical capacity for the public service; (6) previous employment in the public service; (7) business or employment and residence for the previous five years; (8) education. Such other information shall be furnished by the applicant as may reasonably be required by the board touching the applicant's fitness for the public service.

Board to appoint examiner, who shall be ex-officio secretary.

SECTION 8. The said board shall appoint a chief examiner whose duty it shall be, under their direction, to superintend any examinations held in such city under this act, and who shall perform such other duties as the board shall prescribe. Such chief examiner shall be ex-officio secretary of said board, and under the direction of such board he, as such secretary, shall keep minutes of its proceedings, preserve all reports made to it, keep a record of all examinations held under its direction, and perform such other duties as the board may from time to time prescribe.

Salary of examiner.

Such chief examiner shall receive a salary.to be fixed by said board at a sum not exceeding fifteen hundred dollars a year, which shall be paid monthly by the city on the certificate of the president of said board. He shall be subject to removal at any time by the board.

Commissioners may incur expenses.

The said board of commissioners may also incure such expenses, not exceeding five hundred dollars a year, as it may deem necessary, for printing and stationery and other incidental matters.

Board to control examinations.

SECTION 9. The board shall control all examinations, and may, whenever an examination is to take place, designate a suitable number of persons, either in or not in the official services of the city, to be examiners, and it shall be the duty of such examiners, and, if in the service of the city, it shall be a part of their official duty, without extra compensation, to conduct examinations as the board may direct, and make return or report thereof to such board; and the board may at any time substitute any other person, whether or not in such service, in the place of any one so selected, and the board may themselves at any time act as such examiners and without appointing examiners. The examiners at any examination shall not all be members of the same political party, and no person shall serve in an examination of candidates for office under the provisions of this act in case of a relative or connection by marriage within the degree of first cousin.

Examiners not all to be of same political party.

SECTION 10. Notice of the time, place and general scope of every examination shall be given by the board by publication for two weeks preceding such examination, in one or more daily newspapers of general circulation published in such city, and such notice shall also be posted by said board in a conspicuous place in their office two weeks before such examination. Such further notice of examinations may be given as the board shall prescribe.

Notice of examination, how given.

SECTION 11. From the returns or reports of the examiners, or from the examinations made by the board, the board shall prepare and keep a register for each grade or class of position in the service of such city, of the persons whose general average standing upon examination for such grade or class is not less than the minimum fixed by the rules of such board, and who are otherwise eligible; and such persons shall take rank upon the register as candidates in the order of their relative excellence as determined by examination, without reference to priority of time of examination.

Board to keep register.

SECTION 12. Immediate notice in writing shall be given by the appointing power to said board of commissioners of all appointments, permanent or temporary, made in those branches or departments of the civil service of such city which are subject to this act and the rules of said board, and of all transfers, promotions, resignations or vacancies from any cause in such service, and of the date thereof; and a record of the same shall be kept by said board. When any office or place of employment subject to such rules is created or abolished, or the compensation attached thereto is altered, the officer or board making such change shall immediately report in writing to said board of commissioners.

Immediate notice to be given commissioners by appointing power.

SECTION 13. Said board of commissioners shall, on or before the fifteenth day of March in each year, make to the mayor for transmission to the city council, a report showing its own action, the rules in force, the practical effects thereof, and any suggestions it may approve for the more effectual accomplishment of the purposes of this act. The mayor may require a report from said board at any other time.

Board to make annual report to Mayor.

SECTION 14. All officers of any such city shall aid said board in all proper ways in carrying out the provisions of this act, and, at any place where examinations are to be held, shall allow the reasonable use of the public buildings for holding such examinations. The mayor of each city shall cause suitable rooms to be provided for said board at the expense of such city; and a sufficient sum of money shall be appropriated each year by each city to carry out the provisions of this act in such city.

City officers to aid board in all proper ways.

SECTION 15. No person or officer shall wilfully and corruptly, by himself or in co-operation with one or more other persons, defeat, deceive or obstruct any person in respect to his or her right of examination, or corruptly or falsely mark, grade, estimate or report upon the examination or proper standing of any person examined hereunder, or aid in so doing or wilfully or corruptly make any false representations concerning the same or concerning the person examined, or wilfully or corruptly furnish to any person any special or secret information for the purpose of either improving or injuring the prospects or chances of any person so examined, or to be examined, being appointed, employed or promoted.

SECTION 16. No accounting or auditing officer shall allow the claim of any public officer for services of any deputy or other person employed in the public service in violation of the provisions of this act.

Board to certify to comptroller all appointments. SECTION 17. The board of city service commissioners shall certify to the comptroller all appointments to offices and places in the civil service of the city, subject to their rules, and all vacancies occurring therein, whether by dismissal, resignation or death. No comptroller of any such city shall approve the payment of or be in any manner concerned in paying any salary or wages to any person, subject to such rules, for services as an officer or employe of such city, before the appointment of such person to the city service has been certified by the board to the comptroller, nor after the vacation of such person's office or employment shall have been so certified.

Salary of appointee to commence, when. SECTION 18. No paymaster, treasurer or other officer or agent of such city shall wilfully pay, or be in any manner concerned in paying, any person subject to the rules adopted by said commissioners under this act, any salary or wages for services as an officer or employe of such city, before the appointment of such person to the civil service of such city has been certified by the board to the comptroller, nor after the vacation of such person's office or employment shall have been so certified.

Penalty for violation of act. SECTION 19. Any person who shall wilfully, or through culpable negligence, violate any provision of this act or any rule promulgated in accordance with the provisions thereof, shall be guilty of a misdemeanor, and shall, on conviction thereof, be punished by a fine not less than fifty dollars, and not exceeding one thousand dollars, or by imprisonment in the county jail for a term not exceeding six months, or by both such fine and imprisonment in the discretion of the court.

Officers convicted, how punished. SECTION 20. If any person shall be convicted under the next preceding section, any public office which such person may hold shall, by force of such conviction, be rendered vacant, and such person shall be incabable of holding office for the period of five years from the date of such conviction.

Prosecutions, by whom conducted. SECTION 21. Prosecutions for violations of this act may be instituted either by the attorney general, the state's attorney for the county in which the offense is alleged to have been committed, or by the board acting through special counsel. Such prosecution shall be conducted and controlled by the prosecuting officers who institute them, unless they request the aid of other prosecuting officers.

SECTION 22. All acts and parts of acts, including all provisions of any city charter, so far as they conflict or are inconsistent with the provisions of this act, are hereby repealed.

CHAPTER 499, LAWS OF 1889.

SECTION 1. The general law requiring the registration of electors, shall apply to the annual municipal and judicial elections in all towns, villages and cities in which registration is now required at general elections.

Registration of electors, to apply to municipal and judicial elections.

CHAPTER 16, LAWS OF 1887.

SECTION 1. In all cities in this state, which by the census of 1880 contained a population in excess of fifty thousand, the inspectors of election and clerks of election heretofore appointed under the provisions of chapter 389, of the laws of 1885, and by the said chapter constituting the boards of registry in the different wards or election precincts of said city, and all inspectors of election and clerks of election hereafter appointed in any such city, according to the provisions of said chapter, shall hereafter do and perform each and all the duties in said chapter specified and required to be done and performed by them, as such boards of registry in reference to every general election, also in reference to every judicial and annual municipal election held within their precincts during their term of office; provided, that in making the register lists for a municipal election in any such city, it shall be the duty of the board of registry in each election precinct to take and to use the poll lists kept in such precinct at the last previous annual municipal election, for the same purpose and in the same manner as is prescribed in section 3, of said chapter 389, for the taking and use by such boards of the poll list kept at the last preceding general election in making the registry lists for a general election.

Amending chapter 389, laws 1885, regarding the appointment of inspectors and registration of electors in cities of 50,000 inhabitants or over, census 1880.

SECTION 2. In case a new election district shall be formed at any time, by the division of any ward, or in any other way, the inspectors of election in such new district shall make their registry of electors on the days prescribed by this act, and for that purpose they shall procure the poll list or lists or a certified copy of the poll list or lists of the last preceding general or annual municipal election, as the case may be, of the district or districts in which such new district is situated, and shall enter on the registry list made by them, the names of all persons residing in such new district, whose names appear on such poll list, or on either such poll lists, if more than one, the number of the dwelling and name of street or other location, if the same shall be known to, or can be ascertained by such inspectors. In case such new election district shall be formed wholly or in part out of territory not

Section 4, chapter 389, amended, inspectors in new districts to make registry lists, when.

within the city at the last preceding annual municipal election, then the poll list kept at the last preceding general election of the district in which such new district or part of new district is situated, shall be taken and used by the board of registry in making up the registry list for the next annual municipal election.

Separate registry lists to be made of persons qualified to vote at judicial elections, when.

SECTION 3. Whenever there shall be a judicial election on the same day as a municipal election in any such city, and it shall appear to the board of registry of any precinct that any person is a qualified elector to vote at the judicial election in such precinct, but is not a qualified elector to vote for municipal officers at such election, it shall be the duty of the board to make a separate registry list, which shall contain the names, number of dwelling, and name of street, or other location, if the same shall be known to or can be ascertained by such board, of all persons in their precinct qualified to vote at the judicial election, and not qualified to vote for municipal officers, and the vote of such persons may be received, subject to the restrictions and regulations of said chapter 389, at the judicial election, but they shall not be received for municipal officers, and separate poll lists of all such voters shall be made and kept at such election.

CHAPTER 499, LAWS OF 1887.

Clerk or inspector not to issue or write, change or alter any ticket or ballot on election day, or disclose how elector voted, unless required to do so as a witness in judicial proceedings—penalty.

SECTION 1. It shall be unlawful for any clerk or inspector of elections to issue or write, change or alter, for any person on the day of any election any ticket or ballot, and any such officer who shall violate the foregoing provisions, or who shall mark any ballot or ticket except as provided by law, or who shall disclose how any elector shall have voted, unless required to do so as a witness in a judicial proceeding, shall be guilty of a misdemeanor, and upon conviction thereof, shall be punished by a fine not exceeding one hundred dollars, or by imprisonment not exceeding six months, or both, in the discretion of the court.

SECTION 2. This act shall take effect and be in force from and after its passage and publication.

NOTE.—Although not in terms repealed by Chapter 288, Laws of 1893, the three foregoing statutes are rendered practically obsolete by that enactment.

CHAPTER III.

GENERAL POWERS AND DUTIES OF OFFICERS.

Oath of office.

SECTION 1. Every person elected or appointed to any office under this act, shall, before he enters upon the duties of his office, take and subscribe the oath of office prescribed in the constitution of this state, and file the same duly certified by the officer administering the same with the clerk of the city; and the treasurer, comptroller,

clerk, constable, and such other officers as the common
council may direct, shall each, before entering upon the
duties of his office, execute to the city of Milwaukee a
bond, with two or more sureties, the aggregate amount **Official bonds.**
of whose property within this state, over and above all
their respective debts, exemptions and liabilities, as shown
by their affidavits attached to or endorsed on such bond,
shall be at least double the sum named as the penalty in
such bond; and said bonds shall respectively contain
such penal sums and such conditions as the common **How executed, ap-**
council may deem proper, and shall be subject to the **proved and**
approval of said council. And the common council may **deposited.**
from time to time require new or additional bonds, and
remove from office any officer refusing or neglecting to
give the same. All official bonds executed to the city of
Milwaukee, except that of the city clerk, shall be filed
with and safely preserved by the city clerk in his office,
unless the common council shall otherwise direct. The
bonds of all officers who may be charged with the collection or safe keeping, or with the disposition or disbursement of any of the funds of said city, or may have any
control over such funds at any time, shall be duly
witnessed and acknowledged, and recorded in the office
of the register of deeds of the county of Milwaukee. And **Certified copies to**
the city clerk shall, immediately after the filing of any **be delivered to the**
such bond in his office, make and deliver a true copy **comptroller.**
thereof, duly certified by him under the corporate seal of
the city, to the city comptroller, who shall preserve the
same in his office. The said certified copy on file with
the comptroller, or transcripts from the record of such
bonds in the office of the register of deeds duly certified by
said register shall be evidence of the due execution and
contents of the bond so recorded, in case of loss of the
originals. The bond of the city clerk shall be filed with
the city comptroller.

As amended by Section 8, Chapter 144, Laws of 1875.

SECTION 2. The mayor shall take care that the laws **Duties of the**
of the state and the ordinances of the city are duly ob- **Mayor.**
served and enforced; and that all officers of the city discharge their respective duties. He shall from time to
time, give the common council such information, and
recommend such measures, as he may deem advantageous
to the city. The mayor shall be the chief executive

Mayor head of fire and police departments.
Special police.

officer, and the head of the fire department, and of police, of the city; and in case of a riot or other disturbance, or whenever he and the chief of police shall deem it necessary for the prevention of threatened disorder or for the preservation of public peace and the good order of the city, they may appoint as many special or temporary policemen as they may deem necessary. Such special or temporary policemen shall serve for such length of time as the mayor and chief of police shall deem necessary and shall receive such compensation for their services as the common council shall provide or direct, but the term of said special policemen shall in no case exceed the time of two weeks.

As amended by Section 2, Chapter 324, Laws of 1882.

President of the council.

SECTION 3. The common council shall, at the first meeting for organization each year after the annual city election choose by ballot from their number, a president, who shall preside over their meetings for the ensuing year. In case of a vacancy in the office of mayor, or of his being unable to perform the duties of his office by reason of absence or sickness, the president of the common council shall have and exercise all the powers and

May discharge duties of Mayor.

discharge all the duties of the mayor, until the mayor shall resume his office, or the vacancy shall be filled by a new election.

City Clerk.

SECTION 4. The clerk shall be elected by the common council for the term of two years. He shall keep the corporate seal and all papers and records of the city.

It shall be his duty to attend all meetings of the common council and to keep a full record of their proceedings.

His term of office, duties, etc.

He shall draw and sign all orders on the treasury (except as otherwise provided in this act), in pursuance of an order or resolution of the common council, and shall keep a full and correct account thereof, in books provided for that purpose. Copies of any and all books, papers, instruments or documents duly filed and kept in his office, and of the endorsements thereon, and transcripts from the records of the proceedings of the com-

Copies of records when certified by clerk are evidence.

mon council, certified by him under the corporate seal of the city, shall be evidence in all courts and places of the contents thereof and of such endorsements in like manner and with the same force and effect as if the originals were produced. He shall also have power to administer oaths and affirmations, authorized to be taken by and under the laws of this 'state; and shall perform such other duties as may be required of him by the common council. *May administer oaths.*

SECTION 5. The city attorney shall conduct all the law business of the corporation, and of the departments thereof, and all other law business in which the city shall be interested when so ordered by the common council. He shall, when required, furnish written opinions upon subjects submitted to him by the mayor, or the common council, or any of its committees, or any other department of the municipal government. He shall keep a docket of all the cases to which the city may be a party in any court of record, in which shall be briefly entered all steps taken in each cause, and which shall, at all times, be opened to the inspection of the mayor, comptroller, or any committee of the common council. It shall also be the duty of the city attorney to draft all ordinances, bonds, contracts, leases, conveyances, and other such instruments of writing as may be required by the business of the city; to examine and inspect tax and assessment rolls, and all proceedings in reference to the levying and collection of taxes and assessments; and to perform such other duties as may be prescribed by the charter and ordinances of the city. He shall have power to appoint an assistant, who shall be authorized to do all acts required by law of the city attorney: *provided*, that the city attorney shall be responsible to the city for all the acts of such assistant. In case of a vacancy in the office of city attorney of the city of Milwaukee, the assistant city attorney shall have full power and authority, and it is hereby made his duty to exercise the office, and perform the duties of city attorney until such vacancy shall be filled in the manner provided by law at the ensuing general municipal election. *City attorney, duties of the office, etc.* *May appoint an assistant.* *Vacancy of city attorney, how filled.*

As amended by Section 1, Chapter 196, Laws of 1885, and Chapter 188, Laws of 1889. See also section 1, Chapter 103, Laws 1883.

By ordinance No. 85, passed July 10, 1894, the appointment of au additional assistant city attorney was authorized.

SECTION 6. The treasurer shall receive all moneys belonging to the city, and shall keep an accurate account of the same in suitable books to be provided for that purpose. He shall also, on the first Monday of each *City treasurer.*

Shall report receipts, disbursements, etc. month, make a report to the common council, embracing a statement of the receipts and disbursements in his office since the last preceding monthly report, on account of the general fund and of each fund which he is required to keep distinct and separate from other funds in the city treasury; and also the total receipts and disbursements during the same time; and the condition of each of such funds at the date of the report. Such reports when made

Report to be published. shall be published with the proceedings of the common council, when the common council shall so direct.

Annual statement. SECTION 7. On the first Monday in April in each year, the treasurer shall file in the office of the city comptroller a statement showing the monthly receipts and disbursements of the preceding year, on account of the general city and ward funds; such statement to embrace the gross amounts of receipts and disbursements set forth in the monthly reports provided for in the next preceding section.

Other official duties, compensation, etc. SECTION 8. The common council shall have power from time to time to reqnire other and further duties to be performed by any officer whose duties are herein prescribed; and to appoint such other officers as in their judgment may be necessary to carry into effect the provisions of this act, and to prescribe their duties; and to fix the compensation of all officers elected or appointed, when the same shall not be fixed by law; such compensation shall be fixed by resolution or ordinance at the time the office is created, or as soon as practicable after the commencement of the municipal year, and shall not be increased or diminished during the term such officer

Dismissal. shall remain in office. The common council shall also have power to dismiss any officer appointed by said council under the provisions of this section, at any time when in the judgment of the common council the services of such officer are no longer needed.

Proposals to do city printing, when to be made, what to contain. SECTION 9. The common council shall, on or before the first Tuesday in April, A. D., 1891, and on or before the same day in each year thereafter, direct the city clerk of said city to advertise in one English, one German and one Polish newspaper, published in said city, for proposals to do the advertising for the said city for the next ensuing year thereafter, of all ordinances, notices and all the city advertising required by law, or by resolution or ordinance of the common council to be published in a newspaper, and also for proposals to publish the proceedings of the common council as may be ordered by the council; such advertisement shall invite separate bids for the advertising required, and for publishing the proceedings of the common council, and shall invite such bids from the English, the German and the Polish newspapers, published daily in said city for at least two consecutive years prior to the date of the bids, and shall require the delivery of such proposals, stating whether in English, in German or in Polish, in writing duly sealed and directed to said clerk, on or before the third Tuesday of April, of the then current year. No bids for either kind of work shall be considered by said clerk, except from a daily newspaper which has been published in said city at least two years consecutively next before the date of the bid, and no bid shall be considered, unless accompanied by a certificate from the city treasurer, showing that the bidder has deposited with him five hundred dollars in money or United States bonds, and a written agreement executed by said bidder under seal, to the effect that if such bid, either for advertising or publishing proceedings, be accepted; and upon being notified thereof, such bidder shall fail to enter into and execute a contract for the advertising or the publication of proceedings, or for both, as required by this act within the time prescribed by said clerk, said advertisement then and in such case the said five hundred dollars shall become absolutely forfeited to said city. If a bid be rejected in case the bidder makes but one, and if both bids be rejected in case the bidder makes two bids, the said certificate of the city treasurer and such agreement and said five hundred dollars shall be thereupon returned to the bidder. The said clerk shall, on the third Tuesday, in April in each year, at 12 o'clock at noon, in the presence of the mayor, open all such bids or proposals, and shall thereupon, in the presence of the mayor, enter upon a record to be kept by the clerk for that purpose, all the said proposals for either kind of work, either in English, German or Polish, with the respective prices for which such newspapers shall offer to do either the advertising or the publication of the proceedings of the common council. And thereupon said clerk shall transmit all such proposals to the common council, at the next regular

Bids of publishers of daily papers only to be considered, certificate of deposit to accompany bid.

Bids to be opened, when and how.

meeting thereof held after the opening of such proposals and a statement of all such proposals designating therein the English newspaper or newspapers, the German newspaper or newspapers, and the Polish newspaper or newspapers, which shall respectively do such advertising or such publication of proceedings or both of them, at the lowest price, for the year ensuing.   If, however, any two or more bids, either for advertising or for publishing the proceedings either in English, German or Polish, shall be for the same price, then all such facts shall be stated. The common council shall thereupon at said meeting thereof by its resolution designate and award such advertising and such publication of council proceedings to the English newspaper or newspapers, the German newspaper or newspapers and the Polish newspaper or newspapers so published in the said city, which shall respectively offer to do such advertising and such publication of proceedings,

Council to set price. or either at the lowest price for the year then ensuing. Provided, that in case only one Polish paper should bid for the publication of such proceedings and said advertising, and such bid should be higher than the lowest bid for the publication of such proceedings and such advertising in German, then the common council shall set the price for such publication of said proceedings and said advertising in the Polish paper equal to the price to be paid to the German newspaper or newspapers to which contracts for publication of said proceedings and said advertising in German have been or may be at that time awarded. And if two or more bids shall be received for either the advertising or the publication of the proceedings in either English, German or Polish, for the same price, then and in such case such advertising or such publication of the proceedings or both, shall be so let to the newspapers, in either such language, having the largest circulation in

Papers having largest circulation to have preference, when. said city, and the publishers of the newspapers to which such advertising or publication of proceedings, or both, shall be awarded as aforesaid, shall respectively thereupon give bond in the sum of two thousand dollars for the faithful performance of said contract, which bond shall be approved by the comptroller of said city as to the surities therein, and by the city attorney as to the form and execution thereof. Provided, that in case both the advertising and the publication of proceedings, either in English, German or Polish,

shall be let to the same newspaper then the penalty of
such bond shall be four thousand dollars. And whenever the successful bidder for the advertising or for the
publication of proceedings as aforesaid, or for both,
shall have executed the contract and bond aforesaid, and
such bond shall have been duly approved as aforesaid,
the sum of five hundred dollars, deposited with the city
treasurer by such bidder, in accordance with this act shall
be returned to the said bidder in accordance with the provisions hereintofore set forth. Such newspapers shall thereupon become liable to print and publish all such ordinances, notices, council proceedings and other proceeding
as are required by the charter of the city of Milwaukee or by
resolution or ordinance of the common council, to be published in a public newspaper, and which such newspaper
shall have contracted to publish, for the compensation specified in such proposals and contract, and shall receive no
other compensation therefor, provided, however, that said
common council may, in its discretion, reject any or all bids
so made, that by said common council shall be deemed
exorbitant or too high and in case of the rejection of all
bids for either advertising or publication of proceedings,
for such cause it shall thereupon be the duty of the said
common council to direct said city clerk to re-advertise
for proposals for such advertising or publication of proceedings, as the case may be, in the same manner as
hereinbefore in this act provided, and the said clerk shall
thereafter transmit to said common council the proposals
so received by him, in the manner aforesaid. The said
common council shall designate the English, the German,
and Polish newspapers receiving the contract for such
advertising as the proper official newspapers of the said
city.

Council may reject bids, when.

As amended by Chapter 498, 1887.

Previously amended by Chapter 136, 1878; 297, 1877.

As amended by Chapter 66, Laws of 1891.

Chapter 297, Laws of 1877, made a material change in this section, as it appeared in Chapter 184, Laws of 1874. The effect of
the amendment is considered and construed in

Wright vs. Forristal, 65 Wisconsin 341.

SECTION 10. The city printer or printers, immediately after the publication of any notice, ordinance or
resolution, which by this act is required to be published,

Proof of official publication.

shall file with the clerk of the city a copy of such publication, with his or their affidavit, or the affidavit of his or their foreman, of the length of time the same has been published; and such affidavit shall be conclusive evidence of the publication of such notice, ordinance or resolution.

Delivering property to successor in office.

SECTION 11. If any person, having been an officer in said city, shall not, within ten days after notification and request, deliver to his successor in office, all property, books, papers and effects of every description, in his possession, belonging to said city or pertaining to the office he may have held, he shall forfeit and pay to the use of the city one hundred dollars, besides all damages caused by his neglect or refusal so to deliver; and such successor may recover the possession of such books, papers and effects in the manner prescribed by the laws of this state.

CITY COMPTROLLER.

Comptroller shall make annual report.

SECTION. 12. The city comptroller shall report annually on or about the first day of January, to the common council, a statement in detail of the expenses of the city and of the several wards during the preceding year, and likewise a detailed estimate of the revenue necessary to be raised for the ensuing year; and the fiscal year of the city shall commence on the first day of January.

As amended by Section 1, Chapter 311, Laws of 1876.

Shall examine and countersign contracts.

SECTION 13. He shall examine all estimates of work to be done by the board of public works of the city, and countersign all contracts entered into by said board of public works, and all certificates of work given by them; and also all contracts made in behalf of the city; and no contract entered into, or certificate issued against property shall be of any validity unless countersigned by the comptroller, except as otherwise expressly provided in this act.

As amended by section 3, Chapter 324, Laws of 1882.

Shall keep a list of certificates issued against property.

SECTION 14. He shall keep a list of all certificates issued against property in each ward, and at the last regular meeting of the common council in November, shall report to the council a schedule of all the lots or parcels of land within the several wards, which under this act, may be subject to any special tax or assessment, and also the amount of such special tax or assessment which it may be necessary to levy on each such lot or parcel of land, with a full statement of the several acts done and performed in reference to such special taxes or assessments—which said schedule shall be verified by the affidavit of the comptroller, and shall be *prima facie* evidence of the facts therein stated in all cases wherein the validity of such special tax or assessment shall come in question. The common council shall, if from such report they shall deem such special tax legal and just, cause the same to be levied in pursuance of the provisions of this act.

As Amended by Section 9, Chapter 144, Laws of 1875.

SECTION 15. He shall report monthly to the common council the amount of work done, or for which contracts have been entered into, chargeable to the several and respective ward funds, and to the general city fund and to any other fund.

Monthly report to council.

Amended by Section 10, Chapter 144, Laws of 1875, and further amended as by Section 4, Chapter 324, Laws of 1882.

SECTION 16. He shall examine the reports, books, papers, vouchers and accounts of the treasurer, the collector of water rates, the clerk of the municipal court, and of any other officer authorized to collect or receive, or charged with the duty of collecting or receiving moneys for the city and shall perform such other duties as are prescribed in this act, and as the common council may from time to time direct.

Shall examine treasurer's accounts.

As amended by Section 5, Chapter 324, Laws of 1882.

SECTION 17. All claims and demands against the city, before they are allowed by the common council, shall be audited and adjusted by the comptroller, and immediately after the allowance by the common council of any claim or account, it shall be the duty of the clerk to furnish to the comptroller a complete list of the same, and, before any warrant shall be issued therefor, it shall be the duty of the comptroller to countersign the same.

Shall audit and adjust all claims against the city.

SECTION 18. The comptroller shall be authorized to administer oaths and affirmations in all matters arising under the laws and ordinances of the city; and he may

May administer oaths.

require all parties having claims or accounts against the city or either of the wards, to verify the same by affidavit. In all cases of doubt arising under any claim or contract against or with the city or either of the wards, he shall inquire into the same; and for this purpose he may examine parties and others under oath; and if any person shall swear or affirm falsely, touching the expenditure of any of the money of the city or either of the wards, or in support of any claim against the said city or either of the said wards, such person shall be subject to indictment or information, and on conviction thereof, shall be punished as for willful and corrupt perjury.

His record open to inspection.

SECTION 19. The comptroller shall keep a record of all his acts and doings, which record shall be opened to the inspection of all parties interested. He shall not be directly or indirectly interested in any contract or job to which the city or either of the wards is a party.

Comptroller, clerk and treasurer may each appoint deputy.

SECTION 20. The comptroller, clerk and treasurer may each appoint a deputy, for whose acts they shall respectively be responsible. Such deputies, after taking the oath of office required to be taken by their principals, may, in case of the sickness or absence of their principals respectively perform all the duties imposed by law or the ordinances of the city, on said principals respectively; and shall likewise be subject to the same liabilities and penalties.

CHAPTER IV.

THE COMMON COUNCIL,—ITS GENERAL POWERS.

SECTION 1. The municipal government of the city shall be vested in the mayor and common council; and the style of all ordinances shall be "the mayor and common council do ordain," etc.

See Gilman vs. Milwaukee, 61 Wis., 588.

State ex rel., Tibbitts vs. Milwaukee, 86 Wis., 376.

Stated meetings.

SECTION 2. The common council shall hold stated meetings at such times and places as they shall appoint; and the mayor or the president of the board of aldermen may call special meetings thereof by notice of at least twenty-four hours, to each of the members, to be served personally, or left at his usual place of abode. Special meetings shall also be called by the president, at the

written request of five aldermen. The common council **Rules of government.**
shall determine the rules for their own government and
proceedings, provided such rules are consistent with the
provisions of this act. A majority of the members elected
shall be required to constitute a quorum for the transac- **Quorum.**
tion of business, but a smaller number may adjourn; their
session shall be open and public; their proceedings shall
be recorded; and all their papers and records, and all
the election returns shall be deposited with the clerk of
the common council, and the same may be examined at
any time in the presence of the clerk; and each member
of the common council shall have one vote, and no more
on any one question. The ayes and noes may be required **Ayes and noes.**
by any member; and on all questions, ordinances or resolutions for assessing and levying taxes, or for the appropriation or disbursement of money, or creating any
liabilities or charge against said city or any fund thereof,
the vote shall be taken by ayes and noes; and every vote
by ayes and noes shall be entered at length upon the
journal. The common council shall be the judge of the
election and qualifications of its own members, and may
punish its members or other persons present, by fine, for **Compulsory at-**
disorderly behavior; may compel the attendance of its **tendance, fines, etc.**
members upon its sessions, and employ the police of said
city for that purpose; and may fine or expel any member
for neglecting his duty as such member, or for unnecessary absence from the sessions of the board. At all
elections or confirmations by the common council, the **Elections and con-**
vote shall be given viva voce, and shall be duly recorded **firmations.**
by the clerk in the journal; and the concurrence of a
majority of all the members elect shall be necessary to an
election or confirmation. The common council is a
continuing body, and unfinished business pending before
it shall not lapse or go down with the council year, but
all pending business before the common council, or any
committee thereof, at the termination of any council year
shall be considered as pending before the common council
of the next succeeding council year, or the corresponding
committee thereof, and may be acted upon and disposed
of by the council of such succeeding year in the same
manner and with the same effect as if no change in such
common council had taken place, by the expiration of a
council year.

In all cases where by the provisions of the charter of **Relating to local**
said city, matters are referred to a local committee of **committees.**

any ward thereof, and in all cases requiring action by such local committee, including the appointment of school commissioners, if such local committee is unable to agree upon a disposition thereof, or shall fail or neglect to act thereon within thirty days from the date when any such matter shall become subject to the action of such local committee, the common council, on the application of either of the aldermen composing such local commitee, or upon its own motion, shall have power and authority to withdraw the matter so referred or requiring action, and take such further action relating thereto as it may deem proper.

As amended by Section 11, Chapter 144, Laws of 1875; Section 6, Chapter 324, Laws of 1882, and Chapter 117, Laws of 1889.

The common council is a continuing body, and has the control of all its records and papers, while the city clerk has only the custody thereof, and of the corporate seal, and is a mere ministerial officer, without any judicial or *quasi* judicial power.

State, ex rel. Tibbitts vs. Milwaukee, 86 Wis., 376.

The power conferred upon the common council to "judge of the election and qualification of its own members," does not exclude the common law jurisdiction of the courts to determine the right to the office of alderman.

State, ex rel. Anderton vs. Kempf, 69 Wis., 470.

A provision in a city charter that every vote by ayes and noes shall be entered on the journal does not apply to votes to adjourn.

Green Bay vs. Brauns, 50 Wis., 204.

Finances.

SECTION 3. The common council shall have the management and control of the finances, and of all the property of the city, except as in this act otherwise provided, and shall likewise, in addition to all other powers herein vested in them, have full power and authority to

Ordinances.

make, enact, ordain, establish, publish, enforce, alter, modify, amend and repeal all such ordinances, rules, by-laws and regulations for the government and good order of the city—for the benefit of the trade, commerce and health thereof—for the suppression of vice—for the prevention of crime—and for carrying into effect the powers vested in said common council, as they shall deem expedient; and to declare and impose penalties,

Penalties.

and to enforce the same against any person or persons who may violate any of the provisions of such ordinances, rules, by-laws and regulations. And such ordinances, rules, by-laws and regulations are hereby declared to be, and have the force of law: *provided*, that they be not pugnant to the constitution of the United States or of this state. And for these purposes the common council shall have authority—anything in a general law of this state to the contrary nothwithstanding—by ordinances, resolutions, by-laws, rules or regulations:

Council may regulate.

To the mayor and common council is expressly given the management and control of the finances, and of all property of the city, except as otherwise provided. They have also full power and authority to enact and enforce the ordinances, rules, by-laws and regulations therein provided for, which said ordinances, rules, by-laws and regulations are thereby made to have the force of law.
> Gilman vs. Milwaukee, 61 Wisconsin, 588.

Any form of procedure to which the council may resort in order to express its determination as to the fixing of a salary, under a charter provision similar to the above, will be a compliance therewith if such procedure be made to appear upon the records in a permanent written form.
> Green Bay vs. Brauns, 50 Wisconsin, 204.

Whether an ordinance is reasonable or valid is usually a question of law for the court.
> Clason vs. Milwaukee, 30 Wisconsin, 316.

An ordinance prohibiting the sale without license, of lemonade, ice cream, cakes, pies, cheese, nuts, fruits, etc., at temporary stands, *held*, unreasonable, as in restraint of trade.
> Barling vs. West, 29 Wisconsin, 307.

1. To regulate groceries, taverns, victualing houses, saloons, gardens and all other places within said city, where wines and other liquors are sold for any purpose, and whether they are sold to be drank on the premises or otherwise, and to license, regulate and restrain tavern-keepers, grocers, wholesale liquor dealers, druggists, keepers of ordinaries, saloons, victualing houses or other houses or places for the selling or giving away spirituous, vinous or fermented liquors; and to classify, grade and regulate the amount to be paid for licenses for dealing in or vending spirituous, vinous or fermented liquors, in proportion to the amount dealt in or vended; and to prescribe the time for which such license shall be granted; and to restrain any person from vending, giving or dealing in spirituous, vinous or fermented liquors unless duly licensed by authority of the common council; provided, the amount to be charged for any such license shall not, in any case, be less than the minimum sum, nor

Groceries, taverns, saloons, etc.

more than the maximum sum required by the general laws of this state, to be paid for like licenses in its towns and villages of the state, under the general laws which are hereby made applicable to all licenses granted hereunder, nor shall any license be granted for a less term than six months. No license issued under authority of said council shall be transferable from one person to another. And all moneys received by said city for such licenses shall be paid into and be part of the general fund of said city; provided, that nothing in this act contained shall be construed to compel druggists to pay such license fee for the sale of any spirituous, vinous, or fermented liquors contained in any medicine compounded by them.

As amended by Chapter 307, Laws of 1883.

Billiard, pool and pigeon tables, etc. 2. To license, tax, regulate, suppress or prohibit billiard tables, pool tables, pigeon tables, shooting galleries, nine or ten pin alleys, bowling saloons and ball alleys.

As amended by Section 7, Chapter 324, Laws of 1882.

Shows and exhibitions. 3. To license, tax, regulate, suppress or prohibit all exhibitions of common showmen, shows of any and every kind, concerts or other musical entertainments by itinerant persons or companies; exhibition of natural or artificial curiosities, caravans, circuses, theatrical performances, and all other exhibitions and amusements.

See Schultz vs. Milwaukee, 49 Wisconsin, 254.

CHAPTER 410, OF THE LAWS OF 1885, AS AMENDED BY CHAPTER 408, OF THE LAWS OF 1889.

Certain powers conferred upon the mayor. SECTION. 1. The common council of the city of Milwaukee is hereby authorized, by ordinance, to confer upon the mayor of said city power and authority to grant and revoke licenses in the name of said city, and to do any act in respect thereto which the said common council is or may be authorized by law to do, upon the conditions prescribed in the charter of said city, or which are or may be prescribed by any law of the state relating to licenses, and applicabie to said city, and upon such further conditions, not inconsistant with such charter or laws, as may be prescribed in and by such ordinance or ordinances and also to confer upon the said mayor power and authority to determine, subject to the provisions of the charter of said city, the amount of the license fee to be paid in each case by persons or companies authorized to be licensed under sub-section 3, of section 3, of chapter 3 (4)? of the charter of said city, being chapter 184, of the laws of 1874, approved March 10th, 1874, and to empower such mayor to do all acts and exercise all powers which the common council may do or exercise under and by authority of said sub-section 3. Provided, that the action of said mayor, upon any application for any license contemplated in this section, shall be final and conclusive upon all parties, and there shall be no appeal therefrom; and the said mayor shall have the power and authority to revoke and annual any license contemplated in this section without notice to or proceeding against any licensee of said city, whenever in his judgment the good order and welfare of said city will be promoted thereby, and such revocation shall be final and conclusive, and there shall be no appeal therefrom; and no license contemplated in this section shall be transferable from person to person, and such licenses may be issued for any term not less than one month nor more than one year, and the license fee to be paid therefor shall be such pro rata of the annual fee fixed by law as the time for which such license is issued.

Action of mayor on application for licenses to be final—may revoke and annul same.

Not transferable, how issued, fees.

SECTION 2. All acts and parts of acts in conflict with this act are hereby repealed.

4. To restrain or prohibit all descriptions of gaming and fraudulent devices and practices, and all playing of cards, dice and other games of chance, for the purpose of gaming in said city.

Gaming,

5. To prevent any riot, noise, disturbance or disorderly assemblages; to suppress and restrain disorderly houses and groceries, and houses of ill-fame; and to authorize the destruction of all instruments and devices used for the purpose of gaming.

Riots and disturbances,

6. To compel owners or occupants of any grocery, cellar, tallow chandler shop, soap factory, tannery, stable, barn, privy, sewer, sewer connection or other unwholesome house or place, to cleanse, remove, construct, re-construct, abate or locate the same in such place and from time to time as often as it may be deemed necessary, for the health, comfort and convenience of the inhabitants of said city.

Abatement of unwholesome places.

7. To direct the location and management of, and regulate breweries, tanneries, packing houses, livery stables, and sale stables; and to direct the location, management and construction of, and regulate, license, restrain, abate or prohibit, within the city and the distance of four miles therefrom, distilleries, slaughtering establishments, establishments for steaming or rendering lard, tallow, offal, and such other substances as can or may be rendered, soap factories, and all establishments or places where any nauseous, offensive or unwholesome

Breweries, tanneries, distilleries, slaughter houses, etc.

business may be carried on; provided, that for the purpose of this section the Milwaukee, Menomonee and
Kinnickinnick rivers, with their branches, to the outer
limits of the county of Milwaukee, and all canals connected with said rivers, together with the lands adjacent
to said rivers and canals, or within one hundred rods
thereof, shall be deemed to be within the jurisdiction of
the city.

As amended by Section 8, Chapter 324, Laws of 1882.

An ordinance passed under the authority granted by this
section, declaring it unlawful (with certain exceptions) for any
person "to slaughter or dress any animal in any building or yard
within the corporate limits," except at a certain designated "city
slaughter house," *held* not to appear *upon its face* to be so
unreasonable, or so in restraint of trade, as to authorize the court
to pronounce it invalid.

Milwaukee vs. Gross, 21 Wis., 243.
Wahl vs. Milwaukee, 23 Wis., 272.

Public markets. *8.* To establish and regulate public markets, determine their location, and make rules and regulations for
the government of the same; to appoint suitable officers
for overseeing and regulating such markets; and to
restrain all persons from interrupting or interfering with
the due observance of such rules and regulations.

Butchers, game, meat, vegetables, etc. *9.* To regulate butchers, and to regulate and restrain
the sale of game, poultry, fresh meat, vegetables, fish,
butter, fruit, eggs, milk and other provisions in the
city; to restrain and punish the forestalling of poultry,
fruit, milk and eggs; and to cause the seizure and destruction or other disposition, of tainted or unwholesome meat,
butter, vegetables, fruit or provisions.

As amended by Section 9, Chapter 324, Laws of 1882.

Gunpowder. *10.* To direct or prohibit the location and management of houses for the storing of gunpowder or other
combustible and dangerous materials within the city.

11. To regulate and restrain the keeping and conveying of gunpowder and other combustible and dangerous
materials; and the use of candles and lights in barns,
stables and outhouses.

Firearms and fire-works. *12.* To prevent the shooting of firearms and crackers,
and to prevent the exhibition or use of any fireworks, at
any time or in any situation which may be considered

by the council dangerous to the city, or to any property therein, or annoying to any citizen thereof.

13. To prevent the encumbering of the streets, sidewalks, lanes, alleys, public grounds, wharves, and docks with carriages, carts, wagons, sleighs, sleds, wheelbarrows, boxes, lumber, firewood, timber, posts, signs, awnings, or any substance or material, or in any manner whatsoever. **Encumbering streets.**

The owner of a city lot possesses an estate in fee to the center of the street.

        Hundhausen vs. Bond, 36 Wis., 29.

        See Schultz vs. Milwaukee, 49 Wis., 254.

14. To prevent horse-racing and immoderate riding or driving in the streets, and to authorize any person to stop persons immoderately riding or driving as aforesaid; to prohibit and punish the abuse of animals; and to compel persons to fasten their horses, oxen, or other animals, attached to vehicles or otherwise, while standing or remaining in any street, alley or public ground. **Horse racing, fast riding or driving.**

While the use of a public highway for coasting is a nuisance, and its suppression is a police duty, the city is not liable to one injured by collision with a person engaged in coasting.

        Schultz vs. Milwaukee, 49 Wis., 254.

        French vs. Milwaukee, 49 Wis., 584.

        Owens vs. Milwaukee, 47 Wis., 561.

15. To regulate and determine the times and places of bathing and swimming in the canals, rivers, harbors, or other waters, in and adjoining said city, and to prevent any obscene or indecent exhibition, exposure or conduct. **Bathing or swimming.**

16. To restrain and punish vagrants, mendicants, street beggars and prostitutes; and to restrain drunkards, immoderate drinking, or obscenity, in the streets or public places, and to provide for arresting, removing and punishing any person or persons who may be guilty of the same. **Vagrants and beggars.**

17. To restrain and regulate, or prohibit the running at large of cattle, horses, mules, swine, sheep, goats, poultry and geese, and to authorize the distraining, impounding and sale of the same, for the penalty incurred and the costs of the proceedings; and also to impose penalties on the owners of any such animals, for a violation of any ordinance in relation thereto. **Impounding cattle, horses and other animals.**

Dogs.

18. To prevent the running at large of dogs in the said city, and to authorize the destruction of the same in a summary manner, when at large contrary to the ordinances.

Where authority is conferred upon a common council in *permissive* language, it is still *imperative* upon the council to exercise it if other persons have an absolute right to have it exercised. But if the power is properly discretionary, the city is not liable for its refusal to exercise such authority.
Kelly vs. Milwaukee, 18 Wisconsin, 89.

19. To provide for licensing the keeping of dogs in the said city, at a sum or rate of not less than one dollar nor more than ten dollars a year for each dog; and to provide for a badge or token to be carried by each licensed dog; and for the secure muzzling of licensed dogs; and for the killing and destruction, in a summary manner, of all dogs not licensed, wherever the same may be found within the said city, and of licensed dogs running at large in the streets, alleys, or public grounds, in said city; and to punish persons keeping unlicensed dogs.

Hackmen, draymen, etc.

20. To license, regulate and suppress hackmen, draymen, cartmen, porters, omnibus drivers, cabmen, carmen, and all others, whether in the permanent employment of any corporation or otherwise, who may pursue like occupations, with or without vehicles, and to prescribe their compensations.

Hoop, balls, kites, etc.

21. To prevent and regulate the rolling of hoops, flying of kites, playing of ball, or other amusements or practices having a tendency to annoy persons passing in the streets or on the sidewalks, or to frighten teams and horses.

Contagious or infectious diseases.

22. To regulate, control and prevent the landing of persons from boats or vessels wherein are contagious or infectious diseases or disorders, and to make such disposition of such persons as to preserve the health of said city; and also to make regulations to prevent the introduction of contagious diseases into the city, or their spread therein; and to make quarantine laws or regulations, and enforce the same within the city and not to exceed five miles beyond the city bounds.

Abatement of nuisances.

23. To abate all nuisances which are or may be injurious to the public health, in any manner they may deem expedient; to prohibit the leaving of books, pamphlets or other articles or matter by hawkers, peddlers or mercantile agents, at residences or factories for inspection, and to do all acts and make all regulations which may be necessary or expedient for the preservation of health and the suppression of disease.

As amended by Chapter 362, Laws of 1887.

24. To regulate the burial of the dead and registration **Mortuary.** of births and deaths; to provide hospital and cemetery grounds; to direct the returning and keeping of bills of mortality; and to impose penalties on physicians, sextons and others, for any default in the premises.

25. To abate and remove all nuisance under the **Common law** ordinances or at common law, and punish the authors **nuisances.** thereof by penalties, fine and imprisonment; and to define and declare what shall be deemed nuisances, and authorize and direct the summary abatement thereof, but nothing in this act shall be so construed as to oust any court of its jurisdiction to abate and remove nuisances in the streets, or any other parts of said city, or within its jurisdiction, by indictment or otherwise.

26. To prevent any person from bringing, depositing **Putrid carcasses.** or having within the limits of said city, any putrid carcass or other unwholesome substance; and to require the removal or destruction of the same by any person who shall have upon or near his premises any such substances or any putrid or unsound beef, pork, fish, hides, or skin any kind; and, on his default, to authorize the removal or destruction thereof by some officer or officers of the city, at the expense of such person or persons.

27. To erect or establish one or more pest houses, hospitals and dispensaries, and control and regulate the same.

28. To prevent the ringing of bells, blowing of horns **Auctioneers, bells,** and bugles, crying of goods, and all other noises, **etc.** performances and devices tending to the collection of persons on the streets or sidewalks, by auctioneers or others, for the purpose of business, amusement, or otherwise.

29. To control, regulate, or prohibit the use of steam **Steam whistles.** whistles within the limits of the city.

Street sprinkling. *30.* To control and regulate the streets, alleys, and public grounds in said city, and provide for sprinkling the same, and to remove and abate any obstructions and encroachments therein.

As amended by Section 12, Chapter 144, Laws of 1875.

Removing snow from street and sidewalks. *31.* To compel the owners or occupants of buildings or grounds to remove and keep snow, ice, dirt or rubbish from the sidewalk, street, or alley opposite thereto; and to compel such owner or occupants to remove from the lots, owned or occupied by them, all such substances as the board of health shall direct; and on their default, to authorize the removal or destruction thereof by some officer of the city, at the expense of such owners or occupants.

Control of streets and bridges. *32.* To control, regulate, repair, amend and clean the streets and alleys, bridges, and side and cross walks, and open, widen, straighten and vacate streets and alleys, and establish and alter the grade thereof; and prevent the encumbering of the streets and alleys in any manner, and protect the same from any encroachment or injury; and to regulate the manner of using the streets and pavements in the said city, and protect the same from injury by vehicles used thereon.

The power vested in the common council to vacate streets and alleys, "anything in any general law of the state to the contrary notwithstanding," is exclusive, and the circuit court cannot exercise jurisdiction in the city of Milwaukee to vacate an alley.

Brandt vs. Milwaukee, 69 Wis., 386.

33. To prevent all persons from riding or driving any horse, ox, mule, cattle or other animal, on the sidewalks in the said city, or in any way doing any damage to such sidewalks.

Pounds, pumps, wells and cisterns. *34.* To make, establish and regulate public pounds, pumps, wells, cisterns and reservoirs, and provide for the erection and maintenance of water works for the supply of water to the inhabitants, and to prevent the unnecessary waste of water.

See Gilman vs. Milwaukee, 61 Wis., 588.

Street lights. *35.* To erect lamps and regulate the lighting thereof; and to provide for lighting the streets, public grounds and public buildings, with gas or otherwise.

36. To regulate the sale of bread within said city, and **Bread.** prescribe the assize and weight of bread in the loaf, and the quality of the same; and to provide for the seizure and forfeiture of bread baked contrary to such regulations and prescriptions.

37. To require every merchant, retailer, trader and **Weights and** dealer in merchandise or property of any description **measures.** which is sold by measure or weight, to cause his weights and measures to be sealed by the city sealer, and to be subject to his inspection, and to provide for the punishment of persons using false weights and measures. The standards of such weights and measures shall be conformable to those established by law in this state.

38. To regulate the weighing and sale of hay and **Hay, wood and ice.** the places and manner thereof; to regulate the cutting and sale of ice, and to restrain the sale of such ice as is impure; also to regulate the measuring and sale of wood, and the weighing and selling of coal and lime, and the places and manner thereof, and to appoint suitable persons to superintend and conduct the same, and define their duties.

An ordinance passed under the authority conferred by this section is not in restraint of trade, but a salutary regulation of it, and is not repugnant to the constitution or laws of the state.

Yates vs. Milwaukee, 12 Wis., 752.

39. To regulate the times, places and manner of **Auctions, time of** holding public auctions or vendues. **holding.**

An ordinance prohibiting auction sales after sundown is invalid, as being an unreasonable restraint upon trade.

Hayes vs. Appleton, 24 Wis., 542.

40. To tax, license and regulate road vehicles of **Road vehicles and** any and every kind and description, to tax, license, **occupations.** control and regulate auctioneers, distillers, brewers and pawn keepers, pawn brokers, loan brokers, keepers of loan offices, dealers in second hand goods, and all persons who loan money upon the security of chattel mortgages, or other chattel security, and all keepers or proprietors of intelligence offices, junk shops, and places for the sale and purchase of second hand goods, wares and merchandise, and to tax, license, regulate and restrain hawkers, peddlers and venders of milk, and runners or solicitors for steamboats, vessels, cars, railroads, stages, public

houses and other establishments, and keepers or proprietors of gift book stores, gift concerts, and other gift
enterprises, and persons therein engaged; and to fix and
regulate the amount of license under this subdivision, and
to prescribe the time for which such licenses shall be
granted, and to provide and enforce penalties for carrying
on either of said trades, kinds of business or employments,
or using such vehicles without license, and to regulate
the manner in which they shall be carried on or used;
Term and amount of license. provided that no such license shall be granted for a less
term than three months, nor for a longer term than one
year, and that the amount to be so paid for any such
license shall not be less than at the rate of one dollar
per year, nor greater than at the rate of five hundred
dollars per year for the carrying on either of said trades,
kinds of business or employments; provided that the
provisions of this act shall not apply to dealers and
venders in malt, spirituous, ardent or intoxicating liquors.

As amended by Section 2, Chapter 311, Laws of 1876, further
amended by Section 10, Chapter 324, Laws of 1882, and Chapter
308, Laws of 1883, further amended by Chapter 460, Laws of 1885,
and further amended by Chapter 74, Laws of 1891.

CHAPTER 337, LAWS OF 1887.

Grant licenses. SECTION 1. The mayor may, from time to time, grant licenses
under Chapter 308, of the Laws of 1883, to such persons as shall
produce to him satisfactory evidence of their good character to
exercise or carry on the business of a pawn broker, a loan broker,
keeper of a loan office, dealer in second hand goods, or junk shop
keeper, and no person shall exercise or carry on the business of a
pawn broker, loan broker, keeper of a loan office, dealer in second
hand goods or junk shop keeper, without being duly licensed,
under penalty of a fifty dollar fine for each and every day he or she
shall exercise or carry on said business without such license.

Pawnbrokers defined. SECTION 2. Any person who loans money on deposit or pledge
of personal property or other valuable things or who deals in the
purchasing of personal property or other valuable thing on condition of selling the same back again at a stipulated price, is hereby
defined and declared to be a pawn broker within the meaning of
this act. Every person receiving a license under the provisions
of this act shall pay therefor such sum as may be fixed by the
common council of said city of Milwaukee, said license to be paid
to the city treasurer for the use of the city.

Licensee to give bond. SECTION 3. Every person so licensed shall at the time of
receiving such license or at any time thereafter when required by
the mayor, enter with two sufficient sureties into a joint and
several bond to the city of Milwaukee in the penal sum of five
hundred dollars for the due observance of this act, and of all

ordinances of the common council as may be passed or enforced respecting pawn brokers, keepers of loan offices, dealers in second hand goods, and junk shop keepers at any time during the continuance of such license.

SECTION 4.   Every licensed pawn broker, loan broker, keeper of a loan office, every dealer in second hand goods and keeper of a junk shop, shall keep a book in which shall be fairly written in ink at the time of each loan or purchase, an accurate and true discription in the English language of the goods, article or thing pawned, pledged or bought, the amount of money loaned thereon, or paid therefor, the time of pledging or purchasing the same; if a loan, the rate of interest to be paid on such loan, and the name and residence, together with a true description of the person or persons pawning, pledging or selling such goods, article or thing, and no entry made in such book shall be erased, obliterated or, defaced. **Must keep a book.**

SECTION 5.   The said book, as well as every other article or thing of value pawned, pledged or purchased, shall at all reasonable times be open to the inspection of the chief of police or any member of the police force designated by the chief of police for such purpose. **To be open for inspection.**

SECTION 6.   The chief of police may, in his discretion, cause any article or thing of value which has been pawned, pledged or purchased, which he shall have reason to believe was not so pawned, pledged or disposed of by the lawful owner, to be held for the purpose of being identified by such lawful owner for such resonable length of time as the chief of police shall deem necessary for such identification. **Chief of police may hold unpawned things.**

SECTION 7.   It shall be the duty of every licensed person aforesaid, and of every person dealing in second hand goods as aforesaid, to make out and deliver to the chief of police every day, before the hour of twelve noon, a legible and corect copy from the book required by section 4, of this act, of all personal property and other valuable thing received on deposit or purchased during the preceding day, together with the time of the day when the same was received or purchased, and a true description of the person or persons by whom left in pledge, or from whom the same were purchased, and in no case shall such personal property or thing of value be disposed of by said pawn broker, loan broker, keeper of a loan office, second hand dealer or junk shop keeper, within twenty four hours from the time of filing such report with the chief of police as herein provided, except upon written permission of the chief of police for that purpose. **Second hand dealers required to make report daily.**

SECTION 8.   No person licensed under the provision of this act shall bargain for, take, purchase or receive in pawn any property, bonds, notes, securities, article, or other valuable thing from any minor, nor from any intoxicated person. **Can not take property from intoxicated person.**

SECTION 9.   The mayor may forthwith revoke the license of any person who shall have been convicted of any violation of any provision of this act, whether the judgment in such case shall have been appealed from or not. **Mayor may revoke license.**

SECTION 10. Every person violating any of the provisions of this act shall be punished by a fine of not exceeding one hundred dollars, nor less than ten dollars, or by imprisonment in the house of correction of Milwaukee County for a term not exceeding six months, or by both such fine and imprisonment.

Lumber.

41. To regulate or prohibit the keeping of any lumber yard, and the placing, piling, or selling of lumber, timber wood, or other combustible material, within the fire limits of said city.

42. To regulate the measuring and inspecting of lumber, shingles, timber, posts, staves and headings, and all building materials, and to appoint one or more inspectors.

Fish.

43. To regulate the places and manner of selling pickled and other fish.

Whiskey,

44. To regulate the inspection of whiskey and other liquors, to be sold in barrels, hogsheads and other vessels.

45. To provide for the inspection and regulation of stationary steam engines and boilers.

46. To appoint inspectors, weighers and gaugers, and regulate their duties and prescribe their fees.

47. To establish and regulate public pounds.

Locomotive engines, railroad cars, etc.

48. To regulate and prohibit the use of locomotive engines within the city, and to require railroad cars to be propelled by other power than that of steam; to direct and control the location of railroad tracks; and to require railroad companies to construct and maintain, at their own expense, such bridges, viaducts, tunnels, or other conveniences, at public railroad crossings, as the common council may deem necessary; also to regulate the running of horse railway cars, the laying down of tracks for the same, the transportation of passengers thereon, and the kind of rail to be used.

Policemen.

49. To appoint watchmen and policemen, and regulate the police, and prescribe their duties.

Numbering houses.

50. To compel the owners and occupants of all houses, stores and other buildings within the city of Milwaukee, to number the same in such manner as the common council may from time to time prescribe.

51. To declare the weed, commonly called the Canada   Noxious plants. thistle, and other noxious plants and weeds on lots, parts of lots and lands in the said city, a public nuisance, and to proceed to abate the same, as the said city is authorized by law to abate other nuisances.

CHAPTER 313, LAWS OF 1887, AS AMENDED BY
CHAPTER 432, LAWS OF 1889; AS AMENDED
BY CHAPTER 145, LAWS OF 1893, AND
FURTHER AMENDED BY CHAPTER
154, LAWS OF 1895.

SECTION 1. Section 1, of chapter 145, of the laws of 1893, is   **Destruction of** hereby amended so that the same shall read as follows: Section 1.   **weeds.** Every person and corporation shall destroy, upon all lands which he or they shall own, occupy or control, all weeds known as the Canada thistle (circium arvense), burdock (lappa officinalis), white or ox-eye daisy (leucanthemum vulgare), snap dragon or toad flax (linaria vulgaris), cockle burr (zanthium strumarium), sow thistle (souchus arvensis), sour dock and yellow dock (rumex crispus), mustard (sinapis arvensis), wild parsnip (thapsium barbinode), sweet clover (mellilotus alba or mellitotus vulgaris), and Russian thistle (salsola kali), and at such time and in such manner as shall effectually prevent them from bearing seed. In like manner shall he or they destroy any of the above-mentioned weeds standing or growing as far as the center of the highways, lanes or alleys, adjoining the lands owned or controlled by him or them.

SECTION 2. If the occupant of any such lands shall fail to so   **Penalty for failure** destroy such weeds as so required after having six days' notice in   **to destroy.** writing by any commissioner of noxious weeds, such occupant shall be fined five dollars for the first offense and ten dollars for each offense thereafter.

SECTION 3. Whenever it shall become necessary to serve   **Railroad com-** notice as provided in section 2, of this act, upon any railroad or   **panies, service of** other corporation owning or controlling any lands in any town,   **notice upon.** such notice, if served upon any agent of such corporation residing or being in said town, shall be deemed good and sufficient notice, and if no such agent shall reside or be in such town, then such notice may be served upon any agent of such corporation who shall reside or be in any adjoining town.

SECTION 4. It shall be the duty of the chairman of the board   **Commissioners of** of supervisors of each town, the president of the village board of   **noxious weeds,** any village, and the mayor of any city, to appoint some competent   **how appointed—** person or persons, in their town, village or city, to be styled   **duties.** commissioner of noxious weeds, who shall be required to take the same oath as town officers, and shall hold his or their office for one year, and until his or their successors are appointed and qualified. Where more than one commissioner is appointed in any town, city or village, they shall be assigned separate and distinct districts or territories. For any good cause any such commissioner may be removed by the officer appointing him and a successor appointed to serve the unexpired term.

Duties of commissioner.

SECTION 5. The commissioner shall carefully inquire concerning the existence of noxious weeds in his township or precinct, and in case any person, persons or corporations occupying or controlling any lands within this state shall neglect to destroy any Canada thistle, teasel, burdock and snap dragon, white or ox-eye daisy, cockle burr, sow thistle, sour dock and yellow dock, growing on any lands owned or controlled by him or them, or on any highway, lane or alley adjoining such lands, it shall be the duty of the commissioner to destroy or cause to be destroyed all such weeds. He shall spend as many days as the chairman of the town board, president of the village or mayor of the city may deem necessary, and for each day so spent shall receive two dollars, upon presentation of his account therefor, verified by his oath and specifying by separate items against each piece of land, describing the same, and the several amounts shall be placed in the next tax roll in a separate column, headed, "for destruction of weeds," as a tax against the lands upon which such weeds were destroyed and be collected as other taxes.

Destruction of weeds on railroad lands—compensation.

SECTION 6. When any commissioner shall destroy any noxious weed under the provisions of this act, upon any lands owned or controlled by any railroad corporation, the said commissioners shall certify to the amount of money he is entitled to under the provisions of this act, to the board of supervisors of his town, who shall transmit a certified copy of said certificate to the state treasurer, who shall include the amount of money in said certificate in the amount to be paid for a license by said corporation, as provided in section 1213, of the revised statutes of 1878; and the state treasurer shall collect the same from said corporation, as prescribed in the license provided in sections 1212 and 1213, of the revised statutes, and return the said money to the town from which such certificate was transmitted.

Neglect of proper officer to perform duties—penalty.

SECTION 6a. Any chairman of a town board, or any president of a village board, or the mayor of any city, who shall refuse or neglect to appoint one or more thistle commissioners, as provided in section 4, of said chapter, within thirty days next following their election, shall be fined not less than fifty dollars nor more than one hundred dollars and costs, on complaint made in writing by any resident of the county to a justice of the peace, or magistrate in such county. Any weed commissioner, after taking his oath of office, who shall refuse or neglect to perform the duties as prescribed in this chapter, shall be fined not less than ten nor more than twenty-five dollars and costs, on complaint stated as above, for each and every such offense.

Town clerk to read this act aloud at town meeting.

SECTION 7. It shall be the duty of every town clerk, at the annual town meeting in each year, to read aloud to said meeting the whole of this act.

Repeal.

SECTION 8. All previous acts in relation to noxious weeds, and all amendments thereto are hereby repealed.

52. To impose fines for all violations, within the **Fines.**
limits of the said city, of the general laws of the state,
when, in their judgment, it is necessary for the peace
and good order, or for the health of the said city.

53. To direct and regulate the planting and preserving **Trees.**
of ornamental trees in the streets and public grounds.

54. Exclusively to erect and construct, or to permit **Bridges.**
or cause or procure to be erected and constructed, float,
pivot or drawbridges, over the navigable waters within
the jurisdiction of said city, and keep the same in repair;
said bridges to have draws of suitable width; also to erect
and construct, or cause to be erected and constructed,
bridges over ravines within said city.

As amended by Section 13, Chapter 144, Laws of 1875.

55. To preserve the harbor; to prevent any use of **Harbor and river.**
the same, or any act in relation thereto, inconsistent
with or detrimental to the public health, or calculated to
render the waters of the same, or any part thereof, impure
or offensive, or tending in any degree to fill up or obstruct
the same; to prevent and punish the casting or depositing therein of any earth, dead animals, ashes, or other
substance or filth, logs or floating matter; to prevent and
remove all obstructions therein, and punish the authors
thereof; to regulate and prescribe the mode and speed of **Speed of vessels.**
entering and leaving the harbor, of passing the bridges,
and of coming to and departing from the wharves and
streets of the city, by steamboats, canal boats and other
crafts and vessels, and the disposition of the sails, yards,
anchors and appurtenances thereof, while entering,
leaving or abiding in the harbor; and to regulate and
prescribe by such ordinances, or through their harbor
master or other authorized officer, such location of every
canal boat, steamboat, or other craft or vessel afloat, and
such changes of station in, and use of the harbor, as may
be necessary to promote order therein, and the safety and
equal convenience, as near as may be, of all such boats,
vessels, crafts and floats; and to impose penalties, not **Penalties and ex-**
exceeding one hundred dollars, for any offense against **penses.**
any such ordinance; and by such ordinance to change
(*Sic*) such penalties, together with such expenses as may
be incurred by the city in enforcing this section, upon
the steamboat, canal boat, or other vessel, craft or float.

56. To prescribe, regulate and control the time or times, manner and speed of all boats, crafts and vessels passing the bridges over the Milwaukee, Menomonee and Kinnickinnick rivers, and the canals in said city.

Lake piers and wharves.

57. To regulate the construction of piers and wharves extending into Lake Michigan within the limits of said city; and to prescribe and control the prices to be charged for pierage or wharfage thereon; and to regulate, prescribe and control the prices to be charged for dockage and storage within the city.

River piers and wharves.

58. To lease the wharfing privileges of the rivers at the ends of streets, upon such terms and conditions as may be reserved in the leasing of other real estate, reserving such rents as may be agreed upon, and employing such remedies in case of non-performance of any covenants in such case as are given by law in other cases; but no buildings shall be erected thereon, nor shall a lease for any longer period then ten days at any one time be executed; and the owner or owners of the adjoining lot or lots, shall, in all cases, have the preference in leasing such property, and a free passage over the same for all persons with their baggage shall be reserved in such lease: *provided*, nothing in this section shall be so construed as to impair or prejudice any rights which any person may have acquired by the acceptance of any proposition heretofore made by said city respecting such wharfing privileges.

Indigent and destitute children.

59. To authorize the taking up, and to provide for the safe keeping and education, for such periods of time as may be deemed expedient, of all children who are destitute of proper parental care and growing up in mendicancy, ignorance, idleness and vice.

Vagrants.

60. To authorize the arrest, fine and imprisonment, as vagrants, of all persons, who not having visible means to maintain themselves, are without employment, idly loitering or rambling about, or staying in groceries, drinking saloons, houses of ill-fame or houses of bad repute, gambling houses, railroad depots or fire engine houses; or who shall be found trespassing in the night time upon the private premises of others; or begging, or placing themselves in the streets or other thoroughfares or public places to beg or receive alms; also keepers, exhibitors, or visitors at any gaming table, gambling

Swindlers.

house, house of fortune telling, place for cock fighting, or other place of device; and all persons who go about for the purpose of gaming or watch stuffing, or who shall have in their possession any article or thing used for obtaining money under false pretenses, or shall disturb any place where public or private schools are held, either on week day or Sabbath, or places where religious worship is held.

61. To regulate or prohibit the carrying or wearing by any person under his clothes, or concealed about his person of any pistol or colt, or slung shot, or cross knuckles, or knuckles of lead, brass or other metal, or bowie knife, dirk knife, or dirk or dagger, or any other dangerous or deadly weapon, and to provide for the confiscation or sale of such weapons. — **Concealed arms, weapons.**

62. To control and regulate the construction of buidings, chimneys and stacks, and to prevent and prohibit the erection or maintenance of any insecure or unsafe buildings, stack, wall or chimney, in said city, and to declare them to be nuisances, and to provide for their summary abatement. — **Chimneys and smoke stacks.**

63. To declare that it shall be unlawful for any hall, theatre, opera house, church, school house or building of any kind whatsoever, to be used for the assemblage of people, or for any building exceeding three stories in height, to be used as a manufactory, hotel or boarding house, or for any other purpose, unless the same is provided with ample means for the safe and speedy egress of the persons therein assembled, in case of alarm, and may require and regulate the erection of ladders, fire escapes, standpipes, or other appliances for the escape of persons from such buildings, or the extinguishment of fires, and prescribe penalties for the failure, to provide or maintain such means and appliances for the egress and escape of persons from such buildings. — **Height of buildings.** — **Fire escapes.**

As amended by Section 11, Chapter 324, Laws of 1882, as amended by Chapter 75, Laws of 1891.

64. To require the mayor and chief of police to detail a sufficient number of men from the police force of the city to take charge of the public grounds of said city, and to properly enforce the pound ordinances thereof, and to provide for the election of one or more pound — **Public grounds and pounds.**

keepers, and for the payment of such pound keepers, either by salary or fees, or partly by both; and to make all necessary rules and regulations for the enforcement of any pound ordinance of said city.

Common council may provide for erection of guards between curb and walk.

65. The common council of the city of Milwaukee is hereby authorized and empowered to prescribe by ordinance the erection of guards and the kind of guards that shall or may be erected, to protect, the turf laid by the said city or by the owner of the abutting lot or land, by direction or permission of said city, between the curb and the walk laid for the traveling foot passengers, for the purpose of ornamenting or beautifying any street in said city, and to prohibit foot passengers from using the space between the curb and the said sidewalk, for travel, or to tear down or injure such guards, and to prescribe proper penalties for the violation of any of the provisions of such ordinance; and any person who shall hereafter receive any injury by reason of his or her stepping on the said space between the sidewalk and the curb, or by reason of his or her stepping or running against any such guard erected to protect the same, if properly erected, shall be deemed guilty of contributory negligence and shall not recover any damages therefor.

Chapter 430, Laws of 1887.

Vote necessary to pass an ordinance.

SECTION 4. All laws and ordinances shall be passed by an affirmative vote of a majority of the aldermen elect, and shall be signed by the mayor, and by the presiding officer of the council, and shall be published in the official papers of said city before the same shall be in force, and within fifteen days after such publication, they shall be recorded by the city clerk, in books to be provided for that purpose; but, before any of the said laws, ordinances, rules, regulations, or by-laws shall be so recorded, the publication thereof respectively, within the said time, shall be proved by the affidavit of the foreman or publisher of each of such newspapers, and said affidavits shall be recorded therewith, and at all times and in all courts and places, shall be deemed and taken as sufficient evidence of the time and manner of such publication. No ordinance shall be passed, no

Ayes and noes on ordinances and appropriations.

appropriation shall be made, and no act, regulation, resolution or order which may create a debt or liability against said city, or a charge upon any fund thereof, shall be adopted without a vote in its favor of a majority of all the aldermen (entitled to seats in the common council) which vote shall be taken by the ayes and noes, and entered among the proceedings of the council; and when the grade of any street shall have been established by ordinance, and such street shall have been actually made to conform to such established grade, under the direction of the proper authorities of said city, such grade shall not thereafter be changed without a vote of two-thirds of all the members elect of the common council, including the votes of all the members elect representing the ward or wards in which the change is proposed to be made, in favor thereof; the vote in every such case shall be taken by ayes and noes, and shall be entered upon the journal of the common council. All rules, regulations, resolutions and by-laws shall be passed by an affirmative vote of a majority of the aldermen elect, except when otherwise provided in this act. Every ordinance to establish the grade of any street or alley, shall, after its introduction in the common council, be published in full with the proceedings of the council, and shall lay over not less than two weeks after its introduction before it shall be passed.

Vote necessary to change grade of street.

As amended by Section 14, Chapter 144, Laws of 1875; further amended by Section 10, Chapter 311, Laws of 1876.

A provision of the charter requiring all ordinances to be published before they take effect, and within fifteen days thereafter to be recorded, but before recording the publication is to be proved by affidavit, will be construed as not requiring the publication within fifteen days after the enactment, but that the proof must be made within fifteen days after publication.

Janesville vs. Dewey, 3 Wis., 221.

SECTION 5. All resolutions appropriating money, or creating any charge against any of the funds of said city or wards, and all accounts and ordinances, shall be referred to appropriate committees and shall only be acted on by the common council at a subsequent meeting not held on the same day, on the report of the committee to which the same were referred; provided, however, that when a committee shall report by resolution upon a matter referred to them by the common council, action upon such resolution may, in the discretion of the council, be taken without a further reference; and, in either case, if

Appropriation resolution shall be referred.

the report is made upon an ordinance or resolution appropriating money out of, or creating any charge against, any of the funds aforesaid, said report shall be countersigned by the city comptroller, and said comptroller shall not countersign any such report, unless there is a sufficient portion of the proper city or ward fund unappropriated to meet said appropriation or charge. Action upon any report of a committee made to the common council, shall be deferred to the next regular meeting of the same by request of one-fifth of the aldermen present. And no portion of any city or ward fund shall be transferred to, or borrowed from, or by any other of said funds, at any time, or for any purpose whatever, so as to increase any fund to an amount in excess of the estimate for such fund as fixed by the common council.

Amended by Section 15, Chapter 144, Laws of 1875; further amended by Chapter 274, Laws of 1881, and further amended by Section 12, Chapter 324, Laws of 1882.

The word "only" in this section prohibits all action of the common council upon the merits of such resolution, except when the matter is brought before them in one of the ways and upon the conditions prescribed. Such requirements are preliminary to such action on the merits, and are jurisdictional.

Gilman vs. Milwaukee, 61 Wis., 588.

Reconsiderations. SECTION 6. No vote of the common council shall be reconsidered or rescinded at a special meeting, unless at such special meeting there be present as large a number of aldermen as were present when such vote was taken.

Mayor shall approve ordinance in writing. SECTION 7. Every act, ordinance, by-law, regulation, resolution, or appropriation, which shall have been duly passed by the common council, before it shall take effect, and within five days after its passage, shall be duly certified by the city clerk, and presented to the mayor for his approbation. If he approve, he shall sign it; if not, he

Time in which to return them with objections. shall return it within five days, with his objections stated in writing, to the city clerk; and the clerk shall submit said objections to the common council at their next regular meeting thereafter, who shall enter said objections upon the record of their proceedings, and shall proceed to reconsider the matter; and if, after such reconsideration, two-thirds of all the members elected should vote

Vote necessary to override veto. to pass such act, ordinance, by-law, regulation, resolution, or appropriation, it shall take effect and be in force as an act or law of the corporation; otherwise it shall be null and void.   All such votes, after receiving the objections of the mayor, shall be taken by yeas and nays, and entered upon the journal of proceedings of the common council.   If the mayor shall not return any act, ordinance, by-law, resolution, or appropriation, so presented to him, within five days after such presentation thereof, it shall take effect in the same manner as if he had signed it.

May become law without mayor's signature.

SECTION 8.   The powers conferred upon the said common council to provide for the abatement or removal of nuisances, shall not bar or hinder suits, prosecutions or proceedings in the courts, according to law.   Depots, houses, or buildings of any kind wherein more than twenty-five pounds of gunpowder are deposited, stored or kept at one time, gambling houses, houses of ill-fame, disorderly taverns, and houses or places where spirituous, vinous or fermented liquors are sold without license, within the limits of said city, are hereby declared and shall be deemed public or common nuisances.

Suits may be brought to abate nuisances.

As amended by Section 16, Chapter 144, Laws of 1875.

SECTION 9.   The common council shall examine, audit and adjust the accounts of the clerk, treasurer, board of public works, and all other officers or agents of the city, at such time as they may deem proper, and also at the end of each year, and before the term for which the officers of said city are elected or appointed shall have expired.   And the common council shall require each and every such officer and agent to exhibit his books, accounts and vouchers, for such examination and settlement, and if any such officer or agent shall refuse to comply with the orders of said council in the discharge of their duties in pursuance of this section, or shall neglect or refuse to render his accounts or present his books and vouchers to said council, or any authorized committee thereof, it shall be the duty of the common council to declare the office of such person vacant.   The common council shall order suits and proceedings at law against any officer and agent of said city, who may be found delinquent or defaulting in his accounts, or in the discharge of his official duties. And they shall make a full record of all such settlements and adjustments.

Accounts of treasurer, board of public works and others shall be annually examined.

Council may order suits.

CHAPTER 148, LAWS OF 1893.

AN ACT to require the publication of applications to village boards and city councils for private or corporate franchises.

SECTION 1. The provisions of the Revised Statutes of the State of Wisconsin, relating to powers of village boards of incorporated villages, and as to powers of common councils of cities in the state of Wisconsin, in relation to granting franchises, are hereby limited and defined by the following provision: No franchise shall be granted by any village board of any village, or by any common council of any city in the State of Wisconsin, to any person or persons or corporation whatsoever, without first having published such franchise, at the expense of the party applying for the same, in the official newspaper of such city or village, for not less than two weeks previous to taking action thereon by such village board or common council, in order that the people whose interests are at stake may have an opportunity to be heard if they so desire.

SECTION 2. This act shall be construed to be an amendment of every city charter and of every village charter, whether incorporated under the special or general laws of the State of Wisconsin, wherein a similar provision does not already exist, but not otherwise.

CHAPTER V.

BOARD OF PUBLIC WORKS.

Board of public works how created and organized.

SECTION 1. There is hereby established for the city of Milwaukee an executive department to be known as the board of public works, which shall consist of four persons styled commissioners of public works. The city engineer of said city shall be ex-officio one of said commissioners, and president of said board. The members of said board shall be appointed by the mayor of said city, with the approval of a majority of the members elect of the common council. The term of office of the city engineer and of the other commissioners shall be three years, and shall commence on the third Tuesday of April. Each of the present members of said board shall hold his office (unless sooner removed as provided by law) until the expiration of the term for which he was appointed, and annually hereafter a person shall be appointed for three years, as above provided, to succeed the member whose term of office shall then expire, and as often as vacancy shall occur in said board, whether by death, resignation, or otherwise, a person shall be appointed in the manner above provided, to succeed the person whose office shall so become vacant, for the remainder of his term. The members of said board,

Term of office.

except the city engineer, at the time of their appointment, shall respectively reside—one in that part of said city which lies east of the Milwaukee river, one in that part of said city which lies west of the Milwaukee and north of the Menomonee rivers, and one in that part of said city which lies south of the Menomonee and west of the Milwaukee rivers. The commissioners shall elect annually, from their own number, a secretary, who is hereby authorized to administer all oaths required by this act. The city engineer and the other commissioners of said board may be removed for incompetency by the mayor, with the approval of a majority of all the members elect of the common council. *Their residence prescribed.*

As amended by Section 17, Chapter 144, Laws of 1875.

" An *executive* department to be known as the board of public works," was established for the city by the charter, with certain limited powers.

Koch vs. Milwaukee, 89 Wis., 220.

The original act creating the board of public works, being ch. 401, laws of 1869, *held* valid.

State, ex rel. Attorney General vs. O'Neill, 24 Wis., 149.

SECTION 2. The mayor shall on the third Tuesday of April, 1875, or within one week thereafter, and once in three years thereafter, appoint, subject to the approval of a majority of the members elect of the common council, some competent person as city engineer, who shall keep his office in some convenient place, to be designated by the common council, and it shall be his special duty to superintend and to do or cause to be done, all the civil engineering required by the board of public works, in the management and prosecution of all the public improvements committed to their charge and all such other surveying as may be directed by said board, or by the common council. He shall devote his whole time to the duties of his office as city engineer and ex-officio commissioner and president of the board of public works, but he shall not be required to sign any contract, certificate or other paper to be executed or issued by said board of public works under this act. Said engineer shall possess the same powers in making surveys and plats within said city that are given by law to county surveyors, and the like validity and effect shall be given to his acts, and to all plats and surveys made by him, as are or may *City engineer, his duties and powers.*

be given to the acts, plats and surveys of county surveyors. He shall keep a record of all his official acts and doings, shall keep on file a copy of all plats of the lots and blocks and sewers embraced in the city limits, of profiles of streets, alleys and sewers and of the grade thereof, and of all drafts and plans relating to bridges and harbors, and to any public buildings belonging to the city of Milwaukee; and shall keep a record of the location of bench marks and permanent corner stakes from which subsequent surveys shall be started, all of which such records and documents shall be the property of the city, open to the inspection of parties interested, and shall be delivered over by said engineer at the expiration of his term of service to his successor in office, or to the board

Shall make annual report. of public works. He shall make an annual report of all the acts and doings of the engineer's department to the board of public works on or before the first day of February in each year. Said engineer shall appoint such assistants and workmen as he may deem necessary in the discharge of his duties, subject, however, to such regulations respecting the number of assistants and workmen to be appointed, and their compensation, as the common council may prescribe by ordinance.

As amended by Section 18, Chapter 144, Laws of 1875.

Additional employes and workmen. SECTION 3. The said board of public works are authorized to employ, from time to time, such superintendents, clerks, agents, assistants and workmen as they may deem necessary in the discharge of their duties; and may adopt by-laws for the regulation and conduct of all persons in their employ or under their supervision; subject, however, to such regulations respecting the number of persons regularly or permantly employed and their compensation and duties, as the common council may prescribe by ordinance. Any person appointed or employed under the provisions of this or the next preceding section, may at any time be removed or discharged for incompetency by the board of public works or by a majority of the members elect of the common council. The commissioner of public works appointed prior to

Compensation of commissioners. the third Tuesday in April, 1874, and now in office, shall receive an annual salary of $2,250, and the commissioner appointed on the third Tuesday in April of 1874, shall continue to receive the annual salary fixed by the common council on the sixth day of May, 1874. The city

engineer, who may be hereafter appointed, shall receive
such a salary as may be fixed by the common council,
not exceeding four thousand dollars per annum, and the
other commissioners who may be hereafter appointed shall
receive such a salary as may be fixed by the common
council not exceeding three thousand dollars per annum,
but the amount of such salary for the city engineer and
for each of the other commissioners shall not be fixed
until after his appointment shall have been confirmed by
the common council.

As amended by Section 19, Chapter 144, Laws of 1875; further
amended by Chapter 208, Laws of 1881, which was afterward
repealed by Section 58, Chapter 324, Laws of 1882.

SECTION 4. Each of the members of the board of **Official oath and bond.**
public works shall, on entering upon the duties of his
office, take and subscribe an oath of office to support
the constitution and laws of the state of Wisconsin, and
faithfully to perform the duties of his office, and shall
give a bond to the said city, with sufficient sureties to be
approved by the common council, in such penal sum not
less than five thousand dollars, as the common council
shall prescribe, for the faithful performance of his duties.
Said board shall keep their office at some place to be
designated by the common council, and shall fix certain **Office and office hours.**
days and hours when they, or a majority of them, will
be in attendance to hear complaints and transact business.
No estimate, contract or other official paper shall be
signed or executed by said board except at the office so
designated by the common council. Each of the com- **Shall own horse and buggy.**
missioners of the said board shall be required to provide,
at his own expense, a horse and vehicle for use in the
discharge of his duties as such commissioner.

SECTION 5. A majority of said board shall be a quo- **Quorum for business.**
rum to do business. They shall keep a record of all
their acts and doings, and keep and preserve all contracts, plans, estimates and profiles, which at all times
shall be open to the inspection of the common council or
any member thereof, or of any committee appointed by
said council. They shall report their acts and doings in **Annual reports.**
detail to the common council on or before the 1st day
of March in each year, and oftener if required by the
common council.

SECTION 6. It shall be the duty of said board to take special charge and superintendence, subject to such ordinances as may be lawfully passed by the common council, of all streets, alleys, highways, sidewalks, crosswalks, bridges, docks, wharves, public grounds, engine-houses, school houses, and all other public buildings and grounds belonging to the city or to either of the wards, except as otherwise provided in this act; also of all works for the deepening, widening or dredging of the rivers of said city; of all sewers and the work pertaining thereto; and of all public works commenced or undertaken by the city or either of the wards, except as otherwise provided in this act. They shall have power to make contracts in the name and behalf of the city for the purposes, in the manner and under the limitations prescribed by this act. They shall perform all the duties prescribed by this act, and such other duties as the common council may from time to time require.

> The powers of the board of public works under this section are *quasi* judicial, and their exercise cannot be questioned collaterally.
> Robinson vs. Milwaukee, 61 Wis., 585.

> The authority of the board of public works is purely statutory, and the validity of their acts depends upon their having proceeded step by step in strict conformity to the statute.
> Kneeland vs. Milwaukee, 18 Wis., 431.

> The city is responsible for the default of its street commisioners.
> Kittredge vs. Milwaukee, 26 Wis., 46.

> The owner of an adjoining lot, having an estate in fee to the center of the street, has a right to the enjoyment of any use of his estate consistent with the servitude to which it is subjected.
> Hundhausen vs. Bond, 36 Wis., 29.

SECTION 7. All repairs and alterations in the school buildings of said city, and in the premises attached thereto, shall be made by the board of public works in the same manner as the said board is authorized to do other similar work. And whenever any such repairs or alterations are deemed necessary by the school board, it shall be their duty to report the same to the common council of the said city for their order and direction in the premises.

> As amended by Section 13, Chapter 324, Laws of 1882. Chapter 65, Laws of 1881, repealed by Section 58, Chapter 324, Laws of 1882.

Marginal notes:
- What the board shall have special charge of.
- May make contracts.
- Repair of school buildings.

SECTION 8. The said board of public works shall have the exclusive power to grant permits, subject to such regulations and restrictions as may be prescribed by the ordinances of the city, for the moving of houses, along **Moving of houses.** or across streets, alleys or walks, and to regulate the building of vaults under streets, alleys or sidewalks. No building material or other obstruction of any kind shall be placed on the streets, walks, or other public grounds of the city, without the written permit of said board. They shall have power, subject to such ordinances as may be lawfully passed by the common council, to regulate and control the manner of using streets, alleys or walks, for laying down gas or water pipes and sewers, **Laying gas and** and to determine the location and depth thereof, and to **water pipes.** cause the prompt repair in such time and manner as they shall direct, of streets, alleys and walks, whenever such pipes or sewers may be taken up or altered. And in case any corporation or individual shall neglect to repair or restore to its former condition, any street, alley or sidewalk so excavated, taken up or altered, within the time and in the manner directed by said board, the said board shall cause the same to be done at the expense of such corporation or individual.

As amended by Section 20, Chapter 144, Laws of 1875,

See note to Section 16, Chapter VIII.

SECTION 9. Whenever any public work or improve- **Public work to be** ment shall be ordered by the common council, the said **done by contract.** board shall advertise for proposals for doing the same; a plan or profile of the work to be done, accompanied with specifications for doing the same, or other appropriate and sufficient description of the work required to be done, and of the kinds and quality of material to be furnished, being first placed on file in the office of said board for the information of bidders and others. Such advertisement shall be published at least six days in the official city papers, and shall state the work to be done and the time for doing the same, which shall in all cases be such reasonable time as may be necessary to enable a contractor with proper diligence to perform and complete such work. All proposals shall be sealed and directed to said board, and shall be accompanied with a bond to **Contractor to give** the city of Milwaukee in such penal sum, not less than **bond.** thirty per cent. of the amount of the engineer's estimate of the cost of such work, as the board in such advertisement may direct; which bond shall be signed by the bidder and by two or more responsible sureties who shall each make affidavit that he is the owner of real estate in the county of Milwaukee, over and above all incumbrances and subject to execution, of a cash value equal to the penalty of said bond, that he is worth the penal sum of such bond over and above all his debts and liabilities, in property in said county, subject to execution; such bond and sureties to be approved by the board previous to the opening of the accompanying bids or proposals, and shall be conditioned that such bidder will execute and perform the work for the price mentioned in his proposals and according to the plans and specifications on file, in case the contract shall be awarded to him, and in case of default on his part to execute a contract with satisfactory sureties and to perform the work specified, said bond shall be prosecuted in the name of said city, and judgment recovered thereon for the full amount of the penalty thereof, as liquidated damages, in any court having jurisdiction of the action, unless the common council shall, by resolution, direct that no action shall be commenced; provided, that no bond shall be required of any bidder who, at the time he offers his bid or proposal as aforesaid, shall deposit with the board of public works a sum of money equal to fifty per cent. of the penalty required for such bond, under an agreement that the same shall be returned to such bidder in case the contract for the work bid for is not awarded to such bidder, or in case he makes no default in the execution of the contract, with satisfactory sureties, in case it is awarded to such bidder, and that in case the contract is so awarded, and he shall fail to execute a contract with satisfactory sureties, to perform the work specified, for the price named in his bid, within a reasonable time after such contract is prepared and ready for execution, then said sum of money shall become the property of said city, as fixed and liquidated damages for such default, and shall be paid by the said board to the city treasurer.

As amended by Sec. 21, Chap. 144, Laws of 1875, and further amended by Chap. 294, Laws of 1881, Sec. 14, Chap. 324, Laws of 1882, and Sec. 1, Chap. 388, Laws of 1889.

Board of public works cannot initiate erection or construction of public buildings or improvements, but can act only after the work or improvement has been ordered by the council.

Koch vs. Milwaukee, 89 Wis., 220.

See Wright vs. Forristal, 65 Wis., 341.

See Chapter 368, Laws of 1895, in Chapter VIII of this charter.

SECTION 10. All contracts shall be awarded to the lowest bidder, who shall have complied with the foregoing requisitions; provided, that no contract shall be entered into by the board of public works, unless the same shall be executed by two or more sureties for the contractor guaranteeing to the satisfaction of the said board the performance of such contract by the contractor, under the superintendence, and to the satisfaction of said board, each of which sureties shall make an affidavit endorsed on or attached to such contract, that he is the owner of real estate in the county of Milwaukee, over and above all incumbrances and subject to execution, of a cash value equal to the penal sum of such bond, and that he is worth the estimated amount of money to be paid on such contract, over and above all his debts and liabilities, in property, in said county subject to execution. And provided further, that whenever the lowest bid for any work to be let by said board, shall appear to said board to be unreasonably high, the said board is authorized to reject all bids therefor, and to re-let the work anew; and whenever any bidder shall be, in the judgment of said board, incompetent, or otherwise unreliable for the performance of the work for which he bids, the said board shall report to the common council of the said city a schedule of all the bids for such work, with a recommendation to accept the bid of the lowest competent and reliable bidder for such work, with its reasons for such recommendation, and thereupon it shall be lawful for the said common council to direct the said board either to let the work to such lowest competent and reliable bidder, or to re-let the same anew. And provided further, that the said board may reject the bid of any person who shall previously have wilfully or negligently failed to complete any work or contract entered into by him with the city, or any officer or department thereof, or who shall have wilfully or negligently failed to enter into a contract with satisfactory sureties, for any work or improvement that shall have been previously awarded to

Contractor to furnish sureties.

him by said board, and the failure to let such contract to the lowest bidder, in compliance with any provision of this section, shall not invalidate such contract, or any special assessment thereunder, or for the work done in virtue thereof.

As amended by Sections 22, Chapter 144, Laws of 1875 and further amended by Section 15, Chapter 324, Laws of 1882, and Section 2, Chapter 388, Laws of 1889.

The board of public works is authorized to reject all bids for proposed work when the lowest bid shall appear to said board to be unreasonably high. In such case, they may re-let the work anew, and may let the contract for part of the work at one time, and another contract for the remainder at another time, when the board is unable to obtain a satisfactory bid for the whole improvement.

Wright vs. Forristal, 65 Wis., 341.

A contract let without the prescribed notice of letting having been properly given, is void.

Mitchell vs. Milwaukee, 18 Wis., 99.

Where a contract is by law required to be let to the lowest bidder, a violation of that provision will be regarded, *prima facie*, as "affecting the substantial justice of the tax" levied to pay for the work.

Wells vs. Burnham, 20 Wis., 119.

Notice to be given of the letting of contracts should inform bidders, either by the notice or the specifications on file, of the amount of work intended to be included in such contract; the time within which it is to be finished; the manner in which it is to be done; and the quality of the materials, if any, which are to be furnished.

Kneeland vs. Furlong, 20 Wis., 560.

In such contract, the board of public works has no right to "reserve the right to divide the work" after the bids are received.

Ibid.

When a municipal corporation lets a contract in excess of the amount authorized by law, and afterwards procures legislation increasing the amount originally authorized, it will be construed as a ratification of the original contract for an amount exceeding the authority it then possessed.

Hasbrouck vs. Milwaukee, 21 Wis., 219.

Street contractors to put up suitable barriers and lights. SECTION 11. Whenever any board or officer of the city shall let any work or improvement which shall require the digging up, use or occupancy of any street, alley, highway, or public grounds of said city, there shall be inserted in the contract therefor substantial covenants, requiring such contractor, during the night time, to put up and maintain such barriers and lights as will effectually prevent the happening of any accident in consequence of such digging up, use or occupancy of said street, alley, highway, or other public grounds, for which the city might be liable; and also such other covenants and conditions as experience has proved or may prove necessary to save the city harmless from damages. And it shall also be provided in such contracts, that the party contracting with the city shall be liable for all damages occasioned by the digging up, use or occupancy of the street, alley, highway or public grounds, or which may result therefrom, or which may result from the carelessness of such contractor, his agents, employes or workmen.

Shall be liable for damages.

When the city has put up a sufficient barrier, it is only bound to use common care and diligence in maintaining it. If such barrier is afterwards removed or thrown down, without the knowledge or fault of the city authorities, the city is not liable.

Klatt vs. Milwaukee, 53 Wis., 196.

SECTION 12. Whenever any work or improvement shall be let by contract to any person or persons, firm or corporation, covenants shall be inserted in such contract, binding such person or persons, firm or corporation and the sureties to save and indemnify, and keep harmless, the said city against all liabilities, judgments, costs and expenses which may in anywise come against said city in consequence of the granting of such contract, or which may in anywise result from the carelessness or neglect of such person or persons, firm or corporation, or his or its agents, employes or workmen, in any respect whatever; and in every such case where judgment is recovered against the city by reason of the carelessness or negligence of such person, persons, firm or corporation so contracting, or his, their or its agents, employes or workmen, and when due notice has been given of the pendency of such suit, such judgment shall be conclusive against such person, persons, firm or corporation, and his, or their, or its sureties on such bond, not only as to the amount of damages, but as to their liability to said city.

Contractors to indemnify city.

City may recover from them all costs and damages.

SECTION 13. All contracts entered into, and all public notices required by law to be given by the board of public works of the city of Milwaukee, shall be countersigned by the comptroller of the said city, and shall have no force unless so countersigned. All contracts entered into by the said board, and all bonds taken by them, shall be

Contracts and public notices must be countersigned by the comptroller.

entered into in the name of, and shall be executed to the city of Milwaukee; and all such bonds or contracts, when executed, shall be examined and approved, as to form and execution, by the city attorney.

Contracts shall not exceed appropriations.

SECTION 14. The said board of public works shall have no power, by contract or otherwise, to exceed in the doing of any work, in any one year, the sum appropriated for such work by the said common council, or by law, for such year.

Estimates to accompany contracts.

SECTION 15. It shall be the duty of the said board of public works to deliver to the comptroller of said city, with each contract to be countersigned by him, as accurate an estimate as can be made of the aggregate contract price of the work, to be let by such contract; and it shall be the duty of the comptroller to keep a record of such estimates applicable to each fund, and to refuse to countersign any contract the amount of which shall exceed the balance of the fund to which such contract may be chargeable.

All work to be let by contract.

Exception.

SECTION 16. All work and the purchase of supplies or material, chargeable to any ward fund, or to any city fund, including incidental printing, when the cost thereof shall exceed the sum of two hundred dollars, except street cleaning, shall be let by contract, to the lowest bidder in the manner provided by sections 10, 11 and 13 of this chapter; and no indebtedness shall be incurred in excess of the amount herein limited without a formal contract, let to the lowest bidder and all work done or supplies and material purchased, exceeding in cost, two hundred dollars, shall be done and purchased, when practicable, by said board, by contract, which shall be let after due notice, inviting proposals, in the manner provided for the letting of contracts for the doing of public work. All accounts for such work, or for the furnishing of such materials shall, before being allowed by the common council, be audited by the comptroller, and all such accounts for work done or materials furnished, under the supervision of the Board of Public Works, shall be certified by them before being audited.

As amended by Section 16, Chapter 324, Laws of 1882, and further amended by Chapter 437, Laws of 1891.

SECTION 17. Whenever the lowest bidder for incidental city printing for the said city shall appear to the comptroller of the said city and the committee of the common council on printing, to be incompetent or otherwise unreliable for doing the same, the said comptroller and committee shall report to the common council of said city a schedule of all the bids for such printing, together with their objections to accepting the bid of the lowest bidder therefor, and thereupon the common council shall have power either to order such printing to be let to the next lowest bidder who shall appear to be competent and reliable, or to order such printing to be re-let.

When lowest bidder incompetent, etc.

SECTION 18. Whenever the board of public works shall deem it for the interest of the city, or whenever in the prosecution of any public work, said board shall be of the opinion that the proposed work can be better and more cheaply done without the intervention of a formal contract or whenever the board of public works shall deem it advisable, to purchase horses or horse feed for the fire or police departments without the intervention of a formal contract, they shall report the same to the common council with their reasons therefor, and the common council may, by resolution, authorize the said board to procure the necessary materials therefor and to employ workmen to do such work and to purchase such horses or horse feed; provided, that such authority shall not be given unless approved by the votes of at least three-fourths of all the members elect of the common council, and in case of ward work, of two aldermen of the ward; and further provided, that such authority shall not be exercised unless the comptroller shall, as provided in section 19, of this chapter, advise the board that there are sufficient funds available for such proposed work or purchases. Such resolutions which appropriate money for the purchase of horses or horse feed for the fire or police departments shall be duly referred as provided by section 5, of chapter 4, of the charter of the city of Milwaukee as amended, and in case such resolutions shall thereafter be duly passed by the vote aforesaid, by the common council and take effect, the money so appropriated may, upon itemized statements duly audited by the board of public works and city comptroller, be drawn out of the city treasury upon the order

Board of public works to make purchases.

of the mayor and clerk, countersigned by the city comptroller.

Amended by Section 17, Chapter 324, Laws of 1882, and further amended by Chapter 23, Laws of 1887.

Shall deliver comptroller a statement. SECTION 19. It shall be the duty of the said board of public works, before causing such work to be done, to deliver to the comptroller a statement in writing of the work authorized and proposed to be done as provided in the next preceding section, showing the nature and estimated cost thereof, and the fund to which the same is chargeable; and it shall be the duty of the comptroller to enter such statement in the record mentioned in section fifteen of this chapter; and in case the comptroller shall be satisfied that the cost of such proposed work will exceed the amount available for the purpose of the fund out of which the same is to be paid, it shall be his duty to so advise the board of public works, and the resolution of the common council, passed as in the last preceding section, shall be inoperative.

As amended by Section 16, Chapter 324, Laws of 1882.

Shall determine performance of contract. SECTION 20. The said board shall reserve in every contract the right to determine finally all performance of such contract, or doing of the work specified therein; and the right, in case of the improper or imperfect performance thereof, to suspend such work at any time, or to order the entire reconstruction of the same, if improperly done, or to re-let the same to some other competent party; and also the right, in case such work shall not be prosecuted with such diligence, and with such number of men as to-insure its completion within the time limited by the contract, to suspend such work and re-let the same to some other competent party or employ men and secure material for the completion of the same, and charge the cost thereof to the contractor. And power is hereby given to the said board to adjust and determine all questions as to the amount earned under any contract by the contractor or contractors according to the true intent and meaning of the contract; and such adjustment and determination by said board shall be final between the parties and binding upon them. If the amount of damages to be paid to the city shall exceed the amount due from the city to such contractor or contractors, according to such determination and adjustment, then the difference or balance in favor of the city, according to such determination and adjustment, shall be recoverable at law in an action in the name of the city against such contractor or contractors and their sureties, in any court having jurisdiction. Every contract with the city shall be made expressly subject to the powers given to said board by this section, and shall also contain a covenant or agreement on the part of the contractor and his sureties, that in case such contractor shall fail to fully and completely perform his contract within the time therein limited for the performance thereof, such contractor shall pay to the city of Milwaukee as liquidated damages for such default, a certain fixed sum to be named in the contract, which shall not in any case be less than ten per cent. nor more than twenty-five per cent. of the aggregate cost of the work embraced in such contract or shall in lieu of such covenant or agreement contain a covenant or agreement on the part of the contractor and his sureties, that in case such contractor shall fail to fully and completely perform his contract within the time therein limited for the performance thereof, such contractor shall pay to the city of Milwaukee as liquidated damages for such default, a certain and definite sum for each day's delay in completing the contract after the time therein limited for its completion, which daily sum shall be determined and fixed by the board of public works before the contract for the work shall be let, and shall be stated in the advertisement for proposals for the work, and shall be inserted in the contract, and shall in no case be less than one-half of one per cent. of the aggregate cost of the work embraced in such contract.

As amended by Chapter 324, of the Laws of 1882, and further amended by Section 3, Chapter 388, Laws of 1889.

A provision in the contract that the board of public works shall adjudicate the amount earned by the contractor, does not necessitate an adjudication by it as to his damages caused by a breach of the contract by the city.

Markey vs. Milwaukee, 76 Wis., 349.

The provision of the charter making the board of public works the arbiter to adjust and determine all questions as to the amounts earned under contracts with the city, and providing that such determination shall be final and binding on the parties, is valid, and an award made upon a contract which by its terms is subject

to such provisions, cannot be set aside except for fraud, miscon-
duct or mistake.

Forristal vs. Milwaukee, 57 Wis., 628.

Under a somewhat similar form of contract, the court held that
its meaning was to provide for arbitration; and none being had,
the question of the value of the work and materials furnished
should have been submitted to the jury.

Hasbrouck vs. Milwaukee, 17 Wis., 274.

Board may pay on estimates. SECTION 21. In all cases wherein the contractor or
contractors shall proceed properly and with diligence to
perform and complete his or their contract, the said board
may, in its discretion, from time to time, as the work
progresses, grant to him or them an estimate of the
amount already earned—reserving fifteen per cent. thereon
—which shall entitle the holder to the amount due thereon
when the amount applicable to the payment of such work
shall have been collected, and the condition, if any,
annexed to such estimate, shall have been complied with;
provided, that the said board shall have no authority to
grant any such estimate to any contractor when in default;
and that no estimate shall be granted by the said board
to any contractor for any material which has not actually
been put in the work embraced in his contract. And
power is hereby given to the said board to extend or
enlarge the time limited by the terms of the contract for
the performance thereof. Any person entering into any
contract with the city, and who agrees to be paid from
Special assessment. special assessments shall have no claim upon the city in
any event, except from the collection of the special
assessments made for the work contracted for; and no
work proper to be paid for by special assessments shall be
let, except to a contractor who shall so agree.

As amended by Section 4, Chapter 388, Laws of 1889.

Where a charter provision requires work to be done at the
expense of abutting property, the city will not be liable for the
work ordered and contracted to be done at the expense of such
property, although the authorities did not take the necessary steps
to charge such property.

Hall vs. Chippewa Falls, 47 Wis., 267.
Owens vs. Milwaukee, 47 Wis., 461.

Contractors receiving certificates which are to be paid from
special assessments, have no claim upon the city in any event for

the work by them performed, "except from the collection of the special assessments made for doing the work contracted for."
Hoyt vs. Fass, 64 Wis., 273.
See Watkins vs. Milwaukee, 55 Wis., 335.

SECTION 22. In case the prosecution of any public **Defaulting contractors.** work shall be suspended by, or in consequence of the default of any contractor, it shall be the duty of the board of public works to report the fact immediately to the common council, with a statement of the condition of the work, and an estimate of the probable cost of completing the same in the manner required by the contract.

SECTION 23. The said board shall have power, **May contract for use of patented articles.** under the authority of the common council, to make a contract or contracts with the patentee or his licensees or assigns, to use any patent or patented article, process, combination or work for the said city, at a stipulated sum or royalty for the use thereof. And thereupon the said board shall have power to order any work, whether chargeable to the said city or to lots, parts of lots or parcels of land therein, to be done with the use of such patent or patented article, process, combination or work; and whenever the owner or agent of any lot, part of lot or **Users of patented articles, pay city therefor.** parcel of land in said city, or other person authorized by law to do such work, shall do the same and use any such patent or patented article, process, combination or work in doing the same; he shall pay to the said city the sum or royalty chargeable therefor by such patentee, his licensees or assigns, to the city under such contract, and shall be liable to suit by the said city therefor; or the amount of such sum or royalty may be charged as a special assessment upon the respective lots, parts of lots, and parcels of land in front of which such patent was so used, and collected for the use of said city, as other special taxes are collected; and whenever any work, chargeable by special assessment to any lots, parts of **Amount may be charged as** lots, or parcels of land, shall be done with the use of such **special assessment against lots** patent or patented article, process, combination or work, **and lands.** the sum or royalty chargeable therefor by such patentee, his licensee, or assigns, under such contract shall be charged against such lots, parts of lots or parcels of land, for the use of said city, in such special assessment, in addition to the other cost of doing the work, and shall be included in a separate certificate of such special assessment.

Patented article.   See Dean vs. Charlton, 23 Wis., 590.

Separate certificate for patented articles, or royalty —when made, and effect thereof.   SECTION 24.   Whenever the said board of public works shall have let, or shall hereafter let any contract or any work chargeable to lots or land in the said city, to be done with the use of any patent or patented article, in pursuance of the preceding section, and have omitted, or shall omit at the time of making the assessment for such work against property chargeable therewith, to make any assessment, or issue a '' separate certificate '' against such property for the sum or royalty chargeable for the use of such patent or patented article, in pursuance of the provisions of the section last mentioned, the said board of public works shall have power, and it shall be their duty to make such assessment for the sum or royalty chargeable for the use of such patent or patented article, as soon as may be thereafter, and to include the same in a separate certificate for such special assessment for the use of the said city; and such assessment and certificate shall be as binding, and have the same effect when so subsequently made, as if the same had been made at the same time, as the assessment for the contract price of doing such work.

The scope and purpose of the entire chapter relating to the board of public works is to regulate and define the powers and duties of the board, placing them, however, substantially under and subject to the ordinances, direction and control of the common council, especially in the matter of commencing new lines of work and new lines of expenditure.

Gilman vs. Milwaukee, 61 Wis., 588.
Koch vs. Milwaukee, 89 Wis., 220.

The provision contained in the charter of 1852, by which the street commissioners were authorized to require owners to cleanse and repair streets and alleys, and to charge the expense thereof to the respective lots in case they fail to do so, is valid.

Cramer vs. Stone, 33 Wis., 212.

CHAPTER VI.

TAKING PROPERTY FOR STREETS AND OTHER PURPOSES.

SECTION 1.   The common council shall have the power to lay out public squares, grounds, streets and alleys, and to extend, enlarge and widen or vacate the same as follows: any ten or more free holders residing in any ward may, by petition represent to the common council that it is necessary to take certain lands within the ward where such petitioners reside for public use, for the purpose of laying out, extending, enlarging or widening a public square, ground, street or alley, setting forth in such petition the courses, distances, metes and bounds of the lands proposed to be taken, together with the names and residences of the owners and occupants of such premises, so far as the same shall be known to the petitioners, and praying that such lands may be taken for such purpose according to law. Every person signing such petition, shall write after his signature, a brief description of his real estate which makes him such freeholder or of some part thereof, and of the place of his residence in the city, and shall make and annex to such petition his affidavit that he is a resident and freeholder in said ward, and that the names and residences of the owners of the lands proposed to be taken, so far as they are known to him are correctly set forth in such petition, and such signer making such affidavit shall thereupon be taken to be such resident and freeholder, and the names and residences of the owners of the lands proposed to be taken shall be deemed to be correctly stated in such petition, so far as the names and residences of such owners, are known, and such petition shall be valid and effectual although it may afterward appear that such signers or some of them, were not such residents and freeholders, or that the names and residences of the owners and occupants of the lands proposed to be taken were not correctly stated in such petition, so far as known, or both. Persons in actual possession of real estate, under valid contracts for the purchase thereof, shall be deemed to be freeholders within the meaning and for the purposes of this section.

Common council may lay out public squares, grounds, streets, etc.,—petition may be presented for condemnation of lands for public use—what to contain.

As amended by Section 23, Chapter 144, Laws of 1875, further amended by Section 1, Chapter 227, Laws of 1879, and Section 1, Chapter 524, 1887.

The proceedings for determining the value and estimating benefits and damages, where land is to be *taken* for the public use, are entirely distinct from those to *improve* streets or highways *after* they have been laid out and established.

Holton vs. Milwaukee, 31 Wis., 27.

Common council
may open public
street or alley, or
take land for pub-
lic purpose—
when.

SECTION 2. Whenever the said common council with the concurence of three-fourths of the members elected thereto shall declare by their resolution that it is necessary for the public interest to open a public street or alley, or to take land for any public purpose authorized by this aft, the said common council shall have power to open such public street or alley, or to take land for such public purpose, as the case may be, without any petition therefor, and to proceed thereafter in that behalf, as in cases of petition therefor duly made; provided, that in cases of streets and alleys such resolution shall also be approved by both of the aldermen of the ward in which the land proposed to be taken may be situated. The resolution provided for in this section shall declare why it is necessary for the public interest so to proceed; and no such resolution shall be passed by the common council at the same meeting in which it is first considered, but the same shall lie over to a future meeting thereof. And the yeas and nays on the passage of such resolution shall be taken and duly entered in the journal of proceedings of the council.

As amended by Section 24, Chapter 144, Laws of 1875, further amended by Section 2, Chapter 227, Laws of 1879, and Section 2, Chapter 524, Laws 1887.

May direct survey
and plat to be
made and filed—
notice of applica-
tion to be given
to owners of
lands, how—jury
to be selected to
·view premises
and appraise
damages; pro-
ceedings thereon.

SECTION 3. The common council shall thereupon, by resolution, direct the city engineer to make and file with the city clerk an accurate survey and plat of the proposed change or improvement and of the lands proposed to be taken therefor, defining separately each parcel and indicating upon such plat the location of any improvements upon said premises, and said city clerk shall return said plat and survey to the common council. The common council shall thereupon direct the city clerk to cause notice of such application or resolution to be given to owners and occupants of the lands proposed to be taken, which notice shall contain a description of the lands proposed to be taken, and shall state that at a certain time and place therein named, which time shall not be less than four weeks after the first publication thereof, application will be made to the circuit or superior court of Milwaukee county or to the judge of either of said courts for the selection of a jury to view said premises and to determine whether or not it is necessary to take said premises for the purposes specified in said

petition or resolution. Such notice shall be published
in the official papers of said city for four weeks, at least
once in each week, prior to the time therein fixed for the
appointment of jurors, and shall be served at least
twenty days prior to the time therein fixed for the
appointment of jurors, upon each of the owners and   Personal service of
occupants of the land proposed to be taken, residing in   notice on owner
the city of Milwaukee and known as it shall appear by   or occupant.
the petition or resolution, personally by delivering to
and leaving with him a copy of such notice if he can be
found in the city of Milwaukee, and if he cannot be
found in said city, then by leaving a copy of such notice
at his usual place of abode with some member of his
family of suitable age and discretion, or if such place of
abode shall be closed, or no person of suitable age and
discretion found there, then by posting a copy of said
notice on the principal outer door of such place of abode.
Such service shall be made by the chief of police or some   Service of notice
police officer of said city, who shall make return under   may be made by
oath, in writing, of the facts of such service, which   police officer.
return shall have the same effect as a sheriff's return of
the service of a summons in a civil action. As to unknown owners of such land proposed to be taken, and
owners, not residing in the city of Milwaukee, such publication in the official paper shall be a sufficient service
of such notice upon them. At the time and place fixed
for such hearing and upon the presentation of such
application or of such resolution and upon proof of the
publication and service of the notice hereinbefore
required, the said court or the judge thereof, shall thereupon make a list of twenty-four reputable freeholders,   Jurors, how
residents of the city of Milwaukee, but not residents of   obtained.
the ward in which the premises proposed to be taken
may be situated, and not interested in the result of such
taking. The said court or judge shall thereupon hear and
decide any challenge for cause or favor made, as to any
of said freeholders and if sustained shall replace the
name with an unobjectionable juror, until the list shall be
perfected. Thereupon under the direction of such court
or judge, each party, the city of Milwaukee by its representatives constituting one party, and the owners of
land or their agents present, or if none be present or
they disagree, a disinterested person appointed by the
court or judge, constituting the other party, shall chal-

CHAP. 6

Jurors, how summoned.

lenge six names, one at a time alternately, the city beginning. To the twelve jurors remaining such court or judge shall issue a precept requiring them at an hour and day named, not more than fifteen nor less than three days thereafter, to appear before him to be sworn and serve as a jury to view lands, and at the same time shall publicly adjourn the proceedings to the time and place so named; such precept shall be served by the chief of police or any police officer of the city of Milwaukee at least one day before such appointed time, by reading the same to each such juror, or by leaving a copy of such precept at his usual place of abode in said city, in the presence of a member of his family. The jurors summoned shall appear at the time and place named, and if any be excused by the court or judge, or fail

Adjournment for absence of juror.

to attend, he shall publicly adjourn the proceedings to some time and place and name other disinterested freeholders, not residents of the ward in which the premises proposed to be taken or vacated are situated, in their stead to be forthwith in like manner summoned, and to appear at the time and place fixed by said adjournment

Jurors to be sworn.

until twelve jurors shall be obtained. The said jurors shall thereupon, before they proceed to view the premises proposed to be taken or vacated, severally take and subscribe an oath or affirmation before the court or judge, to the effect that they will faithfully and honestly discharge the duties imposed upon them, and determine whether or not it is necessary to take or to vacate the premises in question for the public use designated in the application or resolution. The court or judge shall then issue an order in writing, directed to said jurors, requiring them within thirty days from the date thereof, to view said premises, to be specified in such order, and to make return under their hand to the common council whether or not, in their judgment, it is necessary to take or to vacate said premises for the purposes specified in such

Jurors to act unless excused; penalty for refusal.

application or resolution. It shall be the duty of every person appointed as such juror to act, unless excused for reasonable cause by the court or judge thereof appointing him, and every person duly summoned or notified to act as required by this chapter, who shall, without being so excused, neglect or refuse to perform his duty as such juror shall be guilty of a misdemeanor, and shall, upon conviction thereof, be fined not less than twenty nor more than one hundred dollars; and it shall be the duty of the city attorney to prosecute any person so offending.

As amended by Section 3, Chapter 227, Laws of 1879, and further amended by Section 3, Chapter 524, Laws of 1887.

It is absolutely essential to the validity of the proceeding that the jury should act under the solemnity of an oath.

Lumsden vs. Milwaukee, 8 Wis., 239.

SECTION 4. The said jurors when so selected and sworn, shall immediately proceed in a body to view the premises proposed to be taken or to be vacated, and the city engineer or his deputy shall upon the request of the city attorney, proceed with said jury to said premises and point out to said jurors the several places where the lines of the proposed improvement are located according to the survey hereinbefore directed to be made. The city attorney shall thereupon prepare a notice in the following or some equivalent form: **City attorney to prepare notice.**

In the matter of the application for the (opening, extension, enlarging or widening, as the case may be) of——, in the —— ward of the city of Milwaukee. **Form of.**

Notice is hereby given that the jurors lately appointed and summoned in the above matter, to pass upon the question of the necessity of taking the lands described in said application for the purposes therein prayed, have viewed said lands, and will meet at —— on the —— day of ——, A. D. ——, at which time and place all persons having any interest in the lands proposed to be taken may be heard before such jurors, and all evidence proposed to be taken may be heard before such jurors, and all evidence produced before them upon said question will be considered.

Dated at Milwaukee, the —— day of ——, A. D. ——
———————,
City Attorney.

Such notice shall be published once in the official papers of the city and shall be served upon the owners and occupants of the lands proposed to be taken, and known, the same as the notice provided for in Section 3 of this chapter, and shall be returned in like manner as said notice is therein required to be returned, all of which shall be done prior to the day fixed in said notice for the meeting of the jurors, and publication of said **Notice to be published and served.**

notice shall be sufficient service thereof upon owners of lands proposed to be taken, not known, or not residing in the city of Milwaukee. At the time and place designated in said notice for that purpose, the said jurors shall meet and shall hear all persons interested in the lands proposed to be taken, and shall hear all evidence that shall be produced before them upon the subject of the necessity of taking the land described in the order for the purpose therein stated, and may at the instance of any one or more of their number, summon and examine witnesses upon the same question, and for that purpose either of said jurors may issue a subpoena, and either of the jurors or the city attorney may administer the proper oath to any witness produced before said jury. Said jurors may, if necessary, adjourn such hearing from day to day. If any such jurors shall be absent at the time set for such hearing, and for one hour thereafter, the jurors present shall have power to publicly adjourn their proceedings to the same place. for a period not exceeding twenty-four hours, and the city attorney shall report the names of such absent jurors to the chief of police or to any of the police officers of the city, together with the place and hour to which such jury has adjourned, and the said chief of police or police officer shall thereupon notify such absent juror or jurors of such adjournment and direct them to be present at the time and place fixed by such adjournment. It shall not be necessary for said jurors to reduce the evidence produced before them to writing, nor to return the same with their report. Said jurors shall make a report of their proceedings to the common council within the time limited in the precept, which report shall be signed by them respectively, and shall state whether or not, in their judgment. it is necessary to take the premises in question for the public use proposed in the petition or resolution; provided further, that in all cases where lands shall be condemned without a petition, the city attorney shall prepare a list of the owners and occupants of property to be taken, so far as the same are known, and shall certify the same to be correct, to the best of his knowledge; and notice of the selection of the jury and of the meeting of the jury shall be given, as in the case of condemnation proceedings upon petition; provided further, that no resolution shall be passed or petition

Jurors may issue subpoena; may adjourn from day to day.

Lands condemned without petition— city attorney shall prepare list of owners.

granted in any case for the condemnation of land in said city without the affirmative vote of both the aldermen of the ward in which the land proposed to be taken shall be situated.

As amended by Section 3, Chapter 311, Laws of 1876, further amended by Section 4, Chapter 227, Laws of 1879, and Section 4, Chapter 524, Laws of 1887.

SECTION 5.   Should the jury report that it is necessary to take such premises, the oommon council shall enter an order among its proceedings confirming the whole of said report or any part thereof; and the common council shall direct the board of public works, within one month thereafter, or such further time as may be deemed proper, to view such premises at such time as the board may agree upon, of which at least three days' notice shall be given by publication in the official papers, for the purpose of ascertaining and determining the amount of damages to be paid to the owner or owners of the property proposed to be taken, and also what lands or premises will be benefited by such taking, and to make report of their assessment of such damages and benefits to the common council.   Said board may obtain the testimony of witnessess as to the facts in the case, in the same manner as provided in section 4 of this chapter, and shall hear such testimony as may be offered by any party interested, which testimony shall be reduced to writing by one of the members of said board upon the request of any person so interested; and the said board shall determine and assess and return such damages and benefits in the manner hereinafter directed.   In case either member of said board of public works shall be interested in the premises, or in any property affected by such proceedings, it shall be the duty of the common council to appoint some disinterested person to act in his stead.

Council to confirm report of jury.

As amended by Section 5, Chapter 524, Laws of 1887, and Section 1, Chapter 290, Laws of 1889.

SECTION 6.   Whenever it shall have been determined by the report of the jury, that it is necessary to take certain lands for public use, for the purpose of laying out public squares, grounds, streets or alleys or of enlarging or widening or changing the same, and such report or any part thereof shall have been confirmed by the com-

On confirmation of report by council, board of public works may determine how cost of improvement shall be chargeable.

mon council and referred to the board of public works, the said board of public works shall have power to view the premises so to be taken, and to proceed to assess the damages to the land proposed to be taken and also to assess, against the lands which the said board of public works may deem benefited by the proposed improvement, the amount which it shall determine such property to be benefited in the manner hereinafter provided. If the total amount of damages as assessed, exceeds the total amount of benefits as assessed, the excess of such damages shall be chargeable to and paid out of the general city fund and the ward funds of the wards in which the lands proposed to be taken are situated, in equal proportions.

As amended by Section 6, Chapter 524, Laws of 1887, and Section 2, Chapter 290, Laws of 1889.

Lots situated in one ward may be assessed for the special benefits or damages accruing thereto from the condemnation to public use of lands in another ward.

Gilman vs. Milwaukee, 55 Wis., 328.

Board of public works to examine premises and make assessment.

SECTION 7. The board of public works within the time limited by the common council, shall view and examine the premises proposed to be taken, and all such other premises as will in their judgment be injured or benefited thereby and after hearing such testimony as they may obtain or as may be offered by any party interested, they shall proceed to make their assessment and to determine and appraise the value of the real estate so proposed to be taken, and the injury arising to the owners thereof respectively, in consequence of the taking thereof, taking into consideration the value of any

Value of buildings for removal to be considered.

building situated in whole or in part thereon, less the value to the owner of such building to remove. The amount of said appraisal of real estate and injury to real estate and buildings, so determined, shall be awarded to such owners respectively as damages, after making due allowance therefrom for any benefit which such owners may respectively derive from such improvement.

As amended by Section 25, Chapter 144, Laws of 1875, and further amended by Section 7, Chapter 524, Laws of 1887.

SECTION 8. If the damages to any person be greater than the benefits received, or if the benefits be greater than the damages; in either case the board shall strike a balance, and carry the difference forward to another column so that the assessment will show what amount is to be received or paid by such owner or owners respectively, and the difference only shall in any case be collected of them or payable to them.

Board may strike balance as to difference between benefits and damages to owner.

As amended by Section 8, Chapter 524, Laws of 1887.

SECTION 9.   Whenever there is any building upon the land proposed to be taken, and the land and the building belong to different persons, or if the land be subject to lease, judgment, mortgage or other lien, or if there be any estate in it less than an estate in fee, the injury done to such persons or interest respectively may be awarded to them by the board, less the benefits resulting to them respectively from the proposed improvement.

Same where there is building upon land.

As amended by Section 9, Chapter 524, Laws of 1887.

SECTION 10.   Having ascertained the damages and expenses of the proposed improvement as aforesaid, the board shall thereupon apportion and assess the same, or such portion thereof as shall have been determined to be chargeable to the lots and lands benefited in accordance with the provisions of section 6, of this chapter, together with the costs of the proceedings upon the real estate by them deemed benefited, in proportion to the benefits resulting thereto from the proposed improvement, as nearly as may be, and shall describe the real estate upon which their assessments may be made.

To apportion and assess damages and expense chargeable to lots or lands as provided in section 6.

As amended by Section 10, Chapter 524, Laws of 1887.

See Gilman vs. Milwaukee, 55 Wis., 328.

SECTION 11.   It shall be the duty of the board of public works, after such assessment shall be made and before the same shall be reported by the board to the common council, to give public notice of not less than six days in the official papers of the city, that such assessment has been made, and that the same will be open for review and correction by the board of public works, at the office of the board, for not less than ten days after the first publication of such notice, during certain hours, and not less than two hours of each lay day, and that all will be heard by the said board of public works in objection to such assessments, and generally in the matter of such

To give notice of assessment before making report to council.

review and correction. It shall be sufficient to state in such notice in brief what such assessment has been made for, and in what locality.

As amended by Section 11, Chapter 524, Laws of 1887, and further amended by Chapter 224, Laws of 1889, and Chapter 312, Laws of 1891.

May review, modify and correct assessment.

SECTION 12. During the time specified in the notice mentioned in the last preceding section, it shall be the duty of the board of public works to hear all persons interested in the property assessed, or otherwise personally interested in such assessment, in making objection to any part of such assessment, and to hear all evidence which may be produced in support of such objections; and the board shall thereupon have power to review, modify and correct such assessment in such manner as they shall deem just, at any time during such review and for three days thereafter, and thereupon, it shall be the duty of said board to make report of such assessment in writing signed by them, together with the testimony taken, to the common council within the time limited by said council. Should the time originally limited for making such report prove insufficient, the common council may, in their discretion, from time to time, enlarge or extend the same.

As amended by Section 12, Chapter 524, Laws of 1887.

Assessments to be laid before common council.

SECTION 13. The assessments so reported shall be laid before the common council when in session, and the fact of its presentation shall be entered upon the journal and mentioned in the proceedings of such session, with a statement in brief for what purpose and in what locality such assessment has been made, but the common council shall not have power to act finally upon such report until at least one week from the date of the session at which it was so presented. At or after the expiration of such period of one week last mentioned, the common council may, in its discretion, revise and correct the assessment, and shall confirm the same as corrected by them, or without correction, or refer it back to the said board for revision and correction. If said assessment shall be so referred back, the said board of public works shall proceed to review, correct and report the same in like manner and upon like notice as herein required in relation to the first assessment, and all parties interested

shall have the like rights, and the board of public works
and the common council respectively, shall perform like
duties and have like powers in relation to any such subsequent assessment as are hereby given in relation to the
first. In all cases, however, the excess of damages over
benefits in any such proceeding shall be paid out of the
ward and general city funds as provided in section 6.

As amended by Section 13, Chapter 524, Laws of 1887, and
further amended by Section 3, Chapter 290, Laws of 1889.

SECTION 14. Any person or persons owning or having
any interest in any property affected by such assessment,
may within twenty days after the confirmation of such
assessment by the common council, appeal therefrom to
the circuit court of Milwaukee county, by filing with the
clerk of said circuit court his notice of appeal, setting
forth therein his interests in the premises and the grounds
of his appeal, together with a bond to the city of Milwaukee in the penal sum of five hundred dollars, conditioned for the payment of all costs that shall be adjudged
against him on such appeal, which bond shall be signed
by at least two sufficient sureties, each of whom shall
make affidavit endorsed upon such bond that he is worth
five hundred dollars over and above all his debts, in property not exempt from execution; and said bond and
sureties, if objected to by the city attorney, shall also be
approved by the judge of the said court. Such appeal
shall be ineffectual unless the appellant shall also, within
said twenty days, serve a copy of his notice of appeal
and bond upon the city attorney. In case of any appeal
under the provisions of this section, the city clerk shall
send to the clerk of said circuit court a certified copy of
the assessment of damages and benefits made and reported
by the said board of public works, as confirmed by the
common council, and of all proceedings of the common
council in relation thereto.

Persons owning or having interest in property affected by assessment may appeal to circuit court within twenty days after confirmation by council.

The appeal shall be tried as ordinary issues of facts
are tried in said circuit court; the form of the issue shall
be subject to the direction of the court; and the court
shall permit any person or persons interested in such
damages or benefits to become parties to such appeal,
upon their petition setting forth the nature and extent of
such interest. If on such trial the benefits assessed by
the said board of public works shall be diminished, or
the damages so assessed shall be increased, than and in

Appeal, how tried.

either case the appellant shall recover costs on such appeal, otherwise the city shall recover costs. When the jury shall, by their verdict, award damages to the owner of any lot or part of a lot, and judgment shall have been rendered upon such verdict, the said city shall pay **Judgment against city, when to be paid.** the amount of such judgment, and the costs, if any, recovered therewith, or make provisions for the payment thereof, within one year after the same shall have been rendered; provided, that in case of an appeal from such judgment to the supreme court, the time of the pendency of such appeal shall not form any part of such year. And in case the appellant shall succeed, the difference between the amount assessed and the amount finally adjudged shall be chargeable to and paid out of the proper ward fund.

Amended by Section 26, Chapter 144, Laws of 1875, and further amended by Section 14, Chapter 524, Laws of 1887.

See Van Valkenburgh vs. Milwaukee, 30 Wis., 338.

A city was authorized to issue bonds to pay for building a harbor, and to raise money by taxation to pay principal and interest as they became due. It failed to issue bonds, and the contractor obtained a money judgment for the amount due him. *Held*, that *mandamus* would lie to compel the common council to levy and collect a tax to pay such judgment.

State ex rel. Hasbrouck vs. Milwaukee, 25 Wis., 122.

But the writ must state the exact duty required; and if issued in the alternative, requiring defendant to pay judgment, *or* issue bonds to pay it with, *or* to levy a tax for its payment, the writ will be qnashed

Ibid.

Where a common council has authority to levy a tax to pay a judgment, but refuses to do so, *mandamus* will lie to compel such levy.

State ex rel. Sherman vs. Common Council, 20 Wis., 92.

Appeal the only remedy for damages sustained. SECTION 15. An appeal to the circuit court as provided in and by the foregoing section, shall be the only remedy for damages sustained by the acts or proceedings of the said city or its officers in the matter to which such assessments relate; and no action at law or in equity shall be had or maintained for such injuries or on account of such acts and proceedings.

As amended by Section 15, Chapter 524, Laws of 1887.

On such an appeal, the city is entitled to show a dedication of the lands to public use by acts *in pais* of any owner thereof.

Emmons vs. Milwaukee, 32 Wis., 434.

SECTION 16. Whenever the damages awarded to the owner by the report of the board of public works, as confirmed by the common council, for any property condemned by said city for public use, shall have been paid or tendered to such owner or his agent, or when sufficient money for that purpose shall be provided in the hands of the city treasurer, and ready to be paid over to such owner, and ten days' notice thereof shall have been given by the board of public works, in the official papers, the city may enter upon and appropriate such property to the use for which the same was condemned; and the same shall thereafter be subject to all the laws and ordinances of the city, to the same extent as streets, alleys, and public grounds heretofore opened or laid out. The claimant of such damages shall, in all cases furnish an abstract of title, showing himself entitled to the same before they shall be paid to him. If in any case there shall be any doubt as to who is entitled to the damages for land taken, the city may require of the claimant a bond with good and sufficient sureties to hold said city harmless from all loss, costs and expenses in case any other person should claim such damages. The damages assessed by the board of public works or awarded by the verdict of the jury and judgment rendered thereon in case of appeal, shall be paid or tendered, or provided in the hands of city treasurer and ready to be paid over to the person or persons entitled thereto, and notice thereof given in the official papers as herein provided, within twelve months after the rendering of such judgment, or after the confirmation of such assessment by the common council, in case no appeal shall have been taken; and if not so paid or tendered or provided in the hands of the city treasurer, all the proceedings in any such case shall be void; provided, that such period of twelve months shall be exclusive of the time any such judgment may be pending in the supreme court on appeal; and provided also, that if the common council of said city shall, at any time before the city has actually entered upon and appropriated the property to the use for which it is proposed to be taken, by resolution, determine and declare that the cost of the property proposed to be taken whether ascertained by the board of public works or by the court on appeal in any case from the decision of said board, is unreasonably great or so large as to be burdensome and injurious to the

When city may enter upon and appropriate property condemned.

Abstract to be furnished by claimant.

Bond may be required, when.

Abandonment of proceedings.

owners of the property assessed for benefits thereby, or
that for any reason the taking of any property so proposed to be taken for public use is inexpedient, it shall
be lawful for the common council to direct that the proceedings for taking any or all such property be abandoned,
and thereupon and thereafter such property, or the part
thereof for the taking of which the proceedings are so
abandoned, shall be and remain private property the same
as if no such proceedings had been instituted for the
purpose of taking the same for public use, and the expense
of such proceedings so abandoned, shall be paid by the
said city, out of the fund of the ward or of the wards in
which such property is situated; and provided further,
that no such abandonment of any proceedings shall in
any way hinder or prevent other and subsequent proceedings to take the same property, or any part of it, for
the same or any other public use for which it may be
taken by law. The benefits assessed and reported by
the board of public works, from the confirmation of such
report by the common council, shall be and remain a lien
upon the premises so determined by the board of public
works to be benefited by the taking and appropriation of
lands to the public use as proposed. Whenever the
owner of any building situated in the whole or in part
upon the land proposed to be taken for public use, as in
this act provided, shall not have removed the same from
such land before the city shall desire to enter upon and
appropriate the property to the use for which it is taken,
the common council of said city may direct that notice be
given to such owner requiring him to remove the same
from the premises, so taken for the public use within a
reasonable time, not less than thirty days to be specified
in such notice; and in case such owner shall neglect to
remove such building within the time specified in such
notice, the said board of public works shall report the
facts to the common council, and said common council,
in their discretion, shall have power to sell or direct the
sale of such building at public auction for cash, giving
ten days public notice of such sale in the official papers
of said city, and the purchaser of such building at such
sale shall be authorized to enter upon the said premises
upon which such building is situated adjacent to the land
so taken for public use and to remove such building
therefrom, and he shall not thereby incur any liability to

Assessment to be lien upon premises, when.

Removal of build-ings, how com-pelled.

the owner of such premises as a trespasser thereon. In case of such sale, the proceeds shall be paid by such city to the owner of such building or deposited in the treasury of said city to his use.

As amended by Section 18, Chapter 324, Laws of 1882, and further amended by Section 16, Chapter 524, Laws of 1887.

Before the city can "enter upon and appropriate" property condemned for public use, the damages awarded to the owner must be paid or tendered, or provided for in case of an appeal.
Gilman vs. Milwaukee, 55 Wis., 328.

In an answer interposed by the city in an action to procure payment to plaintiffs of money awarded for taking land for public use, where no right is asserted to an abstract of title before making such payment, the charter provision requiring such abstract is thereby waived.
Kluender vs. Milwaukee, 57 Wis., 636.

When proceedings to condemn land for public use have been lawfully abondoned by the city, it is only liable to the owner for damages caused by *wrongful* acts done by it during the course of such proceedings.
Feiten vs. Milwaukee, 47 Wis,, 494.

The provision of law authorizing the council to abandon proceedings for condemnation theretofore held, is valid, and such abandonment renders inoperative a judgment previously rendered against the city.
Van Valkenburgh vs. Milwaukee, 43 Wis., 574.

SECTION 17. When the whole of any lot or tract of land or other premises, under lease or other contract, shall be taken by virtue of this act, all the covenants, contracts or engagements between landlord and tenant, or any other contracting parties, touching the same, or any part thereof shall upon confirmation of such report, respectively cease and be absolutely discharged. When only part of a lot or tract of land, or other premises, so under lease or other contract, shall be taken for any of the purposes aforesaid, all the covenants, contracts or agreements respecting the part so taken, upon confirmation of such report, shall be absolutely discharged as to the part thereof so taken, but shall remain valid. as to the residue thereof, and the rents, considerations and payments reserved payable and to be paid for or in respect to the same, shall be so apportioned, that part thereof, justly and equitably payable for such residue

When condemned property subject to lease or other contract, such lease or contract to cease and be absolutely discharged on confirmation of report.

thereof, and no more, shall be paid or recoverable for or in respect to the same.

As amended by Section 17, Chapter 524, Laws of 1887.

See Driver vs. W. U. Tel. Co., 32 Wis., 569.

Notices, how served on infants or persons laboring under legal disability.

SECTION 18. When any known owner of lands or tenements affected by any proceedings under this chapter shall be an infant, or labor under any legal disability, the judge of the circuit court of Milwaukee county, or in his absence, the judge of any court of record in said county may upon the application of the city attorney, or of such party or his next friend, appoint a guardian for such party and all notices required by this chapter shall be served upon such guardian.

As amended by Section 18, Chapter 524, Laws of 1887.

Surveys and plats to be made and filed in office of city engineer by board of public works.

SECTION 19. Whenever any public ground, street or alley, or any river, canal or waterway shall be laid out, widened or enlarged, under the provisions of this chapter the board of public works shall cause an accurate survey, plat and profile thereof to be made, and filed in the office of the city engineer.

As amended by section 19, Chapter 524, Laws of 1887.

Condemnation proceedings had previous to this act to be governed by it.

SECTION 20. In all cases where the report or verdict of a jury may have established the necessity of taking private property for any authorized public use in said city, previous to the passage of this act, the damages and benefits arising therefrom may be assessed as required by this act, and all proceedings subsequent to such report or verdict, may be had and continued to final completion, in the same manner as if such proceedings had been originally instituted under this act.

As amended by Section 20, Chapter 524, Laws of 1887.

Directions only directory.

SECTION 21. All the foregoing directions given in this chapter, shall be deemed only directory; and no error, irregularity or informality in any of the proceedings under the provisions of this chapter, not affecting substantial justice, shall in any way affect the validity of the proceedings.

As Amended by Section 21, Chapter 534, Laws of 1887.

See note to Sec. 35, Ch. XVIII.

SECTION 22. The common council shall have the power, and are hereby authorized to vacate, in whole or in part, such highways, streets, alleys and public walks within the corporate limits of the city, as in their opinion the public interest may require to be vacated, or such as in their opinion are of no public utility; provided, however, the necessity of vacating such highway, street, alley or public walk, or any part thereof or their want of public utility shall first be established by a verdict or report of a jury in like manner as is provided for laying out public squares, grounds and streets in this chapter.

Common council may vacate highways, streets, alleys and public walks when required.

As amended by Section 22, Chapter 524, Laws of 1887. See Chapter 374, Laws of 1889, in the foot note.

SECTION 23. Whenever it shall be necessary to change the location or direction of any highways, streets, alleys or public walks within the corporate limits of the city of Milwaukee, and it shall for that purpose be necessary to take lands and to vacate parts of any such highway, street, alley or public walk, such taking of lands and vacating of such parts of such highway, street, alley or public walk may be done by one proceeding, and the jury in such case shall determine the necessity of taking such lands proposed to be taken and the necessity of vacating such parts of such highway, street alley or public walk proposed to be vacated for such purpose, and the board of public works in making the assessment of benefits and damages in such case shall make but one assessment and assess the benefits and damages on account of the change in location or direction of such highway, street, alley or public walk, and the provisions of this chapter in respect to the proceedings for taking lands and for vacating highways, streets, alleys and public walks shall in all respects govern such case.

May change the location or direction of any highway, street, alley, or public walk within corporate limits of city.

As amended by Section 23, Chapter 524, Laws of 1887.

SECTION 24. All provisions of this act relating to the taking of land by said city for public purposes, shall apply to the lands required for the sites of public school buildings, engine houses and other public city buildings, and for the premises attached to such buildings, except that the common council shall not order, and the board of public works shall not make an assessment of benefits, nor shall the cost of such land, or the damages arising by

Provisions of this act to apply to proceedings for condemnation of lands for school sites, engine houses, and other public buildings, or for their enlargement.

reason of the taking of such lands, or any portion of such cost or damage be chargeable to or paid out of the ward fund of any ward, but any and all damages awarded to the owner by the board of public works, as confirmed by the common council for any property condemned by said city for the purposes mentioned in this section, shall be chargeable to and payable out of the general city fund.

As amended by Section 24, Chapter 524, Laws of 1887.

Funds may be advanced from ward funds to pay appropriation.

SECTION 25. Whenever any property shall be condemned for any of the purposes mentioned in this act and after the assessment of benefits and damages shall have been made by the board of public works, and confirmed by the common council, as provided in this chapter the common council shall have power, with the concurrence of the aldermen of the wards, to advance by appropriation from the ward fund of the ward in which the premises to be taken are situated, the amount required to pay the damages so assessed and confirmed, for the purpose of paying or tendering the same to the owner or owners of property so taken, as provided in section sixteen of this chapter; and in case such advance shall have been made the special tax collected from the property benefited, under such assessment, shall be credited to said ward fund, to reimburse said fund, the amount so advanced.

As amended by Section 25, Chapter 524, Laws of 1887.

NOTE:—By chapter 524, Laws of 1887, chapter 6 of the charter was amended throughout; section 25 was inserted and section 25 of the old charter was transposed and made section 31.

The legislature of 1889 overlooked these changes and by chapter 243 amended section 25 so as to read as it appears immediately following hereto. By this error section 25, as given above, is repeated while section 31, which the legislature evidently intended to amend, is left *in statu quo*.

SECTION 25. (In all cases where lands in the city shall hereafter be subdivided into lots or blocks, or where streets, alleys or public grounds shall be donated or granted to the public, the owner or owners thereof shall, in platting the same, cause streets and alleys in such plats to correspond in width and general direction with the streets and alleys through the lots and blocks in said city adjacent to the lot or tract so platted, and shall submit such maps or plats thereof to the board of public works and to the common council of said city for their approval; and if such map or plat shall be approved by said board and by the common council

Board to examine plat.

the party or parties making such plat shall record the same within thirty days from the date of such approval, in the manner prescribed in the Revised Statutes of the state concerning town plats; but except such plat be approved in writing endorsed thereon and subscribed by said board and by resolution adopted by said common council, a copy of which, duly certified by the city clerk, shall be affixed to said plat (and offered for record on or before thirty days from the date of such resolution), it shall not be lawful for the register of deeds of Milwaukee county to receive such plat or map for record, or to record the same, and the same shall have no validity; and the person or persons neglecting or refusing to comply with the requirments of this section shall forfeit and pay a sum not less than one hundred dollars or more than one thousand dollars and the register of deeds who shall record such plat, without such approval of the board of public works indorsed thereon, or without such copy of resolution of the common council thereto attached, approving the same (or after thirty days from the date of such resolution), shall forfeit and pay a sum of not less than fifty dollars or more than one hundred dollars. All forfeitures and liabilities which may be incurred and arising under and by virtue of this section, shall be prosecuted for and recovered in the name of the city of Milwaukee, and paid into the city treasury for the benefit of said city. The provisions of this act shall apply to all maps heretofore approved by the board of public works and common council that shall not be recorded within thirty days after the passage and publication of this act. Every person who shall bargain and sell any lot, piece or parcel of land within the limits of the city of Milwaukee purporting to be described on any unrecorded plat, and such lot, piece or parcel of land shall not have been surveyed, platted and recorded in the office of the register of deeds in the manner provided by law, shall be punished by a fine not exceeding one hundred dollars or less than twenty five dollars).

Penalty.

Chapter 243, Laws of 1889.

SECTION 26. Whenever the common council of the city of Milwaukee shall, with the concurrence of three-fourths of the members elected thereto, declare by resolution that it is necessary for the public interest to extend any water pipe or make or extend any supply tunnel or any sewer below the surface of the ground, upon, along or through any lands either within or without the limits of said city, the said common council shall have the authority to take and acquire the use of such lands for such purposes or for either such purposes, by proceeding in all respects, in relation to such taking and acquiring for such use as is provided in this chapter in reference to the taking of lands for public use without petition, except in those respects in which a different provision is specially made in the next two sections.

Lands may be taken and acquired for purposes of extending water pipe, supply tunnels, etc.

As amended by Section 26, Chapter 524, Laws of 1887.

Board of public
works to deter-
mine injury to
property owners
in consequence
of taking and
acquiring lands
for such use.

SECTION 27. The board of public works in making its award to the owners of the property, in which such use as is herein named, shall be acquired, shall determine the injury arising to the owners thereof, respectively, in consequence of the taking and acquiring of such use, but it shall not be necessary to make any estimate of benefits from such use either to such owner or to other lands.

As amended by Section 27, Chapter 524, Laws of 1887.

When lands may
be used.

SECTION 28. Whenever the damages awarded to the owners of any lands, the use of which for the purposes specified in this act or for either of such purposes, is sought to be taken and acquired by said city, shall have been paid or tendered to such owner or when sufficient money for that purpose shall have been provided in the hands of the city treasurer, and shall be ready to be paid over to such owner, and ten days notice thereof shall have been given by the board of public works, in the official papers, the said city shall thereupon and thereby acquire and have the right to the use of such lands for such purpose forever, and its proper officer and any contractor or other person acting under the authority of said city, or of its proper officers, shall have the right to lay and contract sewers or water-pipes or both, in, through and along such lands and may lawfully enter upon the same with men and teams, as may be necessary or convenient for doing such work, and may dig upon and otherwise prepare such lands for the use for which they are so taken and acquired, doing no unnecessary damage thereby, and may place, lay and maintain water-pipes, or sewers or both therein, and may at any and all times enter upon said lands with men and teams as may be necessary and convenient, for the purpose of taking up, relaying, repairing, removing or in any way modifying such water-pipes or sewers, or both, doing no unnecessary damage thereby; provided, that it shall be the duty of said city or its officers, or any contractor or other person doing any work on lands under the provisions of this act upon the completion of such work, to restore such lands to the same condition in which they were before such work was done, as nearly as is practicable to do so; provided further, that no sewer shall be extended into or through any ward from any other portion of the said city, by virtue of this act without the previous consent of the

aldermen of said ward in writing, filed in the office of the
board of public works.

As amended by Section 28, Chapter 524, Laws of 1887.

When the owner of real estate accepts the damages awarded
him, he is estopped from objecting that the proceedings for laying out a highway are defective.

Karber vs. Nellis, 22 Wis., 207.

SECTION 29.   In addition to the power to acquire the **Lands outside the limits of city may be used and acquired.**
use of lands for the purpose named in this act, by con-
demnation, as hereinbefore provided, the city of Milwaukee is hereby empowered and authorized to acquire such
use of any lands either within or without the city limits
of said city, by grant or conveyance by deed, in all cases
where the terms of a purchase shall be agreed upon
between the city and the owners of any such lands.

As amended by Section 29, Chapter 524, Laws of 1887.

See Tester vs. Sheboygan, 87 Wis., 496.

SECTION 30.   In case it shall be necessary to take any **Lands may be taken for the purpose of opening and constructing canals, water channels and slips established in valley of Menomonee river, or for opening and constructing water channels of Kinnickinnic river.**
property for the purpose of opening and constructing the
canals, water channels and slips, or any part thereof,
laid out and established in the valley of the Menomonee
river, under and in pursuance of chapter 91, of the local
laws of 1869, or to take any property for the purpose of
opening and constructing the water channel of the Kinnickinnick river, when the same shall be adopted and
established, recorded and filed, as provided by section 20,
of chapter 129, of the laws of 1873, the same proceedings
shall be had as are in this chapter prescribed for the taking of property for public squares, grounds, streets and
alleys; the common council shall have power to vacate
any canal or slip or any part thereof for the same reasons
and upon the same proceedings being had that are prescribed in this chapter for vacating streets in said city,
and the said common council is hereby authorized and
empowered to change the location and direction of any
canal, water channel or slip and the location and direction of any river within the corporate limits of said city,
upon the same proceedings being had as are prescribed
in this chapter for changing the location or direction of
any street in said city, and all the provisions of this
chapter relating to assessments of damages and benefits,

appeals and compensation to owners, shall be applicable to cases arising under this section.

As amended by Section 30, Chapter 524, Laws of 1887.

Where hereafter lands are subdivided into lots and blocks, the streets and alleys of such plat must correspond in width and general direction with those adjacent. Map of plat to be submitted to common council for approval.

SECTION 31. In all cases where lands in the city shall hereafter be subdivided into lots and blocks, or where streets, alleys or public grounds shall be donated or granted to the public, the owner or owners thereof shall, in platting the same, cause the streets and alleys in such plat to correspond in width and general direction with the streets and alleys through the lots and blocks in said city adjacent to the lot or tract as platted, and shall submit such maps or plats thereof to the board of public works, and to the common council of said city, for their approval; and if such map or plat shall be approved by the said board of public works and by the common council, it shall be lawful for the party or parties making such plat to record the same, and the evidence of such approval, in the manner prescribed in the revised statutes of the state concerning town plats; but except such plat shall be approved by writing, endorsed thereon and subscribed by said board of public works and by resolution adopted by said common council, a copy of which duly certified by the city clerk, shall be affixed to said plat, it shall not be lawful for the register of deeds of Milwaukee county to receive such plat or map for record, or to record the same, and the same shall have no validity; and the person or persons neglecting or refusing to comply with the requirements of this section, shall forfeit and pay a sum not less than one hundred dollars, nor more than one thousand dollars; and the register of deeds who shall record such plat without the approval of the board of public works endorsed thereon or without such copy of a resolution of the common council thereto attached approving the same, shall forfeit and pay a sum not less than fifty dollars, nor more than one hundred dollars. All forfeitures and liabilities which may be incurred and arise under and by virtue of this section shall be prosecuted for and recovered in the name of the city of Milwaukee, and paid into the city treasury, for the use and benefit of said city.

As amended by Section 31, Chapter 524, Laws of 1887.

Whenever, the common council of the said city of Milwaukee shall have changed and altered the established grade of any street therein in the manner provided by law, after such street shall have been once graded and paved to the established grade, and any part or portion of said street shall have been improved and brought to the grade so altered and changed, it shall be, and is hereby made the duty of the said common council, to cause the remaining portion of said street, the grade of which has been so altered and changed, to be graded and graveled or paved to such altered and changed grade, within one year from the time of the improvement of any portion of said street, to the grade so changed and altered.

Amends chapter 6, charter of the city of Milwaukee.

SECTION 2. It shall not be necessary to give any notice except by publication in the official newspapers of said city in the manner provided by law, to any person, of the vacation or proposed vacation of any street, alley or public place, under the provisions of section 22, of chapter 6, of said charter.

Relating to vacation of streets.

CHAPTER 250, LAWS OF 1881.

SECTION 1. Whenever the common council of the city of Milwaukee, shall with the concurrence of three-fourths of the members elected thereto, declare by resolution that it is necessary for the public interest to extend any water pipe or any sewer below the surface of the ground upon, along or through any lands, either within or without the limits of said city, the said common council shall have the authority to take and acquire the use of such lands for such purposes or for either such purpose, by proceeding in all respects in relation to such taking and acquiring for such use, as is provided in chapter six of the charter of said city, being charter six of chapter one hundred and eighty-four of the laws of 1874, in reference to the taking of lands for public use without petition, except in those respects in which a different provision is especially made in this act.

Common council may take and acquire lands for use in laying pipe.

SECTION 2. The board of public works, in making its award to the owners of the property, in which such use as is herein named shall be acquired, shall determine the injury arising to the owners thereof respectively, in consequence of the taking and acquiring of such use but it shall not be necessary to make any estimate of benefits from such use either to such owners or to other lands.

Board of public works to determine damages.

SECTION 3. Whenever the damages awarded to the owners of any lands, the use of which for the purposes specified in this act or for either of such purposes, is sought to be taken and acquired by said city, shall have been paid or tendered to such owner, or when sufficient money, for that purpose, shall have been provided in the hands of the city treasurer, and shall be ready to be paid over to such owner, and ten days, notice thereof shall have been given by the board of public works, in the official papers, the said city shall thereupon and thereby acquire and have the right to the use of such lands for such purpose forever, and its proper officers

Tender of money for damages, how made.

or any contractor, or other person, acting under the authority of said city, or of its proper officers, shall have the right to lay and construct sewers or water pipes, or both, in, through, and along such lands, and may lawfully enter upon the same with men and teams, as may be necessary or convenient for doing such work, and may dig upon and otherwise prepare such lands for the use for which they are so taken and acquired doing no unnecessary damage thereby, and may place, lay, and maintain waterpipes, or sewers, or both therein, and may, at any and all times, enter upon said lands, with men and teams, as may be necessary or convenient, for the purpose of taking up, relaying, repairing, removing or in any way modifying such water pipes (or) sewers, or both doing no unnecessary damage thereby; provided, that it shall be the duty of said city or its officers, or any contractor or other person doing any work on lands under the provisions of this act upon the completion of such work, to restore such lands to the same condition in which they were before such work was done, as nearly as it is practicable to do so; provided further, that no sewer shall be extended into or through any ward from any other portion of said city, by virtue of this act, without the previous consent of the aldermen of said ward in writing, filed in the office of the board of public works.

Additional powers. SECTION 4. In addition to the power to acquire the use of lands for the purposes named in this act, by condemnation as herein above provided, the city of Milwaukee is hereby empowered and authorized to acquire such use of any lands either within or without the limits of said city, by grant or conveyance by deed, in all cases where the terms of a purchase shall be agreed upon, between the city and the owner of any such lands.

CHAPTER 235, LAWS OF 1881.

Completion of Seventh ward park authorizeo. SECTION 1. The provisions of chapter six, of one hundred and eighty-four, of the laws of 1874, are hereby so amended and enlarged, as to authorize said city to take and acquire the necessary lands and property for the purpose of extending and completing the seventh ward park to the south line of Mason street, as the same are named in chapter one hundred and forty-one, of the private and local laws of 1868, and any acts amendatory thereof, and in addition thereto, such other portions of block one hundred and eight in said seventh ward, as the common council of said city may, by resolution, determine to acquire for said park.

In case of disagreement with owners of lots. SECTION 2. In case said city cannot agree with the owner or owners of any of the land required for said park, on the terms of purchase, it is hereby authorized to condemn and take the same in the manner required by law, to enable said city to take and condemn lands for the purpose of laying out streets, alleys, public squares and grounds; provided, that for the purposes contemplated by this act it shall not be necessary to have any petition of freeholders, or bond; but the common council shall, by resolution adopted by an affirmative vote of a majority of the aldermen of said ward, direct proceedings to be had for such purpose, and

thereafter the proceedings shall be in all respects, as provided by
law, for the taking of property for public use as a street, without
petition or bond.

SECTION 3.   The city of Milwaukee is hereby authorized to pur-   **City may lease or**
chase, or lease with the privilege to purchase, by agreement with   **purchase.**
the owners, any or all of the lands and property contemplated to
be taken for the purpose of such park, but no such purchase shall
be made until the same shall have been ordered by the common
council of said city, by resolution adopted by an affirmative vote
of a majority of the aldermen of said ward, specifying the land to
be purchased, the maximum price to be paid therefor, and the
terms of payment. Any such purchase may be made in whole or
part on credit, and for that purpose the proper officers of said city
may execute and deliver to the vendor of such land or property
purchased, an instrument creating a lien thereon, and any improvements thereon, for such purchase money without creating any
corporate liability therefor, to secure the whole or any part of the
price in installments extending not more than ten years from the
date of such purchase, which installments may bear interest at
such rate as shall be agreed on, not exceeding seven per cent. per
annum.

SECTION 4.   All such lands so taken, purchased or leased, shall   **City to hold lands**
be held by said city in trust for said seventh ward for the purpose   **in trust.**
of a park, to be an extension of the seventh ward park, and shall
be improved, cared for and governed, as is in that respect provided
in chapter one hundred and forty-one, of the private and local
laws of 1868, and the laws amendatory thereof, the same as if such
provisions were herein incorporated and enacted.

SECTION 5.   All moneys required to be paid for the taking of
any lands or property under this act (except such as shall be collected for assessments for benefits), or for the purchasing or
leasing of any lands or property under this act, shall be chargeable
to and payable out of the seventh ward fund, and not otherwise;
and for the purpose of providing such moneys, it shall not be
lawful to exceed the limit now fixed by law for such ward fund,
and for the purpose of special assessments for benefits under this
act, the property lying in said ward, shall be taxable therefor.

SECTION 6.   If the board of public works or common council   **Proceedings may**
of said city shall at any time determine that the cost of the property   **be abandoned,**
proposed to be taken, whether ascertained by the said board or by   **when.**
the court on appeal in any case from the decision of said board, is
unreasonably great, or so large as to be burdensome and injurious
to the owners of the property assessed, to pay for the same, or if
for any reason, the taking of any of the land authorized to be
taken for such park shall be inexpedient, it shall be lawful for the
board or the common council to abandon the proceedings for
taking any or all of such land, which shall therefore remain the
property of the owners thereof, as if such proceedings had not
been commenced, and the expenses of the proceedings so abandoned shall be paid by the ward in which such land lies. Such
abandonment shall not prevent the subsequent resumption of such
proceedings under this act, it being the intention of this act to

authorize the creation of such park, so far as the same can be done to the advantage of the tax payers of the said ward, and at a moderate reasonable cost, and not otherwise.

SECTION 7. This act is hereby declared to be an amendment of the charter of said city, and all acts and parts of acts contravening the provisions of this act, in so far as they conflict herewith, are hereby repealed.

CHAPTER 210, LAWS OF 1883.

May extend Seventh ward park.

SECTION 1. In case the city of Milwaukee shall purchase, by agreement with the owners, any or all of the lands and property contemplated to be taken for the purpose of extending the Seventh Ward park, according to the provisions of Chapter 235, of the Laws of 1881, or shall so purchase by agreement any interest in, or any undivided part or share of any such lands and property, it shall be lawful for said city, and the proper officers of said city are hereby authorized and required to make an assessment of benefits on lands or premises benefited by such purchase by agreement, and to charge such lands or premises with the amount of such benefits in the same manner as is now provided by law for so charging lands or premises benefited, where lands and property are taken by condemnation for such purpose. When said city shall have purchased or determined to purchase by such agreement any undivided interest in, or any undivided part or share of lands or property to be taken for such purpose, it shall be lawful for said city to acquire the remaining interest, share or part of such lands or property by condemnation, as now provided by law for acquiring lands and property for such purpose.

SECTION 2. In case the common council of said city shall determine to purchase, by agreement with the owners, all the lands that shall be acquired for the purpose of the extension of said park under said Chapter 235, the common council shall, upon the adoption of a resolution for that purpose, direct the board of public works to make and report their assessment of benefits to lands or premises that it ascertains and determines to be benefited by the purchase of such property for such purposes, in the same manner as said board would be required to ascertain and determine and make assessment of benefits, upon the confirmation of the report of the jury, in case such property had been taken under proceedings for acquiring property for such purpose by condemnation. In case the common council shall determine to acquire for such purpose, a part only of such lands by purchase by agreement, and the remaining part thereof by condemnation, or in case any undivided interest or interests in any such lands shall be acquired by such purchase, and other interests in the same lands shall be determined to be taken by condemnation, then the common council shall, at the same time that it directs the board of public works to view the premises determined to be taken by condemnation for the purpose of ascertaining and determining the amount of damages to be paid to the owner or owners of the property proposed to be taken, direct said board also to view the premises determined to be acquired by purchase by agreement, and the premises in which any undivided interest is determined to be so acquired, and to ascertain and determine what lands or premises will be benefited by the taking and acquiring of the property for such use, as well that taken by condemnation, as that acquired by purchase by agreement, or in which any interest is so acquired, and to make report of its determination and assessment as now required by law in case of property taken for such purpose by condemnation. After the board of public works shall have been so directed by the common council in either case aforesaid, said board shall proceed as now required by law in a proceeding for the condemnation of such lands and all subsequent proceedings, rights and duties, either of the city or its officers or of private persons or parties in relation to such assessments of benefits, including appeals therefrom, the charging of the property therewith, and the collection of the same, shall be the same and shall be governed by the same laws as are now applicable to cases of assessments of benefits by the taking of such property by condemnation.

SECTION 3. Authority is hereby given to said city to take by condemnation, or to acquire by purchase by agreement for the purpose of extending and completing said park, such portions of the tract of land lying east of the east line of Lake avenue, as laid out and designated on the plat of Diedrich's subdivision of land, lying east of block one hundred (100) in the seventh ward of the city of Milwaukee, as the common council of said city may, by resolution, determine to acquire for such purpose and for that purpose all the provisions of said Chapter 235, and of this act, applicable thereto, are hereby extended so as to include said last named tract of land, and are to be held and construed for all purposes, as if said tract of land had been originally named in and covered by the provisions of said Chapter 235. *How acquired.*

CHAPTER 85, LAWS OF 1881.

SECTION 1. The city of Milwaukee is hereby authorized to sell at the largest practicable price all the interests of said city, or of the fifth ward, in block eighteen, in said fifth ward, and hold the proceeds of such sale in trust for said ward for the purposes hereinafter described. *Sale of block 18, Fifth ward.*

SECTION 2. Whenever the city of Milwaukee shall have sold and conveyed the property described in the first section of this act, as provided in said section, it shall be the duty of the aldermen of said fifth ward, or of a majority of them as soon as practicable after such sale, to proceed to select a suitable site for a public park or market in said ward, and as far as practicable to contract for the necessary land for such park or market, at a price not greater than the aggregate proceeds of the sale provided for in section first of this act; and when said aldermen or a majority of them shall have selected said site and contract for the necessary land for said park or market, or otherwise ascertained the conditions upon which said lands may be obtained as hereinbefore provided, *Aldermen to select public park or market.*

they shall file with the proper officers of said city a description of the site so selected and of said lands with a statement of the probable price at which said land can be obtained, whereupon said city of Milwaukee may purchase and hold in trust for the use of said ward for a public park or market in said ward, all of the said lands so selected and described.

Authority of council and aldermen of Fifth ward.

SECTION 3. No such purchase shall be made until the same shall have been ordered by the common council of said city by resolution adopted by an affirmative vote of a majority of the members of such council and a majority of the aldermen of said ward, specifying the land to be purchased, the maximum price to be paid therefor and the terms of payment.

Condemning lands.

SECTION 4. In case it shall be deemed necessary to condemn any portion of the land selected by said aldermen as a site for said park or market, it shall be the duty of said city to proceed to condemn the same in the same manner that said city is otherwise authorized to condemn lands for public use; and in case such condemnation is made, all amounts assessed to said city for payment in consequence of the taking of such lands for such park or market shall be paid from the proceeds of the sale provided for in the first section of this act.

Liability of city.

SECTION 5. Nothing in this act shall be construed to authorize the city to sell any buildings belonging exclusively to said city and situated in said block; nor shall said city be held liable for the cost of the land taken or purchased, or for the improvement of said park or market in any manner except as provided in this act, provided that the city of Milwaukee may receive donations for the purchase or improvement of said park or market in addition to the proceeds of the sale provided for in the first section of this act; but

Donation required. no part of the proceeds of such sale shall be applied to the purchase or establishment of a market until suitable buildings and other improvements therefor of a total value of at least ten thousand dollars, shall have been previously provided for by donation and without cost to said city or ward.

Amendment.

SECTION 6. This act is hereby declared to be an amendment to the charter of said city and all acts and parts of acts contravening the provisions of this act are hereby repealed.

CHAPTER 488, LAWS OF 1889.

AN ACT to establish a system of public parks within the city of Milwaukee, and to provide for the purchase, payment and government thereof.

City may issue $100,000 park bonds.

SECTION 1. The common council of the city of Milwaukee, is hereby authorized to provide by ordinance for the issue of corporate bonds of said city in amount not exceeding one hundred thousand dollars. Said bonds shall be payable in not more than twenty years after the date of said issue, and shall bear interest not exceeding the rate of five per cent. per annum. Said bonds shall be known as and called park lands [bonds] and shall be issued exclusively to provide funds for establishing and maintaining parks within the city of Milwaukee, embracing one or more parks north of North avenue, in said city, and one or more parks on the south side of the Milwaukee river, in said city. But it shall not be lawful to expend more than one-half of said proceeds from the sale of said bonds upon the park or parks within either of said divisions.

SECTION 2. All bonds issued under the provisions of this act shall be signed by the mayor and clerk of said city, countersigned by the comptroller of said city, attested by the commissioners of public debt of said city, sealed with the corporate seal of said city, made payable in lawful money of the United States of America in the city of Milwaukee or New York, and shall each be for the principal sum of one thousand dollars, or five hundred dollars, or one hundred dollars, and shall have attached thereto interest coupons or warrants for the semi-annual payment of interest thereon, and such bonds and coupons shall be numbered in the form and manner to be designated by said comptroller.

How issued.

SECTION 3. Bonds issued under the provisions of this act shall be issued from time to time, in such amounts as the common council of said city may determine upon; said bonds, when issued and properly signed and sealed, shall be delivered to the commissioners of public debt of said city, and by that body disposed of, the proceeds arising therefrom to be paid into the treasury of said city, and such proceeds shall constitute a separate and distinct fund, to be exclusively applied for the purposes specified in the first section of this act. Provided, that nothing in this act contained shall be construed as authorizing said common council to issue bonds in excess of the limitation prescribed in Section 6, of Chapter 11, of the charter of said city, and the acts amendatory thereof.

To be disposed of by commissioners of public debt.

SECTION 4. The office of commissioners of public debt of said city shall not be abolished while any of the bonds issued under the provisions of this act remain outstanding and unpaid.

Office not to be abolished.

SECTION 5. The provisions of sections 2, 6, 7, 8, 9, 10, 11 and 17, Chapter 87, of the laws of 1861, applicable and not inconsistent with the provisions of this act, shall apply to bonds issued under the provisions of this act, and such sections, if not inconsistent, are incorporated as a part of this act. The true intent and meaning of this act is to provide for the present issue of bonds in the same manner as bonds issued under the provisions of that act are provided for.

Certain provisions of chapter 87, laws of 1861, to apply.

SECTION 6. The common council of said city shall annually cause a tax to be levied upon all taxable property in said city, both personal and real, for the payment of the annual interest on all unpaid bonds issued under the provisions of this act, and for twenty years before the principal of said bonds becomes due, the said common council shall annually cause a tax to be levied upon all taxable property, in said city, both personal and real, equal in amount to five per cent. of all bonds issued under the provisions of this act, for a sinking fund to redeem such bonds as the said commissioners of public debt direct to be cancelled.

Tax levy.

When to cancel.

SECTION 7. As soon as a sinking fund shall have been collected and set aside, the said commissioners of public debt shall proceed to cancel bonds in amount equal to the sinking fund so provided.

How cancelled.

SECTION 8. All bonds directed to be paid by said commissioners of public debt shall be, when paid, stamped, "cancelled" and when so stamped shall be delivered to the common council of said city, and by that body publicly declared cancelled.

Not to be sold for less than par.

SECTION 9. The commissioners of public debt of said city are hereby prohibited from selling or otherwise disposing of any such bonds at a less valuation than par, that is to say, at less than the principal of said bonds, together with the accrued interest thereon.

Mayor to appoint park commissioners.

SECTION 10. It shall be the duty of the mayor of the city of Milwaukee on or before the first day of June, 1889, to appoint, subject to the approval of the common council as in the case of the appointment of other officers, five commissioners who shall constitute a board of park commissioners. Said commissioners shall be chosen from the freeholders of said city, and the mayor shall nominate the chairman of said board and designate the length of the term of each commissioner, one being appointed for one year, one for two years, one for three years, one for four years and one for five years, and the mayor shall in like manner each year appoint a new commissioner who shall hold for five years. In the case of vacancy the mayor

Duties.

shall appoint a commsssioner for the unexpired term. Each of said commissioners before entering upon the duties of his office shall take an oath to well and truly discharge the duties of his office, which oath shall be reduced to writing, subscribed by him and filed in the office of the city clerk. All lands acquired by said city of Milwaukee under the provisions of this act shall be held, managed and controlled by said board of park commissioners as a public park or parks for the recreation, health and benefit of the public and free to all persons, subject to such necessary rules and regulations as shall be from time to time adopted by said board of park commissioners for the well ordering and government of the same. The commissioners appointed under this section shall receive no salary.

Provisions of chapter 6 of chapter 184, laws 1874, relating to acquiring of lands by purchase or lease to apply.

SECTION 11. The provisions of chapter 6, of chapter 184, of the laws of 1874, being the charter of the city of Milwaukee, and the several acts amendatory thereof, are hereby so amended and enlarged as to authorize said city through said board of park commissioners, to take and acquire by purchase, or by lease with the privilege to purchase, by agreement with the owner, in addition to, or in place of the lands to be paid for from the proceeds of said bonds, lands and property for the purpose of establishing the parks herein provided.

May condemn lands when agreement cannot be had.

SECTION 12. In case said city through said board of park commissioners cannot agree with the owner or owners of any of the land required for said parks on the terms of purchase, it is hereby authorized to condemn and take the same in the manner required by law to enable said city to take and condemn lands for the purpose of laying out streets, alleys, public squares, and grounds; provided, that for the purposes contemplated by this act it shall not be necessary to have any petition of freeholders or bond; but the common council shall, by resolution adopted by an affirmative vote of a majority of the aldermen elect, direct proceedings to be had for such purpose, and hereafter the proceedings shall be in all respects as provided by law, for the taking of property for public use as a street without petition or bond.

SECTION 13. No such purchase or lease shall be made until the same shall have been ordered by the common council of said city, by resolution adopted by an affirmative vote of a majority of the aldermen elect, specifying the land to be purchased, the maximum price to be paid therefor and the terms of payment or the terms of option in case of lease by the city with the privilege of purchasing. Any such purchase may be made in whole or part on credit and for that purpose the proper officers of said city may execute and deliver to the vendor of such land or property purchased, an instrument creating a lien thereon and any improvements thereon, for such purchase money, without creating any corporate liabilities therefor, to secure the whole or any part of the price in installments, extending not more than ten years from the date of such purchase, which intallments may bear interest at such rates as shall be agreed on, not exceeding seven per cent. per annum. *When purchase or lease may be made.* *May be on credit.*

CHAPTER 179, LAWS OF 1891.

AN ACT to define the powers and duties of the park commissioners, and establish a fund for the maintenance of parks and boulevards by the city of Milwaukee.

SECTION 1. All lands acquired by the city of Milwaukee under the provisions of Chapter 488, of the laws of 1889, and all lands that shall hereafter be acquired by said city for the purpose of public parks and boulevards, shall be named and controlled by said board of park commissioners and public parks and boulevards, for the recreation, health and benefit of the public, and shall be free to all persons subject to such necessary rules and regulations as shall be from time to time, adopted by said board of park commissioners for the well-ordering and government thereof. *Park commissioners to have control of parks and boulevards.*

SECTION 2. The said board shall have the full and exclusive power to govern, manage, control and improve said parks and boulevards, and to lay out and make rules for the regulation and government thereof; to restrict traffic and prohibit heavy teaming thereon; to appoint such engineers, surveyors, clerks and such other officers as may be necessary for the proper care and management thereof, and the proper preservation of order therein, including special police, who are hereby granted the powers now granted to the police of the city of Milwaukee; and to define and prescribe their respective duties and authorities; to fix the amount of the compensation of all such officers and employees; and generally in regard to said parks and boulevards, the said board of park commis- *Same.*

sioners shall have and possess all powers and authority now by law conferred upon or possessed by the common council and board of public works of the city of Milwaukee, in respect to the public squares and places in said city.

Board to elect a secretary; his salary and bond.

SECTION 3. The said board of park commissioners of the city of Milwaukee shall, at their first meeting after the third Tuesday in April of each year elect a secretary, not a member of the board, and said commissioners may fix the salary of said secretary at a sum not exceeding the sum of $1,500 per year. It shall be the duty of said board to require a bond with satisfactory sureties from their secretary, conditioned in an amount to be fixed by said board, for the faithful performance of his duties, and it shall not be lawful for the said secretary to receive any compensation for his services until he has filed such bond with the city clerk of the city of Milwaukee, with the approval of the city attorney as to the form and execution of said bond endorsed thereon. Each of the sureties shall make affidavit that he is worth the sum named in the penalty of the bond in property liable to execution in the State of Wisconsin over and above all debts, liabilities and exemptions; bond and sureties to be approved by a majority of said board of park commissioners.

Board may establish building lines.

SECTION 4. The said board shall have power to establish building lines for the purpose of regulating the erection of buildings upon property fronting upon any of said parks or boulevards.

Board to make report to common council.

SECTION 5. It shall be the duty of the board of park commissioners within ten days after the appointment of any salaried employee, to report to and file with the city comptroller the name of the person so appointed, with the amount of salary allowed, and the time or times fixed for the payment thereof. All claims and demands against the city, before they are allowed by the said board of park commissioners, shall be audited and adjusted by the comptroller, and immediately after their allowance by sajd board of park commissioners, they shall furnish the said comptroller with a list of all accounts or bills which have been allowed by said board, stating the character of the materials furnished or services rendered, and for which such allowance was made. It shall be the duty of said board to transmit to the common council of said city, at its first regular meeting in April in each year, a full and detailed report of all transactions of said board of park commissioners for the preceding year, together with an itemized account of all expenditures, a list of employees, and an inventory of property, and purchase price thereof, which may be, at the time of making such report, under the control of said board.

Common council to provide by taxation a park and boulevard fund.

SECTION 6. The common council shall include in the tax levy of 1891, and annually thereafter, upon all taxable property of the said city, at the same time and in the same manner as other city taxes are levied and collected by law, a special tax not exceeding one half of a mill upon each dollar of the assessed value of said taxable property, the amount of which tax shall be determined by said board of park commissioners, and certified to the common council and to the city comptroller at the time of making their annual report to said council; and the entire amount of such special tax shall be collected, paid into, and held in the city treasury as a separate and distinct fund, to be known as the " Park and Boulevard Fund " and shall not be used or appropriated, directly or indirectly, for any other purpose than for the improvement, maintenance, and control of the public parks and boulevards, and for the payment of the salaries of the employees and other proper expenses of said board.

SECTION 7. All moneys received or raised in the city of Milwaukee for parks and boulevards, under the control of said park commissioners, shall be paid over to the city treasurer, and shall be disbursed according to resolution of the board of park commissioners authorizing the payment of bills and accounts after the same have been audited and ordered by the board and orders directed to be issued therefor, which shall be signed by the president and secretary of said board; but before the city treasurer pays such orders the resolution of the board, and the accounts and bills shall be presented to the comptroller and audited by him, and thereupon the order shall be countersigned by him. Such orders shall be made payable to the order of the persons in whose favor they shall have been issued, and shall be the only vouchers of the said treasurer for his payment from the park fund. All moneys heretofore paid into the city treasury for park or boulevard purposes, and not used for the purchase of real property, shall be credited to the park and boulevard fund hereby created, and shall be disbursed upon the orders of the president and secretary of the board of park commissioners as herein provided. It shall not be lawful for the board of park commissioners to expend or contract a liability for any sum in excess of the amount levied in any one year for the park fund on account of such fund.

Park and boulevard fund, how disbursed.

SECTION 8. Said board of park commissioners is hereby authorized to contract for the purchase of lands within the county of Milwaukee for the city of Milwaukee, for park or boulevard purposes, and to lease lands therein for such purposes with the privilege of purchasing the same, but no such lease or purchase shall be made until the same shall have been ordered by the common council of said city, by resolution adopted by an affirmative vote of a majority of the aldermen elect, specifying the land to be purchased, the maximum price to be paid therefor and the terms of payment, or the terms of option in case of lease by the city with the privilege of purchasing. Any such purchase may be made in whole or part on credit; and for that purpose the proper officers of said city may execute and deliver to the vendor of such land, or property purchased, an instrument creating a lien thereon and on the improvements thereon, for such purchase money, without creating any corporate liabilities therefor, to secure the whole or any part of the price in one payment, or by installments extending not more than twenty years from the date of such purchase, which installments may bear interest at such rates as shall be agreed on, not exceeding seven per centum per annum. The interest upon, and annual installments of such purchase, heretofore or hereafter made, shall be included by the common council in its annual estimate of expenses.

Powers of board as to purchase and lease of lands.

CHAPTER 231, LAWS OF 1889.

SECTION 1. It is hereby made the duty of the common council of the city of Milwaukee and the officers of said city, immediately upon the passage and publication of this act, to acquire by dedication, purchase or condemnation, the fee simple of a strip of land extending from the intersection of Eleventh avenue with Pierce street in said city, in a northerly direction to the intersection of Sixteenth and Fowler streets in said city, and to be seventy feet wide and of uniform width. And it is hereby made the duty of the city engineer of said city, immediately upon the passage and publication of this act, to cause a survey of the same to be made, and to file said survey in the office of the board of public works of said city, and he shall also file therewith a description of the several parcels of land contained therein, and also a map or plat thereof, showing the location of the same. It is hereby made the duty of the board of public works of said city of Milwaukee, immediately upon the filing of the said plat and description of said strip of land and said survey, to ascertain if the same or any part thereof can be acquired from the owners thereof, by dedication without compensation and to report thereon to the common council without delay, and it is made the further duty of said board of public works to thereupon enter into negotiations with the several owners of the lands to be acquired, for the purchase of the fee simple thereof, and the said board is hereby authorized and empowered to purchase without any delay, from the owners thereof, the fee simple of all the lands described in said survey, which cannot be acquired by gift, and to issue bills therefor against the city of Milwaukee, which shall be paid as are other claims against said city, out of

the general city fund thereof. And it is hereby made the duty of the common council and the proper city officers to provide for the payment of the amounts necessary for such purpose and agreed upon by the said board of public works. It is hereby made the duty of the said board of public works, within sixty days after the filing of said survey and plat, to report to the common council a list of all the lands set off in said survey and plat, which they have been unable to purchase or acquire by gift. And the common council shall thereupon proceed to acquire the fee of the several parcels described in the return of the said board of public works, by condemnation, and shall proceed in that behalf as provided in the charter of said city for the taking of lands for the public use, without petition, excepting that such proceedings shall be to acquire the fee simple of said parcels of land and not the use thereof. And further provided, that there shall be no assessment of benefits, and that the award of damages in all cases shall be paid out of the general city fund. And further provided, that whenever the common council shall have confirmed the assessment of damages in said condemnation proceeding and shall have advertised for six days in the official newspapers of said city, that the amount of damages awarded to the owners of said lands respectively has been provided in the hands of the city treasurer, and is ready to be paid over to such several owners, the said city of Milwaukee shall have full power and authority to enter upon and appropriate the property so taken and condemned, and the same shall thereafter be subject to the provisions of this act and to all the laws and ordinances of the city of Milwaukee applicable thereto. And further provided, that if any person shall appeal from said assessment of damages in the manner provided by said charter, that such appeal shall not prevent the city of Milwaukee from entering upon possession of said lands as hereinbefore provided, and the owners of said lands so appealing may receive and accept the amount so awarded to them without any prejudice whatever to said appeal, and if a greater sum than the amount awarded shall be recovered in any case, the same with costs shall be paid out of the general city fund of said city as other judgments against the said city are paid. In all other respects said proceedings shall be governed by the provisions of said charter relating to the taking of lands for public use.

SECTION 2. The said city of Milwaukee is authorized and empowered to use the lands so acquired for all public purposes of whatever kind, and may construct, erect and maintain thereon any public bridge or bridges, viaducts, abutments, piers or other thing, and to improve the same or any portion thereof as a public street or walk, and to construct therein any sewer, watermain, and for all other public purposes or uses, as the common council of said city of Milwaukee may, from time to time, prescribe. *Empowered to improve such land.*

SECTION 3. All acts and parts of acts in conflict with the provisions of this act are hereby modified, superseded or repealed to the extent that the true meaning of this act may be carried into effect. *Repealed.*

CHAPTER 166, LAWS OF 1893.

AN ACT to amend section 18, of Chapter 392, of the laws of Wisconsin for the year 1856, entitled "An act to incorporate the Milwaukee and Northern Plank Road Company."

SECTION 1. Section 18, of Chapter 392, of the laws of Wisconsin for the year 1856, is hereby amended by striking out all of said section after the word figures "Section 18," and inserting in lieu thereof the following: In case of an extension of the corporate limits of the city of Milwaukee beyond such points and places where toll gates are erected, in such cases toll gates are to be removed beyond the limits of the city of Milwaukee, the distance of one-half of one mile, and in case said company fails and neglects to remove such toll gates, such toll gates shall be thrown open upon complaint by any person being made in writing, in manner provided by sections 19 and 20, of this chapter, and remain open until such removal. *When corporate limits extended, toll gates to be removed.*

CHAPTER 192, LAWS OF 1893.

AN ACT to amend Section 1780 of the Revised Statutes, as amended by Chapter 211, of the laws of 1879, relating to electric light companies.

SECTION 1. Section 1780, of the Revised Statutes, as amended by Chapter 211, of the laws of 1879, is hereby amended by adding

Electric light corporations may use streets and alleys, when.

thereto as follows, to-wit: Any corporation heretofore or hereafter organized for the purpose of furnishing heat, light, power or signals by electricity, is hereby authorized, with the consent of, and in the manner agreed upon with the proper authorities of any city or village, to use any street, alley, lane, park or public grounds for constructing and maintaining and operating its lines with all necessary wires, conduits and appurtenances for the purpose of supplying light, heat, power or signals to such city or village, or to any building, manufactory, industry or public or private house therein; provided, no permanent injury shall be done to such street, alley, lane, park or public grounds. The provisions of this section shall apply to any corporation heretofore organized and now operating an electric light plant by the consent of the authorities of any city or village.

CHAPTER 198, LAWS OF 1895.

AN ACT to provide for the appointment of jurors to be sworn and serve as a jury to view lands in cities operating under special charters.

SECTION 1. Whenever in any city incorporated by and operating under a special charter granted by the Legislature of this state, the requisite number of jurors shall have been summoned to appear before any court or judge, to be sworn and serve as a jury to view lands for the purpose of determining the necessity of taking any lands for public use, or vacating any highways, streets, alleys or public walks, and shall have appeared before said court or judge for the purpose of taking an oath or affirmation in the matter of such taking or vacating, and any of the jurors summoned shall fail to attend or shall be excused by the court or judge, the

Court may appoint jurors to fill vacancies.

court or judge shall thereupon forthwith name and appoint the requisite number of other duly qualified jurors to serve upon said jury in the place of such jurors so excused, or failing to attend. Any juror so named and appointed may be examined by any person interested in such taking or vacating, who shall be present, and if it shall appear to the court or judge that any such juror or jurors are disqualified to act in the matter, he or they shall be excused, and a requisite number of other jurors shall be thereupon named and appointed in his place until the requisite number of jurors shall be obtained, and the said jurors shall thereupon before they proceed to view the premises proposed to be taken or vacated, severally take and subscribe an oath or affirmation before the court or judge to the effect that they will faithfully and honestly discharge the duties imposed upon them, and determine whether or not it is necessary to take or vacate the premises in question for the public use.

When any juror absent, those present may adjourn for not over twenty days.

SECTION 2. Whenever such jurors shall have met in any duly authorized manner for the purpose of hearing persons interested in such taking or vacating, and any such juror or jurors shall be absent at the time set for such hearing and for one hour thereafter, the jurors present shall have power to publicly adjourn their proceedings to the same place for a period not exceeding twenty days, and the city attorney shall report the names of such absent juror or jurors to the chief of police or to any of the police officers of the city, together with the place and the hour to which such jury has adjourned, and the said chief of police or police officer shall thereupon notify said absent juror or jurors of such adjournment and direct them to be present at the time and place fixed by such adjournment. **Police officer to notify absent juror of such adjournment.**

SECTION 3.   All acts and parts of acts inconsistent with this act, are repealed, in so far as they interfere with this act and no further.

CHAPTER 142, LAWS OF 1895.

AN ACT to amend section 12, of chapter 307, of the laws of 1889, entitled "An act to authorize towns, villages and cities to acquire the title to toll roads."

SECTION 1.   Amend section 12, of chapter 307, of the laws of 1889, by adding thereto the following: "Provided, the sale by any toll road company of any portion of its toll road lying within the corporate limits of any city or village shall not affect its charter rights," so that said section, when so amended, shall read as follows: Section 12. Any city or village in this state may acquire the title to that part of a toll road lying within its limits, for the purpose of making the same a public highway, by purchase, or by taking the same by condemnation proceedings in the same manner that each may be authorized to take land of private parties for the purpose of laying out a street; provided, the sale by any toll road company of any portion of its toll road lying within the corporate limits of any city or village shall not affect the charter rights of such toll road company. **City may acquire title to toll road lying in limits.**

CHAPTER VII.

CITY IMPROVEMENTS AND SPECIAL ASSESSMENTS.

SECTION 1.   The board of public works of said city shall, with the concurrence of a majority of the aldermen of the several wards, by the first of May of each year or as soon as practicable thereafter, determine for each ward upon a general system of improvements for the year ensuing, and report the same to the common council, mentioning in said report the most necessary improvements first, and the others in the order of their necessity; and after the same shall have been approved by the common council, the said system shall be carried out, and not materially deviated from except in case of necessity. **Annual estimate of ward improvement.**

Special assessments are distinguished from other impositions in being special taxes levied upon lots to pay for their improvement, with reference to the *special* benefits they derive therefrom.

Hale vs. Kenosha, 29 Wis., 599.

They may be laid for improvements of streets or sidewalks in front of such lots.

> Weeks vs. Milwaukee, 10 Wis., 186.
>
> Lumsden vs. Cross, 10 Wis., 225.

Also to build breakwaters, and other improvements against encroachments by the waves of Lake Michigan.

> Soens vs. Racine, 10 Wis., 214.

Or for abating a nuisance caused by water standing on the lots.

> Smith vs. Milwaukee, 18 Wis., 69.

Or for cleaning streets.

> Cramer vs. Stone, 33 Wis., 212.

Or for improvements on water highways.

> Johnson vs. Milwaukee, 40 Wis., 315.

It is essential that all express provisions of the charter be complied with, such as those requiring notice to lot owners or occupants to do the work before letting the contracts.

> Rogers vs. Milwaukee, 13 Wis., 682.
>
> Johnston vs. Oshkosh, 21 Wis., 186.

And those requiring the making and filing of estimates.

> Myrick vs. La Crosse, 17 Wis., 456.

And those requiring the making and filing of plans and specifications before advertising for proposals.

> Kneeland vs. Milwaukee, 18 Wis., 431.
>
> Kneeland vs. Furlong, 20 Wis., 460.

An assessment of lots for benefits from a street improvement cannot, where no fraud is so shown, be attacked collaterally.

> Fass vs. Seehawer, 60 Wis., 525.

Repairing of streets and sidewalks. SECTION 2. The grading, graveling and planking, macadamizing or paving to the center of any street or alley, and the grading, graveling, macadamizing, planking, paving, sodding and curbing of any sidewalk, and the paving of any gutter, shall be chargeable to and payable by the lots fronting or abutting upon such street, alley or gutter, or fronting, abutting, or adjacent to such sidewalk, to the amount which such grading, graveling, macadamizing, planking, paving, sodding and curbing shall be adjudged by said board to benefit such lots. **Expense of such improvements, how payable.** The expense of all such improvements or work across streets at their intersection with streets and alleys, excepting sidewalks, and the expense of all such improvements or work across public grounds, and to the middle of streets and alleys adjacent to public grounds, and the construction of all crosswalks, shall be paid out of the fund of the ward in which such improvements are made or such works are done. After a street, alley or gutter has been constructed to the grade established by the common council, and graveled, planked, paved or macadamized in compliance with the order of the proper city authorities, the expense of maintaining, renewing, repaving, keeping in repair and cleaning such street, alley or gutter, and the pavement or other surface thereof, and of any other subsequent improvement of such street, alley or gutter, shall be paid out of the fund of the ward in which such work is done or such improvement is made; provided, however, that when a street or alley, which has been graveled, planked or macadamized, is ordered to be paved, the expense of such paving shall be chargeable to and payable by the lots fronting or abutting upon such street or alley to the amount which such paving shall be adjudged by said board to benefit such lots as hereinbefore provided for the improvement of a street or alley; and further provided, that when a change in the grade of any street or alley shall be ordered, the expense of cutting or filling incurred by such change of grade shall be chargeable to and paid by the lots fronting or abutting on the street or alley of which the grade shall be so changed; and provided further, that the provisions of this section in relation to the maintaining, renewing, repaving, keeping in repair and cleaning of streets, alleys and gutters shall not apply to the laying, relaying, cleaning, sodding, curbing, repairing or grading of sidewalks.

As amended by Section 29, Chapter 144, Laws of 1875, and further amended by Section 4, Chapter 311, Laws of 1876, and Section 5, Chapter 388, Laws of 1889.

The tracks and right of way of a railway are not subject to assessment for street improvements.

C. M. & St. P. Ry. Co. vs. Milwaukee, 89 Wis., 506.

Provisions of the charter providing for the repairing of streets and sidewalks at the expense of adjoining lots are not applicable to the repairs which by law railroad companies are required to make.

Oconto vs. C. & N. W. Ry. Co., 44 Wis., 231.

SECTION 3. The construction and keeping in repair of the docks in front of lots or parcels of land along the banks of rivers and public navigable canals in said city, and the dredging of said rivers and canals to a width of fifty feet from their dock lines towards their centers, shall

Relating to docks along rivers and canals.

be chargeable to and payable by the lots or parcels of land so fronting; and after a river or public navigable canal in the city of Milwaukee has been properly docked comformably to specifications on file in the office of the board of public works of said city, and has been dredged to a depth of sixteen feet below the level of the Milwaukee river, as it was in the month of March, 1836, and to a width of fifty feet from its dock line, towards its center, in compliance with the order of the proper city authorities, and at the expense of the lots or parcels of land abutting thereon, and has been duly accepted by the said city engineer, as complying with the above requirements, the expense of re-dredging such rivers or canals to a width of fifty feet from such dock line to its center, shall be charged to, and paid out of the general city fund of said city of Milwaukee, and said board shall have the same authority over said rivers and canals, and lots or lands fronting thereon, as they have over streets and lots or lands fronting thereon, and shall be governed by the same rules in respect thereto as in cases of improvements upon streets, except repairs of the docks in front of lots or parts of land along the banks of rivers and navigable **Repairs to be a** canals in said city, which expenses shall be made a lien **lien upon abutting** and charge upon the lots and parcels of land extending **lots.** to and abutting on said rivers and canals respectively; provided, that dredging chargeable to lots and lands fronting on said rivers and canals shall be ordered and done by said city only when the middle portion of such rivers and canals respectively shall have been dredged or shall be dredged at the same time by the city; and provided, further, that no part of the cost of construction of any of the public navigable canals iu said city shall be chargeable to said city or to any ward thereof, but the whole cost of such construction shall be chargeable exclusively to the lots and land abutting thereon.

As amended by Section 1, Chapter 102, Laws of 1883, and Chapter 180, Laws of 1891.

Common council may order construction of canals. SECTION 4.   The construction of the public navigable canals in said city, including the canals, water channels, and slips, laid out and established in the valley of the Menomonee river shall include all such excavations, dredging and docking as the common council shall by ordinance or resolution in its discretion require, to make the same suitable and convenient for navigation.   The board of public works shall, from time to time, with the approval of the common council, order the construction of the canals, water channels, and slips, in the valley of the Menomonee river, and shall cause the same to be done as they may deem necessary for the public interest, in accordance with the system of canals, water channel and slips, established in said valley pursuant to chapter ninety one of the local laws of 1869. Whenever they shall order any portion of such work to be done, like proceedings shall be had as are provided by this chapter in case of grading streets; and the expense of such construction shall be apportioned by the board of public works among, and shall be a charge and lien upon, the several lots or parcels of land extending to and abutting on said canals, water channels or slips respectively, in proportion to the amount of work done opposite to such lots or parcels of land to be estimated by the city engineer, and shall be collected as other special taxes are levied and collected by and under this act, but no work in the construction of such canals, water channels or slips shall be ordered by said board except on the petition in writing of the persons owning land adjoining the work to be done, to the extent of a majority of the lineal feet of such land, measured on the line of such proposed work; but in case any portion of such adjoining land is owned by persons not residents of the said city of Milwaukee, the said board may order such work to be done on the petition of persons owning a majority of the lineal feet of such land owned by residents of the said city, measured on the line of such proposed work.

Apportionment of costs.

Petitions for canals.

SECTION 5. The docking and dredging of the Milwaukee, Menomonee and Kinnickinnic rivers, and of the public canals in said city, after their construction, opposite to any street or to public grounds abutting thereon, and the dredging of the middle ground of said rivers, and of said canals after their construction, further than fifty feet from either dock line shall be done at the cost of the city. The board of public works, subject to the approval of the common council, shall have the power and are hereby authorized and it shall be their duty when ordered thereto by the common council, without petition in that behalf, to cause the Milwaukee, Menomonee and Kinnickinnic rivers, or any portion thereof, to be docked and dredged; and to proceed therein in like manner as in cases of grad-

Docking and dredging at city expense.

Common council may order docking and dredging.

ing and improving streets, to make the expense of re-con-
structing and repairing the docks of the rivers and canals
in said city, and so much of the expense as is not chargeable to the city a lien and charge upon the lots and parcels of land, extending to and abutting on said rivers
respectively.

As amended by Section 2, Chapter 180, Laws of 1891.

Relating to grading or improving streets.

SECTION 6. Whenever the board of public works
shall deem it necessary to grade or otherwise improve
any street, alley, sidewalk or public ground, or to erect
and construct a bridge or viaduct over any ravine in
said city of Milwaukee, or to dredge or dock any of the
rivers or of the public canals after their first construction, or to abate any nuisance caused by stagnant water
in said city, it shall cause to be made an estimate of the
cost of such work, and shall put the same on file in its
office, and such estimate shall be open to the inspection
of any party interested. Thereupon the said board of

Board of public works to make recommendation to common council.

public works shall make to the common council such
recommendation in relation to the proposed work as
it may deem proper; and upon the same being adopted
by the common council, in whole or in part, the said
board may order so much of the work to be done as
shall have been adopted, provided that no change of any
previously established grade, and no such work, chargeable to lots and parcels of land fronting on or abutting
on the same, except the grading, graveling and paving of
streets, the paving of gutters and making of sidewalks,
and except repairs, and docking and dredging, shall be
ordered by resolution, ordinance or otherwise, unless a
petition therefor shall first be presented to the common
council, signed by residents of said city owning a majority
of the feet in front of all the lots fronting upon such
proposed improvements, owned by residents of such
city, and for that purpose, every person in the actual
possession of any lot or parcel of land fronting upon
such improvements, under a contract in force for the
purchase thereof from the owner, shall be held to be a
freeholder within the meaning of this act, and to be the
owner of such real estate for the purpose of petitioning
as owner thereof. Each person signing such petition

Petitions, what to contain.

as a resident or as the owner of property, shall be
required to write after his signature thereto a brief
description of the property so owned by him, and of

the place of his residence in said city, and to annex
thereto an affidavit that he is such resident and owner,
and thereupon he shall be taken to be such resident and
owner, and such petition shall be as valid and have the
same effect as if such person were the owner of such
property, and a resident of the city or ward, as stated
in his affidavit, although in fact it should thereafter
appear that he was not such owner or resident. The
common council may order the grading, graveling and
paving of streets and alleys, the paving of gutters and
the making of sidewalks, without such petition, provided, however, that in the absence of such petition, the
resolution of the common council ordering the work
shall have been referred by the council to a special
committee of five members, no one of whom shall be a
resident of the ward or any ward in which the grading,
graveling or paving of streets, alleys or gutters, or the
making of sidewalks, mentioned in the resolution is
proposed to be done, and shall have been reported by
such committee to the common council with their recommendation that it be adopted, before a vote shall be
taken upon its adoption, and provided such resolution
shall declare why it is necessary for the public interest to
proceed without such petition, and shall also upon its
passage be supported by the votes of three-fourths of all
the aldermen elected, and of a majority of the aldermen
of the ward or of each ward in which such grading,
graveling or paving, or making of sidewalks, is to be
done; and provided further, that no such resolution
ordering the grading, graveling or paving of a street or
streets or alley, the paving of gutters or the making of
sidewalks, without a petition therefor shall be voted upon
or passed at any meeting of the common council held
within four weeks from the time of its presentation to
the council, and the vote on its passage shall be taken by
yeas and nays, and duly entered in the journal of proceedings. Provided further, that whenever the board of
public works shall deem it necessary to pave or otherwise
improve, any street, alley or gutter, or any part of any
street, alley or gutter, after the same has been once constructed to the grade established by the common council,
and graveled, planked, paved or macadamized, the expense
of maintaining, renewing, repairing or repaving whereof,
shall be a lawful and proper charge against the funds of

Council may order work without petition, how.

Three-fourths vote of all aldermen elect, and of both aldermen of ward necessary.

Petition not to be acted on for four weeks; vote on, to be taken by yeas and nays.

Expense of renewing pavement, etc., chargeable to ward fund.

Petition of property owners, to be granted, when.

the ward, in which such street, alley or gutter is situated, and a majority of the residents of said city of Milwaukee, owning a majority of the feet in front of all the lots, fronting on such proposed improvement, owned by residents of such city, shall file a petition with the said board, for any pavement or other improvement deemed by said board to cost more than the estimate made by the board, of the cost of improving said street, alley or gutter, said cost to be determined by said board, it shall be the duty of said board and of the common council to grant the request of such petition, and to proceed to repave, or otherwise improve, said street, alley or gutter, or any part thereof, named in said petition, according to the prayer of the petition, in the same manner as said board and council are now required to maintain, renew, repair or repave any such street, alley or gutter; provided, however, that all cost and expense of such repavement, or other improvement, in case of such petition, in excess of the estimated cost of the work, made and filed in the office of the board of public works, for the improvement of said street, alley or gutter, or part thereof, shall be chargeable to, and be made payable by, the lots fronting or abutting upon such street, alley or gutter, or part thereof, such excess to be apportioned by such board to said lots respectively, in proportion to the benefits adjudged by said board to have been conferred by said repavement, or other improvement, in the same manner that the original improvement of streets, alleys and gutters are now lawfully chargeable to, and made payable by such lots; provided further, that the petition for such repavement, or other improvement, required in this act, as a condition of increased cost, shall, as to form, qualification of petitioners and otherwise, conform to the requirements in case of petitions for other work chargeable to lots, and requiring a petition therefor, as provided in said Section 20, Chapter 324, Laws of 1882, of which section this act is in part amendatory.

As amended by Section 30, Chapter 144, Laws of 1875, and further amended by Section 2, Chapter 274, Laws of 1881, Section 20, Chapter 324, Laws of 1882, and Chapter 359, Laws of 1887.

One who signs a petition to common council for a change of grade, is not estopped from asserting his claim for damages caused by the new grade, it being *lower* than the one petitioned for.

Luscombe vs. Milwaukee, 36 Wis., 511.

The common council having ordained a change of grade of numerous streets, and having executed the ordinance only in part, plaintiff suffered serious special injury by reason of such *partial* execution; and in order to relieve himself from such a special injury, signed a petition to the council to have the work completed. *Held, not a waiver* of his right to damages for such change of grade.

> Herzer vs. Milwaukee, 39 Wis., 360.

Under the charter provision requiring every resolution ordering work for improving streets to lie over at least four weeks after its introduction, "A resolution introduced on Monday may be acted on the fourth Monday following."

> Wright vs. Forrestal, 65 Wis., 341.

The requirement that the "vote on the passage of every such resolution shall be taken by yeas and nays and duly entered on the journal," etc., is *held*, not to require a separate vote on each such resolution.

> Ibid.

SECTION 7. Before ordering any work to be done by the owners of lots or lands fronting on the same, said board shall view the premises, and consider the amount proposed to be made chargeable against said several lots or pieces of land, and the benefits which, in their opinion, will actually accrue to the owner of the same in consequence of such improvement, and shall assess against the several lots or pieces of lands, or parts of lots or pieces of land, which they may deem benefited by the proposed improvement, the amount of such benefit which those lots or pieces of land will severally, in the opinion of said board, derive from such improvement when completed in the manner contemplated in the estimate of the cost of such work, made as provided by section six of this chapter, taking into consideration in each case any injury which in the opinion of the board, may result to each lot or piece of land from such improvement; and in case the benefits, in their opinion, amount to less than the cost of the improvement, the balance shall be paid out of the ward fund of the ward or wards in which such improvement is made; and said board shall endorse their decision and assessment in every case on the estimate of the cost of such improvement filed in their office. *Assessments of benefits for street work.* *Assessment of damages.*

Assessment made by the board of public works, after confirmation by common council, is not conclusive as to benefits on right of way, but is conclusive as to such railroad property as is not used for railroad purposes, when it appears that the benefits are direct, immediate and certain.

C. M. & St. P. Ry. Co. vs. Milwaukee, 89 Wis., 506.

Abutting property may be assessed for highway improvements only to the extent to which it is *actually* benefited, and must be upon *actual view*. Where such an assessment is based upon the estimated cost of the improvement, and not upon an estimate of actual benefits, the assessment is invalid, and equity will restrain the issue of a certificate to the contractor.

Johnson vs. Milwaukee, 40 Wis., 315.

(This section is substantially the same as Sec. 24, Ch. 401, laws of 1870.)

This section evidently requires a finding by the board of public works upon the question of resulting benefits and of consequent injury, the former to be modified by deducting the amount of the injury; and the lot is to be assessed only to the amount of benefits as thus modified. To this end, therefore, a finding is essential both on benefits and consequent injury to the lot.

Lieberman vs. Milwaukee, 89 Wis., 336.

Where the board of public works arbitrarily added fifty per cent. to the estimated cost of the work, and adopted such amount so determined as the measure of benefits, and the different lots were variously affected, *held*, the assessment was void, there being a failure to exercise the judgment of the board.

Watkins vs. Zwietusch, 47 Wis., 513.

Compensation to lot owners for change of grade.

Assessment therefor.

SECTION 8. In all cases in which the grade of any street has been permanently established by ordinace since February 20, 1852, or shall hereafter be so established, and, after such permanent establishment thereof, and after such street shall have been actually graded to such established grade, the grade so established has been or shall be altered by the city, the owner of any lot or parcel of land which may be affected or injured in consequence of such alteration of grade, shall be entitled to compensation therefor; and it shall be the duty of the board of public works, before ordering to be done the work of actually changing such established grade by excavating or filling such street to the new grade as so altered, and at the time of making their assessment of benefits, as provided in the next preceding section, to consider, determine and assess against the lots which they may deem benefited by the proposed improvement, to the amount of such benefits, the damages, costs and charges, including the cost of such improvement—arising from such alteration of grade to the owner of any lot, parcel of land or tenement, which may be affected or injured in consequence thereof, taking into considera- **Benefits and damages.** tion in each case any advantages and benefits which may be conferred thereby upon such lot, parcel of land or tenement, in common with other property on the street affected by such grade; and the excess of the said damages, costs and charges over the benefits assessed, as provided in the preceding section, shall be paid out of the ward funds of the ward or wards in which such improvement and alteration of grade shall be made; provided. that no owner of any lot. parcel of land or **Petitioners for change of grade not entitled to compensation therefor.** tenement, who shall personally, or by his authorized agent, have signed a petition asking for such alteration of grade, or a petition asking for the grading of a street in comformity with such altered grade, shall be entitled to compensation, but every such owner shall be deemed thereby to have waived and relinquished all claim to compensation for any injury in consequence thereof; and no damages, costs or charges arising to such owner from such alteration of grade, shall be assessed or paid to such owner.

Compensation for the injury to lots caused by raising the street, under the facts alleged, *held*, on demurrer, to be presumed to have been fully made by filling up the lots, there being no allegation to the contrary.

> Watkins vs. Milwaukee, 55 Wis., 335.
> See Anderton vs. Milwaukee, 82 Wis., 279.

Ch. 254, Laws of 1891, held invalid in

> Anderton vs. Milwaukee, 82 Wis., 279.
> Koeffler vs. Milwaukee, 85 Wis., 397.

Any *peculiar* or *special* benefit conferred on plaintiff's lot, not common to other lots in the neighborhood, and not increasing its market value, cannot be considered by the jury in fixing damages; but if such lot, by reason of the changed grade is appreciated in value in common with other property in that vicinity, the city is entitled to have such increase of value deducted in the estimate of damages.

> Church vs. Milwaukee, 31 Wis., 512.
> Stowell vs. Milwaukee, 31 Wis., 523.

The liability of the city to pay damages to lot owner for change of grade is not affected by the fact that the owner did the work himself, in obedience to an order duly made by the street commissioners.

> Pearce vs. Milwaukee, 18 Wis., 450.

When the city, in grading a public street then in the use and occupation of the public as a highway, leaves the same in a dangerous condition, and without lights, guards or warning to passengers, it is liable for all damages accruing to any person injured because of such negligence.

Milwaukee vs. Davis, 6 Wis., 374.

See also French vs. Milwaukee, 49 Wis., 584.

Owens vs. Milwaukee, 47 Wis., 461.

Where a grade is duly established by an ordinance, which also provides that the faith of the city is pledged that such grade shall not be altered, the city is liable for damages caused by change of grade some years thereafter, where the grade is lowered twenty feet, and buildings erected with reference to the first grade are rendered valueless.

Goodall vs. Milwaukee, 5 Wis., 32.

It is only by statute that a municipal corporation is liable for injuries caused by an *authorized* change of grade, and the statutory remedy providing specific means for recovering damages, is *exclusive*.

Dore vs. Milwaukee, 42 Wis., 108.

The plaintiff *held*, entitled to recover the expense of grading down that part of lot fronting on the alley, the ordinances implying that the grades of alleys must conform to those of adjoining streets.

Church vs. Milwaukee, 34 Wis., 66.

The right to damages is purely statutory. Damages to the soil or building may be recovered, but not for injury to the trade or business carried on.

Stadler vs. Milwaukee, 34 Wis., 98.

The purpose to be subserved by this section is to secure to the lot owner, in the case therein mentioned, a proper allowance for damages, costs and charges arising from the change of grade, by way of compensation therefor, and payment thereof, if it exceeds the benefits, out of the ward funds.

Liebermann vs. Milwaukee, 89 Wis., 336.

SECTION 9. As soon as any assessment of benefits or damages, or both, shall be made, as in the preceding sections of this chapter provided, the said board shall give notice to all parties interested, by advertisement for not less than four days in the official papers of the said city, that such assessment has been made and is ready for inspection in its office, and that the same will be open for review and correction by the said board, at its office, for not less than four days after the first publication of such notice during certain hours, not less than two hours of each lay day, and that all persons interested will be heard by said board in objection to such assessment, and generally, in the matter of such review and correction. It shall be sufficient to state in such notice, in brief, what such assessment has been made for, and in what locality, and no further notice or publication of such assessment shall be necessary. During the time mentioned in such notice, the said board shall hear objections and evidence, and they shall have power to review, modify and correct such assessment, in such manner as they shall deem just, at any time during such review, and for three days thereafter; and thereupon said board shall endorse such corrected and completed assessment upon or annex the same to the estimate of the cost of such improvement, made and filed in its office, as provided in section 6, of this chapter, and shall file a duplicate of such estimate and assessment in the office of the city clerk, who shall lay the same before the common council at its next meeting; and thereupon the common council may confirm or correct said assessments, or any of them, or may refer the same back to the board of public works for revision and correction; and the said common council, and the said board of public works shall respectively have the like powers, and perform the like duties, in relation to such assessment, and any subsequent assessment made pursuant to such reference by the common council, as are prescribed and conferred in relation to the first assessment.

Duplicate assessment to be filed with city clerk.

As amended by Section 31, Chapter 144, Laws of 1875, and further amended by Section 6, Chapter 388, Laws of 1889.

SECTION 10. Thereupon, as soon as the common council shall have confirmed such assessments of benefits and damages, the said board shall enter into a contract for the doing of the same, as hereinbefore provided. Such contract shall require the contractor to receive certificates upon or against the several lots, parts of lots, or parcels of land, which may be assessed with benefits on account of the same, to apply in payment of the contract price, as now provided by law; provided that in any case where the contract price of the work to the center of the street or alley, done opposite to any lot or parcel of ground, shall exceed the benefits assessed to such lot, the excess shall be paid out of the ward fund of the ward in which such lot, part of lot or parcel of land shall be situated.

Relating to payment for work done on streets.

Excess of damages to be paid out of ward fund.

As amended by Section 1, Chapter 308, Laws of 1882.

The board of public works cannot proceed under this section without a previous ordinance or resolution of the common council.

Koch vs. Milwaukee, 89 Wis., 220.

Where the board of public works has issued a special assessment certificate, until the money has been collected therefor and paid into the treasury, *it seems* that the treasurer is the agent of the owner of the certificate. The city will only be liable to the holder after the treasurer has refused to pay over the money on demand, after it has been collected and placed in the treasury.

Silkman vs. Milwaukee, 31 Wis., 555.

Appeals from assessments, how and when taken.

SECTION 11. The owner of any lot, or tract of land, or tenement, who feels himself aggrieved by such assessment, as confirmed by the common council, as to the amount of benefits thereby adjudged to accrue to him by reason of any improvements charged against his lot or parcel of land, or the amount of damages, costs and charges, arising to such owner from an alteration of grade, may, within twenty days after such confirmation by the common council, appeal therefrom to the circuit court of Milwaukee county; and such appeal shall be taken, tried and determined, and bonds for costs shall be given, and costs awarded therein, in like manner as in cases of appeals to the said circuit court provided for in chapter six of this act. Such appeal shall not affect the rights of the contractor, or the proceedings in reference to his contract, but the certificate against the lot or parcel of land in question, shall be given as if no appeal had been taken; and in case the appellant shall succeed, the difference between the amount charged in the certificate and the amount of the benefit finally adjudged, shall be paid by the city out of the proper ward fund, to the appellant, but not until he shall have done the work in question, or have paid the certificate issued

Assessments for damages, when to be paid.

for doing the same. The amount assessed by the board of public works, or finally adjudged on appeal, for damages, costs, and charges arising from an alteration of the grade, in excess of the amount charged against property deemed benefited, shall be paid by the city out of the proper ward fund, to the person or persons thereto entitled, within one year after the confirmation of the assessment by the common council, or after final adjudgment therefor rendered by the court on appeal, as aforesaid; provided, that the time during which an appeal from such judgment may be pending in the supreme court shall not be deemed part of the year so limited.

The remedy by appeal is not exclusive, as equity will set aside an invalid assessment, a sale under it, the certificate of sale, and restrain the issue of a deed upon such certificate.
Watkins vs. Milwaukee, 52 Wis., 98.

Where the assessment is void, the provisions of this and the following section, as to appeal being the only remedy, do not apply.
Lieberman vs. Milwaukee, 89 Wis., 336.

An original action at law for damages cannot be brought by a lot owner injured by change of grade, but he must proceed by appeal from the assessment of benefits and damages within the time limited.
Owens vs. Milwaukee, 47 Wis., 461.
See, also, Benton vs. Milwaukee, 50 Wis., 368.

SECTION 12. The appeal given by the last preceding section, from the assessment of the board of public works, as confirmed by the common council, to the said circuit court, shall be the only remedy for the recovery of any damages, costs and charges arising from any alteration of grade by the said city, or sustained by reason of any proceedings or acts of the said city or its officers, in the matter to which such assessment of damages or benefits relates; and no action at law shall be maintained for such damages or injuries, whether arising from an alteration of grade or otherwise. *(Limiting right of action.)*

Existing remedies, either common law or statutory will not be regarded as taken away by subsequent statutes granting new remedies, unless such purpose is expressed, or *clearly* implied.
Goodrich vs. Milwaukee, 24 Wis., 422.

Damages for an *unauthorized* change of grade may be recovered in an ordinary civil action, but the complaint must show the want of authority.
Dore vs. Milwaukee, 42 Wis., 108.
Crossett vs. Janesville, 28 Wis., 420.
See also, Liebermann vs. Milwaukee, 89 Wis., 336.

SECTION 13. After the completion and performance of any contract entered into by the board of public works for work chargeable to the lots or lands fronting thereon, or to other lots upon which assessments of benefits have been made therefor by virtue of this act, *(Contractor shall receive a certificate stating amount of work done.)*

they shall give to the contractor or contractors a certificate signed by the board or the president thereof, and countersigned by the comptroller, stating the amount of work done by such contractor, the nature thereof, and the description of the lot or parcel of land upon which the same is chargeable. It shall be the duty of the comptroller to keep a register of all certificates issued by the board of public works against lots, and countersigned by him, which said certificates may be paid by the owner or owners of such lots at any time before the sale of such lots for the non-payment of taxes, to the city treasurer, who shall receive the amounts paid on such certificate and hold the same for the benefit of the owners of such certificates, and such owner shall be entitled thereto on producing and surrendering such certificates to be canceled.

As amended by Section 2, Chapter 308, Laws of 1882.

Where the lot owner pays the amount of the certificates to the city treasurer, the latter receives and holds the amounts so paid on such certificates for the benefit of the owners thereof, and such owners respectively are entitled to the same on their producing and surrendering such certificates for cancellation.

Hoyt vs. Fass, 64 Wis., 273.

Certificates issued under this section are liens upon the lots, draw interest at twenty five per cent. per annum from the time when the lot was sold by the city treasurer on account of such certificate liens, and are transferable by endorsement.

Ibid.

Certificates, when lots subdivided.

SECTION 14. In all cases where the board of public works shall have issued a certificate for work done on any street, sidewalk or alley, chargeable to lots or lands according to the provisions of this act, and the lot or tract of land described in such certificate shall have been subdivided prior to the date of such certificate, then the work certified to in such certificate shall be chargeable to that subdivision of such lot or tract of land which fronts on the streets, sidewalk or alley on which such work shall have been done according to law; and it shall be lawful for the city treasurer, in collecting the special taxes assessed by reason of the issue of such certificates, to collect the amount named in such certificates from that subdivision of lot or tract of land, which fronts on the street or alley named in such certificates, and on which said work was done according to law.

Collectable from subdivisions.

SECTION 15. Whenever snow shall fall upon any of **Removing snow** the sidewalks of the said city, so that the same shall be **from sidewalks.** encumbered thereby, and such snow shall not be removed therefrom within twenty-four hours after the snow shall have ceased falling, the said board shall have power, forthwith, without notice or letting, to employ persons or to make contract or contracts to remove such snow from any sidewalk or part of sidewalk in said city, where they shall by resolution declare it to be necessary, and to assess the cost thereof against all lots, parts of lots and **Cost of removal to** parcels of land abutting on such sidewalk or part of side- **be assessed upon** walk in the manner hereinafter directed. **abutting lots.**

SECTION 16. It is hereby made the duty of the board **Repair of streets** of public works with the consent of the aldermen of the **and sidewalks.** proper ward, unless otherwise provided by ordinance of the common council, to cause the streets, alleys and side- walks in the city to be kept in proper repair, and in a cleanly and wholesome condition at all times, and for this purpose they are empowered with the consent of the aldermen of the ward in which such street, alley or side- walk is located, to employ the necessary labor, or to con- tract pursuant to law, for such cleaning and repairing as they may deem necessary for the safety and health of the people, the expense of such cleaning and repairing, except of sidewalks, shall be chargeable to and paid out of the fund of the ward in which such work is done; and the said board is also hereby empowered to cause side- walks to be repaired, or to be taken up and relaid with new materials or with part new and part old materials, and to be restored to grade and to assess the expense thereof against the lot or piece of land in front of which such work may be done, in the manner provided by section 19, of said sub-chapter 7, of said chapter 184, of the laws of 1874.

As amended by Section 32, Chapter 144, Laws of 1876, further amended by Section 21, Chapter 324, Laws of 1882, and Section 7, Chapter 388, Laws of 1889.

CHAPTER 374, LAWS OF 1895.

AN ACT providing for keeping sidewalks clear of snow and ice in cities and villages incorporated under special charters, and collecting the expense thereof.

SECTION 1. The common council of every city and the board of trustees of every village incorporated under any special charter

Common council may cause sidewalks to be kept clear of snow and ice.

may cause the sidewalks within such cities and villages to be kept clear of snow and ice and the expense thereof to be charged as a special tax against the abutting lots or parcels of land, when the owner or occupant fail to keep the same clean. It shall be lawful for the common council of such city and the board of trustees of such village, by ordinance, to designate some officer whose duty it shall be to keep the sidewalks clear of snow and ice in all cases where the owner or occupants of abutting lots or parcels of land fail to do so.

May appoint officer for such purpose.

Duty of officer so appointed.

SECTION 2. It shall be the duty of the officer designated as provided in the preceding section, under such rules or ordinance as the common council or board of trustees may make therefor, to keep the sidewalks in such city or village clear of snow and ice in all cases where the owners or occupants of abutting lots fail to do so, and the expense of clearing the snow or ice from sidewalks in front (and along the side of a corner lot or parcel of land) of any such lot or parcel of land shall be a lien thereon. And said officer shall keep an account of such expense and make a report of the same to the city or village clerk, who shall enter the amount therein charged to each lot or parcel of land in the next or subsequent tax roll, as a special tax against said lot or parcel of land, and the same shall be collected in all respects like other city or village taxes upon real estate, and no lot or parcel of land in such city or village shall be exempt from the payment thereof.

SECTION 3. This act shall not be construed as prohibiting the authorities from imposing a fine or penalty in addition to the collecting of the expenses for neglecting to keep such sidewalks clear of snow and ice.

SECTION 17. Whenever any sidewalk, or part of any sidewalk, shall in the judgment of the said board, declared by resolution to that effect, be in a dangerous condition to persons passing over it, for want of being repaired or remade, or on account of being above or below the grade established by the common council, the said board shall have power to order the same to be forthwith repaired or remade, and thereupon forthwith to employ fit persons to repair or remake the same for a fair price, and charge the expense thereof to the lots, parts of lots, or parcels of land abutting thereon, by a special assessment; and such assessment shall be a valid charge and lien upon such lots, parts of lots or parcels of land, without any estimate, notice, letting or other proceeding preliminary to the doing of such work, except the resolution of said board so declaring such sidewalks to be dangerous.

How repaired.

As amended by Section 5, Chapter 311, Laws of 1876.

SECTION 18.   Whenever any nuisance, source of filth, or cause of sickness shall be found on private property, or in the alley in front or rear of such property, the common council may order the owner or occupant thereof, at his own expense, to remove or abate the same within twenty-four hours from the date of the order, or within such time as may be named in such order; and if the owner or occupant shall refuse or neglect so to do, within the time named in said order, then the board of public works shall forthwith cause said nuisance, source of filth, or cause of sickness to be abated or removed, at the expense of the lot or tract of land in the front or rear of which, or upon which · such nuisance, source of filth or cause of sickness may be found.

Relating to nuisances.

Amended by Section 1, Chapter 80, Laws of 1877, which was repealed by Section 58, Chapter 324, Laws of 1882. As amended by Section 22, Chapter 324, Laws of 1882.

Where by a neglect to provide proper sewerage in the grading of a street, a nuisance is created upon a private lot, the city may provide for abating it as for other similar improvements; and where the work for that purpose has been done by contract in a regular manner, an assessment upon the lot for the cost of the work is valid at law.

Smith vs. Milwaukee, 18 Wis., 69.

A special assessment for the cost of abating a nuisance created upon a private lot by the act of the city is illegal, and will be set aside.

Weeks vs. Milwaukee, 10 Wis., 186.

SECTION 19.   In all cases mentioned in sections 15, 16, 17 and 18 of this chapter, or in either of said sections, wherein the board of public works are authorized to do any work or cause the same to be done, and to charge or assess the expense thereof upon the lots, parts of lots or parcels of land upon or in front or rear of which such work may be done, the expense of such work shall, in the first place, be defrayed out of the ward fund of the proper ward. It shall be the duty of said board to keep a strict account of the labor expended upon such work in front or rear of each such lot, part of lot or parcel of land, and of the cost thereof, and to make a report to the comptroller monthly, on the first of each month for each ward in said city, stating and certifying the description of the lots, parts of lots or parcels of land, in front or rear of, or upon

Relating to work done by board of public works.

Board to report to comptroller monthly.

which work chargeable thereto under either of said sections, shall have been done by said board, under authority thereof, during the preceding month, the nature of the work so chargeable to each lot or parcel, and the amount actually expended therefor, and the comptroller shall, at the time of making his annual report to the common council of the lots or parcels of land subject to special tax or assessment, required by section 14 of chapter 3 of this act, include therein the said lots or parcels of land so reported to him by said board of public works, with the aggregate amount chargeable thereto, according to such reports, for work done during the preceding year, under said section 15, 16, 17 and 18, of this chapter, and such amounts shall be levied on the lots or parcels of land respectively, to which they are so chargeable, in like manner as other special taxes are levied in said city; and when collected, the same shall be credited to the account of the ward fund of the ward in which such property is situated.

As amended by Section 23, Chapter 324, Laws of 1882. Amended by Section 2, Chapter 80, Laws of 1877, which was repealed in Section 58, Chapter 324, Laws of 1882.

Commissioners of public works not to be interested in contracts or improvements.

SECTION 20. If any commissioner of public works shall in any case be directly interested in any property liable to be assessed with benefits, on account of any public improvements, or entitled to an assessment of damages arising from an alteration of grade, the common council shall in such case appoint some disinterested person to act in his stead; and the person so appointed shall, for the particular case in which he is so appointed, possess all the powers and authority of, and be subject to all the duties and restrictions imposed by law upon a member of said board.

Canada thistles.

SECTION 21. The said board, under direction of the common council, shall have power to make contracts for the removal of Canada thistles and other noxious plants and weeds from streets, alleys and public grounds, in any ward of the city; the cost thereof to be chargeable to the ward fund of the proper ward.

Sprinkling of streets—how contract shall be let.

SECTION 22. Whenever a petition shall be presented to the common council, signed by a majority of the owners of lots or parcels of land, fronting or abutting on any street, or part of a street, actually residing on such lots, or parcels of land, and approved by a majority of the aldermen of the ward or wards in which such street or part of such street shall be located requesting such or part of such street to be sprinkled, the common council shall order the board of public works to advertise for sealed proposals for sprinkling such street or part of such street. Such advertisement shall be published for at least six days in the official city papers, and shall state the street or part of the street to be sprinkled, and for what length of time. All contracts shall be awarded by said board to the lowest bidder in compliance with the provisious of section ten, of chapter five of this act, and shall be expressly subject to the powers given to said board by said chapter.

As enacted by Section 33, Chapter 144, Laws of 1875.

SECTION 23. The board of public works shall assess against the several lots, parts of lots, or parcels of land, fronting or abutting on such street, or part of such street, the cost of sprinkling such street, or part of such street in front of such lots, parts of lots, or parcels of land. The cost of sprinkling such street, or part of such street, at its intersection with streets and alleys, and across public grounds, and to the middle of such street, adjacent to public grounds, shall be paid out of the fund of the ward in which such work is done.

Cost of sprinkling to be assessed against adjoining lots.

As enacted by Section 33, Chapter 144, Laws of 1875.

SECTION 24. After the completion and performance of any contract for sprinkling, entered into by the board of public works for work chargeable to lots or lands fronting on streets or alleys upon which such work has been done, the cost of such work shall in the first place be paid out of the ward fund of the proper ward.

Cost of sprinkling to be first paid out of ward fund.

It shall be the duty of the said board to keep a strict account of the cost of such work done in front of such lot or parcel of land, and report to the city comptroller on the completion of each such contract, stating and certifying the description of the lots, parts of lots or parcels of land, in front of which, work chargeable thereto under such contract, has been done, and the amount chargeable to each such piece of property, and the said comptroller shall, at the time of making his annual report to the common council of the lots or parcels of land

Board to make report to comptroller.

subject to special tax, or assessment, include therein the said lots or parcels of land so reported to him by said board of public works, with the amount chargeable thereto for sprinkling, done under such contracts, during the preceding year; and such amounts shall be levied on the lots or parcels of land, respectively, to which they are so chargeable, in like manner as other special taxes are levied in said city, and when collected the same shall be credited to the ward fund in which such property is situated.

As enacted by Section 33, Chapter 144, Laws of 1875, and amended by Chapter 254, Laws of 1881.

CHAPTER 226, LAWS OF 1895.

AN ACT to enable cities to cause streets to be sprinkled at the expense of abutting owners.

Common council may cause streets to be sprinkled.

Expense to be assessed to abutting owners.

SECTION 1. Whenever there shall be presented to the common council of any city organized under any special laws of this state, a petition signed by the owners of a majority of the frontage upon any street or part of street in such city, praying for such street or part of street shall be sprinkled during a term in such petition to be set forth, not exceeding eight months, such common council may order such sprinkling to be done upon such requirements and in such manner as it shall establish; and shall assess the expense of such sprinkling to the owners of the property fronting upon such street or part of street in the same manner as other special charges, in proportion to the frontage of each owner's property thereon, excepting street crossings, which shall be paid for by such city.

SECTION 2. The common council of any such city may let to the lowest bidder the contract for doing all sprinkling to be done pursuant of this act; which contract shall be awarded upon public notice to be published in some newspaper to be designated by such common council at least ten days prior to the date of awarding such contract. Such contract shall be in such form and with such conditions as such common council shall find to be convenient and just for carying such work into effect.

Power of council to order planting of shade trees.

SECTION 25. The common council shall have power to order by resolution, adopted by a vote of the majority of the members elect, and a majority of the aldermen of the proper ward, the planting and preserving of shade trees in the streets of the city, at the cost of the lots, parts of lots and parcels of land, fronting or abutting on such improvements, and in pursuance of such resolution the board of public works shall prepare plans and specifications and require such work to be done by the owners of property in front of which such work is to be done, and in default thereof to let the work by contract and assess the cost against such lots, parts of lots, and parcels of land and all the provisions of this act in relation to notices, proposals, contracts, payments and certificates for street improvements shall be applicable to the work provided for in this section, but no assessment of benefits and damages shall be made in such cases and no notices in relation thereto shall be published; provided, however, that no such resolution for the planting or preserving of shade trees in the streets of the city shall be passed by the common council unless a petition therefor shall first **Petition to be pre-sented.** be presented to said common council signed by the residents of the city owning a majority of the feet in front of all the lots fronting upon such proposed improvement owned by residents of such city.

As enacted by Section 33, Chapter 144, Laws of 1875.

SECTION 26. The common council is hereby author- **Relating to purchase of sprinkling tanks, etc.** ized, in its discretion, to provide for the purchase of tanks, suitable for the sprinkling of streets, to be kept and owned by the city, and may cause the work of sprinkling the streets to be done by men and teams employed for that purpose by the board of public works, and under its direction, using the said sprinkling tanks of the city; and in such case it shall be the duty of the board of public works to keep a strict account of the cost of such sprinkling done in front of each lot or parcel of land, and to make a report thereof to the comptroller on or before the 15th day of November, in each year, and such cost shall be charged and assessed upon the property in front of which such sprinkling is done, in like manner as provided in and by section 24, of the sub-chapter hereby amended. as amended by Chapter 254, of the Laws of 1881; provided, however, that in the First, Second, Third, Fourth, Fifth, Six, Seventh, Eighth, Eleventh, Twelfth and Thirteenth wards of the city, the cost of such sprinkling done in said wards shall be charged to and paid out of the ward funds of said wards respectively, and no assessment upon the property in front of which said sprinkling is done shall be made therefor.

As enacted by Section 24, Chapter 324, Laws of 1882, as amended by Chapter 420, Laws of 1887, and further amended by Chapter 372, Laws of 1891.

The corporate authorities are not vested of the fee of land dedicated to public use, but only of the use of it for the purposes for which it was dedicated.

Goodall vs. Milwaukee, 5 Wis., 32.

Milwaukee vs. R. R. Co., 7 Wis., 76.

CHAPTER 310, LAWS OF 1893.

AN ACT relating to special assessments for grading, paving and improving streets, and the issue of improvement bonds therefor, in cities of twenty thousand inhabitants and upwards.

Extension of payment of assessment of benefits, how made. SECTION 1. Whenever, in any city having a population of twenty thousand inhabitants or more, the grading, paving, or repaving of any street or avenue, with a permanent paving, having a concrete foundation, shall, in any manner, have been duly authorized, and a specification, together with an estimate of the cost of such work, has been prepared and filed, and the necessary assessments of benefits and damages against the several lots, parts of lots or parcels of land, which may be deemed benefited or damaged by the proposed permanent improvements, shall have been made and approved or confirmed, and the contract for such improvement shall have been entered into, the board of public works, or in the absence of the existence of such board, the common council, is hereby authorized, within two weeks, after the letting of such contract, by resolution to determine that any owner or owners of any lots, parts of lots or parcels of land which may be assessed with benefits on account of such permanent improvement, shall have the option at any time within thirty days after the passage and publication of such resolution to apply for an extension of the payments of such assessments of benefits to his or their property by paying therefor in equal annual installments for such a period as the board of public works or the common council may in such resolution determine, not less than five and not exceeding ten years, the first installment to become due and payable, without interest, immediately after the completion of the first tax sale succeeding the date of the bond hereinafter provided for.

Application for extension, when to be made.

What to contain. SECTION 2. Any owner or owners of any lots, parts of lots or parcels of land, which may be assessed with benefits on account of any such permanent improvement, may, within thirty days after the passage and publication of such resolution, make application to the board of public works, or, in the absence of the existence of such board, to the city clerk, for the extension of the payment of such assessment of benefits to his or their property, and such application shall contain an agreement that in consideration of the privilege granted by such resolution, he or they will make no objection to any illegality or irregularity in regard to the assessments against his or their property, and will pay the same in equal annual installments, together with interest upon the unpaid balances, at a rate of interest not exceeding six per centum per anum, and for such a term of years as in such resolution may have been provided. Such application shall also contain a brief description of the property and that the applicant is the owner thereof. After the expiration of the time within which such application may be made, an assessment list shall be prepared containing a description of each piece of property, the owner or owners of which have agreed to pay for such improvement in installments, showing the amounts chargeable to such property, together with the necessary columns to which the installment assessment shall be extended, showing the amount of each installment and interest, and when payable, and a copy of each such assessment list shall be filed with the city clerk, the city comptroller and the city treasurer. In all cases where such agreement has not been signed within the time limited, the entire assessment shall be payable in the manner and at the time as is now provided for the payments of assessments on account of street or other improvements.

Assessment list to be prepared; what to contain.

SECTION 3. Whenever any contract is entered into for such permanent improvement, such contract shall, in addition to the requirements now provided for by law in such cases, stipulate that the contractor shall receive, to apply in payment of the contract price, street improvement bonds upon or against the several lots, parts of lots or parcels of land, the owner or owners of which have agreed, as hereinbefore provided, to avail themselves of the privilege of paying for such improvement in equal annual installments; and upon the completion and performance of such contract, the contractor shall receive on account and in payment for his work, said bond or bonds upon or against said several lots, parts of lots or parcels of land, to an amount not exceeding the assessment of benefits against such lots, parts of lots or parcels of land by reason of such permanent improvement.

Contract for improvement to contain agreement to accept bonds in payment.

SECTION 4. After the performance and completion of any contract for the grading or the paving and repaving of any street or avenue with a permanent pavement, having a concrete foundation, and in case the owner or owners off any lot, parts of lots or parcels of land fronting or abutting on such street or avenue shall have applied for an extension of time for the payment of assessments as provided in section 2, of this act, the board of public works, or, in the absence of the existence of such board, the city clerk, shall issue bonds against said lots, parts of lots, or parcels of land, for the amounts chargeable against such property, said bonds to be made payable within the time limited in the resolution, which may have been passed in accordance with section 1, of this act. Such bonds shall be designated as "Street Improvement Bonds;" shall bear the name of the street or avenue for which they are issued; shall be made payable to the contractor doing the work, or bearer; shall be made negotiable; shall state the amount of work done by the contractor, the nature thereof, and a description of the property upon which the same is chargeable; shall be issued in the name of the city and countersigned by its comptroller, but neither the city nor any officer thereof shall become liable or holden for any part thereof, either principal or interest, excepting for so much as has been actually collected by the city treasurer for the payment of such part of the improvement for which such bonds have been issued. Such bonds shall bear interest at a rate not exceeding six per centum per annum, from and after the first day of February succeeding the

Street improvement bonds, when may be issued against lots, etc.

Bonds, form of.

Rate of interest.

date of issue, and shall have attached thereto coupons, each in amount equal to the annual payment due on such bond, together with the accrued interest. Said coupons and bonds shall be payable at the office of the city treasurer, immediately after the completion of the tax collection each year to the extent of the moneys received by him on account of the improvements for which such bonds have been issued. Said bonds shall be a first lien against any lots, parts of lots, or parcels of land, and in case of failure of the payment of any installment or interest thereon, when the same becomes due, the whole amount of such bond, together with the interest chargeable against any such lot, parts of lots or parcels of land, the owner or owners of which has failed to pay the annual assessment or interest, shall, at the election of the holder of such bond, to be exercised within thirty days after such default, forthwith become due and payable and may be recovered in any court of competent jurisdiction, as mortgages are foreclosed, recovering a reasonable attorney's fee and costs. The owner or owners of any lots, part of lots, or parcels of land upon which bonds are issued, may at any time pay to the city treasurer the entire unpaid assessment and accrued interest, and receive a release of the lien and assessment against his property by paying to the city treasurer, in addition to said assessment and accrued interest, interest on said bonds for the period of three months after such payment of the assessment. The issuance of said bonds shall be conclusive evidence of the regularity of all previous proceedings and the validity of said lien. No error or irregularity upon the part of any taxing or other officer in connection with the making of such assessments or issue of such bonds, not going to the substantial justice of the case, shall invalidate said bonds.

Bonds to be first lien; when may be foreclosed.

Assessment may be paid at any time.

Annual installment assessment to be entered on tax roll.

SECTION 5. The proper city official shall, in preparing the annual tax roll, enter the amount of the annual installment assessment together with the accrued interest, against the several pieces of property on said tax roll according to the assessment list prepared and filed in the office of the city clerk for the term of years that such installment assessment list may cover, and until the entire amount chargeable to such property on account of the permanent pavement improvement, and the interest thereon, shall have been taxed and levied against such property; and such assessment shall be collectable by the city treasurer, as other taxes are collected by him. The city treasurer shall keep a separate account of the funds arising from the collection of such installment assessments and interest, and such funds shall not be diverted to the payment of any other improvement than that for which the same were collected, and he shall enter upon each assessment list, in its proper column and place, such amounts as have been paid, and such lists shall be open to the public examination. As soon as the coupons or bonds shall have been paid by the city treasurer, he shall cancel the same and turn them over to the city comptroller, by whom they shall be kept on file.

Treasurer to keep separate account.

Property fronting on street, when to be exempt from assessment.

SECTION 6. No property fronting on any street or avenue shall be exempt from any assessment of benefits on account of the paving of such street or avenue with a permanent pavement having a concrete foundation, until such property shall have paid in the aggregate in assessments for street pavements in front thereof, the sum of three dollars per square yard for all that part of the roadway directly in front of or abutting such property, and lying between the curb line and the center of such roadway of said street. Where any property has paid less than said amount it shall be liable for any difference up to the amount of three dollars.

SECTION 7. All acts or parts of acts which are inconsistent with this act, or not in harmony with its provisions and operation, are hereby declared to be modified, amended, superseded or repealed in so far as they interfere or are at variance with the true intent, meaning and operation of this act. This act shall take effect and be in force from and after its passage and publication.

CHAPTER 479, LAWS OF 1891.

SECTION 1. The common council of the city of Milwaukee is hereby authorized and directed within sixty days after the passage and publication of this act, by resolution or ordinance to direct the board of public works of said city to proceed and complete within a time limited to five years, to fill up and improve the low and marsh land upon which there may be stagnant water in parts and portions of the southwest and southeast quarters of section 30, and the northwest and northeast quarters of section 31, what is called and known as the Menomonee valley, in the Eighth and Sixteenth wards of the city of Milwaukee, and to abate and remove any nuisance, source of filth or cause of sickness therein, proceeding and completing the filling and improvement of one-fifth thereof as near as may be each year.

Common council may improve low and marsh lands in Menomonee valley.

SECTION 2. Whenever the board of public works of the city of Milwaukee shall be directed by the common council thereof, as herein provided, to fill up or improve the low and marsh land upon which there may be stagnant water in the so called valley of the Menomonee of said city, hereinbefore designated, and to abate and remove any nuisance, source of filth or cause of sickness therein, said board shall cause to be made an estimate of the cost of said work and shall put the same on file in its office, and such estimate shall be open to the inspection of any party interested. Thereupon the said board of public works shall make to the common council such recommendation in relation to the proposed work as it may deem proper; and upon the same being adopted by the common council in whole or in part the said board shall order so much of the work to be done as shall have been adopted; and shall enter into a contract for the doing of the same as other contracts for city work are made. Provided, that the owner of any lot or parcel of land so proposed to be filled or improved, or upon which any nuisance, source of filth or cause of sickness may exist, which said city may order abated or removed, may enter into an agreement with the said city of Milwaukee, to fill up and improve said lot or parcel of land so owned by him, or abate and remove any nuisance, source of filth or cause of sickness thereon, within the time limited in such resolution or ordinance, such work

Board of public works to recommend work done, when.

to be so done by such owner under the direction and to the satisfaction of said board of public works.

Duty of board in ordering work done.

SECTION 3. Before ordering any work to be done pursuant
to such resolution or ordinance, the said board of public works
shall view the premises, and consider the amount proposed to be
made chargeable against said several lots or pieces of land, and
the benefits which, in their opinion, will actually accrue to the
owner or owners of the same in consequence of such improvement, and shall assess against the several lots or pieces of land, or
parts of lots or pieces of land which they may deem benefited by
the proposed improvement, the amount of such benefit which
such lots or pieces of land will severally, in the opinion of said
board, derive from the improvement when completed in the
manner contemplated and the estimate of the cost of said work
made and provided in section 2, of this act, taking into consideration in each case any injury, which in the opinion of the board,
may result to each lot or piece of land from such improvement;
and in case the benefits, in their opinion, amount to less than the
cost of the improvement, the balance shall be paid out of the ward
fund, in which such lot or tract of land is situated, and the said
board shall endorse their decision and assessment in every case on
the estimate of the cost of such improvement filed in their office.
Provided, any owner of any lot or parcel of land, who shall
personally, or by his authorized agent, have signed a petition
asking for such improvement, shall not be entitled to compensation, but every such owner shall be deemed thereby to have
waived and relinquished all claim to compensation for any injury
in consequence thereof, and no damages, cost or charges arising
to such owners from such improvement shall be assessed or paid.
No action shall lie against any officer, agent, servant or employe
of the city of Milwaukee or any contractor or his servants or
employes who may enter upon, in or upon any of the premises
herein intended to be improved pursuant to the provisions thereof
for trespass or otherwise.

Notice of assess-ment of benefits and damages, when and how given.

SECTION 4. As soon as any assessment of benefits or damages,
or both, shall be made, as in the preceding sections of this chapter
provided, the said board shall give notice to all parties interested,
by advertisement for not less than four days in the official papers
of the said city, that such assessment has been made and is ready
for inspection in its office, and that the same will be open for
review and correction by the said board, at its office, for not less
than four days after the first publication of such notice, during
certain hours, not less than two hours of each day, and that all
persons interested will be heard by said board, in objection to
such assessment, and generally in the matter of such review and
correction. It shall be sufficient to state in such notice, in brief,
that such assessment has been made for, and in what locality, and
no further notice or publication of such assessment shall be
necessary. During the time mentioned in such notice, the said
board shall hear objections and evidence, and they shall have
power to review, modify and correct such assessment, in such
manner as they shall deem just, at any time during such review,
and for three days thereafter; and thereupon said board shall

endorse such corrected and completed assessment upon or annex the same to the estimate of the cost of such improvement, made and filed in its office, as provided in section 3, of this act, and shall file a duplicate of such estimate and assessment in the office of the city clerk, who shall lay the same before the common council at its meeting; and thereupon the common council may confirm or correct said assessments, or any of them, or may refer the same back to the board of public works for revision and correction; and the said common council, and the said board of public works shall respectively have the like powers and perform the like duties in relation to such assessment, and any subsequent assessment made pursuant to such reference by the common council as are prescribed and conferred in relation to the first assessment.

SECTION 5. Such contract shall require the contractor to receive certificates upon or against the several lots, parts of lots, or pieces of land which may be assessed with benefits on account of such improvement, such certificates to apply in payment of the contract price for the doing of said work, and they shall be a lien upon said lot or tract of land; provided that in any case if the contract price of the work shall exceed the benefits assessed, such excess shall be paid out of the ward fund in which such lot or tract of land is situated in the city of Milwaukee.

Contracts, what to require.

SECTION 6. The owner of any lot or tract of land, or tenement, who feels himself aggrieved by such assessment, as confirmed by the common council, as to the amount of benefits thereby adjudged to him by reason of any improvement charged against his lot or parcel of land more than twenty days after such confirmation by the common council may appeal therefrom to the circuit court of Milwaukee county and such appeal shall be taken, tried and determined, and bonds for costs shall be given, and costs awarded therein in like manner as in cases of appeals to the circuit court in chapter 6, of the charter of said city. Such appeal shall not affect the rights of the contractor, or the proceedings in reference to his contract, but the certificate against the lot or parcel of land in question, shall be given as if no appeal had been taken; and in case the appellant shall succeed, the difference between the amount charged and the certificate and the amount of the benefit finally adjudged, shall be paid by the city out of the proper ward fund to the appellant, but not until he shall have done the work in question or have paid the certificate issued for doing the same. The amount assessed by the board of public works or finally adjudged on appeal for damages, costs and charges arising from such improvement in excess of the charges against property deemed benefited, shall be paid by the city out of the proper ward fund to the person or persons thereto entitled, within one year after the confirmation of the assessment by the common council or after final judgment therefor by the court on appeal as aforesaid; provided, that the time during which an appeal from said confirmation may be pending shall not be deemed part of the year so limited.

Owner may appeal from assessment.

SECTION 7. The appeal given by the last preceding section from the assessment of the board of public works, as confirmed by

Appeal the only remedy.

the common council to the said circuit court, shall be the only remedy for the recovery of any damages, costs and charges arising from any works done by virtue of this act by the said city or sustained by reason of any proceedings or acts of said city, or its officers, in the matter to which such assessment of damages or benefits relates; and no action at law shall be maintained for such damages or injuries arising, whether arising from the filling of said lot or parcel of land or the abatement of any nuisance in any manner which may be caused by stagnant water or otherwise.

Certificates, how issued.

SECTION 8. After the completion and performance of any contract entered into by the board of public works for work done pursuant to the provisions of this act, they shall give to the contractor or contractors a certificate signed by the board of public works or the president thereof, countersigned by the comptroller, stating the amount of work done by such contractor, the nature thereof, and the description of the lots and parcels of land upon which the same is chargeable; which said certificate shall be a lien upon said lot, part of lot or tract of land; it shall be the duty of the comptroller to keep a register of all certificates issued by the board of public works against lots, and countersigned by him, which said certificate may be paid by the owner or owners of such lots at any time before the sale of such lots for the non-payment of taxes, and the city treasurer who shall receive the amount paid on such certificates and hold the same for the benefit of the owners of such certificates, and such owners shall be entitled thereto on producing and surrendering such certificates to be cancelled.

Assessments to be a lien.

SECTION 9. In all cases where' by the provisions of this act, any special charge or assessment is made a lien upon land, the amount of such charge or assessment shall be carried out on the tax roll in a separate column or columns, opposite the lot or tract upon which the same may be a lien; and the treasurer may collect and sell, and do all other acts in relation thereto, in the same manner as if the amount of such lien was a general tax.

Amends chapter 184, laws of 1874.

SECTION 10. This act shall be amendatory of the charter of the city of Milwaukee, being chapter 184, of the laws of 1874, entitled, "an act to revise, consolidate and amend the charter of the city of Milwaukee, approved February 20, 1852, and the several acts amendatory thereof," and the several acts amendatory thereof

CHAPTER 302, LAWS OF 1895.

AN ACT relating to legalizing special assessments for street improvements and providing for re-assessments of special taxes in certain cases in all cities of the first and second class in this state.

In any action to set aside assessment, court may stay proceedings.

SECTION 1. In case, in any action, now pending or hereafter brought to set aside or vacate any special assessment against property, for opening, widening or extending any street or alley or part thereof, or for grading, graveling, macadamizing, paving or repaving any street or alley, or part thereof, or making any other improvement thereof, or for constructing any sewer therein, in any city of this state, or to set aside or vacate any special assessment certificate, tax sale or tax sale certificate, based upon such special assessment, the court shall be of the opinion, after a hearing in that behalf had, that such assessment is invalid by reason of a defective assessment of benefits and damages, it shall stay all proceedings in such action until a new assessment thereof is had in the manner hereinafter mentioned. Thereupon, the proper city authorities shall proceed to make a new assessment of benefits and damages against the property of the plaintiff in such action, in like manner as required by law in the case of such original assessment, and such plaintiff shall have the same right to appeal from such new assessment as he or his grantors would have had from such original assessment. If the plaintiff shall desire to contest the validity of such new assessment, he shall, within ten days after its confirmation by the common council, file with the clerk of the court, and serve upon the defendant's attorneys, his objections in writing to such new assessment, and thereupon the court shall direct an issue to be made up involving the objections aforesaid, which issue shall be tried summarily by the court, and thereupon the court shall file an order sustaining or overruling the objections of the plaintiff aforesaid. When by such order such new assessment of benefits and damages shall be held invalid, subsequent assessments may be had, in the manner and form as hereinbefore provided, and the same proceedings may be resorted to, to determine the validity of such assessments. When the amount to be assessed against the plaintiff's property has been finally determined by an assessment of benefits and damages to which no objections are filed, as aforesaid, or which, if objections are so filed, the court shall hold to be valid and regular, or, when an appeal is taken, upon such appeal, the court shall make an order requiring the plaintiff to pay into court, within a time to be fixed by such order, for the use and benefit of the defendant, or the parties entitled thereto, the amount which, based upon such valid new assessment, he ought justly to pay, or which should be justly and equitably assessed against the property in question, and the court shall, upon the plaintiff's complying with said order, within the time so limited, order judgment for the plaintiff with costs, and in default of plaintiff complying with such order within the time so limited, the action shall be dismissed with costs in favor of the defendant.

SECTION 2. If, in any action now pending or hereafter commenced, the validity of any special assessment certificate, or tax sale or tax sale certificate, based upon an assessment for any of the purposes mentioned in section 1, of this act, is attacked and sought to be set aside, upon grounds other than those affecting the validity of the assessment of benefits and damages, or in addition thereto, the court after hearing in that behalf had, shall be of opinion that the same is void by reason of any failure to observe any provision of law, or by reasons of any act or defect in the proceedings upon which such special assessment certificate, tax sale or tax sale certificate is based, which has intervened to the prejudice of the plaintiff, it shall immediately stay all proceedings in the action, and shall cause an issue to be made up involving the extent of the injury which the plaintiff has suffered by reason

City authorities to make new assessment.

Plaintiff contesting validity of new assessment, to file objections.

Court may cause issue to be made up, when.

of such failure or such act or defect, and such issue shall be tried summarily by the court. In the event that in such action the validity of the assessment of benefits and damages upon which such special assessment certificate, tax sale or tax sale certificate is based, is attacked and such assessment shall be set aside, such issue shall only be tried after a new assessment has been had, as provided by section 1 of this act.

Court may require plaintiff to pay into court the amount he should justly pay, when. When such issue has been tried and determined, the court shall make an order requiring the plaintiff to pay into court, within the time to be limited in such order, for the use and benefit of the defendant, or parties entitled thereto, the amount which he ought justly to pay, or which should be justly and equitably assessed against the property in question, based upon the finding of the court upon such issue, or in case a new assessment of benefits and damages is had, upon such new assessment and such finding, and upon such payment being made within such time, the court shall order judgment for the plaintiff with costs, but, in the event that the plaintiff fails to pay such amount within the time so fixed by the court, the action shall be dismissed with costs in favor of the defendant.

No special assessment to be invalid by reason of guarantee to keep work good for term of years. SECTION 3. No special assessment or certificate thereof or tax sale certificate based thereon shall be held to be invalid for the reason that any contract which has been heretofore or may hereafter be let, contains on the part of the contractor a guarantee or any provision to keep the work done under such contract in good order or repair for a limited number of years, when such guaranty or provision was inserted therein for the purpose of insuring the proper performance of such work in the first instance. All such provisions in contracts for doing public work, inserted for the purpose aforesaid, are hereby legalized, and all such provisions shall be deemed prima facie to have been inserted for that purpose, unless the time during which the contractor is required to keep the work in good order or repair shall exceed five years.

SECTION 4. All acts or parts of acts which are inconsistent with this act, or not in harmony with its provisions and operations, are hereby declared to be modified, amended, superseded or repealed, in so far as they interfere with or are at variance with the true intent, meaning and operation of this act.

SECTION 5. The provisions of this act shall not apply to cities of the third or fourth class, whether operating under general or special charters.

CHAPTER VIII.

SEWERS.

Sewerage districts. SECTION 1. The city of Milwaukee is hereby divided into three sewerage districts, as follows: All that part of the city embraced in the First, Third and Seventh wards, shall constitute one district, to be known as the East sewerage district. All that part of said city embraced in the Second, Fourth, Sixth, Ninth, Tenth and Thirteenth wards, shall constitute one district, to be known as the West sewerage district. All that part of said city embraced in the Fifth, Eighth, Eleventh and Twelfth wards, shall constitute one district, to be known as the South sewerage district.

The Bay View sewerage district, comprising the Seventeenth ward, was created by chapter 37, laws of 1887.

SECTION 2. The board of public works of said city shall cause to be made, from time to time, as fast as the preliminary surveys can be completed, diagrams for each such district, in addition to an extension of those already made and adopted under and pursuant to the provisions of chapter two hundred and seventy-four, of the local laws of 1870, which diagrams shall conform to the system of sewerage in the district and show the plan thereof, and contain, as nearly as practicable, the lots, blocks, and tracts of land, the main sewers to be constructed, the branch and minor sewers, the man-holes, the catch basins and their connections, through overflow pipes with the sewers, the sewers already constructed, and any other data deemed by them necessary for information; provided, that the plans for sewerage heretofore made and adopted pursuant to said chapter two hundred and seventy-four, shall remain in full force and be deviated from only by authority of the common council, and that all sewers already constructed under chapter three hundred and ninety-nine of the local laws of 1869, or chapter two hundred and seventy-four of the local laws of 1870, shall be considered as part of the plan, to be in no respect altered or changed, and that no other sewers previously constructed may be included in the diagrams to be prepared, so far as the same can be used in the proposed system of drainage.

Diagrams for each district

Present sewerage plan to remain in force.

Present sewers not to be disturbed.

SECTION 3. On the completion of any such diagram, said board shall give notice in the official papers of the city for at least six days, that a plan of sewerage is open at their office for inspection. Any person owning real estate in such district, may file with said board written objections to the said plan, stating therein the nature and reason of his objections, and may also suggest improvements to said plan.

Notice of diagram to be given.

Plan may be modified by board.

SECTION 4. The said board may reconsider and modify said plan, and at the expiration of ten days after the time such notice shall have been given to said resident freeholders of the district, shall report such plan to the common council for its approval.

Municipalities have same rights to repel surface waters as private persons have, and they may discontinue and abandon sewers, if the land owners are not thereby left in a worse condition than if the sewers had never been made.

Waters vs. Bay View, 61 Wis., 642.

Hoyt vs. Hudson, 27 Wis., 656.

Council to ratify or condemn.

SECTION 5. The common council shall take such plan into consideration, and within thirty days after receiving the same, shall return it to the board approved, or if objected to, with a statement in writing of such objections, or of any alteration or improvements thereof which they may deem desirable.

Plan may be changed or a new one prepared.

SECTION 6. The said board may, on return of such plan by the common council, modify or change the same in accordance with the suggestions of the common council, or may prepare a different plan, which shall be again submitted to the common council, and may generally modify and change their action in the premises, until a plan shall be mutually agreed upon by the board and common council; provided, that no plan shall take effect until approved by the common council, and no plan thus approved shall be deviated from except by consent of the common council; and provided further, that sewers may be ordered and constructed in any district without the plans of such district being completed in their whole extent and all their details.

Board to annually report the sewers necessary in each district.

SECTION 7. On or before the first day of March in each year, the board of public works shall report to the common council the sewers necessary, in their judgment, to be built in each district, during the current year, in accordance with the plan, stating the precise location and extent of the same, and the kind of material of which they should be composed. The common council shall take such report into consideration, and may approve the same, and make such additions to it, or alterations in it in any respect as to them may seem best, and return the same to the board, and it shall be the duty of the board to carry out the work as directed in the report thus returned from the common council.   The board may also from time to time, during the year, as may be necessary, recommend to the common council the construc- **May recommend** tion of other sewers than those contained in the general **others.** report, which recommendation the common council shall take into consideration and return to the board approved, negatived or altered, as may to them seem best, and the board shall carry out the work, as prescribed in the action of the common council; provided, that said board of public works shall, at least five days before the presentation of such recommendation to the common council, give notice by publication in the official paper or papers of the city, stating the day when such recom- mendation will be presented to the common council, and giving a general description of the proposed improve- ment and extension.   Upon the presentation of such recommendation to said common council, with proper proof of publication of the notice above described, the same shall be referred to the appropriate committee, and con- sidered and disposed of in the same manner and under the same rules, as are provided in the case of ordinances or resolutions creating a charge or liability against any city or ward fund; and provided further, that no sewer shall **Sewers to be built** be built or contracted for by the board until the same **only upon order** has been authorized or ordered by the common council. **council.**

As amended by Section 3, Chapter 274, Laws of 1881, and further amended by Section 25, Chapter 324, Laws of 1882.

SECTION 8.   After the common council shall, by reso- **Board shall adver-** lution or otherwise, have ordered the construction of any **tise for proposals.** sewer, the board shall advertise for and receive bids to do the work so ordered, having first procured to be care- fully prepared, and put on file in their office, for the examination and guidance of bidders, plans and specifica- tions describing the particular work to be done, and the kinds and qualities of materials to be used, as directed by the common council, and shall let the contract to the **Contract shall be** lowest responsible and reliable bidder, subject, however, **let to lowest bid-** to the provisions of chapter five of this act.   Provided, **ders.** that any contractor for such work may procure **Contractor may** from the board of public works a license as a sewer **procure license** contractor, and at the time of procuring such license he **upon giving bond.** shall file with said board a bond in the penal sum of five thousand dollars, which bond shall be approved as to form

**Bond, how con-
ditioned.**

**Bond to be renewed
when required.**

and manner of execution by the city attorney and as to the sufficiency of the sureties therein by said board of public works prior to their accepting and filing the same, which said bond shall be conditioned that such contractor and bidder will execute and perform the work for the price mentioned in his proposals and according to the plans and specifications on file in case the contract shall be awarded to him, and in case of default on his part to execute a contract with satisfactory sureties and to perform the work for which he bid, said bond shall be prosecuted in the name of the city, and judgment recovered thereon for the full amount of the penalty thereof; which penalty shall be agreed upon as liquidated damages, unless the common council shall by resolution direct that no action shall be commenced.   The bond herein provided for shall be renewed as often as required by said board, and shall be taken and accepted by said board until the license hereinbefore mentioned is revoked by said board, as and in lieu of the preliminary bond accompanying bids and proposals, provided for in section 9, of chapter 5, of the Charter of the city of Milwaukee; nothing herein contained, however, shall prevent any person from making and presenting a bid and proposals pursuant to the provisions of chapter five, of the charter of said city.

As amended by Chapter 316, Laws of 1891.

CHAPTER 368, LAWS OF 1895.

AN ACT to provide for the manner of asking and receiving bids for public work or improvements ordered by the common council of any city of the first class in the State of Wisconsin.

**When sewer work
to be done, board
of public works
shall advertise for
proposals.**

**Advertisement to
be published six
days.**

SECTION 1. Whenever the laying and building of any sewer or the grading or making of any street or alley shall be ordered by the common council of any city of the first class as classified in Chapter 40 of Sanborn & Berryman's annotated statutes of the state of Wisconsin, and by chapter 238 laws of 1895, the board of public works of said city shall advertise for proposals for doing the same; a plan or profile of the work to be done, accompanied with specifications for doing the same, or other appropriate and sufficient description of the work required to be done and of the kinds and quality of material to be furnished being first placed on the file in the office of said board of public works for the information of bidders and others. Such advertisements shall be published at least six days in the official city papers, and shall state the work to be done and the time for doing the same, which time shall in all cases be such a reasonable time as may be necessary to enable a contractor with proper diligence to perform and complete such work.

SECTION 2.   All proposals for such work shall be sealed and
directed to such board of public works and shall be accompanied
at the time of such bid or proposal with a sum of money equal to
at least fifteen per cent. of the amount of the engineer's estimate
of the cost of such work, as the board of public works in such
advertisement may direct, under an agreement that such sum of
money shall be returned to such bidder in case the contract for the
work bid for is not awarded to such bidder, or which sum of money
shall also be returned to such bidder in case such bidder will execute
the contract for such work pursuant to his bid and accompany
such contract with good and sufficient bond with satisfactory
sureties in case the contract is awarded to such bidder, and also
that in case the contract is so awarded and he shall [fail] to execute
a bond with satisfactory sureties to perform the work specified for
the price named in his bid within a reasonable time after such
contract is prepared and ready for execution, then such sum of
money shall become the property of said city as fixed and liquidated damages for such default, and shall be paid by said board to
the city treasurer of such city.   All bids unless fulfilling the
requirements of this act shall be rejected.

Proposals to be accompanied by deposit of fifteen per cent.

SECTION 3.   All acts or parts of acts contravening the provisions
of this act are hereby repealed.

SECTION 9.   Such contracts shall require the contractor
to receive as payment for so much of the work as has
been assessed against the lots opposite to the front of
which any such sewer shall extend, certificates against
such lots respectively; and the residue of such contract
shall be paid out of the proceeds of the general sewerage
tax, to be levied on the real estate and personal property
within the sewerage district, by the common council, on
the recommendation of the board of public works.

Contractor to take certificate in part payment.

SECTION 10.   After any contract for work, under this
act, to be paid for in whole or in part by special assessments, shall have been entered into, the board of public
works shall make, or cause to be made, an assessment
against all lots, parts of lots and parcels of land, fronting
or abutting on the work so contracted to be done, on
each side of the same for its whole length, and which
have not before been so assessed for sewerage purposes,
at the rate of eighty cents per lineal foot of the whole
frontage of each lot, part of lot or lots, or parcel of land,
fronting or abutting on either side of such sewer, except
corner lots, which shall be assessed therefor as follows:
corner lots not subdivided in ownership and subdivisions
of corner lots, constituting the actual corner of corner
lots subdivided in ownership, shall be entitled to deduc-

Sewerage assess-ment, when and how made, and for what amounts.

tion in making such assessment, of one-third from the aggregate of the street lines of such corner lots, or corner subdivisions thereof, on all the streets in front thereof;

Deductions, what lots entitled to, and for what amount. such deduction to be made in the assessment of the longest street line of such corner lots, or corner subdivisions thereof, or in case of equal street lines thereof, in the assessment for the second sewer to which they are liable; provided, however, that when the actual cost of any sewer shall be less than one dollar and sixty cents per lineal foot, then, and in that case, the assessment shall be for the actual cost of such sewer per lineal foot, one-half thereof to be chargeable against the property fronting or abutting thereon, on each side thereof. Whenever

Subdivisions, how charged. any lot which, as originally platted, fronts or abuts on any sewer, is subdivided, and the subdivisions thereof are owned by different persons, no subdivision of such lot, not fronting or abutting on such sewer, and not owned by the same person who owns the subdivision fronting or abutting on such sewer, shall be assessed for the cost of such sewer.

Notice of subdivisions, duties of board when given. SECTION 11. Whenever any lot or parcel of land, shall be subdivided by sale or any other contract, after the assessment of benefits accruing to it by a system of sewerage, shall have been made, and before such system shall have been fully carried out and extended to such lot—and the assessment on such work paid—any party interested may give notice to the board of such subdivision, and in such case, or when the said board shall in any other way become cognizant of the fact of such subdivision, they may make an equitable apportionment of the said benefit tax against any said lot, between the different parcels of it, but if, by neglect of the owners of the lot so subdivided, no such apportionment shall be made, then the entire lot shall be liable for the entire tax.

Sewers in streets and alley crossing chargeable to sewerage fund. SECTION 12. The cost of all sewers in street and alley crossings, and of all sewers, in excess of one dollar and sixty cents per lineal foot, chargeable to lots and lands, as provided in section ten of this chapter—of all catch basins for receiving the water from the gutters, and of the overflow pipes connecting them with the sewers—of all temporary catch basins—and of the repairing and cleaning of sewers—and all expenditures for temporary work necessary to carry out the system of sewerage herein provided, and all costs for constructing sewers, not provided for by special assessment, shall be paid out of the fund of the proper sewerage district; and all cleaning and repairing of sewers and catch. basins, and all temporary work necessary to be done as above stated, shall be done by the authority of the board of public works, as may be necessary. *Cleaning and repairing.*

SECTION 13.   The board of public works shall report to the common council, on or before the 15th day of December in each year, as accurately as may be, the amount of money required for sewerage purposes for the ensuing year, in each district, in addition to the special assessments made; and the common council are hereby authorized to direct the levy and collection of a tax for sewerage purposes in each district, for such amount as may be necessary, not, however, to exceed in any one year the sum of one and one-half mills on the dollar, on all the property, real and personal, subject to taxation within any such sewerage district; which tax, so levied, shall, when collected, be paid into the city treasury, and be placed in the fund of the sewerage district in which the same has been collected; and the city comptroller is hereby directed and required to keep a separate and distinct account with each sewerage district. The tax to be levied under the provisions of this section may be added on the tax roll to the general city tax assessed against such property. *Board to make annual report of money required for that year in each district.* *Sewerage tax, how levied and collected.*

As amended by Section 34, Chapter 144, Laws of 1875, and further amended by Section 26, Chapter 324, Laws of 1882.

SECTION 14.   Any person to whom a contract is awarded for the construction of a sewer, shall receive in payment certificates against the lots, parts of lots, or parcels of land, so as heretofore directed to be assessed, so far as the same will go in liquidation of the amount of such contract, and shall be entitled to receive city orders for the balance due, payable only out of the fund of the proper district; and it shall be the duty of the board of public works, after the completion of any contract, and acceptance of the work, to issue such certificates on the request of the person entitled to receive them; and where any sum is found to be due a contractor over and above the amount of certificates so to be issued and received in . part payment, to certify the same to the common council, which may direct an order to be drawn on the *Contractor entitled to certificate on completion of work.*

Certificate of special assessment, how executed.

proper fund for the payment of the same. All certificates of special assessment for building sewers, shall be made by the board of public works, and signed by the board or the president thereof, and countersigned by the comptroller of the said city, and delivered by the said board of public works to the person entitled to receive the same, in the same manner as certificates of assessments for other work in the said city.

Certificates issued under this section are liens upon the lots, draw interest at the rate of twenty-five per cent. from the time of sale by the city treasurer on account of such certificate liens, and are transferable by endorsement.

Hoyt vs. Fass, 64 Wis., 273.

Where the construction of a sewer is duly authorized under a law requiring plan, specifications and estimate to be first filed before letting the contract, it is sufficient, to sustain a tax for the work, to leave in the proper office a plan, with specifications and estimate which are sufficiently accurate to enable persons of ordinary skill to bid intelligently thereon.

Houghton vs. Burnham, 22 Wis., 289.

Contracts to be approved by city attorney and by president of board.

SECTION 15. All contracts entered into by the board of public works under this chapter shall be approved as to form and execution by the city attorney, and before taking effect shall be signed by a majority of the board of public works, or by the president of said board, and countersigned by the comptroller, and all bonds taken by them shall be entered into in the name of, and shall be executed to the city of Milwaukee, and shall be approved by the board. All contracts entered into under this chapter, shall be expressly subject to the powers given to said board by chapter five of this act. And in

In case of suspension or default.

case any work shall be suspended, in consequence of the default of any contractor, or in case the bids shall be deemed excessive, or the parties making proposals for any work shall not be deemed responsible or proper parties to be entrusted with its performance, or shall have failed to complete any contract within the meaning of section ten of said chapter five, the said board shall proceed as provided in said chapter.

As amended by Section 35, Chapter 144, Laws of 1875.

Grades of sewers.

SECTION 16. The grades of sewers to be constructed shall be fixed by the board of public works, with the approval of the common council, and the said board shall make or cause to be made a profile of such grades upon

the plans of the sewer to be constructed, giving a sufficient number of bench marks and their elevation, and
such other data as may be necessary to make future surveys.   And in all cases the work shall be subject to the
superintendence and direction of the said board; and no
contractor shall be entitled to recover compensation for
any work executed by him, in any form of action, unless
such work shall have been approved by the said board:
provided, that the said board may from time to time, as
the work progresses, at their discretion, grant to any
contractor for a sewer an estimate of the amount and
proportionate value of the work already done, withhold-
ing in all cases twenty-five per cent. of said estimate,
which shall entitle the holder to receive the amount
thereof, less such twenty-five per cent. from the
public fund.

*Work to be ap-
proved by board.*

*Board may grant
estimates.*

The powers granted to the board of public works and the common council by this section are *quasi* judicial, and the exercise of
such powers by those bodies cannot be collaterally attacked.

Robinson vs. Milwaukee, 61 .Wis., 585.

SECTION 17.   Whenever the common council shall
order the paving or repairing of any street in the city of
Milwaukee, in which water and gas mains and sewers, or
either of them, shall have been previously laid and constructed, they may also by resolution require the board
of public works to cause water and gas service pipes and
house drains to be first laid in such street, at the cost
of the property fronting such street, from the main sewer
and water and gas mains in such street, to the curb line
on either side of the street, at intervals not less than
twenty feet, along the whole length of such paved street,
except at street and alley crossings; and the board of public works shall thereupon give notice to the owners or
occupants of the property adjoining such paved street, by
publication thereof for six days in the official papers,
requiring them to do such work opposite their respective
lots, according to a plan and specification to be before
prepared and on file in the office of said board, showing
the location and size, and the kind and quality of materials of such lateral sewers or drains, and water and gas
service pipe; and if such owners or occupants shall refuse
or neglect to do the same before the paving or repairing
of said street so ordered, and within ten days after the
publication of such notice, the said board may procure

*Board may order
sewer pipe laid
before paving any
street.*

*Notice thereof to
be given.*

If not done by owners, may be assessed against property.

the same to be done, and charge and assess the expense thereof to the lots or parts of lots fronting upon such work in the manner provided in and by section nineteen of chapter seven of this act; and the same shall be levied and collected as other special assessments are levied and

No street to be paved until gas and water mains and sewer pipe be laid.

collected in said city; provided, no street shall be paved or repaved by order of the common council, unless the water and gas mains and service pipes, and necessary sewers and their connections shall, as required by the common council, be first laid and constructed in that portion of such street so to be paved or repaved.

Contractors for paving a street will be enjoined from unnecessarily interfering with the operation of a street railway thereon, where the city has not attempted to exercise the power of stopping the running of the cars.

Mil. St. R'y. Co. vs. Adlam, 85 Wis., 142.

Board to see that all proper drains are made.

SECTION 18.   It shall be the duty of the said board to see that proper drains or sewers are constructed from every lot in said city, which in their judgment requires it; and that such private drains or sewers are made to communicate with the public sewers in a proper manner; and they shall have power to require such number of private drains and sewers to be constructed as they may deem expedient.

The city is not liable for injuries to property of an owner of a private sewer, caused by the negligence of the board of public works in re-connecting such private sewer with the main sewer after the lowering of the latter, it not being an act within the line of any corporate duty.

Streiff vs. Milwaukee, 89 Wis., 218.

Board to have control, etc.

SECTION 19.   The said board shall prescribe the location, arrangement, form, materials and construction of every drain and sewer, for every lot in the city emptying into the public sewers, and shall determine the manner and plan of the connection of the same; the work of construction shall be in all cases subject to the superintendence and control of said board, and shall be executed strictly in compliance with their orders; but the cost of such private sewers shall not be included in the estimate of the cost of the general plan of sewerage in any district, and shall be charged upon the lot or lots for the benefit of which such private sewers shall be constructed.

SECTION 20. The said board shall have at their office, **Specifications of private drains and sewers to be kept open for examination.** ready for the examination of the parties interested, the specifications of any private drains or sewers so ordered to be constructed, and they shall give to the lot owners six days' notice, in the official papers, to construct the same, designating therein a reasonable time within which the work shall be completed; and in case any lot owner neglects to do the work required of him to be done, within the time specified in said notice, they shall advertise for proposals, and let the same by contract; and at the completion of the contract, shall give to the contractor a certificate or certificates against such lot or **Certificates.** lots, which shall be proceeded with, and shall have the like effect as other certificates given for work chargeable to lots.

SECTION 21. Any person who has taken such contract from said board to construct a private drain or **Contractor may enter premises, etc.** sewer from any lot, shall be authorized to enter upon such lots, and construct thereon such drain or sewer, and shall have free ingress and egress upon the same, with men and teams for that purpose, and to deposit all the necessary building materials, and generally to do and perform all things necessary to a complete execution of the work.

SECTION 22. No private drain shall be connected with **Permit to connect private with public sewers.** any public sewer without the said board first issuing their order or permit for such connection; and there shall be paid for such order or permit, into the general fund of the sewerage district, by the owner of any lot from which a private drain is led into a public sewer, an amount to be fixed by said board, proportioned to the size of such private drain, but not less than two and a half, nor more than five dollars for every drain from any lot or parcel of a lot; and in case such amount is not paid, it shall be a lien upon such lot, and shall be collected as other taxes **Fee therefor.** on real estate are collected; provided, that no charge shall be made for the order or permit herein referred to, when the connection for which it is used is made before the sewer is finished in front of the premises to be connected.

SECTION 23. No person shall break open or make **Penalty for breaking or obstructing sewers.** connections with any public sewer, except by the consent and under the direction of the board of public works; and any person who shall do so, or shall wilfully or maliciously obstruct, damage or injure any public or private sewer or drain in said city, or wilfully injure any of the materials employed or used in said city for the purposes of sewerage, shall be deemed guilty of a misdemeanor, and upon conviction thereof, shall be fined not more than five hundred dollars, or imprisoned in the county jail not to exceed three months.

Contractors to restore streets and alleys to former condition. SECTION 24. Any contractor, or other person, acting under the direction of the board of public works, may lay sewers in and through any alleys and streets of said city, and through any breakwater into Lake Michigan, and also in any highways of Milwaukee county, whether within the limits of said city or not; provided, that it shall be the duty of such contractor to repair such streets, alleys, breakwaters, and highways, and to restore the same to their former condition, upon the completion of such sewers.

Chapter 322, laws of 1875, entitled "an act to authorize the improvement of certain streets in the third ward of the city of Milwaukee, and to authorize the levy of a special tax in said ward," is in the nature of an amendment to the city charter, and is a grant of corporate powers to the city. It is not a "special act for the assessment or collection of taxes" within the inhibition of Subd. 6, Sec. 31, Art. IV, of the Constitution of Wisconsin.

Such an act does not embrace "more than one subject," and the title is sufficient to express the subject.

Warner vs. Knox, 50 Wis., 429.

CHAPTER 88, LAWS OF 1891.

Common council may raise money for sewerage purposes in Bay View sewerage district. SECTION 1. The common council of the city of Milwaukee is hereby authorized to levy and raise by taxation upon all taxable property, real and personal, within the Bay View sewerage district of said city, in addition to the amount authorized to be raised for a sewerage fund in said district, and in addition to the amount of money authorized to be raised by taxation for all purposes within said district, now limited by law, for each of the years 1891, 1892 and 1893, a sum of money not exceeding one and one half mills on the dollar, in each of said years, upon all the taxable property within said district, for the purpose of continuing and completing the sewers contemplated by the plans for sewers in said Bay View sewerage district of said city, now on file in the office of the proper officers of said city of Milwaukee and for the purpose of constructing and continuing the construction of such sewers as shall or may be included in any amendments to or changes of the plans in said district during the years 1891, 1892 and 1893.

Section 1. The common council of the city of Milwaukee is hereby authorized to levy and raise by taxation upon all taxable property, real and personal, within the south sewerage district of said city in addition to the amount authorized to be raised for a sewerage fund in said district, and in addition to the amount of money authorized to be raised by taxation for all purposes within said district, now limited by law, for each of the years 1892 and 1893, a sum of money not exceeding one and one half mills on the dollar in each of said years, upon all the taxable property within said district, for the purpose of continuing and completing the sewers contemplated by the plans for sewers in said south sewerage district of said city, now on file in the office of the proper officers of said city of Milwaukee, and for the purpose of constructing and continuing the construction of such sewers as shall or may be included in any amendments to or change of the plans in said district during the years 1892 and 1893.

Common council may raise money for sewerage purposes in south sewerage district.

CHAPTER 224, LAWS OF 1893.

AN ACT to authorize the division of certain cities into sewer districts, and to provide means for perfecting the sewer systems therein by special taxation and by the issue of corporate bonds of such cities.

Section 1. The common council of any city operating under a special charter granted by the legislature of this state, and authorized by such charter to construct sewers, is hereby empowered to divide such city into sewer districts, and to levy a special tax of not more than one mill and a half of a mill on the dollar of the assessed value of the taxable property in any such sewer district, if in the opinion of such common council such special tax shall be needed for the extension or improvement of the sewer system for such district.

Common council may divide city into sewer districts.

Section 2. If in the opinion of such common council any such sewer district shall require an extraordinary outlay of money for the construction of outlets or pumping stations to perfect its sewer system, such common council is hereby authorized to provide by ordinance for issuing corporate bonds of such city payable within twenty years from the time of their issue in lawful money of the United States, bearing interest at a rate not exceeding five per cent. per annum.

Corporate bonds, when may be issued.

Section 3. The bonds authorized to be issued under the provisions of this act shall be executed in the manner prescribed by the charter of the city issuing the same, or if no provision for the execution of the same is contained in the charter of such city, then in the manner which may be prescribed by ordinance or resolution of the common council thereof. Such bonds shall be called sewer bonds and shall be consecutively numbered, and shall have interest coupons attached, and shall show on their face the district for the benefit of which they are issued.

Form of bonds.

Section 4. There shall be annually levied a direct tax upon all taxable property in the district for the benefit of which any

Direct tax, what to be levied.

sewer bonds are issued, to pay the annual interest thereon, and to raise a sinking fund each year of five per cent. on the principal of such bonds remaining unpaid and outstanding, for the payment of such principal as the same may become due.

Limit of indebtedness.

SECTION 5. No bonds shall be issued under the provisions of this act in excess of the limit fixed for indebtedness by the charter of the city issuing the same, or by the constitution of this state.

A statute granting certain powers to "any city operating under a special charter * * * and authorized by such charter to construct sewers," may be construed to apply to all cities whose special charters, *either expressly or by implication*, authorize them to construct sewers. Such cities, being authorized by their charters to repair and keep in order their streets, are "authorized by such charters to construct sewers," within the meaning of Ch. 224, laws of 1893, since the authority first mentioned carries with it the latter.

Johnson vs. Milwaukee, 88 Wis., 383.

CHAPTER IX.

HARBOR AND RIVERS.

Milwaukee harbor, what it includes.

SECTION 1. The harbor of Milwaukee shall include the Milwaukee river from lake Michigan to the dam across said river, in said city, and all those portions of the Kinnickinnick river, and of the Menomonee river, and the canals, water channels and slips laid out and established in the valley of said Menomonee river, under and in pursuance of chapter ninety-one of the local laws of 1869, which are in the limits of the city of Milwaukee, and also lake Michigan, to a distance of one mile from the shore along the east front of said city; and said rivers, and said canals, water channels and slips, are hereby declared to be public highways, and navigable from lake Michigan to said dam, and to the western and southern limits of said city.

It is not within the powers of a municipal corporation to engage in works of internal improvement, such as the construction of harbors, canals, railroads and the like without being specifically authorized by the legislature.

Hasbrouck vs. Milwaukee, 13 Wis., 42.

Soens vs. Racine, 10 Wis., 214.

Kinnickinnick a navigable river.

SECTION 2. Whenever the survey and plat of the Kinnickinnick river, describing the channel and dock lines of said river shall be made, adopted and established, recorded and filed, as provided by section twenty, chapter one hundred and twenty-nine of the laws of 1873, the water channel of said river, as described and represented by such survey and plat, shall be deemed to be and is hereby declared to be a public navigable river, subject to all laws and regulations applicable to it as such.

SECTION 3. The common council of said city shall have power, by ordinance, to establish dock and wharf lines upon the banks of the Milwaukee, Menomonee and Kinnickinnick rivers, and the public canals in said city, wherever the same are not established by statute; to restrain and prevent encroachments upon said rivers and canals, and obstructions thereto; and to construct, alter and maintain, or cause to be canstructed, altered and maintained, at the expense of the city, docks or wharves along the banks of said rivers and canals, where the same are not by law required to be constructed and maintained at the expense of the owners of the lots bounded on said rivers and canals respectively. *Dock and wharf lines.*

SECTION 4. The board of public works shall annually, in the month of April, appoint one or more harbor masters, subject to the approval of the common council. The duties and compensation of such harbor masters, shall be prescribed by the common council, by ordinance. Their term of office shall be one year, and until their successors are appointed and qualified; but they shall be subject to removal at any time by the board of public works, with the approval of the common council. *Harbor masters.* *Term of office.*

SECTION 5. The board of public works shall appoint, subject to the approval of the common council, all bridge tenders, whose number, duties and compensation, shall be fixed and determined by the common council. Any bridge tender may be removed at pleasure by the board of public works, or by the mayor. *Bridge tenders.*

BRIDGES.

SECTION 6. Draw or swing bridges, with openings sufficient for the passage of vessels, shall be maintained and supported at the expense of the city, at the following places in said city, to-wit: *Location of draw or swing bridges.*

ACROSS THE MILWAUKEE RIVER.

From Pleasant street, in the First ward, to Dock street, in the Sixth ward;

From Water street, in the First ward, to Cherry street, in the Sixth ward;

From Division street, in the First and Seventh wards, to Chestnut street, in the Second ward;

From Martin street, in the Seventh ward, to State street, in the Second ward;

From Oneida street, in the Seventh ward, to Wells street, in the Fourth ward;

From Wisconsin street, in the Third and Seventh wards, to Grand avenue, in the Fourth ward;

From Michigan street, in the Third ward, to Sycamore street, in the Fourth ward;

From Huron street, in the Third ward, to Clybourn street, in the Fourth ward;

From East Water street, in the Third ward, to Ferry street in the Fifth ward;

From Broadway, in the Third ward, to Lake street in the Fifth ward;

ACROSS THE MENOMONEE RIVER AND CANALS.

From West Water street, in the Fourth ward, to Reed street, in the Fourth ward;

On First avenue, in the Fifth and Eighth wards;

On Sixth street, in the Fourth ward;

On Muskego road, in the Fourth ward;

ACROSS THE SOUTH MENOMONEE CANAL.

On Sixth avenue, in the Eight ward;

ACROSS THE KINNICKINNIC RIVER.

On Clinton street, and on Kinnickinnic avenue, in the Twelfth ward; and

ACROSS THE BAYOU.

In the Sixth ward.

Buffalo street bridge approaches. It shall be the duty of the common council to perfect, as soon as practicable, the arrangement now pending for the conveyance to the city of Milwaukee of a strip of land not less than sixty feet in width, extending from the west dock line of the Milwaukee river, to West Water street, in the Fourth ward, at the point located for the western approach of the bridge proposed to be constructed across said river, from Buffalo street, in said Third ward, to the Fourth ward; and as soon as such strip of land shall

be duly conveyed to said city, the common council shall
proceed to construct and complete a draw or swing bridge,
and to maintain the same, across said river, from said
Buffalo street to the Fourth ward, as provided by chapter
129 of the laws of 1873.

As amended by Section 27, Chapter 324, Laws of 1882, and
Section 1, Chapter 182, Laws of 1889.

SECTION 7. Stationary bridges shall also be main- **Stationary bridges.**
tained at the expense of the city, across the Milwaukee
river, from Racine street, in the first ward, to Humboldt
avenue, in the sixth ward, and on North street, from the
first ward to the sixth ward; also across the Milwaukee
and Rock River Canal, at the foot of Humboldt avenue,
at the foot of Walnut street, and at the foot of Cherry
street, and across the bayou, on Dock street, in the sixth
ward; across Holton's canal, on Canal street, in the
Fourth and Eighth wards; in the valley of the Menomonee
river on the Muskego road, in the Eighth ward; across
the Kinnickinnic river, at the intersection of Clinton
street and Lincoln avenue; and across the old channel of
the Menomonee river, at Canal street, in the Fourth and
Eighth wards.

As amended by Section 27, Chapter 324, Laws of 1882.

In an action against the city for damages in failing to maintain
and repair a bridge which, by its charter, the city is required to
maintain, the complaint must show that the city has sufficient
funds on hand to do the work, which are lawfully applicable
thereto, and must also show that there has been an unreasonable
delay in doing the work. Such delay will not be presumed from
an averment that the city has neglected "for the space of about
one year" to repair the bridge.
Orth vs. Milwaukee, 59 Wis., 336.

SECTION 8. The common council of said city shall **Other swing**
have the power to construct swinging or stationary bridges **bridges may be**
across any of the rivers or canals in the city, in addition **constructed by a**
to those mentioned and provided for in section seven of **two-thirds vote.**
this chapter, whenever in their judgment public conveni-
ence may require the same; provided, that the same
shall be so constructed as not unnecessarily to impede
the navigation of the river or canal over which the same
may be constructed; and provided, further, that the act,
resolution or ordinance for the construction of any such
bridge, shall require for its passage or adoption a vote of

two-thirds of all the members elect of the common council, and shall have no force or validity without such two-thirds vote.

As amended by Section 36, Chapter 144, Laws of 1875.

Board to advertise for plans.

SECTION 9.   Whenever the common council shall, by ordinance or resolution, order the construction of any ·bridge, the board of public works shall have power to advertise for plans, with bids thereon, allowing each and every contractor to present his own plan and bid; also to prepare or procure plans, and to advertise for bids thereon; and the authority is hereby extended to the board of public works to select therefrom such bid and plan as shall seem to them to be the best for the interest of the city, and to report the same, together with all other plans and bids for such bridge, to said council, with their reasons for their choice; and the said council **Council to select and approve plans.** may approve said selection, and order contracts to be entered into accordingly, or may disapprove of the same, and by a vote of two-thirds of the council in favor thereof may select any other of the plans and bids so reported, and direct the board of public works to enter into contract on the same; provided, that no contract shall be entered into under this section without the authority of the council, expressed by ordinance or resolution.

¡Preservation of bridges.

SECTION 10.   The general laws for the preservation of bridges, and the punishment by such laws provided for willful and malicious injuries done thereto, are hereby extended to and shall include all of said bridges, and shall apply to any willful or malicious damage which may be done to either of them, by any person or persons whomsoever; and the common council may from time to time make such by-laws or ordinances as they may deem necessary for the preservation of such bridges, and enforce the same by adequate penalties.   In case of any damage **Prosecution for damages thereto.** being done to any of said bridges, by any vessel or water-craft or by the master, or any person in command thereof, such vessel or water-craft may be proceeded against under the law to provide for the collection of demands against boats and vessels.

CHAPTER 285, LAWS OF 1893.

AN ACT to repeal all acts heretofore passed prohibiting the erection of bridges by cities.

SECTION 1. All those parts of the different city charters of this state, heretofore passed, prohibiting any city from erecting bridges over waters in whole or in part in this state, are hereby repealed.

Cities may build bridges.

CHAPTER X.

WATER WORKS.

SECTION 1. From and after the first day in January, A. D. 1875, or whenever, before that time, the board of water commissioners of said city shall, by resolution, surrender the water works and property now in their charge to the city, and the common council shall consent to accept the same, all the powers, duties and functions of the board of water commissioners of the city of Milwaukee, and of the engineer and assistants, the treasurer and secretary, and all other officers, agents, employes and servants, appointed and employed by said board, shall cease and determine; and said board and its officers, agents, employes and servants, shall on that day, or at the time of such surrender and acceptance, deliver the possession of the water works, and of all property pertaining thereto, and of all their records, contracts, transactions, reports, accounts, surveys, maps, plats, estimates, profiles, plans and documents, of whatsoever nature, to the board of public works, who shall thereupon assume and have the exclusive charge and superintendence, subject to the direction of the common council, of the water works of said city; provided, that the common council may by resolution extend the time herein limited, to such later date as to them may seem best, and the powers, duties and functions of said water commissioners, and of their appointees and employes, shall continue till the expiration of the time so extended.

Surrender of water works to city.

Delivery of property pertaining thereto.

Time may be extended.

SECTION 2. It shall be the duty of said board of public works to examine and consider all matters relative to supplying the city of Milwaukee with a sufficient quantity of pure and wholesome water to be taken from lake Michigan, for the use of its inhabitants.

Water matters.

SECTION 3. The said board shall have power to construct jets and fire hydrants for public use, and

Public hydrants.

fountains at such places in the said city as the said board
with the approval of the common council, shall determine,
and also to lay water pipes in and through all the alleys,
streets and public grounds in the said city, and generally
to do all such work as may be found necessary or
convenient, from time to time, for the purposes of this
chapter.

See Gilman vs. Milwaukee, 61 Wis., 588.

May enter on pre-mises for surveys and examina-tions. SECTION 4. The said board shall have power, by
themselves, their officers, agents and servants, to enter
upon any land or water in the said city for the purpose
of making examinations or surveys in the performance
of their duties under this chapter, without liability
therefor; and said board shall have power with the
approval of the common council, to purchase and acquire
for the said city all real and personal property which may
be necessary for the construction of the works hereby
provided for.

Taking of real estate for use of water works. SECTION 5. Whenever any real estate or any easement therein or use thereof, shall, in the judgment of
said board, be necessary for the construction of the said
works, and for any cause an agreement for the purchase
thereof cannot be made with the owner thereof, they
shall report the same to the common council, and thereupon the said common council shall proceed to take such
real estate, easement or use, as provided in chapter six
of this act in the case of taking lands for public squares,
grounds, streets and alleys, except that no petition or bond
shall be necessary; but all the other provisions of the said
chapter six shall apply to the taking of such real estate,
easement or use, for the construction of such works, so
far as the same may be applicable.

Water works property of city. SECTION 6. All property, real, personal and mixed,
acquired for the construction of said water works,—and
all plans, specifications, diagrams, papers, books and
records connected therewith,—and the said water works
and all buildings, machinery and fixtures appertaining
thereto, shall be the property of the said city of Milwaukee.

Water fund. SECTION 7. There is hereby created for the said city
a separate fund, to be called the water fund. There
shall belong to such fund all bonds and proceeds thereof,
authorized by law to be issued for the construction of

the said water works, all proceeds of all taxes levied for
the construction of the said water works, all water rates
assessed and collected for water proceeding from such
water works, and all other proceeds, revenue and income
of said water works,—and all other moneys and property
in any way derived by the said city in aid of the said
water works, or appropriated by the said common council
toward the same; and the said fund is hereby exclusively
devoted and appropriated to the construction and
maintenance of the said water works—and to the payment
of said water bonds, until the said works shall be
wholly completed and the said bonds wholly paid.
Said water fund shall be kept in the city treasury in the **How kept.**
custody of the city treasurer, and shall be disbursed by
him on vouchers drawn for the same in the manner
provided in this act; and said city treasurer and the sureties
on his official bond shall be liable for the safe keeping
and disbursement thereof. It shall be the duty of the **Special report.**
treasurer of said board of water commissioners to submit
his account of the water funds in his hands on the first
day of January, 1875, or at such time as the water works
shall be surrendered, as provided in section one of this
chapter, and to settle and adjust such accounts with the
city comptroller, and to pay over any balance remaining
in his hands on that day to the city treasurer, to the
credit of the water fund.

SECTION 8. It shall be the duty of the said board of **Quarterly reports.**
public works to report to the common council once in
three months, all their doings under this chapter, and the
state of the said water fund and the general condition of
the said water works; and such reports, after being
submitted to the common council, shall be filed in the
office of the comptroller of the said city.

SECTION 9. It shall be the duty of the comptroller of **Separate account.**
said city to keep separate accounts of all the funds,
receipts, and payments on account of said water works,
and a separate record of all the contracts made by the said
board touching said water works, and of the estimates of
the cost of such contracts, and generally to keep separate
books for the said water fund and water works, as he is
or may be by law required to keep of other property,
funds and interests of the said city.

Control of water
works.

SECTION 10. The said water works, and all the grounds, buildings, fixtures, machinery and other things appertaining thereto, shall be under the control of the said board, who shall have the power to regulate and control and have a general supervision over the same, subject to the authority of the said common council.

The authority of the board of public works to regulate, control and supervise the water works and appurtanances is subject to the authority of the common council.

Gilman vs. Milwaukee, 61 Wis., 588.

Water rules and
regulations.

SECTION 11. The said board shall have power, from time to time, to make and enforce by-laws, rules and regulations, in relation to the said water works, and, before the actual introduction of water, they shall make by-laws, rules and regulations, fixing uniform water rates to be paid for the use of water furnished by the said water works, and fixing the manner of distributing and supplying water for use or consumption, and for with-holding or shutting off the same for cause, and they shall have power, from time to time, to alter, modify, or

To be approved by
council.

repeal such by-laws, rules and regulations; provided, however, that no such by-law, rule or regulation, and no alteration, modification or repeal thereof, shall have any force until submitted to and approved by the said common council.

Collection of water
rates.

SECTION 12. All regular water-rates shall be due and payable on the first days of May and November in each year semi-annually in advance, and metered and measured water-rates shall be due and payable on the first days of January, April, July and October in each year, for the three months preceding such days. To all water-rates remaining unpaid on the twenty-first day of the month in which they become due, the water registrar shall add

Penalty.

a penalty of five per cent. of the amount of such rates, and if such rates shall remain unpaid for ten days there-after, he shall forthwith report the same to the city engineer who shall cause the water to be shut off the premises so reported, subject to the payment of such delinquent rates, and in all cases where the supply of water shall be shut off as above provided, the said city engineer shall not cause the water to be again turned on to said premises until the said water registrar shall duly certify to him, that all delinquent rates and penalties,

and the sum of two dollars as expenses for turning the
water off and on, shall have been paid.   Whenever two
or more dwellings or tenements or buildings are connected
with a street main by one pipe only, the owner or owners
of such premises shall provide a separate cut-off for each
of said dwellings, tenements or buildings in such locality
as the board of public works shall deem most efficient
and expedient, and all such cut-offs shall be conveniently
accessible to and shall be controlled exclusively by the
proper officer of the water department.   Said water
registrar shall, on or before each day when such rates
become due and payable as aforesaid, cause a written or
printed notice to be mailed or personally delivered to the
owner or occupant of all premises subject to the payment
of water-rates, directed to the place where such water is
consumed, stating the amount due, the time when and
the place where such rates can be paid, and the penalty
of neglect of payment.   All water-rates for water furnished
to any building or premises shall be a lien on the lot, part **Shall be a lien on property.**
of lot, or parcel of land on which such building or
premises shall be situated.   If any water-rates or
fractional parts thereof remain unpaid on the first day of
October in any year, the same shall be certified by said
water registrar to the city comptroller on or before the
first day of November next following, and shall be by
him placed upon the tax roll and collected in the same
manner as other taxes on real estate are collected in said
city.   The charge of water supplied by the city in all
premises where meters are or shall be attached and
connected, shall be at rates fixed by the board of public
works with the approval of the common council; if in
any case the water registrar shall determine that the
quantity indicated by the meter is materially incorrect,
then in such case the said water registrar in conjunction
with the board of public works, shall determine in the
best manner in their power the quantity used, and such
determination shall be conclusive; no water-rate or rates
duly assessed by said water registrar against any property
shall be thereafter remitted or changed except by the
common council of said city.

As amended by Section 2, Chapter 258, Laws of 1889; also
amended by Section 6, Chapter 311, Laws of 1876, and Section 29,
Chapter 324, Laws of 1882.

SECTION 13. Any person, who shall wilfully pollute
or otherwise injure any water supplied by the said water
works, in any tunnel, aqueduct, reservoir, pipe or other
thing, or shall wilfully injure the said water works, or
any building, machinery or fixtures appertaining thereto,
or shall wilfully, and without authority of the said board,
impede or derange the flow of water in any tunnel,
aqueduct, pipe or other thing belonging to the said water
works, or shall wilfully and without authority of the said
board, bore or otherwise cause to leak, any tunnel, aqueduct, reservoir, pipe or other thing used in the said water
works for holding, conveying or distributing water, shall
be deemed guilty of a misdemeanor, and upon conviction
thereof, shall be punished by a fine not exceeding one
thousand dollars; or by imprisonment for a term not
exceeding two years, or by both such fine and imprisonment, in the discretion of the court.

SECTION 14. It shall be the duty of the said common
council, and they are hereby empowered, from time to
time, to pass such ordinances as may be deemed necessary
or expedient to protect said water works and the use
thereof, and to enforce the by-laws, rules and regulations
of the said board of public works.

SECTION 15. The board of public works for the city of
Milwaukee, before laying water pipe along a street, alley,
or other line in said city, shall assess against the several
lots, parts of lots or parcels of land which may front or
abut on the proposed line of water pipe, or which may
be contiguous to and used in connection with any lot or
parcel of land so fronting and abutting, the amounts
which the said several lots, parts of lots or parcels of
land may, in the judgment of the said board, be specially
benefited by reason of laying such water pipe, not to
exceed, however, the amount prescribed in the next
section; provided, that no lot, parcel of land or part
thereof, shall be subjected to the payment of more than
one assessment for water pipe laid in the same street or
alley.

As amended by Section 30, Chapter 324, Laws of 1882, and
Section 58, Chapter 324, Laws of 1882, which repealed Section 1,
Chapter 268, Laws of 1880.

See Gilman vs. Milwaukee, 61 Wis., 588.

SECTION 16.   A regular lot (not corner) which may   Assessment for
front or abut on the line of water pipe, shall be assessed   minor water pipe.
an amount equal to one-half of the cost, as estimated by
the said board of public works, of furnishing and laying
a regular minor water pipe of approved materials and
manufacture, with the required openings for connections
with private service water pipe along the front of such lot,
such minor pipe to be not less than four nor more than
six inches in diameter, as the said board may determine.
Every irregular lot, part of lot, or other parcel of land   Irregular lots.
fronting or abutting on such line of water pipe, and likewise any parcel of land, or lot, which shall be contiguous
to any parcel of land, or lot, or part of lot so fronting or
abutting, and which in the judgment of the said board is
or may be most advantageously used in connection therewith, shall be assessed for such water pipe the amount
which, in the judgment of said board, shall be as nearly
as may be in just proportion to the amount assessed for
regular lots as compared with the special benefits derived
by each from the laying of the said water pipe.

As amended by Section 31, Chapter 324, Laws of 1882, and
Section 58, Chapter 324, Laws of 1882, which repealed Section
2, Chapter 268, Laws of 1880.

It is not a voluntary payment where one pays the entire cost
of laying water pipe, not knowing what the actual cost was, but
acting under the belief induced by fraudulent representations of
city officers that she was being charged only half cost.

Harrison vs. Milwaukee, 49 Wis., 247.

See Gilman vs. Milwaukee, 61 Wis., 588.

SECTION 17.   Every corner lot, and every lot, part of   Corner lot assess-
lot or parcel of land, which may front or abut on more   ments.
than one street on which a line of water pipe shall be
proposed to be laid, shall be assessed for every such
line of water pipe; but the aggregate of the assessment
therefor on any such lot or parcel of land, shall be as
nearly as may be in just proportion to the amount
assessed for regular lots, as compared with the special
benefits derived by them respectively, from the laying
of such water pipe; and in making such assessment, the
said board shall take into consideration the situation of
such lot or parcel of land, with respect to its different
fronts and all subdivisions thereof by sale, contract, use
or occupation in severalty and may assess subdivisions
separately; and may also assess any subdivision of

May assess subdivision of corner lots. such lot or parcel of land in connection with any other part of such lot or other lot or land contiguous thereto and most advantageously used in connection therewith.

As amended by Section 32, Chapter 324, Laws of 1882, and Section 58, Chapter 324, Laws of 1882, which repealed Section 3, Chapter 268, Laws of 1880.

Apportionment to such subdivision. SECTION 18. Whenever any lot or parcel of land shall be subdivided by sale or contract, or by use or occupation in severalty, whether such subdivision shall occur before or after the assessment of special benefits as herein provided, the said board of public works may, after ascertaining such fact, at any time before the sale of such lot for the non-payment of the assessment, make an equitable apportionment of the benefit tax against such lot or parcel of land, among the different subdivisions thereof.

Report of such assessment to be filed, and published. SECTION 19. The said board of public works shall file reports of such assessments with the comptroller, who shall record the same in a book to be kept for that purpose, and give notice thereof to the parties interested, by publishing the same for three successive days in the official papers. Any person feeling himself aggrieved by the report of said board, may, within twenty days after the completion of the publication of notice by the comptroller, appeal from such report to the **Appeals, how taken and conducted.** circuit court of Milwaukee county. Such appeal shall be entered and conducted in like manner, and like security for costs shall be required as provided by law in cases of appeals from the decision of the common council of said city to said court, on the returns of assessments of benefits for street improvements. In the making and signing of all reports or returns, under this chapter, by the said board of public works to the comptroller or any other officer of said city, the official signatures of the president and secretary of said board shall be sufficient.

The remedy by appeal within twenty days is not exclusive, so as to prevent recovery by action, of the excess paid in ignorance of facts through fraudulent misrepresentations of municipal officers.

Harrison vs. Milwaukee, 49 Wis., 247.

Comptroller shall keep record of assessments. SECTION 20. The said board of public works shall, from time to time, make reports to the comptroller of all work done, for which assessments shall have been made,

as hereinbefore provided, and the comptroller shall file
such reports, and enter the same in his book of records
of assessments; and of all assessments for work so
reported to have been done, the comptroller shall, if
possible, make certified returns to the city clerk, in time
to have the same included in the tax levy for the current
year; and the same shall be entered on the tax roll in a   To be entered on
separate column, under the head of "water pipe assess-   tax roll as "water
pipe assess-
ments;" and the same shall be collected, and the payment   ments."
thereof shall be enforced by sale, deed, and other
proceedings, in like manner as is now provided by law
in cases of assessments for street improvements. No
certificates shall be issued by the comptroller for such
assessments, but all such assessments, and the proceeds
thereof, when collected, shall belong to the fund for the
construction of water works, and shall be credited to
said fund on the books of the comptroller and treasnrer
of said city.

SECTION 21. On the third Tuesday of April, 1890,   Water registrar,
and every three years thereafter, the mayor of the city of   duties and
powers.
Milwaukee shall appoint, subject to the confirmation of
the common council, a proper person to be the water
registrar of said city, who shall hold his office for three
years and until his successor is appointed and has
qualified. Said water registrar shall receive an annual
salary of twenty-five hundred dollars from the time he
enters upon his duties. Said water registrar shall have
authority to collect and receive all water-rates in said
department, and shall have charge of all books and papers
relating to the assessment and collection of water-rates,
and shall cause the water-rates to be duly assessed and
listed, and shall also keep proper books of account of the
business of his said office and shall account to and pay
over to the city treasurer of said city daily, all moneys
which may come into his hands by virue of the provisions
of law relating to said office. Said water registrar shall
appoint, subject to the confirmation of the common
council, all subordinate officers in his said department,
and he may require such subordinate officers to give
reasonable bonds for the faithful discharge of their official
duties. Said water registrar shall before entering upon
his official duties prescribed in this act, take the oath of
office required of other city officers by the charter of said
city, and shall also execute a bond to the city of

Milwaukee, with sufficient sureties, to be approved by the mayor and comptroller, in the penal sum of twenty thousand dollars, conditioned that he will faithfully discharge his duties of his said office, and account to and pay over to the city treasurer of said city, as required by law, all moneys which may come into his hands by virtue of said office.   The water registrar shall file with said comptroller on the first day of May and November in each year, a report containing a statement of the amount of assessments for the succeeding six months, stating the amount of each and every bill issued by him, also a statement of the amounts received by him for regular water-rates in each ward during the six months preceding said days, and of any and all changes made in the assessment for said period, and of all amount of regular water-rates uncollected during such period; also a separate statement of all the metered and measured water-rates collected by him during the preceding six months, and of the amounts of water-rates remaining uncollected at such time, and of all penalties and other moneys that may have been received by him.   He shall also on the first day of each month furnish to the city engineer a statement of the amount of money received by him during the preceding month.   The present collector of water-rates of said city of Milwaukee shall, from and after the passage and publication of this act, exercise and hold the office of water-registrar of the water department of said city under the provisions of this act, and receive the compensation hereinbefore provided, until his successor shall be appointed and have qualified as provided in this section.

As enacted by Section 33, Chapter 324, Laws of 1882, and amended by Section 1, Chapter 258, Laws of 1889.

Water permits may be granted to National Home for disabled soldiers.   SECTION 22.   It shall be lawful for the board of public works of the city of Milwaukee, subject to the approval of the common council of said city, to issue a permit to the county of Milwaukee, national home for disabled soldiers, or any other party, to obtain water from the water works in the said city for use outside of the limits of said city; and for that purpose to connect any pipe that shall be laid outside of the city limits with any water pipe in said city: provided, however, that no such permit shall be issued until the party making application therefor shall first file with the board of public works a bond in such sum and with such surety as the said board shall

approve, conditioned that the said party will obey all rules
and regulations that may from time to time be prescribed
by the board of public works for the use of such water,
that he will pay all charges fixed by said board for the
use of such water as measured by a meter to be approved
by said board, which charges shall not be less than one-
quarter more than that charged to the inhabitants of the
city for like use of water; and further, that he will pay
the city of Milwaukee all damages whatever that it may
sustain, arising in any way out of the manner in which
such connection is made or water supplied is used.   In
case of granting a permit to the county of Milwaukee or
to the national home for disabled soldiers, the board of
public works may waive the giving of such a bond.
Every such permit shall be issued upon the understanding
that the city of Milwaukee shall in no event ever be liable
for any damage in case of failure to supply water; and it
shall be lawful for the said board of public works, at any
time to cancel such permit, to cut off the supply of water
and break such connection when in their judgment the
interests of the city shall require; and in case the party
to whom such permit shall have been granted, shall
refuse or neglect to obey the rules and regulations
prescribed by said board for the use of such water, or in
case the common council of the said city shall so direct,
it shall be the duty of the said board to do so.

As enacted by Chapter 54, Laws of 1887, approved March 16,
1887.

SECTION 22. The board of public works, with the
approval of the common council, may require the attaching and connecting of water-meters to all service pipes
supplying water from the city water works to hydraulic
elevators or to manufactories and other places of
business where water is used for manufacturing or
other purposes, and the board, with the approval of the
common council, may prescribe and regulate the kind of
water meters to be used in said city and the manner
of attaching and connecting the same, and may in like
manner make such other rules for the use and control
of water meters attached and connected as herein provided
as shall be necessary to secure reliable and just measure-
ment of the quality of water used for any such elevator
or manufactory or other business place; and may alter
and amend such rules from time to time, as shall

Board of public works may require water meters to be attached to service pipes, when.

be necessary for the purpose named; provided, that
all such rules and all amendments and alterations
thereof, shall be approved by the common council before
the same shall have effect. If the owner or occupant
of any premises, where the attaching and connection
of a water meter may lawfully be required, shall
neglect or fail to attach and connect such water meter,
as is required according to the rules of the board, for
thirty days after the expiration of the time in which
such owner or occupant shall have been notified by said
board to attach and connect such meter, said board may
cause the water supply by the city to be cut off from the
premises, and it shall not be restored except upon such
terms and conditions as the board, with the approval of
the common council, shall prescribe. The charge for
water supplied by the city in all premises where meters
are or shall be attached and connected shall be at rates
fixed by the board with the approval of the council, and
for the quantity indicated by the meter, unless in any
case the board shall determine that the quantity indicated
by the meter is materially incorrect, and in such
case the board shall determine in the best way in their
power the quantity used, and such determination shall
be conclusive.

As enacted by Chapter 463, Laws of 1887, approved April
13th, 1887.

**May make rules
and regulations
for ventilating
and trapping
drains, etc.**

SECTION 23. The board of public works with the
approval of the common council, may also make rules
and regulations for the proper ventilating and trapping
of all drains, soil-pipes and fixtures hereafter constructed
to connect with or be used in connection with the sewerage
or water supply of the city, and the common council
may provide by ordinance for the enforcement of
such rules and regulations, and may prescribe proper
penalties and punishment for disobedience of the same.
The board of public works, with the approval of the
common council, may also make rules to regulate the
use of vent, soil, drain, sewer and water pipes in all
buildings in said city, which hereafter shall be proposed
to be connected with the city water supply or sewerage,
specifying the dimensions, strength and material of
which the same shall be made, and which may prohibit
the introduction into any building of any style of water
fixture, trap or connection, the use of which shall have

been determined to be dangerous to health or for any reason unfit to be used, and the board shall require a rigid inspection by a skilled and competent inspector under the direction of the board, of all plumbing and draining work, and water and sewer connections hereafter done or made in any building in the city, and unless the same are done or made, and made according to the rules of the board and approved by the board, no connection of the premises with the city sewerage or water supply shall be allowed.

As enacted by Chapter 463, Laws of 1887.

CHAPTER 90, LAWS OF 1891.

SECTION 1. The common council of the city of Milwaukee is hereby authorized to provide by ordinance for the issue of corporate bonds of said city not exceeding in amount one hundred thousand dollars, payable in not more than twenty years after date of said issue. Said bonds shall bear interest not exceeding the rate of five per cent. per annum, and shall be known as and called "city water bonds," and shall be issued to provide funds for the extension of the system of water works in said city. Provided, that not more than fifty thousand dollars worth of said bonds shall be issued in the year 1891, and not more than fifty thousand dollars worth of said bonds shall be issued in the year 1892. *Common council may issue bonds.*

SECTION 2. All bonds issued under the provisions of this act, shall be signed by the mayor and clerk of said city, countersigned by the comptroller of said city, attested by the commissioners of public debt of said city, sealed with the corporate seal of said city, made payable in lawful money of the United States of America in the city of Milwaukee or New York, and shall each be for the principal sum of one thousand dollars, or five hundred dollars, or one hundred dollars, and shall have attached thereto interest coupons or warrants for the semi-annual payment of interest thereon and such bonds and coupons shall be numbered in the form and manner to be designated by said comptroller. *How issued.*

SECTION 3. Bonds issued under the provisions of this act shall be issued from time to time, in such amount as the common council of said city may determine upon; said bonds when issued and properly signed and sealed, shall be delivered to the commissioners of public debt of said city, and by that body disposed of; the proceeds arising therefrom to be paid into the treasury of said city, and such proceeds shall constitute a separate and distinct fund, to be exclusively applied for the purposes specified in the first section of this act. *How disposed of.*

SECTION 4. The office of commissioners of public debt of said city shall not be abolished while any bonds issued under the provisions of this act remain outstanding and unpaid. *Office of commissioners of public debt not to be abolished.*

Certain sections of chapter 87, laws of 1861, made a part of this act.

SECTION 5.   The provisions of sections 2, 6, 7, 8, 9, 10, 11 and 17, chapter 87, of the laws of 1861 applicable and not inconsistent with the provisions of this act, shall apply to bonds issued under the provisions of this act and such sections, if not inconsistent, are incorporated as a part of this act.   The true intent and meaning of this act is to provide for the present issue of bonds in the same manner as bonds issued under the provisions of that act are provided for, unless the common council upon the recommendation of the commissioners of public debt shall elect by ordinance to specify, what particular bonds shall expire and be retired in each year not less than five per cent. of the whole issue, and said common council is hereby authorized to so elect.

Tax to be levied to pay interest and principal of bonds.

SECTION 6.   The common council of said city shall annually cause a tax to be levied upon all taxable property in said city, both personal and real, for the payment of the annual interest on all unpaid bonds issued under the provisions of this act, and for twenty years before the principal of said bonds becomes due, the said common council shall annually cause a tax to be levied upon all taxable property, both personal and real, equal in amount to five per cent. of all bonds issued and outstanding under the provisions of this act, for a sinking fund to redeem such bonds as the said commissioners of public debt direct to be cancelled or which shall have matured.

Bonds to be cancelled.

SECTION 7.   As soon as a sinking fund shall have been collected and set aside, the said commissioners of public debt shall proceed to cancel bonds in amount equal to the sinking fund so provided.

Same.

SECTION 8.   All bonds directed to be paid by said commissioners of public debt shall be, when paid, stamped, "cancelled," and when so stamped shall be delivered to the common council of said city and by that body publicly declared cancelled.

Bonds not to be sold for less than par value.

SECTION 9.   The commissioners of public debt of said city are hereby prohibited from selling or otherwise disposing of any such bonds at a less valuation than par, that is to say, at less than the principal of said bonds, together with the accrued interest thereon, and said commissioners of public debt are further prohibited from issuing bonds under the provisions of this act, which, together with the bonds heretofore issued, shall exceed the limit of the bonded indebtedness of said city.

CHAPTER 182, LAWS OF 1895.

AN ACT in relation to municipal ownership or control of water-works and lighting works.

Cities may lease or purchase water works or lighting works, how.

SECTION 1.   Any city, when authorized so to do by ordinance adopted by a vote, in favor of the same, of a majority of all the members elect of its common council, after the same has been submitted to a vote of the people and a majority have voted in favor of such purchase or lease, may purchase or lease the water-works or lighting works, or both, owned by any corporation in such city and having a contract with such city for public service, or purchase or lease the interest of such corporation in such works, or obtain the control of such works by purchasing the stock of such corporation and keeping up its organization, and in any such case such council, by majority vote, may provide for the payment for such purchase by the issuance of bonds or otherwise in such manner as the common council of such city may deem for its best interests, not contravening, however, the provisions of the constitution in respect to municipal indebtedness; and in such case such city shall provide, by appropriate ordinances for a non-partisan management of such works, and to that end, may create a board of commissioners, to be non-partisan and elected by the common council, fix the term of office of the members thereof, and invest such board with appropriate powers. Provided the authority hereby granted shall extend only to the purchase 'or lease of water works or lighting works already erected and established and in operation and only to cities in which there exists one such system for such purpose or purposes.

SECTION 2. All acts and parts of acts so far as they conflict with the provisions of this act, are hereby repealed.

CHAPTER XI.

PUBLIC DEBT.

SECTION 1. There shall be in the city of Milwaukee a board composed of three persons, who shall be residents of said city, shall be styled "commissioners of the public debt," shall be appointed by the mayor, with the approval of the common council, and shall respectively hold the office for the term of three years, and till their successors are appointed and qualified. Each of the present commissioners of the public debt of said city shall continue to hold his office until the expiration of the term for which he was appointed, and until his successor is appointed and qualified. The mayor shall, within one month after the expiration of the term of any commissioner, appoint his successor, and within one month after any vacancy shall occur by death, resignation, or otherwise, shall appoint some person to fill the vacant office for the unexpired term, all such appointments being subject to the approval of the common council.

Commissioners of public debt.

Appointments, how made; vacancies, how filled.

SECTION 2. The commissioners of the public debt shall fix their own times of meeting, and the mode of calling their meetings. The action of a majority of them shall be deemed the action of the commissioners. They shall transact all their business at the office of the comp-

Transaction of business.

troller, and that officer shall be ex-officio the secretary of the commissioners and shall preserve a full record of all their proceedings.

Duties of commissioners.

SECTION 3.   It shall be the duty of the commissioners of the public debt to superintend the execution, issue, and use of all bonds issued or to be issued by the city, and the levy, collection and disbursement of the taxes provided for by law for the interest upon such bonds and for the sinking fund for the payment of the principal thereof, and to perform such other services and duties in respect to the same as are or may be prescribed by law.

All city bonds hereafter issued to be attested by commissioners of public debt.

SECTION 4.   All bonds hereafter issued by said city shall be numbered consecutively in such manner as the common council may by ordinance prescribe, shall be signed by the mayor and clerk, sealed with the corporate seal, countersigned by the comptroller, and attested by the commissioners of the public debt of the said city, and

Face of bonds shall show, etc.

each and every bond issued shall show on its face for what purpose, and by authority of what law it was issued, and shall have plainly engraved or printed in figures, on some convenient place thereon, a statement of the several amounts of the assessed value of the taxable property in the city of Milwaukee, for the five several years next preceding the issue of such bonds, and also of the principal sum of the bonded debt of the said city of Milwaukee, issued and yet outstanding—exclusive of the bonds heretofore issued by the said city to railroad companies—specifying severally the amount of each issue of such bonds, including the issue of which the bonds bearing such statement shall be a part.

Account of city bonds to be kept.

SECTION 5.   An accurate account shall be kept by the comptroller, or by such other officer as may be appointed by law for that purpose, of the issue of all the bonds by the said city, of their numbers, dates and amounts, of the dates of payment of interest and principal thereon, and of the particular purpose for which each bond is issued.   All bonds issued by the said city shall be negotiated and disposed of by the said commissioners of the public debt, and such bonds, and the proceeds thereof, shall be used solely and only for the purposes defined in the law authorizing their issue, and in amount shall not exceed the limits fixed by law for the respective purposes so defined. The commissioners of the public debt shall from time to time, or when requested by the common council, report to the common council of the said city the sale or other disposition of any city bonds issued by said city.

Commissioners of public debt shall negotiate all city bonds.

SECTION 6. The principal of the aggregate funded debt of the city of Milwaukee, exclusive of bonds heretofore issued to railroad companies, and bonds which may be issued in settlement and liquidition thereof, shall never exceed a sum equal to five per centum on the amount of the assessed value of the taxable property in the said city, which value shall be ascertained and determined by the average annual amount of the assessment rolls thereof for the next preceding five years, and all bonds hereafter issued by said city shall contain a covenant to that effect, and all bonds, notes or other evidences of debt, payable at a future day, which shall be issued by the said city contrary to this section, and in excess of the limitation herein prescribed, either with or without statutory authority, shall be void; provided, that the foregoing limitation shall not apply to or include orders drawn upon the city treasurer, payable out of the revenues of the current year, nor to the certificates or scrip issued or authorized to be issued by said city, by and under section three of chapter two hundred and fifty-one of the laws of 1873, for the settlement and payment of its bonds, heretofore issued to certain railroad companies; and provided, further, that the common council may, as provided in chapter seventeen of this act, borrow money to be paid out of the revenues of the current year. If in any case, the city, or any city officer shall hereafter threaten or attempt to issue any such bonds, notes, or other evidences of debt, in contravention of the provisions of this section, they shall be restrained by injunction from so doing, upon the application of any holder of bonds of the said city, or of any citizen who shall have paid city taxes in said city for two years then next preceding.

Aggregate funded debt limited.

Bonds void when limit exceeded.

City orders and scrip excepted.

Officers may be restrained from issuing excess.

Where bonds for $100,000 are authorized to be issued, the proceeds to be used in constructing a harbor, a contract providing for a greater expenditure is void as to the excess; and subsequent ratification of such contract by the legislature, without the assent of the corporation, will not make the contract valid.

Hasbrouck vs. Milwaukee, 13 Wis., 42.

SECTION 7. A tax upon all of the taxable property, real and personal, in the said city shall be annually levied and collected, at the same time, and in the same manner as other taxes are levied and collected in said city, sufficient in amount for the following purposes, to-wit: to pay the interest and provide for the sinking fund upon the bonds and scrip authorized by and issued under sections 1 and 3 of an act entitled "an act to enable the city of Milwaukee to readjust its corporate debts," approved March 19, 1861, as stipulated and provided in and by section 4 of the same act. Also to pay the annual interest, and to provide the sinking fund upon all bonds of the said city, issued or to be issued to provide means for the construction of water works for said city, or for other purposes, under and in accordance with the provisions of chapter 406 of the private and local laws of 1871, entitled "an act authorizing the city of Milwaukee to issue bonds," approved March 23, 1871, and the several acts amendatory thereof, as specially stipulated and provided in and by section 11 of said chapter 406. Also to pay the interest on all other bonds of said city, issued, or that may be issued under legal authority, and outstanding according to the terms thereof, and to provide a sinking fund equal to not less than five per centum each year of the principal of such bonds actually issued for the payment of such principal; provided, that this section shall not include or apply to any bonds heretofore issued by said city to any railroad company or companies. The common council shall, on or before the first day of October in each year, determine by resolution the amount of the net revenue or income of the said water works, over and above the expenses thereof, which shall be appropriated and applied to the payment of interest on the said water bonds or to the sinking fund for the payment of the principal thereof, and the amount of such net revenue or income so appropriated in and for any year to the fund for the payment of such interest, or to such sinking fund, may be deducted from the amount of tax to be levied in that year for the payment of the principal or interest of such water bonds.

As amended by Section 34, Chapter 324, Laws of 1882.

SECTION 8. The commissioners of the public debt shall, at least ten days before the levy of general city taxes in each year, certify to the common council the amounts necessary to be levied that year for the interest and sinking funds, on bonds and scrip of the said city. It shall be the duty of the common council to levy the tax for interest and sinking funds in this act provided for, to the amount so certified by the said commissioners, at the same time in each year that the common council levy the tax for general city purposes; and if they refuse or neglect so to levy in any case for five days after the levy of the tax for general city purposes, the commissioners of the public debt shall levy the same, and certify the amount thereof forthwith to the city clerk; and if the commissioners of the public debt should likewise fail to levy such tax for interest and sinking funds within ten days after the levy of the general city taxes in any year, then the judge of any court of record in Milwaukee county, either in term time or vacation, either in open court or at chambers, may, upon summary application of any holder or holders of bonds of the said city, other than bonds heretofore issued to any railroad company, to the amount of ten thousand dollars or more, by order, levy such tax to such amount as he shall deem necessary, and certify the amount thereof to the city clerk, who shall in all cases cause such tax, however levied, to be extended upon the tax roll in like manner as other taxes levied by the common council, but in a separate column, suitably marked, to distinguish the same. And it shall be the duty of the city treasurer, or other collector of taxes, to proceed to collect and enforce such tax in the same manner as other general city taxes are collected and enforced by law. In fixing the amount of the treasurer's bond, at the beginning of his term of office, the fact that he has to collect this tax for interest and sinking funds shall be taken into consideration.

Commissioners of public debt shall annually certify amount necessary to raise tax, and council shall order it levied.

In default, judge of any court of record may order tax levied.

To be enforced and collected as other taxes.

SECTION 9. Money only shall be received by the treasurer or other collecting officer in payment of said tax for interest and sinking funds, and the same shall be kept in and disbursed from the treasury strictly as a separate and distinct fund, not subject to the order of the common council, and shall be paid out only upon orders signed by the mayor, countersigned by the comptroller and approved in writing by a majority of the commissioners of the public debt and specifying the purpose for which they are drawn; and such money shall be

Money only to be received in payment of such taxes.

Money to be used for no other purpose.

drawn out only for the purpose of paying interest on the bonds and scrip provided for by section seven of this chapter, and for retiring such bonds and scrip in the manner hereinafter provided.

City shall purchase.

SECTION 10. If upon the sale of any property for delinquent taxes the city shall become the purchaser, it shall appropriate and add to the fund raised for interest and sinking funds, a sum equal to the amount of such delinquent tax which was levied for interest and sinking funds out of the first moneys which shall be in or come into the treasury from any source whatever.

City treasurer to report condition of interest and sinking funds.

SECTION 11. The city treasurer shall every year, immediately after the sale of land for delinquent taxes, and whenever else he shall be thereto requested by the commissioners of the public debt, in addition to any other report which he shall be required by law to make, report to said commissioners the condition of the interest and sinking funds, embracing a statement of all sums collected and held or disbursed by him for those funds, and no settlement by the treasurer with the common council as to those funds shall be of any validity unless confirmed by said commissioners.

Commissioners of public debt to advertise for proposals for retirement and cancelation of scrip or bonds.

SECTION 12. Once in each year, immediately after the coming of the report mentioned in the last section, the commissioners of the public debt shall cause notice to be given by the comptroller, or otherwise by publication in one daily newspaper printed in the city of New York, and one daily newspaper printed in the city of Milwaukee, each of general circulation, for twenty days at least, of the time and place of receiving bids or proposals from bondholders or scripholders to surrender their bonds or scrip for cancellation on payment out of the sinking fund applicable thereto, the manner of directing such proposals, and such other things as the commissioners shall direct to be inserted in such notice.

Proposals how received and opened.

The proposals received shall be opened by the commissioners of the public debt, in the presence of the mayor and such other persons as shall choose to attend; and the lowest rates offered, provided the same be at or below par, shall be accepted to the extent of the fund on hand to pay the same at those rates; and the bonds or scrip so offered at the lowest rates, shall be paid at those rates on being surrendered for cancellation. When the funds shall not be sufficient to pay all the bonds and scrip which are offered at equal rates and lower than all others, the commissioners shall select at once, and publicly, as aforesaid, among such bonds and scrip, by lot, so many as they shall have the means to pay. In case any parties, whose proposals shall be accepted, shall not, within such reasonable time as the commissioners, with the approval of the mayor, shall fix, surrender their bonds or scrip, the commissioners may, with the approval in writing of the mayor, accept the next best proposal, provided they are below par, or they may advertise and proceed throughout anew, in the manner provided in this section. and so in like manner again and again, as often as the last named contingency shall arise.   All bids or proposals by bondholders or scripholders, under this section, shall particularly specify the numbers of the bonds or scrip so proposed to be retired, and shall be accompanied by a certificate in each case, of the president or cashier of some reputable bank, or some person, in either case to be approved by the commissioners of the public debt, to the effect that the bonds or scrip specified in such bid are all deposited in such bank, or with such person, and will be delivered up for cancellation if such bid shall be accepted by the commissioners.

May advertise anew.

What bids shall specify.

SECTION 13.   In any case when no proposals, or not sufficient in amount to consume the moneys on hand belonging to the sinking funds, shall be received to retire bonds or scrip at or below par, the commissioners may advertise and proceed throughout again, as provided in the last section above, or with the approval of the mayor, shall in their discretion determine by lot, publicly as aforesaid, which bond or bonds, or scrip, shall be paid out of the moneys then in the sinking fund provided therefor, at par, including interest, and shall notify the holders of their readiness to pay the same, by advertisement for twenty days in one daily newspaper printed in the city of New York, and one daily newspaper printed in the city of Milwaukee, each of general circulation, and from the time of the completion of such notice in both papers, such bonds or scrip so determined by lot, shall cease to bear interest, unless the city shall neglect to pay the same for ten days after payment thereof shall afterwards be demanded; and the money shall be kept constantly on hand by the treasurer, to pay the same on

What proposals insufficient.

Interest on bonds or scrip to cease, when.

presentment, unless the commissioners of the public debt, with the approval of the mayor, shall otherwise order.

Sinking fund money to be a trust fund.

SECTION 14.   The moneys levied and collected for, or belonging to the interest and sinking funds, shall be held in trust for those purposes only, or for the benefit of the holders of the bonds of the different issues or classes for which such funds are specially provided, and shall in no way be diverted from the specific purposes for which they are provided; nor shall the same, or any part thereof, be subject to attachment or execution, or be liable by any process or proceeding, to be subject to the payment of any other debt than that to meet which they were specially raised or appropriated under this act.

Cancellation.

SECTION 15.   All bonds and interest coupons, paid or otherwise retired, shall be forthwith marked cancelled, by the commissioners of the public debt, and by them returned to the common council of the said city, who shall forthwith publicly cancel the same.

NOTE.—As to constitutionality of certain legislation authorizing issuance of bonds, consult Johnson vs. Milwaukee, 88 Wis., 383.

CHAPTER XII.
PUBLIC SCHOOLS.

School board, how elected, term of office, etc.

SECTION 1.   The public schools of the city of Milwaukee shall be under the general management, control and supervision of a school board, consisting of two persons from each ward, to be appointed by the aldermen of such ward, subject to confirmation by the common council. The members of said board shall hold their offices for three years unless sooner removed; provided, that the present school commissioners shall remain in office for the terms for which they have been elected respectively.

President, how elected.

A president shall be elected by said board, who shall be a member thereof, and in his absence shall elect a president for the time.   The seat of any member shall be declared vacant and the common council shall proceed to choose a successor to any member who shall be reported to the common council as having been absent for four successive meetings of the school board without a satisfactory excuse.

SECTION 2.   The members of the school board shall take the official oath, and be subject to all the restrictions, disabilities, liabilities, punishments and limitations prescribed by the law as to the aldermen in said city of Milwaukee, and they shall be exempt from jury duty. The council may remove any member of the board for causes for which aldermen are removable. The school board shall not in any one year contract any debt or incur any expense greater than the amount of the school funds subject to their order, without any previous ordinance or resolution of the common council. A majority of the members of the board who have duly qualified shall constitute a quorum for the transaction of business, but a smaller number may adjourn.

SECTION 3. The school board of the city of Milwau- kee is hereby authorized and required, subject to the approval of the common council, to establish and organize so many public or common schools in addition to those already established in said city, as may be necessary for the accomodation of the children of the city entitled by the constitution and laws of this state to instruction therein; and the common council shall erect, purchase, hire or lease buildings and furniture, and lots for the accommodation of such schools, and the high schools of said city, and shall improve and enlarge such school buildings. The school board shall also have power to establish and define, from time to time, the boundaries of all common school districts, in the city in such manner as they may deem best calculated to promote the interests of the schools. The school board shall also have power to employ all janitors necessary in the school houses, and to fix their compensation.

SECTION 4. The school houses now erected, and the lots on which they are situated, and the lots now or hereafter purchased for school purposes, and the school houses thereon erected, shall be the property of the city; and no lot shall be purchased or leased, nor shall any school house be erected, without an ordinance or resolution duly passed by the common council. Deeds of conveyance and leases shall be made to the city of Milwaukee.

SECTION 5. The school board shall have power to adopt for use in the several public schools in the city suitable text books which shall be uniform, and when the school board shall have adopted for use in the public

Discipline and
management of
schools.

schools of the city any text-book, or text-books, the
same shall not be changed by the board for five years
next thereafter; and the school board shall require that
the system of instruction in the several public schools of
the city shall be as nearly uniform as possible.

And shall adopt, at their discretion, modify or repeal
by-laws, rules and regulations for their own government,
and for the organization, discipline and management of
the public schools of said city, and generally adopt such
measures as shall promote the good order and public
utility of the said schools; provided, that such by-laws,
rules and regulations shall not conflict with the constitution and laws of the state.

Superintendent of
schools.

SECTION 6. The school board shall biennially elect by
ballot on the first Tuesday in March, a person of suitable
learning and experience in the art of instruction and
practical familiarity with the most approved methods of
organizing and conducting a system of public schools, for
superintendent of schools, and he shall hold his office for
two years, or until his successor is elected, unless sooner
removed.

His powers and
duties.

The superintendent of schools shall, under direction of
the school board, have a general supervision of the public
schools of the city and the manner of conducting and
grading them, of the teachers, and in connection with a
committee of the board, of the purchase of school
apparatus. He shall, in connection with a committee of
the board, and subject to confirmation by the board,
examine, employ, certificate and classify and transfer
teachers. He shall, also in connection with a committee
of the board and subject to confirmation by the board,
dismiss them for incompetency or inattention to duty, and
he shall do and perform all such other duties as may be
required by the board; provided, that in case of disagreement between himself and a committee, the school board
may determine the matter by a vote of a majority of all
its qualified members.

Salary.

He shall receive a salary not exceeding four thousand
dollars per annum, to be fixed by the school board. The
superintendent of schools shall appoint, subject to confirmation by the board, an assistant superintendent, who
shall hold his position, during the term for which the
superintendent is elected, unless sooner removed, and

whose salary shall be fixed by the board, not to exceed twenty-five hundred dollars per annum.

SECTION 7. Any person feeling himself aggrieved by any act of the superintendent may within ten days after the time of such act, appeal to the school board, who shall dispose of such appeal as may be deemed right. *Appeals.*

SECTION 8. The board shall also appoint biennially some suitable person to act as secretary of the board, who shall receive a salary not exceeding two thousand dollars per annum, to be fixed by such board. It shall be his duty to attend the meetings of the board, to keep a record of the proceedings, and a full and fair account of all receipts and expenditures of the board, and to do and perform all such other duties as shall be required of him by said board. The secretary of the school board shall, before entering upon the duties of his office, execute a bond to the city of Milwaukee, in such form and penalty, and with such conditions as the board shall prescribe, with sureties to be approved by said board, which bond shall be filed with and kept in the office of the city clerk of said city; and the school board may require security to be given for the faithful performance of his duties by any officer or employe of said board, in such form and amount as the board shall deem best, and may at any time require of any officer or employe additional bonds and sureties, in its discretion. The secretary of the board shall also take the annual enumeration of the children of school age in the city of Milwaukee, required by law, and shall at the same time collect such further statistics and information relating to schools and to the population entitled to school privileges in said city, as may be directed and required by the school board, and he shall receive for such service a compensation or fee of two cents per capita upon the entire enumeration of persons between the ages of four and twenty, residing in said city, to be audited by the school board, and paid out of the funds provided for the support of the schools. *Secretary of the school board.*

SECTION 9. The superintendent of schools, or the secretary of the school board, may be removed from office, for misdemeanor in office, incompetency or inattention to the duties of his office, by a vote of two thirds of the school board; provided, that notice in writing of charges against him and of the time and place of hearing and *May be removed by a two-thirds vote.*

acting upon the same, shall be served upon the accused
at least five days before the time of hearing and before
any action shall be taken by the board thereon.

Accused shall be heard.
And the accused shall be heard by himself or counsel,
and either party shall produce witnesses who shall be
sworn and give testimony subject to the pains and penalties of perjury.

Certified list of teachers and salaries to be filed with comptroller.
SECTION 10.   It shall be the duty of the secretary of the
school boord, within thirty days after the annual appointment of teachers and other salaried employes, to report to
and file with the city comptroller a duly certified list of
the teachers and employes so appointed, with the salaries
allowed to each, and a statement of the time or times fixed
for the payment thereof. He shall also, as often as any action
shall be taken by said school board, changing the salaries
of either of the officers of said board, or any of such teachers
and employes, or making a new election or appointment to
any position entitling the person appointed to receive a
stated salary, within thirty days after such action is had,
in like manner file with the comptroller a certified statement and list of all such changes and appointments.   A
list of all accounts which may be allowed by said school
board, stating the character of the materials of service for
which the same were rendered, shall be furnished to said
comptroller for his information, immediately after the
meeting of said board at which such allowance was made.
And said secretary shall also make and file with the said
comptroller quarterly statements of the condition of the
fund for the support of schools and of the financial transactions of the school board during the three months next
preceding such statement.

High school site and buildings.
SECTION 11.   The school board are hereby authorized,
and it shall be their duty to maintain the high school
now established in said city, and establish and maintain
such other high schools as may from time to time be
found necessary, and whenever more than one high school
is so established, said board may divide said city into high
school districts, and said schools shall be open to students
residing within the said district, and for that purpose the
common council of the city of Milwaukee are hereby
authorized to purchase suitable sites and erect or purchase
all necessary buildings for the use of said schools and to
enter into all contracts necessary for the accomplishment
of the purpose of this section.

Section 12. The said high schools shall be public **Teachers.** schools of Milwaukee, and as such shall be under the same supervision and control, except as herein provided, as other public schools of said city. The said board shall have power, and it shall be their duty to employ a principal and such other teachers as may be necessary for each of said high schools. The president of the board shall annually appoint a committee of said board of high schools, which, together with the superintendent, who shall be a member of said committee, shall employ or appoint all teachers in said high schools, subject to the approval of the board.

Section 13. The course of study in the high schools **Course of study.** shall be liberal, and shall embrace such studies as the said school board may deem proper; and the said board shall have power to grant diplomas and to confer degrees in testimony of scholarship and literary acquirements.

. Section 14. The said school board shall have power **Management of** to make rules and regulations for the government of **high schools.** teachers and students of said high schools, to prescribe terms of admission, to determine the text books to be used, to fix the number of classes and the conditions of graduation, and all other matters relating to the management of said high schools; provided, that no rule, order or regulation made by said board shall be valid, if inconsistent with the laws of this state.

Section 15. In case of the absence or inability from any cause, of the officers, appointed by said school board to perform the duties of their respective offices, said board may appoint some suitable person to act in their place and stead during their absence or inability, and such person shall have and possess the same power or authority as the officer whose place he is appointed temporarily to fill.

Section 16. The school board shall report to the **Support of the** common council of said city at or before the first meeting **public schools.** of the council in January in each year, the amount of money required for the support of all the public schools in said city, including the high schools for the next fiscal year.

And it shall be the duty of said common council to **Tax shall be levied.** levy and collect a tax, in addition to the tax to be levied for general city purposes upon all the taxable property of the said city, at the same time and in the same manner as other taxes are levied and collected by law, which, with the other funds provided for the same purpose, shall be equal to the amount of money required by said school board for the support of said schools; provided, that the said common council may, by the votes of two-thirds of all the members elect, levy a tax for a greater or less amount for such purpose.

School moneys shall not be used for any other purpose.

The said tax and the entire school fund of the city shall not be used or appropriated directly or indirectly for any other purpose than the payment of the salaries of the superintendent of schools, the secretary of the board and . the teachers, and such other employes as the board may deem necessary, and the necessary and current expenses of schools, including the purchase of school supplies, apparatus, and fuel, and the ordinary and necessary repairs of school furniture.

School moneys— how disbursed.

SECTION 17. All moneys received by or raised in the city of Milwaukee for school purposes shall be paid over to the city treasurer, to be disbursed by him on the orders of the president and secretary of the school, board countersigned by the city comptroller; provided, that the president, instead of signing each order, may certify upon the pay-rolls furnished by the secretary to the comptroller to the fact that the amounts therein are correct as allowed by the school board.

Orders drawn upon city treasurer by the president and secretary of the school board, and payable out of school fund, for amounts duly allowed by the board, are evidences of indebtedness, for which an action will lie against the city.

Terry vs. Milwaukee, 15 Wis., 543.

School board to report annually.

SECTION 18. The school board shall be governed in all things by the school laws of the state, except as they are altered or modified by this act. They shall report to the common council annually the general proceedings and acts of said board, the number and condition of the public schools kept in said city during the year, the time they have severally been taught, the number and names of teachers, and the amount of salary of each; the number of children taught in said schools, respectively; the result of the annual enumeration required by law; the extent of school accommodations in the several schools;

the amount of school moneys raised or received during the year, distinguishing the amount received from the state fund from the amounts derived from taxes levied by the county board of supervisors and by the common council respectively, and the accounts allowed by them against the school fund in detail, together with such other information as they may deem useful, or as the common council may require. A copy of said report shall be transmitted to the state superintendent of public instruction, and a like copy to the librarian of the state historical society at Madison.

The entire chapter relating to public schools is Chapter 386, Laws of 1891.

CHAPTER 73, LAWS OF 1891.

AN ACT to amend Section 10, of Chapter 12, of Chapter 184, of the Laws of 1874, entitled "An act to revise, consolidate and amend the charter of the city of Milwaukee, approved February 20, 1852, and the several acts amendatory thereof," and the several acts amendatory thereof.

Amends chapter 184, laws of 1874.

SECTION 1. All claims and demands against the city or the school board, before they are allowed by the school board, shall be audited and adjusted by the comptroller and immediately after the allowance by the school board of any claim or account, it shall be the duty of the secretary of said board to furnish to the comptroller a complete list of the same, stating the character of the material or service for which the same were rendered; and before a warrant shall be issued therefor, it shall be the duty of the comptroller to countersign same. And the said secretary shall also make and file with the said comptroller, quarterly statements of the condition of the fund for the support of schools and of the financial transactions of the school board during the three months next preceding such statement, so that said section, when amended, shall read as follows: Section 10. It shall be the duty of the secretary of the school board, within ten days after the annual appointment of teachers and other salaried employes, to report to and file with the city comptroller, a duly certified list of the teachers and employes so appointed, with the salary allowed to each, and a statement of the time or times fixed for the payment thereof. He shall also, as often as any action shall be taken by said school board changing the salaries of either of the officers of said board, or of any of such teachers or employes, or making a new election or appointment to any position entitling the person appointed to receive a stated salary, immediately after such action is had, in like manner file with the comptroller a certified statement and list of all changes and appointments. All claims and demands against the city or school board before they are allowed by the school board shall be audited and adjusted by the comptroller and immediately after the allowance by the school board of

Secretary of school board to file with comptroller certified list of teachers with salary; comptroller to audit all claims before allowance and countersign warrants.

any claim or account it shall be the duty of the secretary of said board to furnish to the comptroller a complete list of the same stating the character of the materials and services for which the same were rendered; and before a warrant shall be issued therefor it shall be the duty of the comptroller to countersign the same. And the said secretary shall also make and file with the said comptroller quarterly statements of the condition of the fund for the support of schools and of the financial transactions of the school board during the three months next preceding such statements.

CHAPTER 141, LAWS OF 1891.

AN ACT to amend Section 3, of Chapter 12, of Chapter 184, laws of 1874, entitled "An act to revise and consolidate the charter of the city of Milwaukee and the several acts amendatory thereof."

Amends chapter 184, laws of 1874.

School board authorized to organize and establish additional public schools; janitor having charge of steam boiler to pass examination.

SECTION 1. Section 3. The school board of the city of Milwaukee is hereby authorized and required, subject to the approval of the common council, to establish and organize so many public or common schools in addition to those already established in said city as may be necessary for the accommodation of the children of the city, entitled by the constitution and laws of the state to instruction therein, and the common council shall erect, purchase, hire or lease buildings and furniture and lots for the accommodation of such schools and of the high school of said city; and shall improve and enlarge such school buildings. The school board shall have power to establish and define, from time to time, the boundaries of all common school districts in the city in such a manner as they may deem best calculated to promote the interest of the schools. No janitor having charge of any steam boiler in any school building shall hereafter be employed or retained in the employ of the school board of the city of Milwaukee, unless he has a certificate signed by the board of public works of said city, signifying that he has passed a sufficient examination therefor.

CHAPTER XIII.

BOARD OF HEALTH.

Duties of commissioner of health.

SECTION 1. It shall be the duty of the commissioner of health to examine into and consider all measures necessary to the preservation of the public health in the city of Milwaukee, and to see that all ordinances and regulations in relation thereto be observed and enforced.

As amended by Chapter 470, Laws of 1885.

Powers of commissioner of health.

SECTION 2. The commissioner of health shall have power to appoint, subject to confirmation by said common council, such assistants, clerks, agents and

workmen as may be necessary for the proper discharge of
his duties, and they shall receive such salary or compensation for their services as the said common council may
fix.   The said commissioner of health shall also have
power to appoint from time to time, as they may be
needed, temporary special assistants for the purpose of
maintaining quarantine, under his direction over houses
and premises in the city in which are persons affected
with the small-pox or any other pestilential, contagious
or infectious disease, subject to quarantine under the
ordinances of the city.   He shall also have power to cause
all children attending private schools in the city, who shall
not have been previously vaccinated, for the prevention
of small-pox, to be so vaccinated, and to cause such
children, upon refusal to be vaccinated, to be excluded
from such private schools.

As amended by Chapter 470, Laws of 1885.

SECTION 3.   The said commissioner of health, or any **Further power of**
person under him, have authority to enter into and **commissioner.**
examine at any time, all buildings, lots and places of all
descriptions within the city, for the purpose of ascertaining
the condition thereof so far as the public health may
be affected thereby.

As amended by Chapter 470, Laws of 1885.

SECTION 4.   The commissioner of health shall give **Commissioner of**
such directions and adopt all such measures for cleansing **health to cause**
and purifying all such buildings, lots and other places, **unwholesome**
and for causing the removal therefrom of any wells, **places to be**
cisterns, privy-vaults, urinals, sinks, slop-hoppers, defec- **cleaned.**
tive plumbing or any sewer connection and of nauseous
substances producing a disagreeable smell or tending to
cause sickness or disease, as in his opinion may be deemed
necessary; and he may do or cause to be done whatever
in his judgment shall be needful to carry out such
measures for the preservation of the public health.   Any
person who shall disobey any order of the commissioner
of health, which shall have been personally served upon
him requiring him to abate or remove any nuisance or to
cleanse or purify any premises owned or occupied by him
in the manner or at the time described in the order shall
on complaint of the commissioner of health or any persons
serving such order before the municipal court of said

city, be liable to arrest and summary trial and punishment by fine, not exceeding five hundred dollars ($500) or by imprisonment not exceeding six months, or by both such fine and imprisonment in the discretion of the court.

As amended by Chapter 470, Laws of 1885, and Chapter 183, Laws of 1891.

Abatement of nuisances.

SECTION 5.   It shall be lawful for the commissioner of health in all cases where he may deem it necessary for the more speedy execution of his orders, to cause any such nuisance or nuisances, to be abated or removed at the expense of the city, and also to cause any such nuisance or nuisances which may exist upon the property of non-resident owners, or upon property, the owners of which cannot be found, or unknown and cannot be ascertained, to be abated or removed in like manner, at the **Cost of abatement** expense of the city, and the sum or sums so expended in **to be lien on** the abatement or removal of such nuisance or.nuisances **premises.** in such cases shall be a lien, in the same manner as any tax upon real estate, upon the lots or premises from or upon which such nuisances shall be abated or removed; the commissioner of health shall certify to the comptroller the description of such property, and the cost of abating and removing such nuisance or nuisances thereon, and the comptroller shall include the same in the annual schedule of lots subject to special taxation; and payment thereof may be enforced in like manner as other special taxes upon real estate are levied and collected in said city; provided, that the common council shall, from time to time, on application of said commissioner of health, appropriate and set apart out of the general fund of said city such sums as the council in its discretion shall deem necessary for the purposes of this chapter; and the expenses which the said commissioner is authorized by the section to incur, shall be paid exclusively out of the funds so provided by said city; and said commissioner shall not be authorized to create any liability on the part of said city in excess of the sums which shall have been so appropriated and set apart as aforesaid for his use.

As amended by Chapter 470, Laws of 1885.

Destruction of infected clothing.

SECTION 6.   It shall be the duty of the commissioner of health, by resolution, to direct any bedding, clothing putrid or unsound meat, pork, fish, hides, or skins of any kind, or any other article found within said city which in his opinion, will be dangerous to the health of the inhabitants thereof, to be destroyed or buried, and he may employ such persons as he may deem proper to remove or destroy such article, and every person who shall in any manner resist or hinder any person so employed, shall be deemed guilty of a misdemeanor, and on conviction thereof, shall be punished by a fine not exceeding two hundred and fifty dollars, or imprisonment not exceeding six months or both. It shall also be his duty to procure suitable places for the reception of persons sick of any pestilential or infectious disease, and in all cases where sick persons cannot otherwise be provided for, to procure for them proper medical attendance and provisions and to forbid and prevent all communication with any house, or family infected with any contagious or pestilential disease, except by means of physicians or nurses.

As amended by Chapter 470, Laws of 1885.

The powers conferred by this section are judicial in their nature' and the officer exercising them is not responsible in an action for damages to any one for any judgment he may render within his jurisdiction, however erroneously, negligently, ignorantly, corruptly or maliciously he may act.

Fath vs. Koeppel, 72 Wis., 289.

SECTION 7. It shall be the duty of the commissioner of health, on complaint being made to him, or whenever he shall deem any business, trade or profession carried on by any person or persons, or corporation in the city of Milwaukee, detrimental to the public health, to notify such persons or corporations, to show cause before the commissioner of health, at a time and place specified in such notice, why such business, trade or profession, should not be discontinued or removed, which notice shall not be less than three days (except that in cases of epidemic or pestilence the commissioner of health may by general order direct a shorter time not less than twenty-four hours) and may be served on the parties to be affected thereby by the commissioner of health or any of the employes in his department or by any police officer in said city in the same manner as provided by law for the service of a summons in civil actions. Cause may be shown by affidavit, and if in the opinion of the commissioner of health, no good and sufficient cause be shown why such business, trade or

Commissioner to give notice to parties to show cause.

profession should not be discontinued or removed, the commissioner shall order said parties to discontinue or remove the same within such time as the commissioner may deem reasonable and necessary, and the order of the commissioner shall be final and conclusive.

As amended by Chapter 470, Laws of 1885.

Penalty for refusing to obey lawful order.

SECTION 8.   Any person or persons failing or refusing to obey such lawful order of the commissioner of health, shall be deemed guilty of a misdemeanor, and upon conviction thereof, shall be punished by a fine of not more than two hundred and fifty dollars, or by imprisonment not more than one year or by both such fine and imprisonment and such person or persons shall be subject to like punishment for each and every day that he, she, or they shall continue such business, trade or profession, after the expiration of the time specified in the order of the commissioner of health for the discontinuance or removal of the same.

As amended by Chapter 470, Laws of 1885.

Ex parte affidavit deemed good.

SECTION 9.   In all trials for the violation of the provisions of this chapter, the *ex-parte* affidavit of service of any order, notice or requirement of the said commissioner of health, purporting to be made by the person who made such service, and stating the time, place and manner of the service, shall be deemed and taken as *prima facie* evidence of the due service of such order, notice or requirement in all trials in any court.

As amended by Chapter 470, Laws of 1885.

Disposition of fines.

SECTION 10.   All fines mentioned in this chapter shall be collected as other fines, and when so collected shall be paid into the city treasury.

As amended by Chapter 470, Laws of 1885.

Temporary hospitals.

SECTION 11.   The commissioner during the prevalence of the Asiatic cholera, or of any epidemic disease, shall have power when by him it is deemed necessary, to take possession of, and occupy as temporary hospitals, any building or buildings in the said city; but the city of Milwaukee shall pay for the use of such property, so taken, a just compensation.

As amended by Chapter 470, Laws of 1885.

SECTION 12.   It shall be the duty of each and every
practicing physician in the city of Milwaukee:

1.   Whenever required by the commissioner of health
of said city to report to said commissioner, at such times
and in such forms as they may prescribe, the number of
persons attacked with any pestilential, contagious or infectious disease attended by such physicians for the twenty-
four hours next preceding, and the number of persons
attended by such physician who shall have died
within the twenty-four hours next preceding such
report, of any such pestilential, contagious or infectious
disease.

2.   To report in writing to said commissioner of health
every patient he shall have laboring under any pestilential, contagious or infectious disease, within twenty-four
hours after he shall ascertain or suspect the nature of
such disease.

3.   To report in writing to the commissioner of health
when by them [him] required, the death of any person who
shall have died of any disease, within twenty four hours
thereafter, and to state in such report the specific nature
and type of such disease.

As amended by Chapter 470, Laws of 1885.

SECTION 13.   Any practicing physician, who shall
neglect or refuse to perform the duties required of him by
or in any section of this chapter shall be considered guilty
of a misdemeanor and upon conviction thereof shall be
punished by a fine of not more than two hundred and
fifty dollars for each offense.   Any person prescribing for
another person, shall, for the purpose of this chapter, be
deemed a practicing physician, and shall not be allowed
to plead ignorance for failure to perform any duty herein
required of a practicing physician.

As amended by Chapter 470, Laws of 1885.

SECTION 14.   Any person who shall deposit or knowingly cause to be deposited in any open stream or river
in the city of Milwaukee, after June 1, 1880, any offal,
garbage or filth or any refuse, obnoxious, odious, or
unhealthful matter of any kind or nature whatever, from
any factory, brewery, distillery, stock-yards, slaughter
house, tannery, gas factory, glue factory or other building
or establishment of whatever kind located in said city, or

the contents of any privy, privy vault or water closet located within any residence or dwelling house, and connected with or emptying into any of the sewers of said city, unless means are provided and employed for the abundant flushing of the same with clear water every time it may be used, shall be deemed guilty of a misdemeanor, and for every such offense shall be punished by imprisonment in the county jail not more then three months, or by a fine not exceeding one hundred dollars or by both fine and imprisonment, as the court may determine. It shall be the duty of the commissioner of health to rigidly enforce this provision of law.

As amended by Chapter 470, Laws of 1885.

Compensation of health officers. SECTION 15. The common council of said city shall, in making their annual estimates and levy for the expenses of the city government, estimate and provide such sums as may be necessary for the compensation of such officers and all other employes which the said commissioner of health is authorized to appoint by this chapter, and for all other expenses incurred by said commissioner in the performance of the duties prescribed in this chapter, and such expenses shall be audited and allowed and paid as other expenses of said city.

As amended by Chapter 470, Laws of 1885.

Duties of commissioner of health. SECTION 16. The common council of the city of Milwaukee shall have power to further define the duties of the commissioner of health; and to pass such ordinances in aid of the powers of the commissioner of health as may tend to promote and secure the general health of the inhabitants of said city.

As amended by Chapter 470, Laws of 1885.

Special duties of police officers. SECTION 17. It shall be the special duty of the members of the police force of said city, and of all magistrates and civil officers and all citizens of the state, to aid to the utmost of their power, the commissioner of health and the officers mentioned in this chapter, in the performance of their respective duties, and on requisition of the commissioner of health, it shall be the duty of the chief of police to detail one or more of the policemen of said city to serve the notices of said commissioner and

to perform such other duties as such commissioner may
require.

As amended by Chapter 470, Laws of 1885.

CHAPTER 361, LAWS OF 1887.

SECTION 1. No person or persons or corporation, shall sell or **Relating to sale of**
offer for sale or suffer or permit to be sold to any family, hotel, **ice in city of Mil-**
restaurant, saloon or individual, for drinking or eating purposes, **waukee.**
any ice cut from any river, canal, bayou, basin or slip within the
limits of the county of Milwaukee, except north of North street
in Milwaukee river in said county.

SECTION 2. No person shall knowingly use or cause to be used, **Use of, prohibited.**
or give or offer to others for use, for drinking or eating purposes,
any ice cut in or taken from any river, canal, bayou, basin or slip
within the limits of the county of Milwaukee, except north of
North street in the Milwaukee river, in said county.

SECTION 3. This act shall not be construed to prohibit the **How law to be con-**
cutting of ice upon any waters within the county of Milwaukee **strued.**
and the selling thereof for cooling purposes, but any person
dealing in such ice shall keep the same stored in a separate
building, wholly removed, distinct and separate from, and without
any connection or communication whatever with any place,
building or enclosure wherein shall be kept or stored ice cut from
waters outside of the county of Milwaukee.

SECTION 4. Any person violating the provisions of the first or **Penalty.**
third sections of this act shall, upon conviction thereof, be punished
by a fine of not less than one hundred dollars nor more than five
hundred dollars, and by imprisonment in the house of correction
of said county of not less than ten nor more than thirty days.
Any person who shall violate the second section of this act shall
be punished by fine of not less than twenty-five dollars nor more
than fifty dollars.

SECTION 5. It is hereby made the duty of the president of the **Duty of board of**
state board of health, and of the health officers of each town, **health.**
village or city in Milwaukee county, who shall have knowledge or
to whom any notice of any violation of this act shall be given, to
forthwith investigate the known or alleged violation thereof, and
if reasonable cause exists therefor to make complaint against the
person or persons so offending and to forthwith notify the district
attorney thereof and to assist such prosecuting officer in procuring
the requisite proofs to secure the conviction of such offenders.

CHAPTER 36, OF THE LAWS OF 1878, AS AMENDED
BY CHAPTER 217, AND SECTION 41, CHAPTER
324, OF THE LAWS OF 1882.

SECTION 1. It shall be the duty of the mayor of the city of **Mayor to appoint**
Milwaukee to appoint on the third Tuesday of April, 1882, and **commissioner of**
every four years thereafter, subject to the confirmation by the **health.**

common council of said city, a commissioner of health whose duty it shall be to examine into and consider all measures necessary to the preservation of the public health in said city and to see that all ordinances and regulations in relation thereto be observed and enforced.

Duty of commissioner.

SECTION 2. Such commissioner shall before he enters upon the duties of his office, take and subscribe the usual oath of office; and shall receive for his services such salary as the common council of said city by ordinance fix and determine.

Vacancy, how filled.

SECTION 3. Any vacancy in the office of commissioner of health shall be filled by appointment of the mayor with the approval of said common council; such appointment to be for the unexpired term.

Power of commissioner to appoint subordinates.

SECTION 4. The commissioner of health shall have power to appoint, subject to confirmation by said common council, such assistants, clerks, agents, and workmen as may be necessary for the proper discharge of his duties, and they shall receive such salary or compensation for their services as said common council may fix. The said commissioner of health shall also have power to appoint from time to time, as they may be needed, temporary special assistants for the purpose of maintaining quarantine under his direction, over houses and premises in the city in which are persons affected with the small pox or any other pestilential, contagious or infectious disease, subject to the quarantine under the ordinances of the city. He shall also have power to cause all children attending private schools in the city, who shall not have been previously vaccinated for the prevention of small pox, to be so vaccinated, and to cause such children, upon refusal to be vaccinated, to be excluded from such private schools.

Powers of commissioner.

SECTION 5. All powers vested in the board of health and the health officer of said city, are hereby conferred upon the commissioner of health, and all the duties of said board and of said health officer shall, from and after the taking effect of this act, devolve upon and be vested in the said commissioner of health.

Acts repealed.

SECTION 6. Sections one, two and three of sub-chapter thirteen, of chapter one hundred and eighty-four, of the laws of 1874, entitled "an act to revise, consolidate and amend the charter of the city of Milwaukee, approved February 20, 1852, and the several acts amendatory thereof;" also chapter three hundred and sixty-nine of the laws of 1876, amendatory of said chapter one hundred and eighty-four, and all other acts and parts of acts contravening the provisions of this act, are hereby repealed.

CHAPTER 232, LAWS OF 1893.

AN ACT to amend Chapter 41, Revised Statutes of Wisconsin for 1878, entitled "General provisions relating to municipalities, and the several acts amendatory thereof, and pertaining to public health in cities of one hundred and fifty thousand inhabitants or more."

Registrar of vital statistics.

SECTION 1. The commissioner of health in cities of one hundred thousand or more, is hereby authorized and instructed to appoint a registrar of vital statistics for any such city for a like term as that of such commissioner of health, whose salary shall be fixed by the common council of such city, and paid as other city officials are paid.

SECTION 2. The registrar's office shall be located with the office of the health department, and shall be subject to such rules as the commissioner of health shall prescribe, and all deaths reported to the health office shall be arranged by dates, and indexed in alphabetical order and recorded, after being numbered, commencing with number one at the beginning of each month, and all births reported to the registrar, as hereinafter provided for, shall also be kept in like manner as is required in the recording of deaths, including indexing the same.

Office; duties and location of.

SECTION 3. For the purpose of simplifying the work of physicians and other professional persons in recording births and deaths, and at the same time enabling them to collect the fee provided in section 1, of Chapter 287, entitled "An act to provide for the payment of fees for the recording of births and deaths," approved March 30th, 1882, it is hereby enacted that it shall be the duty of the registrar of vital statistics to transmit every week all reports of births received for record from physicians and other professional persons to the register of deeds of any county in which such city may be located, taking his receipt therefor, and the delivery of such reports to the registrar of vital statistics, with the receipt of the register of deeds, for the same, shall be sufficient evidence of compliance with the provisions of said chapter 287, laws of 1882, and of section 1023 and 102, of the Revised Statutes of Wisconsin, and chapter 264 laws of 1885.

Reports of births, record to be given register of deeds weekly.

SECTION 4. Before the delivery of said certificates of births, the registrar of vital statistics is hereby required to make correct entries in a book in the form prescribed in a succeeding section, giving each certificate a number commencing with number one and continuing through the year, said number to correspond with those on the record books.

Certificates of birth, record to be made.

SECTION 5. It shall be the duty of the person attending the birth of any child in any such city, or in case of non-attendance by a physician or midwife, the father of the child, to report on blanks to be furnished free, personally, at the office of the registrar of vital statistics, and to be filled out by him as hereinafter provided, corresponding to those furnished by the secretary of state, all the facts concerning said birth, and particularly the name of the child, color, sex, name of father and his occupation, name of mother previous to marriage, date and place of birth, number of street, place of nativity of father and mother, within six days after the birth of a child which was born alive. Any person failing to so report the birth of any child in any such city, shall be guilty of a misdemeanor, and upon conviction thereof, shall be punished by a fine not exceeding fifty dollars for each and every offense, or by confinement in the county jail for a period not exceeding thirty days, or by both such fine and imprisonment, at the discretion of the court; provided however, that this section

Birth of child to be reported.

Failure to report, a misdemeanor.

shall not apply to the record of still-births, which are to be reported as deaths only.

Record book of births.

SECTION 6.   The birth shall be recorded in a book in a similar manner to the death record kept at the health office, and a dating stamp shall be provided with the words, "Registrar of vital statistics of" (naming the city), and the registrar shall make an impression of such stamp on every certificate of birth upon receipt of the same.

CHAPTER 143, LAWS OF 1895.

AN ACT to authorize cities, towns and villages to pay for personal property destroyed to prevent the spread of contagious or infectious diseases.

City may pay for personal property destroyed to prevent spread of contagious diseases.

SECTION 1.   Whenever personal property is destroyed by order of the public authorities of any city, town or village, in order to stamp out or prevent the spread of contagious or infectious diseases, the proper city, town or village authorities may, for the purpose of paying therefor, appropriate money from the city, town or village treasury, to an amount not exceeding one hundred dollars to any one family; provided, however, that no money shall be appropriated without the certificate of the local board of health or commissioner of health as to the necessary destruction of such property and the amount and value thereof; and in no case shall an amount greater than the actual value of the destroyed property as determined by the said certificate be appropriated or paid under the provisions of this act.

CHAPTER 262, LAWS OF 1895.

AN ACT relating to commissioners of health in all cities having a population exceeding one hundred thousand.

Commissioner of health to procure proper places for care of persons suffering from contagious diseases.

SECTION 1.   It shall be the duty of the commissioner of health in all cities having a population exceeding one hundred thousand inhabitants, wherever the office of commissioner of health shall be provided for by law, or by the ordinances of such city, to procure suitable places for the reception of persons sick with any pestilential, contagious or infectious disease, and in all places where sick persons cannot otherwise be provided for, to procure for them proper medical attendance and provisions, and to forbid and prevent all communication with any house or family infected with any such disease.   It shall be the duty of such commissioner of health to place in a proper isolation hospital, under the care of competent nurses, any person who may be found in such city laboring under any of the following diseases, towit: Small pox, diphtheria, scarlet fever, measles, typhus fever, or any other dangerous, contagious or infectious disease, or when such person is a non-resident of such city, a traveler, a guest at a hotel, or has no residence of his own in the city, where he can be taken care

What persons not to be removed.

of; provided, however, that no such person or persons shall be removed to any isolation hospital in such city who can be nursed and cared for during such illness in his or her home, except upon the recommendation and advice of such commissioner of health, or one of his assistant commissioners of health, and the physician attending upon such child or person not being a member of the board of health of such city; and in case such commissioner or assistant commissioner, and such physician, shall be unable to agree as to the advisability of removing such child or person, then they shall call in and appoint another physician not a member of said board of health, or health department, and the decision of the majority of such commissioners and physicians shall be decisive of the question. The third physician called in as above provided shall not receive or be entitled to any fees from such city for such consultation or services, in the decision of the case submitted to the board of such physician; and provided further, that no child eight years of age or under shall be so removed unless permission is granted its mother, or some person akin to it, if such there be, to attend upon such child in such isolation hospital.

SECTION 2. All laws conflicting with the provisions of this act are hereby repealed.

CHAPTER XIV.

FIRE DEPARTMENT.

SECTION 1. The common council, for the purpose of guarding against the calamities of fire, shall have power, and it shall be their duty, to prescribe the limits within which wooden buildings, or buildings of other materials that shall not be considered fire proof, shall not be erected, placed or repaired; and to direct that all and any buildings within the limits prescribed, shall be made and constructed of fire-proof materials; and to prohibit the repairing or rebuilding of wooden buildings within the fire limits, when the same shall have been damaged to the extent of fifty per cent. of the value thereof, and to prescribe the manner of ascertaining such damage. *Fire limits. Repairing and rebuilding.*

SECTION 2. The common council shall have power to prevent the dangerous construction and condition of chimneys, fire places, hearths, stoves, stove pipes, ovens, boilers and apparatus used in and about any building, and to cause the same to be removed, or placed in a safe and secure condition, when considered dangerous;— *Preventive powers of the common council.*

To prevent the deposit of ashes in unsafe places;— *Ashes.*

To require the inhabitants to provide as many fire buckets, and in such manner and time, as they shall prescribe; and to regulate the use of them in time of fire;— *Fire buckets.*

Manufactories.

To regulate and prevent the carrying on of manufactories dangerous in causing or promoting fires;—

Fireworks.

To regulate and prevent the use of fire works or fire arms;—

Scuttles and ladders.

To compel the owners and occupants of buildings to have scuttles in the roofs, and stairs or ladders leading to the same;—

Idle and suspected persons.

To authorize the mayor, aldermen and other officers of the city to keep away from the vicinity of any fire all idle and suspected persons, and to compel all bystanders to aid in the extinguishment of fires, and in the preservation of property exposed to danger thereat; and generally to establish such regulations for the prevention and extinguishment of fires, and for the safety and protection of persons from injury thereby, as the common council may deem expedient.

Fire engines and fire companies.

SECTION 3.   The common council shall have power to purchase fire engines and other fire apparatus, and to organize a fire department, composed of a chief engineer, one or more assistant engineers, and such other officers and men as shall be required and employed in the management and conduct of such fire-engines and apparatus, and to establish rules and regulations for such department.

Apparatus and number of men to each company.

SECTION 4.   The city of Milwaukee is hereby authorized and empowered to purchase for the use of said city, steam fire engines and all necessary hose and apparatus for running and conducting the same in said city, and to employ engineers, and all other necessary help, to run and conduct said steam fire-engines, at stated salaries or monthly wages; provided, that there shall be employed not to exceed ten persons to care for, run and conduct each steam fire-engine, and the hose cart therewith, and that the number of persons employed as hook and ladder men shall number not to exceed eight persons for each

Salaries.

company.   The salary of the foreman of each fire company, of said city, shall be twelve hundred dollars per annum; of the first pipeman nine hundred dollars per annum; of each stoker eight hundred dollars per annum for the first year of his service in the department, nine hundred dollars per annum thereafter; of each pipeman seven hundred dollars per annum, for the first year of his service in the department, eight hundred dollars per annum for the second year, and nine hundred dollars

per annum thereafter; the salary of each driver in the
department, after the end of the second year of service
shall hereafter be nine hundred dollars per annum.   All   Repealing act.
parts of the charter of the city of Milwaukee conflicting
with any of the provisions of this act are hereby repealed;
provided, that nothing contained in this act shall in any
manner modify, amend, supersede, or repeal any of the
provisions of chapter 378, of the laws of A. D. 1885.

As amended by Chapter 405, Laws of 1885, and also Section 3,
Chapter 336, Laws of 1887.

NOTE.—Some of the salaries above fixed were changed by
ordinance passed January 9, 1893, pursuant to authority conferred
by Section 10, Chapter 378, Laws of 1885.

SECTION 5.   The chief engineer of the fire department   Chief engineer, how
shall be appointed by the mayor, subject to the confirm-   appointed.
ation of the common council, and shall hold his office for
two years subject to removal by the mayor with the
approval of the common council.   All other members of   Other members,
the fire department shall be appointed by the chief   how appointed.
engineer, subject to the written approval of the mayor,
and shall hold office during the pleasure of such chief
engineer.   The common council may provide by ordinance for the performance of police or other duties by the
members of such department.

Amended by Chapter 378, Laws of 1885 (Police and Fire Commissioners' Act), which see in foot note to Chapter XV hereof.

SECTION 6.   There shall be paid to the treasurer of   Tax on fire insur-
the city of Milwaukee, on or before the first day of Feb-   ance agents.
ruary in each year, by every person who shall act in said
city as agent for or in behalf of any individual or association or association of individuals, whether incorporated,
by the laws of this state or by the laws of any other state,
territory or county, to effect insurance against losses or
injury by fire, the sum of two dollars upon each hundred
dollars—and at that rate upon the amount of all premiums,—which during the year or part of the year ending
on the next preceding first day of January, shall have
been received by such agent or person or company,
or by any other person or persons for him or it, or which
shall have been agreed to be paid for any insurance
effected or agreed to be effected or promised by him as
such agent or otherwise, or by such company, against loss

Money paid by fire insurance companies to go to use of fire department.

or injury by fire in said city.   All moneys hereafter paid to the treasurer of the city of Milwaukee by fire insurance companies, or their agents, under section six of chapter fourteen of said chapter one hundred and eighty four, of the laws of 1874, shall be appropriated and used by said city of Milwaukee exclusively for the use and benefit of the fire department of said city.

As amended by Section 8, Chapter 311, Laws of 1876.

The percentage required to be paid by this section is not a tax upon the agent or his occupation, nor are its requirements an exercise of the power of taxation as to the companies, but of the police power inherent in the sovereignty of the state.

Fire Department vs. Helfenstein, 16 Wis., 142.

Insurance.

SECTION 7.   No person shall in said city of Milwaukee, as the agent or otherwise for any individual, individuals, association, or corporation, agree to effect, or effect any insurance upon which the duty mentioned in the next preceding section is required to be paid, or as an agent or otherwise procure such insurance to be effected unless he shall have first executed to said city of Milwaukee and delivered to the comptroller of said city a bond to be approved by such comptroller in the penal sum of five thousand dollars, with sureties to be approved by said comptroller, conditioned that he will render to said comptroller, on or before the first day of February of each succeeding year, a just and true account verified by his oath that the same is just and true, of all premiums which during the year ending on the first day of January preceding such report, shall have been received by him, or by any other person for him, or agreed to be paid, for any insurance against loss or injury by fire in said city which shallhave been effected, or promised by him, or agreed or promised by him to be effected, from any individual, individuals, association or corporation, and that he will, on such first day of February in each year, pay to the treasurer of said city for the use of said city, two dollars upon every hundred dollars, and at that rate upon the amount of such premiums.

As amended by Section 42, Chapter 324, Laws of 1882.

The legislature may permit or prohibit foreign insurance companies from doing business in this state; and if it permits, it may impose such conditions and restrictions as it sees fit.

Fire Department vs. Helfenstein, 16 Wis., 142.

SECTION 8.   Every person who shall in said city effect, **Penalty for effecting insurance.** agree to effect, promise or procure any insurance contrary to the provisions of the preceding section of this chapter, shall forfeit and pay to the city of Milwaukee, for each offense, and for each insurance so effected, or agreed, or promised to be effected, the sum of one hundred and fifty dollars; such sums may be recovered by said city in a civil action, and said city may maintain an action on such bond, or against such agent, to recover all moneys required by section six of this chapter, to be paid into the city treasury.

As amended by Section 43, Chapter 324, Laws of 1882.

SECTION 9.   Whenever any person shall refuse to **Penalty for disobeying lawful order of officers at fires.** obey any lawful order of the mayor, or of any engineer, alderman or policeman, at any fire, it shall be lawful for the officer giving such order, to arrest, or to direct orally any policeman, constable, watchman, or any citizen, to arrest such person, or to confine him temporarily in any safe place until such fires shall be extinguished; and in the same manner, such officers, or any of them, may arrest or direct the arrest or confinement of any person at such fire, who shall be intoxicated or disorderly; and any person who shall refuse to obey any such lawful order, who shall refuse to arrest, or aid in arresting, any person so refusing, shall be liable to such penalty as the common council may prescribe, not exceeding fifteen dollars.

CHAPTER 336, LAWS OF 1887.

SECTION 1.   In addition to the officers and men now authorized **Officers of fire department.** to be employed in the fire department of the city of Milwaukee, including the assistant superintendent of fire-alarm telegraph, the superintendent of machinery and apparatus and the secretary now appointed and employed under ordinances of said city; and which several officers last named are hereby constituted and confirmed as officers of the department; there may also be appointed hereafter by the chief, with the approval of the board of fire and police commissioners, as provided by law, a third assistant engineer, a chief operator of fire-alarm telegraph and two assistant operators of fire-alarm telegraph.

SECTION 2.   The salary of the third assistant engineer shall be **Salary of officers.** fifteen hundred dollars per annum; the salary of the chief operator of fire-alarm telegraph shall be eight hundred dollars per annum; the salary of each of the two assistant operators of the fire-alarm telegraph shall be seven hundred dollars per annum.

SECTION 3.   The salary of each driver in the department, after the end of the second year of service, shall hereafter be nine hundred dollars per annum.

Amendment.   SECTION 4.   This act shall be taken as an amendment to the charter of said city and the acts amendatory of chapter 184, of the laws of 1874, and any provision contained in said charter or the amendments thereof, which are necessarily inconsistent with the provisions of this act are declared to be hereby amended or repealed, as the true intent and meaning of this act shall require.

CHAPTER 176, LAWS OF 1885.

AN ACT relating to the "Firemen's Relief Fund," of the city of Milwaukee; and to repeal chapter 37, of the laws of 1878.

Relating to fire-   SECTION 1.   The members of the paid fire department of the
men's relief fund. city of Milwaukee, shall on or before the first day of June, A. D. 1885, form an association, and shall organize, under the provisions of sections 1987 and 1988, of the revised statutes, and shall adopt by-laws and regulations for the government thereof, and when so organized and the officers therof shall have been duly elected and shall have qualified according to the by-laws of such corporation or association, the city treasurer of the city of Milwaukee, shall upon receiving written notice of such organization, and of the election and qualification of the officers of such association, pay over to the treasurer thereof, the whole amount of the fund in his hands as city treasurer, known as the "Firemen's Relief Fund," created and held by virtue of chapter 37, of the laws of 1878; and thereafter such fund shall be the property of such corporation or association, and shall be held, enjoyed or disposed of by it, subject to its by-laws and regulations.

Duties of city   SECTION 2.   The city treasurer of the city of Milwaukee shall
treasurer. pay to the treasurer of such corporation for the benefit of the persons entitled to relief from such corporation, on or before the first day of March in each year, one-eighth of the amount of all fire insurance rate, now annually paid into the treasury of the city of Milwaukee, under section 6, of chapter 14, of the charter of the city of Milwaukee, being chapter 184, of the laws of 1874, and the various laws amendatory thereof.

Who are eligible.   SECTION 3.   No person shall be elected to, or hold any office, in such corporation, unless he be in the active employment of the fire department of the city of Milwaukee; and if his employment with the city shall be terminated while holding the office of trustee, or any other office of such corporation, his term of office shall thereupon cease and determine, and the members of such corporation as shall, by the by-laws thereof, be entitled to vote, shall forthwith elect his successor.

Repealed.   SECTION 4.   Chapter 37, of the laws of 1878, is hereby repealed, and the trustees therein named are hereby discharged from the trusts thereby created.

Repealed.   SECTION 5.   All acts and parts of acts contravening the provisions of this act are hereby repealed.

CHAPTER 147, LAWS OF 1893.

AN ACT defining the name in which actions may be brought to collect the two per centum and forfeitures mentioned in Section 1926, Revised Statutes, as amended.

SECTION 1. Actions to collect the two per centum and forfeits mentioned in section 1926, Revised Statutes, as amended, may be brought in the name of the town, city or village in which the fire department therein mentioned is located. **Name in which action may be brought.**

SECTION 2. This act shall take effect and be in force from and after its passage and publication.

CHAPTER 102, LAWS OF 1895.

AN ACT to amend Section 1987, of the Revised Statutes of 1878, as amended by chapter 328, laws of 1889, relating to paid fire departments in cities.

SECTION 1. Section 1987, of the revised statutes for 1878, as amended by chapter 328, of the laws of 1889, is hereby amended by inserting after the word "families" where it occurs in the tenth line of said section as amended, the words "under and in accordance with such reasonable rules and regulations as may be adopted by such association and of paying to the representatives or beneficiaries of deceased members such sums of money as they may be entitled to receive in accordance with the constitution and by-laws of the association," so that said section, when amended, will read as follows: Section 1987. The members of the paid fire department of any city now or hereafter organized, are constituted a body corporate in such city, under the name of the Firemen's Relief Association of the city of ———, for the purpose of giving relief to its sick and disabled members and their families, under and in accordance with such reasonable rules and regulations as may be adopted by such association, and of paying to the representatives or beneficiaries of deceased members such sums of money as they may be entitled to receive in accordance with the constitution and by-laws of the association; and in case any member of any such association shall cease to act with the fire department, of which he has been a member, he shall continue to enjoy all the advantages and benefits of the association so long as he complies with the rules, regulations and by-laws of the same and pays his dues; and every such association shall have all the usual powers of a corporation necessary and proper for the purpose of its organization, and may take by gift, grant, purchase or otherwise, real and personal estate not exceeding fifty thousand dollars in value, and hold, enjoy, lease, convey and dispose of the same, subject to the by-laws and regulations of such corporation; and such property shall be devoted solely to the purposes of, and objects of such corporation.

CHAPTER 163, LAWS OF 1895.

AN ACT to amend section 1987, of the revised statutes, relating to fire and police relief associations.

SECTION 1. Section 1987 of Sanborn & Berryman's annotated statutes is hereby amended by inserting after the word "fire" in

the second line of said section the words "or police," and by
inserting after the words "of the city of ——," in the fourth
line of said section, the words, "or the policemen relief association of the city of ——, as the case may be," and by striking
out after the words "relief to," in said fourth line of said section
1987, the words "its sick and disabled members and their
families," and inserting in lieu thereof the words "the sick and
disabled members of such associations, and their families, and to
the persons dependent upon the deceased members, and no
others," and by inserting after the word "fire" in the sixth line
of said section 1987 the words, "or police," and by inserting after
the word "member" in the seventh line of said section 1987, the
words "after five years of service," and by inserting after the
word "dues" in the ninth line of said section 1987 the words
"unless the connection of such person with either of said departments was discontinued for the good of the service. Each person
on becoming a member of either of said departments may be
required to pay an initiation fee not exceeding fifty dollars, and
annual dues, as long as he remains a member," so that said section
1987 when amended shall read as follows: Section 1987. The
members of the paid fire or police departments in any city, now
or hereafter organized, are constituted a body corporate in such
city under the name of "The Firemen Relief Association of the
city of ——," or "The Policemen Relief Association of the city
of ——," as the case may be, for the purpose of giving relief to
the sick and disabled members of such associations and their
families and to the persons dependent upon the deceased members,
and no others. In case any member of such association shall
cease to act with the fire or police department of which he has
been a member, after five years of service, he shall continue to
enjoy all the advantages and benefits of the association, as long as
he complies with the rules, regulations and by-laws of the same
and pays his dues, unless the connection of such person with
either of said departments, was discontinued for the good of the
service. Each person on becoming a member of either of said
departments, may be required to pay an initiation fee not exceeding
fifty dollars and annual dues as long as he remains a member.
Every such association shall have all the usual powers of a corporation, necessary and proper for the purposes of its organization,
and may take by gift, grant, purchase or otherwise, real and
personal estate, and hold, enjoy, lease, convey and dispose of the
same, subject to the by-laws and regulations of such corporation,
and all of such property and the rents, issues and profits thereof,
shall be devoted solely to the purposes and objects of such
corporation.

SECTION 2. All acts or parts of acts conflicting with the
provisions of this act are hereby repealed, so far as they conflict
with this act, and no further.

CHAPTER XV.

POLICE DEPARTMENT.

SECTION 1. The police force of the city of Milwaukee **Strength of police force.** shall consist of one chief of police, two lieutenants, and such number of detectives and patrolmen as the common council shall from time to time by ordinance determine and prescribe.

See amendment made by Chapter 483, Laws of 1887, in foot note hereto.

SECTION 2. The chief of police shall be appointed by the mayor subject to the approval of the common council, on the third Tuesday in April, A. D. 1882, and biennially thereafter, and may be removed by the mayor, with the approval of the common council. The chief of police shall nominate, and subject to the written approval of the mayor, appoint all other members of the police force, who shall hold office during the pleasure of such chief of police; and all appointments in the police shall be reported to the common council from time to time as changes are made, and also annually.

As amended by Section 3, Chapter 308, Laws of 1882; practically repealed by Chapter 378, 1885, which see *post.*

SECTION 3. The mayor or common council may direct **Detailed police.** the chief of police to detail any of the policemen to perform such official duties as he or they deem proper, and no extra compensation shall be allowed therefor.

SECTION 4. The mayor and aldermen, and the harbor master and bridge tenders of the city, and the commissioner of health and his assistants, the meat inspector, and the special assistants appointed by said commissioner of health for quarantine service while engaged in such service, shall severally and respectively have and exercise, within said city, all the powers of policemen of said city, without any compensation or claim to compensation therefor.

As amended by Section 44, Chapter 324, Laws of 1882.

SECTION 5. The members of the police force shall **Duties of policemen.** perform such duties as shall be prescribed by the common council, for the preservation of the public peace, and the good order and health of the city; they shall possess the powers of constables at common law, and all powers given to constables by the law of this state, and may within the county of Milwaukee execute all process issued by the municipal court of Milwaukee county or any justice of the peace of said county in criminal cases, but shall not serve civil process except when the city is a party.

As amended by Chapter 216, Laws of 1882.

Officers of the peace.

SECTION 6. The mayor or acting mayor, the sheriff of Milwaukee county, and each and every alderman, justice of the peace, policemen, constable and watchman shall be officers of the peace, and may command the peace, and suppress in a summary manner all rioting and disorderly behavior within the limits of the city; and for such purposes they may command the assistance of all bystanders, and, if need be, of all citizens and military companies; and if any person, bystander, military officer or private, shall refuse to aid in maintaining the peace when so required, each such person shall forfeit and pay a fine of fifty dollars; and in cases where the civil power may be required to suppress riotous and disorderly behavior, the superior or senior officer present, in the order above mentioned in this section, shall direct the proceedings.

Penalty for disobeying officers of peace.

Chief of police to annually report names of liquor dealers.

SECTION 7. It shall be the duty of the chief of police, on or before the first day of May in each year, to report to the clerk and attorney the names and places of business of all parties selling or dealing in spirituous, vinous or fermented liquors, and to give notice to such parties that they are required to pay the city treasurer such license money as may be fixed by law for the selling or dealing in spirituous, vinous or fermented liquors; and from time to time the chief of police shall report the names and places of business of all other parties who, subsequent to or not embraced in such report, shall be, or may have been engaged in the selling or dealing in spirituous, vinous or fermented liquors. Every license for the sale of such liquors shall expire on the first day of May following the date of its issue; and in case such license shall be issued prior to the first day of November, the fee for a full year shall be paid therefor; but if issued on or after the first day of November, one-half the fee for a full year shall be paid therefor.

License for selling liquors.

SECTION 8.   No extra compensation shall be paid the chief of police for the performance of the services specified in the foregoing section.

SECTION 9.   It shall be the duty of the city attorney to prosecute all persons whose names are embraced in such annual report, who shall not have taken out the proper license on or before the fifteenth day of May, and he shall prosecute all parties not embraced in such reports, who shall not have taken out their licenses within two weeks from the time they shall have been notified by the chief of police.

City attorney shall prosecute viola-tion of license ordinance.

CHAPTER 204, LAWS OF 1875.

SECTION 1.   The authority of the police department of the city of Milwankee, is hereby extended so as to embrace the county of Milwaukee, and policemen of said city shall have like authority to make arrests and serve process within the county of Milwaukee as are now possessed by them within the city of Milwaukee.

SECTION 2.   In order to facilitate the transactions of business and performance of duty by policemen in the county of Milwaukee, beyond the limits of the city of Milwaukee, the county board of the county supervisors of the county of Milwaukee may supply the police department of the city of Milwaukee with sufficient authority and conveyance to travel through the county of Milwaukee.

CHAPTER 56, LAWS OF 1880.

SECTION 1.   The salary of the chief of police of the city of Milwaukee is hereby fixed at three thousand dollars per annum, on and after the second Tuesday of April, A. D. 1880, which salary shall be in full of all demands for his services as chief of police and for collecting delinquent taxes on personal property.

Salary of chief of police.

SECTION 2.   The said chief of police shall collect with the delin-quent taxes on personal property, put into his hands for collection, the same collection fees now established by law, and shall pay the same into the treasury of said city.

Shall pay over.

SECTION 3.   No police officer or other officer of said city shall receive any fees for travel or attendance as a witness in any case in which said city shall be a party tried in any court sitting in said city, but in all such cases, when such fees are properly taxable in favor of said city, they shall be taxed and collected with the other costs in the case and be paid into the treasury of said city.

Fees now estab-lished by law.

When officers of city not to receive fees.

SECTION 4.   All acts and parts of acts contravening the provis-ious of this act, in so far as they conflict herewith, are hereby repealed.

Repealed.

SECTION 5.   This act shall take effect and be in force on and after the second Tuesday of April, A. D. 1880.

SECTIONS 4, 5, 6, OF CHAPTER 308, LAWS OF 1882, AS
AMENDED BY SECTION 1, CHAPTER 8,
LAWS OF 1883.

**Regulating qualifi-
cations, etc., of
police force.**

SECTION 4. The common council may make regulations relative to the appointment, qualifications, government and duties of
the members of the police force, and may provide thereby that all
patrolmen shall be first appointed upon trial or probation; but such
regulations shall not conflict with the provisions of the next
preceding section.

**May serve and
return process.**

SECTION 5. The officers and members of the police force shall
have authority to serve and return process returnable in any court
in the county of Milwaukee, in cases in which the city of Milwaukee, or the state of Wisconsin is plaintiff or prosecutor, with
the same force and effect as the same may be done by the sheriff
of said county or his deputies.

**Weapons and con-
traband articles.**

SECTION 6. Authority is hereby given to the common council
of said city to provide by ordinance, for the sale, destruction or
other disposition, of weapons and other contraband articles taken
from persons under arrest, that are now, or hereafter may be in
possession of the chief of police, and also for the sale of all articles
of personal property of whatever nature, which now, or hereafter
may be in the custody of the chief of police, and not claimed by
the owners thereof, for the period of six months after their seizure;
and the proceeds of all articles so sold under such ordinance, shall
be paid into the city treasury of the city of Milwaukee to the
credit of the general fund. Witness fees taxed for the testimony
of any police officer or policeman in any case, either criminal, or
arising from violation of any city ordinance, as witness or
interpreter shall be paid into the general city fund of said city.

CHAPTER 378, LAWS OF 1885.

**Board of fire and
police commis-
sioners.**

SECTION 1. There shall be in the city of Milwaukee, a board
of fire and police commissioners, consisting of four citizens, not
more than two of whom shall belong to the same political party,
when appointed. No salary or other compensation for services
shall be paid to any member of such board. Three members of
the board shall constitute a quorum necessary for the transaction
of business. It shall be the duty of the mayor of said city, before
the first Monday of July, 1885, to appoint four members of said
board, designating the term of office of each, one to hold one
year, one to hold two years, one to hold three years and one to
hold four years from the first Monday in July, 1885, and all until
their respective successors shall be appointed and qualified. After
the present year it shall be the duty of the mayor, each year
before the first Monday in July, to appoint one member of said
board, whose term of office shall be four years from the first
Monday in July in that year, and until his successor is appointed
and qualified. Every person appointed a member of said board
shall, before entering upon the duty of his office, take and
subscribe the oath of office prescribed by the constitution of the
state, and file the same duly certified by the officer administering
it, with the clerk of said city.

SECTION 2. After the first Monday in July, 1885, no person shall be appointed to any position, either on the police force or in the fire department of said city, except with the approval of said board.

No appointments to be made except with approval of board.

SECTION 3. As soon as possible after the first members of said board shall enter upon their offices, said board shall prepare and adopt such rules and regulations to govern the selection and appointment of persons to be thereafter employed on either the police force or the fire department of said city, as in the judgment of said board shall be adapted to secure the best service for the public in each department. Such rules and regulations shall provide for ascertaining, as far as possible, the physical qualifications, the habits and the reputation, and standing and experience of all applicants for positions, and they may provide for the competitive examination of some or all in such subjects as shall be deemed proper for the purpose of best determining their qualifications for the positions sought. Such rules and regulations may provide for the classification of positions in the service and for a special course of inquiry and examination of candidates for each class. All rules and regulations adopted shall be subject to modification or repeal by the board at any time.

Adoption of rules and regulations.

SECTION 4. The board shall cause the rules and regulations so prepared and adopted and all changes therein, to be printed and distributed as they shall deem necessary, and the expense thereof shall be certified by the board to the city comptroller and shall be paid by the city. Such rules and regulations shall specify the date when they will take effect, and thereafter all selections of persons for employment, or appointment or promotion, either in the police force or the fire department of said city, except of the chief and first lieutenant of the police and the chief engineer and first assistant of the fire department, shall be made in accordance with such rules and regulations.

Examination to be free to all citizens of the U. S.

SECTION 5. The examinations which the rules and regulations shall provide for shall be public and free to all citizens of the United States with proper limitations as to residence, age, health, habits and moral character. The examinations shall be practical in their character and shall relate to those matters which will fairly test the relative capacity of the candidates to discharge the duties of the positions in which they seek employment or to which they seek to be appointed, and may include tests of manual skill and physical strength. The board shall control all examinations and may designate suitable persons, either in the official service of the city or not, to conduct such examinations, or any of them, and may change such examiners at any time, as shall seem best.

Examinations shall be public.

SECTION 6. Whenever after the first Monday in July, 1885, a vacancy shall exist in the office of chief of police or in the office of chief engineer of the fire department it shall be the duty of said board to appoint proper persons to fill such offices respectfully [respectively] during good behaviour subject to suspension and removal as hereinafter provided.

In case of vacancy, how filled.

Vacancy in office of lieutenant of police.

SECTION 7. Whenever after the first Monday in July, 1885, a vacancy shall exist in the office of first lieutenant of the police, the chief of the police shall nominate and with the approval of said board, shall appoint a suitable person to such office, to hold during good behavior, subject to suspension and removal as hereinafter provided.

Vacancy in office of first assistant engineer.

SECTION 8. Whenever after the first Monday in July, 1885, a vacancy shall exist in the office of first assistant engineer of the fire department, the chief engineer shall nominate and with the approval of the board shall appoint a suitable person to that office, to hold during good behavior, subject to suspension and removal as hereinafter provided.

All other members shall hold at pleasure of chief.

SECTION 9. All other members of the force in either department named, at the time when the rules and regulations shall go into effect shall continue to hold their respective positions and employments at the pleasure of their respective chiefs, and all persons subsequently appointed shall so hold. All vacancies in either department shall be filled and all new appointments shall be made by the respective chiefs with the approval of the board. Where vacancies in old offices or newly created offices can, with safety to the department, be filled by the promotion of officers or men already in the service and who have proved their fitness for the promotion, the vacancies and newly created offices shall be so filled by promotion by the respective chiefs with the approval of the board.

Salaries to be according to length of service; common council may change.

SECTION 10. Provisions may be made by the common council of said city by general ordinance that the salaries of officers and men in the police and fire departments of the city shall increase with the length of the term of service. The salary and compensation of all officers and men in said departments shall be at all times subject to change by the common council, provided that the salary or compensation of no officer or man in the service of either department shall be decreased, except upon the previous recommendation of such change made in writing by the board to the common council. The common council shall have the power to provide for an annual pension for life for such members of either service as shall be honorably discharged from the same.

Common council has power to pension.

Suspension from office.

SECTION 11. The chief of police, the first lieutenant of police, the chief engineer of the fire department, and the first assistant engineer of the fire department, each and all of them, shall be subject to a suspension from office for cause by the mayor at any time. Any officer so suspended shall thereupon cease to exercise the functions of his office until he shall be reinstated. In case of such suspension, the mayor shall, at once, communicate to said board the charge or charges against the officer suspended, and the board shall at once consider and examine the same, giving the suspended officer opportunity to meet the charges and be heard in his own defense. After hearing the matter, the board shall determine whether the charges are sustained. If the charges shall not be sustained by the board the officer shall be immediately reinstated. If the board shall determine that the charges are sustained, they shall at once determine whether the good of the service requires that the suspended officer shall be removed from office, or shall be suspended from office without pay for a fixed period. The board shall communicate their decision to the mayor in writing. The mayor shall make it public, and the decision shall be final and conclusive in all cases.

SECTION 12. The board shall have power and it shall be the duty of the board when all the four members thereof concur in the opinion that the good of the service, in either of the departments aforesaid, will be subserved by the removal from office of any of the officers named in section 11 to remove such officer. In such cases the removal shall be made by a notice to the officer, signed by all the members of the board, and it shall not be necessary to state any cause for such removal.

When it is duty of board to remove from office.

SECTION 13. The board shall have the power to appoint an officer to be called a chief examiner. The board shall prescribe his duties and his compensation, which shall be paid by the city on the certiffcate of the board. He shall be subject to removal at any time by the board, and they shall have power to change his duties and his compensation at any time, as they may deem proper. The board shall have power to fix and alter at will a compensation for any other examiners appointed by the board, and such compensation shall be paid by the city on a certificate of the board.

Power of appointment.

SECTION 14. This act is to be taken as an amendment to the charter of the city of Milwaukee, being chapter 184, of the laws of 1874, and the various laws amendatory therof, and any parts or portions of said chapter, and any provisions therein which are inconsistent with this act, or not in harmony with its provisions, are declared to be modified, amended, superseded or repealed by this act, as the intention herein declared may require.

Charter amended.

CHAPTER 483, LAWS OF 1887.

SECTION 1. From and after the fifteenth day of April, next, the two lieutenants of police in the city of Milwaukee, now known as the first and second lieutenants, shall be designated and known respectively as the inspector of police and the captain of police, and under those designations and names, such officers, respectively, and their successors shall have all the powers and rights, and shall perform the duties, and be subject to the same regulations and provisions of law as now pertain to the offices of first and second lieutenants of police.

Relating to police force.

SECTION 2. From and after the fifteenth day of April next, in addition to the chief, the inspector and the captain, and such number of detectives, sergeants, roundsmen, and patrolmen as the common council may from time to time prescribe, constituting the police force of said city, there shall be also four lieutenants of police who shall be appointed as the law provides, and shall each receive a salary of twelve hundred dollars per year to be paid as provided for the payment of the salaries of other officers upon the police force.

Salary of lieutenant of police.

SECTION 3. This act shall be taken as an amendment to the charter of the city of Milwaukee, being chapter 184, of the laws of 1874, and the various laws amendatory thereof, and any parts of said chapter or of the amendments thereto, and any provisions therein which are necessarily inconsistent with the provisions of this act, are declared to be hereby amended or repealed by this act as the intention herein declared may require.

As amended by Chapter 136, Laws of 1889.

CHAPTER 137, LAWS OF 1889.

AN ACT to create, regulate and control the policemen's relief fund of the city of Milwaukee.

SECTION 1. The members of the paid police department of the city of Milwaukee shall on or before the first day of June, 1889, form an association and shall organize under the provisions of section 1987 and 1988, of the revised statutes, and shall adopt by-laws and regulations for the government thereof, and when so organized and the officers thereof, shall have been duly elected and shall have qualified according to the by-laws of such association, the city treasurer of the city of Milwaukee shall, upon receiving written notice of such organization and of the election and qualification of the officers of said association and on the first Monday in May, 1890, and on the first Monday in May of each year thereafter, pay over to the treasurer of said association, for the benefit of the persons entitled to relief from said association, one per centum of the amount of all fees received by said city for licenses issued by said city for the sale of intoxicating liquors during the preceding year; provided, however, that such amount shall not exceed the sum of two thousand five hundred dollars in any year, and the proper officers of said city of Milwaukee are hereby authorized and directed from time to time to issue to the treasurer of said association an order on the city treasurer therefor, and thereafter such amount shall be the property of the said association, and shall be held, and enjoyed by and disposed of by it, subject to its by-laws and regulations.

SECTION 2. It is hereby made the duty of every member of said department, including the chief of police, to execute to the said policemen relief association of the city of Milwaukee, on or before the first day of June, 1889, a written assignment of all of his right, title and interest of, in and to all moneys received, and to be received as rewards during the period of his membership in said department; and it shall be the duty of every person appointed as a member of said department thereafter, to execute such an assignment upon entering upon his duties; and it is hereby made the duty of the chief of police to forthwith remove from said department any member who shall fail to comply with the provisions of this section.

SECTION 3. It is hereby made the duty of all persons during their membership in said department, to pay or deliver over without delay to the treasurer of said association all property, money or things of value other than their salaries, received by such

Rewards, etc., received to be paid or turned over to treasurer.

persons as reward or compensation in the performance of official duty or special services in said department; and it is hereby made the duty of the chief of police to forthwith remove any member of said department who shall fail to comply with this provision.

SECTION 4. The proceeds hereafter realized from the sales of unclaimed goods and property disposed of under the provisions of chapter 8, of the laws of 1883, and the ordinances of said city, shall be paid by the chief of police to the treasurer of said association, and all money that shall be unclaimed for the space of one year shall be delivered by the chief of police to the treasurer of said association.

Proceeds, how applied.

SECTION 5. It is hereby made the duty of the clerk of the municipal court of Milwaukee county to tax witness fees in all cases in said court wherein the members of said department are witnesses for the prosecution, and he shall pay the same, when collected on the first Mondays of January, April, July and October, to the treasurer of said association.

Witness fees of members of, to be paid to treasurer by clerk of municipal court.

SECTION 6. All funds that shall come into the hands of the treasurer of said association by virtue of this act shall be the property of said association, and shall be held and enjoyed by and disposed of by it subject to its by-laws and regulations.

Duty of treasurer respecting funds.

SECTION 7. The treasurer of said association shall give a bond, with at least two sureties, in the penal sum to be fixed by said association, not to be less, however, than five thousand dollars, which shall be approved by the comptroller of the city of Milwaukee before such treasurer shall enter upon the duties of his office.

Treasurer to give bond.

SECTION 8. No person shall be elected to or hold any office in said association unless he be in the active service of the police department of the city of Milwaukee, and if such active service shall be terminated while holding the office of trustee or any other office of said association his term shall thereupon cease and determine, and the members of said association who shall by the by-laws thereof be entitled to vote, shall forthwith elect his successor. The city attorney of the city of Milwaukee shall be ex-officio one of the trustees of the policemen's relief association and also a trustee of the firemen's relief association of the said city of Milwaukee.

Who eligible to office in association.

City attorney shall be ex-officio trustee.

As amended by Chapter 163, Laws of 1895.

CHAPTER 202, LAWS OF 1889.

AN ACT to authorize the city of Milwaukee to pension widows and children of members of the fire and police departments.

SECTION 1. The common council of the city of Milwaukee is hereby authorized to pay annually to the widow and children and dependent widowed mother of any member of the fire or police departments of said city, who have been killed since the first day of February, 1889, or who may hereafter be killed in the actual

Common council may pension widows, children and dependent widowed mothers

of members of
police and fire
departments
killed in dis-
charge of duty.

discharge of his duties, such sum of money as a pension for such time as it may deem proper; such sum not to exceed one-half of the annual salary drawn by said member; provided, that such pension shall cease upon the remarriage of said widow or upon other cessation of dependency of such children or widowed mother.

SECTION 2. This act shall take effect and be in force from and after the date of its passage and publication.

CHAPTER 370, LAWS OF 1895.

AN ACT to provide pensions for the members of the paid fire and police departments and to the widows and minor children of deceased members in cities having a population of one hundred and fifty thousand and over in certain cases and to repeal conflicting laws.

Board of fire and
police commis-
sioners to decide
applications for
pensions.

SECTION 1. The board of fire and police commissioners in any city having a population of one hundred and fifty thousand and over and having paid fire and police departments shall hear and decide all applications for pensions under this act, and its decisions on such applications shall be final and conclusive and not subject to review, modification or reversal except by the board itself at its own discretion. The board shall cause to be kept a record of all such applications and of all its proceedings under this act.

Member of depart-
ment, when
retired; duty of
commissioners.

SECTION 2. If any member of the paid fire or police department of any such city shall, while engaged in the performance of his duty as such fireman or policeman, be injured and be found upon examination by a medical officer ordered by said board of fire and police commissioners to be physically or mentally permanently disabled by reason of service in such department so as to render necessary his retirement from service in such fire or police department, said board of fire and police commissioners shall retire such disabled member from service in such fire or police department, provided no such retirement on account of such disability shall occur unless said member has contracted said disability while in the service of such fire or police department. Upon such retirement the said board of fire and police commissioners shall order the payment to such disabled member of such fire or police department, monthly, by the treasurer of said city of a sum equal to one-half the monthly compensation allowed to such member as salary at the date of such retirement.

Pensions, who
entitled to, upon
death of member.

SECTION 3. If any member of the paid fire or police department of such city shall, while in the performance of his duty, be killed or die as the result of an injury received in the line of his duty or any disease contracted by reason of his occupation, or if any member of such paid fire or police department, after ten years' service in such department, shall die from any cause whatever while in said service, or if any member of such paid fire or police department shall die from any cause whatever after having been retired upon a pension under any of the provisions of this act, or of chapter 287 of the laws of 1891, and shall leave a widow or minor child or minor children under 16 years of age surviving him, said board of fire and police commissioners shall direct the payment by the treasurer of said city of the following sums monthly, to-wit: to such widow, while unmarried, thirty dollars; to the guardian of such minor child or children, six dollars for each of said children while under the age of sixteen years; provided, however, that there shall not be paid to a family of a deceased member a total pension exceeding one-half the amount of the monthly salary of such deceased member at the time of his decease, or, if retired upon a pension under any of the provisions of this act, or of said chapter 287, of the laws of 1891, a sum not exceeding one-half the amount of the monthly salary of such retired member at the date of his retirement; but nothing in this act shall warrant the payment of any pension to the widow of any member or retired member of such fire or police department after she shall have re-married. **Pensions, amount of.** **Widow not entitled to pension after re-marriage.**

SECTION 4. Any member of the paid fire or police department of such city after becoming fifty years of age and having served twenty-two years or more in such fire or police department, of which the last five years of service shall have been continuous, may make application to be retired from such fire or police department, such application to be decided by the board of fire and police commissioners in accordance with the authority conferred upon it by this act; or such member may be retired from such fire or police department, without any application, by the board of fire and police commissioners whenever in its judgment advisable; and in either case the said board of fire and police commissioners shall order and direct that such person shall be paid a monthly pension equal to one-half the amount of salary attached to the rank which he may have held in such fire or police department at the date of such retirement, to be paid by the treasurer of such city; and the said board upon the recommendation of the chief officer of such fire or police department shall have the power to assign members of the fire or police department retired and drawing pensions under this act or under said chapter 287, of the laws of 1891, to the performance of light duties in such fire or police department in case of extraordinary emergencies. **When member of department may retire.**

SECTION 5. Any persons now drawing pensions under any of the provisions of chapter 287, of the laws of 1891, entitled "An act to create a pension fund for members of fire and police departments in certain cities of Wisconsin," shall continue to receive monthly the same sums as they are now receiving under any of the provisions of said chapter 287; but such sums shall be paid to them hereafter by the treasurers of such cities in the same manner and under the same provisions of law which govern the payment of pensions under the present act and not otherwise. **Persons drawing pensions to be paid by city treasurer.**

SECTION 6. The pensions provided for in this act shall be paid monthly, on the first day of the month, in the same manner and under the same provisions of law which govern the payment of the salaries of active members of such fire and police departments so far as the same may be applicable, and the provisions of any law or ordinance for monthly pay-rolls in such fire or police **Pension to be paid monthly.**

departments shall apply to the persons and pensions provided for in this act.

Old board to report and thereafter cease to exist.   SECTION 7.   The board of trustees of the firemen's and policemen's pension fund heretofore organized under the provisions of chapter 287, of the laws of 1891, in any city having a population of one hundred and fifty thousand and over, and having a board of fire and police commissioners, shall immediately upon the passage and publication of this act make report to the common council of said city of the condition of such pension fund, and any funds remaining in the possession or under the control of any such board of trustees, or of its treasurer, shall be transferred to the treasurer of such city and be by him turned into the general fund of such city, and thereupon such board of trustees shall cease to exist in such city.

SECTION 8.   The provisions of any act or law or ordinance now in force or effect so far as they conflict with the provisions of this act are hereby repealed.

CHAPTER XVI.

SALARIES.

Salaries of city officials.   SECTION 1.   Salaries shall be paid to the several and respective officers of the said city mentioned in this section, for all services during the time of their service, at the following rates per annum, to-wit:

To the mayor four thousand dollars;
(Chapter 349, Laws of 1889.)

To the city treasurer five thousand dollars;
(Section 5, Chapter 161, Laws of 1889.)

To the comptroller four thousand dollars;
(Chapter 352, Laws of 1889.)

To the deputy comptroller twenty-two hundred dollars;
(Chapter 375, Laws of 1891.)

To the city attorney four thousand dollars;

To the assistant city attorney twenty-four hundred dollars.
(Chapter 36, Laws of 1889.)

To the city clerk two thousand five hundred dollars;
(Chapter 303, Laws of 1889.)

To the deputy city clerk eighteen hundred dollars;
(Chapter 189, Laws of 1891.)

To the tax commissioner twenty-five hundred dollars;
(Chapter 323, Laws of 1889.)

To the assessors each seven hundred and twenty dollars;
(Chapter 489, Laws of 1887.)

To the chief engineer of the fire department three thousand dollars.
(Chapter 419, Laws of 1885.)

To the first and second assistant engineers of the fire department eighteen hundred dollars;
(Chapter 136, Laws of 1889.)

To the third assistant engineer of the fire department fifteen hundred dollars;
(Chapter 336, Laws of 1887.)

To the assistant superintendent of fire alarm telegraph fifteen hundred dollars.
(Chapter 136, Laws of 1889.)

To the superintendent of machinery and apparatus fifteen hundred dollars;
(Chapter 136, Laws of 1889.)

To the secretary of the fire department twelve hundred dollars;
(Chapter 136, Laws of 1889.)

To the chief operator of fire alarm telegraph eight hundred dollars;
(Chapter 336, Laws of 1887.)

To the assistant operators of fire alarm telegraph seven hundred dollars;
(Chapter 336, Laws of 1887.)

To the foreman of each company twelve hundred dollars;
(Chapter 405, Laws of 1885.)

To the first pipeman each nine hundred dollars;
(Chapter 405, Laws of 1885.)

To the firemen each eight hundred dollars;

To the engineers of fire steamers each twelve hundred dollars;

To the stokers each eight hundred dollars for the first year of service in the department and nine hundred dollars, thereafter;
(Chapter 405, Laws of 1885.)

To the drivers each nine hundred dollars, after the second year of service in the department;
* (Section 3, Chapter 336, Laws of 1889.)

To the pipemen each seven hundred dollars for the first year of service in the department, and eight hundred dollars for the second, and nine hundred dollars thereafter;
(Chapter 405, Laws of 1885.)

To the chief of police three thousand dollars;
(Chapter 56, Laws of 1880.)

To the inspector of police eighteen hundred dollars;
(Chapter 136, Laws of 1889.)

To the captain of police fifteen hundred dollars;
(Chapter 136, Laws of 1889.)

To the four lieutenants of police each twelve hundred dollars;
(Chapter 136, Laws of 1889.)

To the detectives each one thousand dollars;

To the sergeants each nine hundred dollars;

To the roundsmen each eight hundred dollars;

To the patrolmen each eight hundred dollars;

To the harbormaster one thousand dollars;

In addition to his salary, as above, the city treasurer shall be allowed such sum each year, for clerk hire, as the common council shall deem to be reasonable, and shall fix or determine by resolution. All salaries of officers and others, which are not fixed absolutely by this act, shall be fixed by the common council, by ordinance, subject to the limitations herein prescribed.

The salaries and allowance above mentioned, and which shall be fixed as aforesaid by the common council, shall be accepted by such officers and others, respectively, as their sole compensation for the services for which such salaries are allowed.

As amended by Section 45, Chapter 324, Laws of 1882.

NOTE.—Under the authority granted by Section 10, Chapter 378, Laws of 1885, the common council has passed various ordinances changing the compensation of officers and men of the fire and police departments, so that the charter salaries for those departments have been greatly varied, and considerably increased.

SECTION 2. All salaries paid by the said city to officers or others shall be payable monthly, at the end of each and every month, by warrants on the city treasurer, signed by the mayor and city clerk, and countersigned by the comptroller.

Salaries paid monthly.

SECTION 3. The city treasurer shall keep an accurate account of all moneys received by him for fees, commissions, and percentages, which he is required by section thirty-six of chapter eighteen of this act, to pay into the city treasury for the use of the city; and the city clerk and the city attorney shall each keep a like account of all moneys received by him for and in behalf of said city; and said treasurer, clerk and attorney shall each, at the end of each and every three months during his term of office, pay into the city treasury all such moneys remaining in his hands, and file a transcript of such account with the city comptroller, accompanied by his affidavit that the same is a just, true and complete account of all moneys so received by him during the three months then next preceding, and by the city treasurer's receipt showing that all such moneys have actually been paid into the city treasury; and it shall not be lawful for the mayor, city comptroller, or common council, to pass or settle the accounts, or to order, or draw, countersign or deliver any warrant for the payment of any portion of the salary or allowance of either of said officers, after any failure by him to file such verified quarterly transscript of account with the city comptroller, or to pay such moneys into the city treasury so long as such officer shall continue to be so delinquent.

Treasurer to keep account of fees, percentages and commissions received.

City clerk and city attorney to pay every three months.

Such payments how enforced.

SECTION 4. If either said treasurer, attorney or clerk of said city, shall wilfully neglect or violate any provision or requirement of the preceding section, or any duty therein or thereby imposed upon him, he shall be deemed guilty of a misdemeanor, and upon conviction thereof shall be punished by a fine of not less than five hundred dollars nor more than five thousand dollars, or by imprisonment in the county jail of said county of Milwaukee not less than two months nor more than one year, or by both fine and imprisonment, in the

Penalty for neglect or violation of duty.

discretion of the court; and it shall be the duty of the **Council shall order actions for recovery of moneys.** common council to cause an action to be forthwith commenced and prosecuted to final judgment against such officer and the sureties on his official bond, if any, for the recovery of all moneys in his hands, which, by the terms of the preceding section, and the section therein referred to, he is required to pay into the city treasury. In case said common council shall neglect to cause such action to be commenced within thirty days after any delinquency shall occur in the payment of any moneys required to be paid into the city treasury by any officer under said sections, such action may be brought and prosecuted by **Any taxpayer may commence the action on giving bond.** any taxpayer of the said city, in the name and for the benefit of said city; provided, that before commencing such action, a bond to said city shall be executed and filed in the office of the city comptroller, in the penal sum of five hundred dollars, with sufficient sureties approved by the judge of the circuit court of said county of Milwaukee, conditioned to pay all costs and damages which may be recovered against said city in such action, and to indemnify the city against any and all costs, expenses and damages by reason of said action; and such action when so commenced by a taxpayer shall not be subject to the control or management of said city or of any officer thereof.

CHAPTER XVII.

FINANCE AND TAXATION.

City orders, how drawn and signed. SECTION 1. All funds in the city treasury, except school funds and the fund created and set apart for the payment of interest and principal of the funded debt of said city, shall be under the control of the common council and shall be drawn out upon the order of the mayor and clerk, duly authorized by vote of the common council and countersigned by the city comptroller, except in the cases in this section mentioned, to-wit: The common council may provide by ordinance for the **Monthly pay-rolls.** payment of such persons as may be employed by the board of public works and by the fire and police departments or by the common council in the service of the city, upon monthly pay-rolls, and shall prescribe the form of such pay-rolls and the manner in which the same shall be certified, audited, approved, and payment made thereon; provided, that such pay-rolls shall in all cases be certified by the board of public works or chiefs of the fire and police departments as the case may be, and countersigned by the city comptroller. All orders drawn upon the treasury shall specify the purposes for which **Orders to specify.** they were drawn and shall be drawn payable generally out of any funds in the treasury belonging to the city and not otherwise appropriated, and all such orders shall be received in payment of any tax or assessment levied by the authority of the city, except the tax for interest and the sinking fund. All orders shall be payable to the **Orders** order of the person in whose favor they may be drawn **transferable.** and shall be transferable by indorsement. Certificates issued in payment for work done or improvements made **Certificates receiv-** chargeable specially to lots, parts of lots or parcels of **able for special** land shall be receivable for the special taxes levied **taxes.** therefor upon such lots, parts of lots or parcels of land respectively.

As amended by Chapter 144, Laws of 1875, also amended by Chapter 19, Laws of 1889.

CHAPTER 170, LAWS OF 1889.

The provisions of chapter 19, of the laws of Wisconsin, of the **Amendment to** year 1889, shall not apply to the funds appropriated to the public **chapter 19, laws** library and public museum of the city of Milwaukee, the trustees **1889.** of which institution shall have charge of the funds thereof to the same extent as if said chapter had never been enacted.

SECTION 2. The common council of said city shall **Levy for general** have power to levy annually, for the general city fund, **city fund.** exclusive of the amounts required for the support of schools, and for the payment of interest and principal on the funded debt of the city, and other special funds authorized by law, a sum not exceeding six mills on the dollar of the total assessed valuation of all property, real and personal, in said city subject to taxation; also for contingent fund a sum not exceeding one-half of one **Contingent fund.** mill on the dollar of such assessed valuation; also for a sewerage fund in each sewerage district, a sum not exceeding one and one-half mills upon the dollar of the total assessed valuation of all property, real and personal, in such sewerage district subject to taxation; also for the special sewerage fund for said city, a sum not exceeding one mill upon the dollar of the total assessed valuation **Special sewerage** of property, real and personal, in said city, subject to **fund.**

Ward fund.

School fund.

Levy not to exceed estimates.

taxation: also, for a fund for ward purposes in each ward, a further sum not exceeding six mills upon the dollar of the total assessed valuation of all property, real and personal, in such ward, subject to taxation; and also for the support of all the public schools in said city, including the high school, for the next fiscal year, a further sum not exceeding three and one-half mills upon the dollar of the total assessed valuation of all property, real and personal, in said city subject to taxation; provided, however, whenever the comptroller and board of public works, to meet current and necessary ward expenses, shall deem it necessary or expedient for the common council to levy a larger amount than six mills upon the dollar as aforesaid, in any ward for a ward fund as aforesaid, and shall so certify to the common council on or before the first day of July in any year, it shall be competent for the common council to levy for a ward fund in any such ward, in any such year, a percentage upon the dollar of the total assessed valuation of all property, real and personal, in such ward subject to taxation, not exceeding ten mills; provided, also, that the percentage which shall be levied in each ward for ward purposes shall in no case exceed the amount estimated and required by the comptroller and board of public works; and, provided further, that the aggregate amount of general taxes for all purposes levied by the common council and collected upon the city tax roll for municipal purposes under this section inclusive of taxes, for the support of the public library and the public museum and for the payment of principal and interest of the funded debt of the city, but not inclusive of the tax for the support of schools, shall not, in the whole, for any one year, exceed fourteen (14) mills on the dollar of the total valuation of property, real and personal, in said city subject to taxation; and also provided, that it shall not be lawful for the county board of supervisors of Milwaukee county, in determining the amount to be raised by tax in the city of Milwaukee for the support of common schools therein, for any year, to fix an amount greater than the amount apportioned to said city in the last apportionment of the income of the school fund of the state.

As amended by Chapter 310, Laws of 1883.

SECTION 3. It shall be the duty of the common council, before the first day of February in each year, to estimate, and by resolution determine what sums, in their judgment, will be required to meet the expenses and disbursements of said city for the current fiscal year, specifying in such resolution the sum required for each of the several funds authorized or created by law; and it shall not be lawful for said city to expend or contract a liability for any sum in excess of the amount so determined, on account of either or any of the funds of said city, except on the written recommendation of some department of the city government, specifying the reasons for such increased expenditure, which must be approved by a vote of three-fourths of the members elect of the common council. No debt or liability on the part of said city shall be contracted or created by any officer, board or department of said city, or by any subordinate or employe in the service of the city, in excess of the amount so determined and approved by the common council, on account of either or any of the funds of the said city, and every officer and employe of the city who shall participate in a violation of this section shall be personally liable to the city for all loss and damages resulting from such violation. *Annual estimates for expenses and disbursements.*

SECTION 4. All election expenses for city, ward, or general elections, shall be chargeable to the ward fund of the proper ward. *Election expenses.*

SECTION 5. The common council shall have power to appropriate sums, from time to time, out of the contingent fund, by a vote of at least three-fourths of all the aldermen elect, for any purpose or purposes which they shall declare, by their resolution, to be a proper expense to be defrayed by the said city. *Contingent fund, how appropriated.*

SECTION 6. As often as the common council shall think best for the safety or interest of the city, they shall select some bank or banks, or banking associations, with which all funds in the treasury of the city, or which shall be thereafter collected or received by the treasurer, shall be deposited; provided, however, that such bank, banks, or banking associations so selected shall, before receiving such funds, give securety in the same manner as is now required of the treasurer of said city, for the safe keeping and proper distribution of such funds, which security shall be approved by the common council. *City depository.*

Shall give bond.

Treasurer's weekly statement.

SECTION 7. The city treasurer shall render weekly statements to the common council of the amounts received and disbursed by him; and the balance over five thousand dollars on hand in the treasury, at the end of each week, shall be deposited with the bank or banks, or banking associations so selected, it or they giving proper vouchers therefor. From the time of so depositing such funds, the said treasurer shall be relieved from all liability to the city, arising from the failure of the bank or banks, or banking associations, safely to keep said funds. Such funds shall be drawn out only upon the check of the said treasurer, countersigned by the comptroller of said city.

His liability.

Funds, how drawn.

Balance in treasury.

SECTION 8. The treasurer and comptroller may, whenever the balance in the treasury does not amount to five thousand dollars, increase it by their check, as aforesaid, in favor of the treasurer. The true object of this is to enable the treasurer to have funds under his control with which to pay such demands upon the treasury as he is, or shall be required by law to pay.

Interest on deposits.

SECTION 9. The common council may, before or after so selecting a depository or depositories, contract with such bank or banks, or banking associations, that it or they shall pay to the city such interest upon said funds, so to be deposited, as they may mutually agree upon.

Limiting city treasurer.

SECTION 10. Nothing in this act contained shall be so construed as to authorize the treasurer to apply funds so retained by him, or so to be drawn from the bank on his check countersigned by the comptroller, to purposes other than those to which the same funds are appropriated by law. The common council may at any time when, in their opinion, the safety or interests of the city require it, direct all sums so deposited, to be paid into the treasury of the city, or to such other bank or banks as they may select under the law.

Common council may borrow on notes of city.

SECTION 11. The common council may from time to time borrow upon the notes of the city, signed by the mayor and city comptroller, such sums of money, in anticipation of the incoming taxes of the year, as they shall deem necessary to pay accruing interest on the funded debt, and to meet the current expenses of the city.

All such notes shall be paid out of the taxes of the current year, at such time as may be agreed on—not later than the first day of February next following their date. And the said common council may provide by resolution at any time for receiving moneys into the city treasury in advance payment of the taxes of the current year, and for the payment of interest thereon, at a rate not exceeding seven per cent. per annum from the time of the receipt of such taxes until the 15th day of January next ensuing and no longer. The receipts given by the treasurer of the city for such advance payment shall be countersigned by the city comptroller, and the excess of such advances, if any, over the amount of taxes of the year, payable by the party making the same shall be returned to such party with the interest thereon, between the 15th and 31st days of January next, after the making of the same.

SECTION 12. At the first meeting of the common council succeeding the charter election in each year, the city clerk shall prepare and present to the common council, a descriptive list, giving the dates, amounts and names of payees of all city orders drawn, which shall have remained in his office three years uncalled for by such payees. The common council shall cause such orders to be compared with such list, and when found or made correct, such list shall be filed and preserved in the office of such clerk, and a copy thereof, duly certified by said clerk, shall be delivered by him to the comptroller, and all such orders shall be cancelled and destroyed. The person entitled to any such order may, upon application to the common council, have a new order issued to him for the amount named in the original order so canceled, without interest, at any time within six years from the date of such original order, and not afterwards.

List of payees of unclaimed city orders.

Limiting time for new orders.

CHAPTER 161, LAWS OF 1889.

SECTION 1. It shall be lawful for the common council of the city of Milwaukee to provide, either by resolution or by ordinance, for the appointment by the city treasurer, subject to confirmation by the council, of such number of deputies as the council may at any time determine to be necessary, and each deputy so appointed shall, before entering upon his duties, take the oath required of the city officers and give such official bonds as the common council may require. Each deputy so appointed shall receive such compensation or salary as the common council shall determine. Each

Amendment to the charter of Milwaukee relating to the collection of taxes.

such deputy shall have authority to collect and receive any and all taxes and other moneys which the treasurer is authorized to collect and receive, and receipt for any such moneys, signed by any such deputy, shall have the same force and effect for all purposes as if signed by the city treasurer.

Tax districts.

SECTION 2.   It shall be lawful for said common council, whenever it shall be for the convenience of the public to do so, to divide the city in two or more districts for the purpose of collecting taxes, and to direct that the taxes upon real estate in each district, and upon personal property of owners residing in each district may be paid to and received by the treasurer or by a deputy at a particular place either within said district or without said district, to be specified by the council and mentioned in the notice required to be published by the treasurer upon the receipt of the tax roll All sales of real estate in case of the non-payment of taxes thereon, shall be made at the treasurer's office as heretofore.

Tax roll may be bound in volumes.

SECTION 3.   It shall be lawful for the common council of said city to cause the tax roll of said city to be so made out that it may be bound in two or more volumes so that the different volumes shall contain the descriptions of the real estate situated in the different districts, and the taxes thereon, and the names of the owners of personal property residing in the different districts, and the taxes thereon.   Each of said volumes shall be so numbered or paged that it may be designated and referred to by number or pages, or by both, in the warrant and in the clerk's certificate, which are attached or appended to the tax roll as required by law, or the warrant and certificate may be attached to each such volume.

Duplicate tax roll.

SECTION 4.   Whenever the common council of said city shall direct the tax roll for any year to be made out so as to be bound in two or more volumes, as provided in the preceding section, it shall be lawful for the city clerk of said city, and it shall be his duty to make out in the same manner the duplicate tax roll containing the state, county and school taxes, as required by law.

Salary of city treasurer.

SECTION 5.   The salary of the city treasurer shall be five thousand dollars a year, and he shall not be held responsible for any funds deposited by him in any bank designated as the city depository.

SECTION 6.   This act shall be taken and held to be an amendment to the charter of the city of Milwaukee, and shall be in force from and after its passage and publication.

CHAPTER 302, LAWS OF 1881.

AN ACT to restrict taxation in the city of Milwaukee.

Taxation limited to two per centum.

SECTION 1.   The aggregate amount of taxes levied or collected from the taxable property of any ward in the city of Milwaukee, for any one year, for all purposes, including state, county, city, school, ward, special, and all other taxes, shall not exceed two per centum of the assessed valuation of all the real and personal property of said ward, provided, that whenever, in any year, three-

fourths of all the members of the common council of said city, shall
declare by resolution, that an urgent public necessity exists for a
larger aggregate amount of taxation, than would be derived from
the taxable property of said city under the limitations hereinbefore
prescribed, then and in that case, the aggregate amount of said
taxes levied and collected from the taxable property of the several **Exception.**
wards in said city, for said years, may be increased to an amount
not exceeding two and one-half per cent. of the assessed valuation
of all the real and personal property in any ward of said city.

SECTION 2. This act is hereby declared to be an amendment
of the charter of said city, and all acts or parts of acts contrary to
the provisions of this act, so far as they conflict herewith, are
hereby repealed.

CHAPTER 87, LAWS OF 1861.

AN ACT to enable the city of Milwaukee to re-adjust its corporate
  debts.

SECTION 1. The city of Milwaukee is hereby authorized (by **City may issue**
ordinance, and with the approval of the commissioners of the public **bonds.**
debt), to issue new bonds to the amount, and for the purposes
following, that is to say:

First. For re-adjusting its bonded debt, incurred for strictly **For what purposes.**
municipal purposes, and of retiring all its outstanding bonds, exept
those which were issued to aid in the construction of railroads, to
any amount not exceeding the amount, including principal and
interest up to June 1, 1861, of the municipal bonds so to be retired,
and not exceeding eight hundred and twenty-five thousand
dollars.

Second. For the purpose of funding and retiring all city orders, **Ibid.**
city notes, treasury warrants and school orders, which shall have
been issued prior to February 1, 1861, and all judgments now
existing against the city, and all claims against the city heretofore
acknowledged and liquidated, whether secured or not (except
bonds and coupons thereon) to any amount not exceeding the
aggregate amount (including principal and interest up to June
1, 1861), of all such notes and other debt, (except bonds and
coupons as above), and not exceeding three hundred and twenty
thousand dollars.

SECTION 2. All the bonds issued under this act shall be **Bonds—how num-**
numbered consecutively from No. 1, upwards in the order in which **bered, what to**
they shall issue.· Each and every bond so issued, shall show on **show, and ac-**
its face for which of the purposes mentioned in section one of this **count of them**
act, it was issued. An accurate account shall be kept by the **kept.**
comptroller or by such other officer as shall be appointed by law
for that purpose, of the issue of all such bonds, of their numbers and
of the particular purpose, as above described, for which each bond
is issued. Such bonds shall be issued and used solely and only for
the purposes in section one of this act described, and in amount
shall not exceed the limit fixed in said section one, for any one of
the purposes so enumerated.

How signed, where and when payable, interest, etc.

SECTION 3.   All bonds issued under this act shall be signed by the mayor, countersigned by the comptroller, and attested by the commissioners of the public debt, and shall in terms be made payable in the city of New York, and all such bonds shall be payable at the end of thirty years from the date thereof, and shall each be for the principal sum of either one thousand dollars, or five hundred dollars. The commissioners of the public debt may, however, to facilitate exchanges, issue certificates or scrip, countersigned by the comptroller, for smaller sums, in exchange for which bonds of the denominations above mentioned may be given at par. No bond issued under this act shall bear a greater interest than at the rate of five per centum per annum, and no new bonds so to be issued shall be exchanged for old bonds or other evidence of debt at less than par, or dollar for dollar, except that in cases where they shall be issued and given to retire old bonds which bear ten per cent. interest, or such as are now secured by collateral pledge or deposit, the commissioners may in their discretion add to the principal sum of bonds so given, such amount as they shall deem equitable and just by reason of the circumstances last named.

Annual tax for interest.

SECTION 4.   A tax upon all taxable property of said city shall be annually levied and collected, commencing with the year 1861, sufficient in amount to pay annual interest at the rate provided in the section last above, upon the amount of all bonds authorized by this act to be issued for the purpose specified in section one hereof, and in addition thereto for sinking fund upon the same amount for each of the first five years after 1860, one-half of one per centum and for each year thereafter one per centum per annum, until all of the bonds issued under this act shall have been satisfied or provided for; and so much of the tax so levied for interest as shall not be required for that purpose, from year to year, as bonds shall be gradually retired, shall be added to and considered part of the sinking fund.

Commissioners of public debt.

SECTION 5.   On or before May 1st, A. D. 1861, three persons to be styled "commissioners of the public debt," shall be appointed, whose term of office shall be respectively for one, two and three years, as the mayor shall indicate in their appointment. Such commissioners shall continue while any of the bonds to be issued under this act shall be outstanding and unprovided for, and except in the case of two of those first appointed as aforesaid, their term of office shall be three years, and each shall hold over till his successor is appointed and qualified. The appointment of such commissioners, whether for full terms or for vacancies, shall be made by the mayor within one month after the expiration of their term of office, or after any vacancy shall occur, with the approval of the common council, and their duty shall be to superintend the execution, issue and use of the bonds to be issued under this act, and the levy, collection and disbursement of the tax herein provided for, for interest and sinking fund.

Their duty.

How tax for interest and sinking fund to be levied.

SECTION 6.   The commissioners of the public debt shall, at least ten days before the levy of general city taxes in each year, certify to the common council the amount necessary to be levied that year for interest and sinking fund. It shall be the duty of the common council to levy the tax for interest and sinking fund. It shall be the duty of the common council to levy the tax for interest and sinking fund in this act provided for, to the amount so certified by the commissioners, at the same time in each year that the common council levy the tax for general city purposes; and if they refuse or neglect to do so in any case for five days after the levy of the tax for general city purposes, the commissioners of the public debt shall levy the same and certify the amount thereof forthwith to the city clerk; and if the commissioners should likewise fail to levy such tax for interest and sinking fund within ten days after the levy of the general city taxes in any year, then the judge of any court of record of Milwaukee county, either in term time or in vacation, either in open court or at chambers, may, upon summary application of any holder or holders of bonds issued under this act, to the amount of ten thousand dollars or more, by order, levy such tax to such amount as he shall deem necessary, and to certify the amount thereof to said city clerk, who shall in all cases cause such tax, however levied, to be extended upon the tax lists in like manner as other taxes levied by the common council, but in a separate column, suitably marked to distinguish the same. And it shall be the duty of the treasurer, or other collector of taxes, to proceed to collect and enforce such tax in the same manner as other general city taxes are collected and enforced by law. In fixing the amount of the treasurer's bond, at the beginning of his term of office, the fact that he has to collect this tax for interest and sinking fund, shall be taken into consideration.

How collected.

SECTION 7. Money only shall be received by the treasurer or other collecting officer, in payment of said tax for interest and sinking fund, and the same shall be kept in and disbursed from the treasury strictly as a separate and distinct fund, not subject to the order or disposal of the common council, and shall be paid out only upon orders signed by the mayor, countersigned by the comptroller, and approved in writing by a majority of the commissioners of the public debt, specifying the purpose for which they are drawn; and such moneys shall be drawn out only for the purpose of paying interest on bonds issued under this act, and for retiring such bonds in the manner hereinafter provided. The commissioners of the public debt shall fix their own times of meeting and the mode of calling their meetings. The action of a majority of them shall be deemed the action of the commissioners. They shall transact all their business at the office of the comptroller, and that officer shall be ex-officio the secretary of the commissioners, and shall preserve a full record of all their proceedings.

Money only to be received.

Meetings of the commissioners.

SECTION 8. If upon the sale of any property for delinquent taxes, the city shall become the purchaser, it shall appropriate and add the amount of that portion of such delinquent tax which shall have been levied under this act for interest and sinking fund, to the fund raised under this act for interest and sinking fund, out of the first moneys which shall be or come into the treasury from any source whatever.

Delinquent taxes.

Treasurer to report to commis-sioners.

SECTION 9. The city treasurer shall, every year, immediately after the sale of land for delinquent taxes, and whenever else he shall be thereto requested by the commissioners of the public debt, in addition to any other report which he shall be required by law to make, report to said commissioners the condition of the interest and sinking fund, embracing a statement of all sums collected and held or disbursed by him for that fund; and no settlement by the treasurer with the common council as to that fund, shall be of any validity unless confirmed by said commissioners.

Cancellation of bonds.

SECTION 10. Once in each year, immediately after the coming in of the report mentioned in the last section, the commissioners of the public debt shall cause notice to be given by the comp-troller or otherwise, by publication in one daily newspaper printed in the city of New York, and one daily newspaper printed in the city of Milwaukee, each of general circulation, for twenty days at least, of the time and place of receiving bids or proposals from bond-holders to surrender their bonds for cancellation on payment out of the sinking fund, the manner of directing such proposals, and such other things as the commissioners shall direct to be inserted in such notice. The proposals received shall be opened by the commissioners of the public debt, in the presence of the mayor and of such other persons as shall choose to attend, and the lowest rates offered, provided the same be at or below par, shall be accepted to the extent of the fund on hand to pay the same at those rates, on being surrendered for cancellation. When the fund shall not be sufficient to pay all the bonds which are offered at equal rates and lower than all the others, the commis-sioners shall select at once and publicly, as aforesaid, among those bonds by lot, so many as they shall then have the means to pay. In case any parties, whose proposals shall be accepted, shall not within such reasonable time as the commissioners, with the approval of the mayor, shall fix, surrender their bonds, the commis-sioners may, with the approval in writing of the mayor, accept the next best proposals, provided they are below par, or they may advertise and proceed throughout anew, in the manner provided in this section, and so in like manner again and again, as often as the last named contingency shall arise. All bids or proposals by bond holders, under this section, shall particularly specify the numbers of the bonds so proposed to be retired, and shall be accompanied by a certificate in each case of the president or cashier, of some reputable bank, or of some person, in either case to be approved by the commissioners of the public debt, to the effect that the bonds specified in such bid are all deposited in such bank or with such person, and will be delivered up for cancellation, if such bid shall be accepted by the commissioners.

When bonds to cease to draw interest.

SECTION 11. In any case when no proposals, or not sufficient in amount to consume the moneys on hand belonging to the sinking fund shall be received to retire bonds at or below par, the commissioners may advertise and proceed throughout again as provided in the last section above, or with the approval of the mayor, shall in their discretion, determine by lot publicly, as aforesaid, which bond shall be paid out of the moneys then in the sinking fund at par, including interest, and shall notify the holders of their readiness to pay the same, by advertisement for twenty days in one daily newspaper printed in the city of New York, and one daily newspaper printed in the city of Milwaukee, each of general circulation, and from the time of the completion of such notice in both papers, such bonds so determined by lot, shall cease to bear interest, unless the city shall neglect to pay the same for ten days after payment thereof shall afterwards be demanded, and the money shall be kept constantly on hand by the treasurer to pay the same on presentment, unless the commissioners of the public debt, with the approval of the mayor, shall otherwise order.

SECTION 12. The bonds issued under this act shall contain a covenant to the effect that said city shall issue no bonds except under or consistently with this act, until the aggregate amount of bonds issued under this act and outstanding, shall have been reduced to five hundred thousand dollars or under. All bonds, notes or other evidences of debt payable at a future day, hereafter issued by said city, contrary to the provisions of this act, during the period last named, either with or without the color of statutory authority, shall be void. *No bonds to be issued inconsistent with this act.*

If in any case, the city or city officer shall hereafter threaten or attempt to issue any such bonds, or other evidences of debt in contravention of the provisions of this act, they shall be restrained by injunction from so doing, upon the application of any holder of bonds issued under this act, or any citizen who shall have paid city taxes in said city for two years then next preceding; provided, however, that nothing in this act contained shall prevent the city from issuing orders on the treasury, payable out of the revenue of the current year, or from carrying out the existing contract for the building of school houses now in process of erection. *Injunction.* *Proviso.*

SECTION 13. No city or school order or scrip issued prior to the first day of February, 1861, nor any such order or scrip drawn for any such debt or liability contracted prior to such date, shall be receivable in payment of any tax or in redemption of any property sold for delinquent taxes, unless it be for delinquent taxes prior to 1861. *City and school orders not receivable for taxes.*

SECTION 14. Common council, with the approval of the commissioners of the public debt, may at any time, to meet interest falling due, but for no other purpose, anticipate by temporary loan on the comptroller's note, a portion of the incoming tax for the current year; provided, that in no case shall such notes be issued in any one year to exceed ten thousand dollars. It is, however, further provided, that whenever the city shall have returned to the cash system in its finances, that is to say, whenever it shall commence to act upon the plan, and shall be so circumstanced in the opinion of the common council and of the commissioners of the public debt, that it can adhere permanently to the plan of receiving nothing except money into the treasury in payment of taxes, and of allowing no city or school orders or scrip to issue except when there is money in the treasury to meet and pay the same, then the common council may, with the approval of the commissioners of the public debt, anticipate, by temporary loan *How interest may be met.*

on the comptroller's note, a portion of the incoming tax not exceeding $20,000 in any year, to meet current expenses.

Retiring of railroad bonds.   SECTION 15. Nothing in this act shall be construed so as to prevent said city of Milwaukee, with the approval of the commissioners of the public debt, and upon authority to be hereafter attained from the legislature, from issuing bonds strictly and only for the purpose of settling and retiring any balance or remainder of city bonds heretofore issued in aid of railroad companies which shall not be met or provided for by the companies. Such new bonds shall not in any event exceed in amount, altogether, the sum of two hundred and fifty thousand dollars, shall run thirty years from their date, and shall bear interest at a rate not exceeding five pei centum per annum.   But no such bonds shall be issued or used for the purpose of settling or retiring any of the city bonds issued to any railroad company until all the security of every kind and nature taken by the city from that company on account of those city bonds, shall have been exhausted, or shall have become in the opinion of both the common council and the commissioners of the public debt, clearly and hopelessly inadequate to the protection of the city.   If any of the bonds authorized by this act to be issued for the purposes specified in section one hereof, shall not be accepted by the parties for whom they are so intended, and so in consequence thereof the sum raised for annual interest in any year shall be in excess of the amount required for that purpose, then such excess shall be added to the sinking fund, and used to retire bonds in the manner in this act provided.

The moneys levied and collected for or belonging to the interest and sinking fund under this act, shall be held in trust for those purposes only, for the benefit of the holders of the bonds issued under this act for the purposes specified in section one hereof, shall in no way be diverted from that purpose, nor shall the same or any part thereof be subject to attachment or execution, nor be liable by any process or proceeding to be subjected to the payment of any other debt than that to meet which it was specially raised under this act.

Acts repealed.   SECTION 16. All acts and parts of acts passed at any former session of the legislature, authorizing said city to issue bonds or to raise a sinking fund, are hereby repealed, and neither the said city nor any ward or wards, or any part or subdivision thereof, shall have power to issue bonds or other evidence of debt, except under or consistently with the provisions of this act.

Re-levy of unpaid taxes.   SECTION 17. Whenever any portion of the tax levied for any one year, shall be unpaid and shall remain delinquent, and the lands sold therefor shall be unredeemed, an amount equal to such delinquent tax may in the discretion of the common council, with the approval of the commissioners of the public debt, at the time of levying city taxes for the next year, be added tot he amount of taxes which would otherwise be levied for the same purposes, and levied and collected as the other taxes are levied and collected by law.

SECTION 18. After so many of the bonds issued under this act shall have been satisfied and retired as to leave less than five hundred thousand dollars in amount thereof outstanding, nothing **Limits to amount of** in this act contained shall be construed so as to prevent said city, **bonds that may be** under authority thereto then obtained from the legislature, **subsequently** from issuing her bonds to any extent, so that the aggregate **issued.** amount of the bonds so then issued and those issued under this act and then still outstanding, shall not exceed five hundred thousand dollars, nor from issuing bonds at any time for the purpose of extending the time of payment of the amounts of any of the bonds issued under this act at the same or less rate of interest at the maturity thereof.

SECTION 19. This act shall take effect from and after its passage.

CHAPTER 91, LAWS OF 1891.

SECTION 1. The common council of the city of Milwaukee is **Common council** hereby authorized to provide by ordinance for the issue of corporate **may issue bonds.** bonds of said.city not exceeding in amount six hundred thousand dollars, payable in not more than twenty years after date of said issue. Such bonds shall bear interest not exceeding the rate of five per cent. per annum and shall be known as and called "City Hall Bonds," and shall be issued to provide funds for the erection of a building suitable for the accommodation of the city departments. Said bonds to be issued as follows: Two hundred thousand dollars within 1891, two hundred thousand dollars within 1892, and two hundred thousand dollars within 1893.

SECTION 2. All bonds issued under the provisions of this act **Bonds, how issued.** shall be signed by the mayor and clerk of said city, countersigned by the comptroller of said city, attested by the commissioners of public debt of said city, sealed with the corporate seal of said city, made payable in lawful money of the United States of America in the city of Milwaukee or New York, and shall each be for the principal sum of one thousand dollars, or five hundred dollars, or one hundred dollars, and shall have attached thereto interest coupons or warrants for the semi-annual payment of interest thereon and such bonds and coupons shall be numbered in the form and manner to be designated by said comptroller.

SECTION 3. Bonds issued under the provisions of this act shall **Bonds, how dis-** be issued from time to time in such amount as the common council **posed of.** of said city may determine upon; said bonds when issued and properly signed and sealed, shall be delivered to the commissioners of public debt of said city, and by that body disposed of, the proceeds arising therefrom to be paid into the treasury of said city, and such proceeds shall constitute a separate and distinct fund, to be exclusively applied for the purposes specified in the first section of this act.

SECTION 4. The office of commissioners of public debt of **Office of commis-** said city shall not be abolished while any of the bonds issued **sioners of public** under the provisions of this act remain outstanding and unpaid. **debt not to be** **abolished.**

Certain sections of chapter 87, laws of 1861, made a part of this act.

SECTION 5. The provisions of sections 2, 6, 7, 8, 9, 10, 11, and 17, chapter 87, of the laws of 1861, applicable and not inconsistent with the provisions of this act, shall apply to bonds issued under the provisions of this act, and such sections, if not inconsistent, are incorporated as a part of this act. The true intent and meaning of this act is to provide for the present issue of bonds in the same manner as bonds issued under the provisions of that act are provided for, unless the common council upon the recommendation of the commissioners of public debt, shall elect by ordinance to specify what particular bonds shall expire and be retired in each year not less than five per cent. of the whole issue, and said common council is hereby authorized to so elect.

Tax to be levied to pay interest and principal of bonds.

SECTION 6. The common council of said city shall annually cause a tax to be levied upon all taxable property in said city, both personal and real, for the payment of the annual interest on all unpaid bonds issued under the provisions of this act, and for twenty years before the principal of said bonds becomes due, the said common council shall annually cause a tax to be levied upon all taxable property, both personal and real, equal in amount to five per cent. of all bonds issued and outstanding under the provisions of this act, for a sinking fund to redeem such bonds as the said commissioners of public debt direct to be cancelled, or which shall have matured.

Bonds to be cancelled.

SECTION 7. As soon as a sinking fund shall have been collected and set aside, the said commissioners of public debt shall proceed to cancel bonds in amount equal to the sinking fund so provided.

Same.

SECTION 8. All bonds directed to be paid by said commissioners of public debt shall be, when paid, stamped "cancelled," and when so stamped shall be delivered to the common council of said city, and by that body publicly declared cancelled.

Bonds not to be sold for less than par value.

SECTION 9. The commissioners of public debt of said city are hereby prohibited from selling or otherwise disposing of any such bonds at a less valuation than par, that is to say, at less than the principal of said bonds together with the accrued interest thereon.

Board of public works may make contracts.

SECTION 10. The board of public works shall have power and authority by and under the direction of the common council to enter into contract or contracts for doing all the work of erecting and constructing the city hall building, without any other appropriation for doing such work than is herein provided and in advance of and prior to the issuance and disposal of the bonds herein authorized to be issued and disposed of during the years 1892 and 1893. The common council shall, from time to time, during the progress of said work in the erection and construction of said building, appropriate out of the funds realized from the proceeds of the sale of the bonds as herein provided, such sum or sums of money as may become necessary and required for defraying the cost of the erection of said building, not exceeding in any one year the amount realized from the sale of said bonds.

Comptroller to countersign contracts.

SECTION 11. It shall be the duty of the comptroller to countersign any contract or contracts for doing the work of erecting and constructing the said city hall building which shall be made and entered into by the said board of public works, as aforesaid; provided however, that the amount of money to be expended and the liability to be incurred by such contract or contracts shall not exceed the amount of bonds authorized to be issued for the purpose of such contract or contracts, and the amount of the fund to be realized from the sale of such bonds.

SECTION 12. The provisions of sections 14 and 15 of chapter 5 of the charter of the city of Milwaukee, as revised and amended, any other provision or provisions of said charter which are inconsistent with the provisions this act shall not apply to the contract or contracts to be made and entered into for the purposes and under the provisions of this act.

Provisions of sections 14 and 15, of chapter 5, of charter not to apply to said contracts.

CHAPTER 92, LAWS OF 1891.

SECTION 1. The common council of the city of Milwaukee is hereby authorized to provide by ordinance for the issue of corporate bonds of said city, not exceeding in amount two hundred and twenty thousand dollars, payable in not more then twenty years after date of said issue. Said bonds shall bear interest not exceeding the rate of five per cent. per annum, and shall be known as and called "public park bonds" and shall be issued to provide funds for the purchase and improvement of public parks, and for the paying of installments of principal and interest upon the parks already purchased under the provisions of chapter 488, of the laws of 1889, and of parks to be hereafter purchased, as they may become due; provided, that not more than one hundred and fifty thousand dollars worth of said bonds shall be issued in the year 1891, and seventy thousand dollars worth of said bonds shall be issued in the year 1892, not less than fifty thousand dollars of which shall be used for the purchase of park grounds on the west side of the city of Milwaukee and north of the Menomonee river.

Common council may issue bonds.

SECTION 2. All bonds issued under the provisions of this act shall be signed by the mayor and clerk of said city, countersigned by the comptroller of said city, attested by the commissioners of public debt of said city, sealed with the corporate seal of said city, made payable in lawful money of the United States of America in the city of Milwaukee or of New York, and shall each be for the principal sum of one thousand dollars, or five hundred dollars, or one hundred dollars, and shall have attached thereto interest coupons or warrants for the semi-annual payment of interest thereon, and such bonds and coupons shall be numbered in the form and manner to be designated by said comptroller.

Bonds, how issued.

SECTION 3. Bonds issued under the provisions of this act shall be issued from time to time in such amount as the common council of said city may determine upon; said bonds when issued and properly signed and sealed, shall be delivered to the commissioners of public debt of said city, and by that body disposed of; the proceeds arising therefrom to be paid into the treasury of said city, and such proceeds shall continue a separate and distinct fund to be exclusively applied for the purposes specified in the first section of this act.

Bonds, how disposed of.

Office not to be abolished.

SECTION 4.   The office of commissioners of public debt of said city shall not be abolished while any of the bonds issued under the provisions of this act remain outstanding and unpaid.

Certain laws made a part of this act.

SECTION 5.   The provisions of sections 2, 6, 7, 8, 9, 10, 11, and 17, chapter 87, of the laws of 1861 applicable and not inconsistent with the provisions of this act shall apply to bonds issued under the provisions of this act, and such sections, if not inconsistent, are incorporated as a part of this act.   The true intent and meaning of this act is to provide for the present issue of bonds in the same manner as bonds issued under the provisions of that act are provided for, unless the common council upon the recommendation of the commissioners of public debt shall elect by ordinance to specify what particular bonds shall expire and be retired in each year, not less than five per cent. of the whole issue, and said common council is hereby authorized to so elect.

Tax to be levied to pay interest and principal of bonds.

SECTION 6.   The common council of said city shall annually cause a tax to be levied upon all taxable property in said city, both personal and real, for the payment of the annual interest on all unpaid bonds issued under the provisions of this act, and for twenty years before the principal of said bonds becomes due, the said common council shall annually cause a tax to be levied upon all taxable property, both personal and real, equal in amount to five per cent. of all bonds issued and outstanding under the provisions of this act, for a sinking fund to redeem such bonds as the said commissioners of public debt direct to be cancelled or which shall have matured.

Bonds to be cancelled.

SECTION 7.   As soon as a sinking fund shall have been collected and set aside, the said commissioners of public debt shall proceed to cancel bonds in amount equal to the sinking fund so provided.

Same.

SECTION 8.   All bonds directed to be paid by said commissioners of public debt shall be, when paid, stamped "cancelled," and when so stamped shall be delivered to the common council of said city, and by that body publicly declared cancelled.

Bonds not to be sold for less than par value.

SECTION 9.   The commissioners of public debt of said city are hereby prohibited from selling or otherwise disposing of any such bonds at a less valuation than par, that is to say, at less than the principal of said bonds, together with the accrued interest thereon; and said commissioners of public debt are further prohibited from issuing bonds under the provisions of this act, which, together with the bonds heretofore issued shall exceed the limit of the bonded indebtedness of said city.

CHAPTER 93, LAWS OF 1891,

Common council may issue bonds.

SECTION 1.   The common council of the city of Milwaukee is hereby authorized to provide by ordinance for the issue of corporate bonds of said city not exceeding in amount two hundred and fifty thousand dollars, payable in not more than twenty years after date of said issue.   Said bonds shall bear interest not exceeding the rate of five per cent. per annum, and shall be known as, and called "library and museum bonds," and shall be issued to provide funds for the erection of a public library and public museum in the city of Milwaukee, and to purchase additional grounds therefor, if deemed necessary. Provided, that not more than one hundred thousand dollars worth of said bonds shall be issued in the year 1891, and one hundred and fifty thousand dollars worth of said bonds shall be issued in the year 1892.

SECTION 2. All bonds issued under the provisions of this act shall be signed by the mayor and clerk of said city, countersigned by the comptroller of said city, attested by the commissioners of public debt of said city, sealed with the corporate seal of said city, made payable in lawful money of the United States of America in the city of Milwaukee or New York, and shall each be for the principal sum of one thousand dollars, or five hundred dollars, or one hundred dollars, and shall have attached thereto interest coupons or warrants for the semi-annual payment of interest thereon, and such bonds and coupons shall be numbered in the form and manner to be designated by said comptroller. **Bonds, how issued.**

SECTION 3. Bonds issued under the provisions of this act shall be issued from time to time in such amounts as the common council of said city may determine upon; said bonds when issued and properly signed and sealed shall be delivered to the commissioners of public debt of said city, and by that body disposed of; the proceeds arising therefrom to be paid into the treasury of said city, and such proceeds shall constitute a separate and distinct fund, to be exclusively applied for the purposes specified in the first section of this act. **Bonds, how disposed of.**

SECTION 4. The office of commissioners of public debt of said city shall not be abolished while any of the bonds issued under the provisions of this act remain outstanding and unpaid. **Office not to be abolished.**

SECTION 5. The provisions of sections 2, 6, 7, 8, 9, 10, 11, and 17, chapter 87, of the laws of 1861, applicable and not inconsistent with the provisions of this act, shall apply to bonds issued under the provisions of this act, and such sections, if not inconsistent, are incorporated as a part of this act. The true intent and meaning of this act is to provide for the present issue of bonds in the same manner as bonds issued under the provisions of that act are provided for, unless the common council, upon the recommendation of the commissioners of public debt shall elect by ordinance to specify what particular bonds shall expire and be retired in each year, not less than five per cent. of the whole issue and said common council is hereby authorized to so elect. **Certain laws made a part of this act.**

SECTION 6. The common council of said city shall annually cause a tax to be levied upon all taxable property in said city, both personal and real, for the payment of the annual interest on all unpaid bonds issued under the provisions of this act, and for twenty years before the principal of said bonds becomes due, the said common council shall, annually, cause a tax to be levied upon all taxable property, both personal and real, equal in amount to five per cent. of all bonds issued and outstanding under the provisions of this act, for a sinking fund to redeem such bonds as the **Tax to be levied to pay interest and principal of bonds.**

said commissioners of public debt direct to be cancelled, or which shall have matured.

Bonds to be cancelled.

SECTION 7. As soon as a sinking fund shall have been collected and set aside, the said commissioners of public debt shall proceed to cancel bonds in amount equal to the sinking fund so provided.

Same.

SECTION 8. All bonds directed to be paid by said commissioners of public debt shall be, when paid, stamped "cancelled," and when so stamped shall be delivered to the common council of said city, and by that body publicly declared cancelled.

Bonds not to be sold for less than par value.

SECTION 9. The commissioners of public debt of said city are hereby prohibited from selling or otherwise disposing of any such bonds at a less valuation than par, that is to say, at less than the principal of said bonds, together with the accrued interest thereon; and said commissioners of public debt are further prohibited from issuing bonds under the provisions of this act, which, together with the bonds heretofore issued shall exceed the limit of the bonded indebtedness of said city.

Board of public works may make contracts.

SECTION 10. The board of public works shall have power and authority by, and under the direction of the common council, to enter into contract or contracts for doing all the work of erecting and constructing the library and museum building without any other appropriation for doing such work than is herein provided, and in advance of and prior to the issuance and disposal of the bonds herein authorized to be issued and disposed of during the year 1892. The common council shall, from time to time, during the progress of said work in the erection and construction of said building, appropriate out of the funds realized from the proceeds of the sale of the bonds, as herein provided, such sum or sums of money as may become necessary and required for defraying the cost of the erection of said building, not exceeding in any one year the amount realized from the sale of said bonds.

Comptroller to countersign contracts.

SECTION 11. It shall be the duty of the comptroller to countersign any contract or contracts for doing the work of erecting and constructing the said library and museum building which shall be made and entered into by the said board of public works as aforesaid; provided, however, that the amount of money to be expended and the liability to be incurred by such contract or contracts shall not exceed the amount of bonds authorized to be issued for the purpose of such contract or contracts and the amount of the fund to be realized from the sale of such bonds.

Sections 14 and 15, of chapter 5, of Milwaukee charter, not to apply to said contracts.

SECTION 12. The provisions of sections 14 and 15 of chapter 5 of the charter of the city of Milwaukee as revised and amended, and any other provision or provisions of said charter which are inconsistent with the provisions of this act, shall not apply to the contract or contracts to be made and entered into for the purposes and under the provisions of this act.

CHAPTER 120, LAWS OF 1891.

Common council may issue bonds to build bridges.

SECTION 1. The common council of the city of Milwaukee is hereby authorized to provide by ordinance for the issue of corporate bonds of said city in amount not exceeding fifty-five thousand dollars, said bonds shall be payable not more than twenty years after the date of said issue, and shall bear interest not exceeding the rate of five per centum per annum. Said bonds shall be known as and called "park bridge bonds," and shall be issued exclusively to provide funds for erecting and constructing a bridge across the Milwaukee river in the thirteenth and eighteenth wards of said city.

SECTION 2. All bonds issued under the provisions of this act shall be signed by the mayor and clerk of said city, countersigned by the comptroller of said city, attested by the commissioners of public debt of said city, sealed with the corporate seal of said city, made payable in lawful money of the United States of America in the city of Milwaukee or New York, and shall each be for the principal sum of one thousand dollars, or five hundred dollars, or one hundred dollars, and shall have attached thereto interest coupons or warrants for the semi-annual payment of interest thereon, and such bonds and coupons shall be numbered in the form and manner to be designated by said comptroller. *Bonds, how issued.*

SECTION 3. Bonds issued under the provisions of this act shall be issued from time to time in such amounts as the common council of said city may determine upon; said bonds, when issued and properly signed and sealed, shall be delivered to the commissioners of public debt of said city, and by that body disposed of, the proceeds arising therefrom to be paid into the treasury of said city, and such proceeds shall constitute a separate and distinct fund, to be exclusively applied for the purposes specified in the first section of this act. Provided, that nothing in this act contained shall be construed as authorizing said common council to issue bonds in excess of the limitation prescribed in section 6 of chapter 11 of the charter of said city and the acts amendatory thereof. *Bonds, how disposed of.*

SECTION 4. The office of commissioners of public debt of said city shall not be abolished while any of the bonds issued under the provisions of this act remain outstanding and unpaid. *Office not to be abolished.*

SECTION 5. The provisions of sections 2, 6, 7, 8, 9, 10, 11, and 17, chapter 87, of the laws of 1861, applicable and not inconsistent with the provisions of this act, shall apply to bonds issued under the provisions of this act, and such sections, if not inconsistent are incorporated as a part of this act. The true intent and meaning of this act is to provide for the present issue of bonds in the same manner as bonds issued under the provisions of that act are provided for, unless the common council upon the recommendation of the commissioners of public debt shall elect by ordinance to specify what particular bonds shall expire and be retired in each year, not less than five per centum of the whole issue; and said common council is hereby authorized to so elect. *Certain former laws made part of this act.*

SECTION 6. The common council of said city shall annually cause a tax to be levied upon all taxable property in said city, both personal and real, for the payment of the annual interest on all unpaid bonds issued under the provisions of this act, and for twenty years before the principal of said bonds become due, the *Tax to be levied to pay bonds.*

said common council shall annually cause a tax to be levied upon all taxable property in said city, both personal and real, equal in amount to five per centum of all bonds issued and outstanding under the provisions of this act, for a sinking fund to redeem such bonds as the said commissioners of public debt direct to be cancelled, or which shall have matured.

Bonds to be cancelled.

SECTION 7. As soon as a sinking fund shall have been collected and set aside, the said commissioners of public debt shall proceed to cancel bonds in amount equal to the sinking fund so provided.

Same.

SECTION 8. All bonds directed to be paid by said commissioners of public debt shall be, when paid, stamped "cancelled," and when so stamped shall be delivered to the common council of said city, and by that body publicly declared cancelled.

Bonds not to be sold at less than par value.

SECTION 9. The commissioners of public debt of said city are hereby prohibited from selling or otherwise disposing of any such bonds at a less valuation than par, that is to say, at less than the principal of said bonds, together with the accrued interest thereon.

CHAPTER 122, LAWS OF 1891.

Common council to acquire certain lands.

SECTION 1. It is hereby made the duty of the common council of the city of Milwaukee and the officers of said city, immediately upon the passage and publication of this act, to acquire by dedication, purchase, or condemnation a strip of land extending from the intersection of Eleventh avenue with Pierce street in said city, in a northerly direction to the intersection of Sixteenth and Fowler streets in said city, to be seventy feet wide, and of uniform width. And it is hereby made the duty of the city engineer of said city, immediately upon the passage and publication of this act, to cause

City engineer to make survey.

a survey of the same to be made, and to file said survey in the office of the board of public works of said city, and he shall also file therewith a description of the several parcels of land contained therein, and also a map or plat thereof, showing the location of the same. It is hereby made the duty of the board of public works of said city of Milwaukee, immediately upon the filing of the said plat, and description of said strip of land and said survey to ascertain if the same or any part thereof can be acquired from the owners thereof, by dedication without compensation, and it is made the further duty of said board of public works also to enter into negotiations with the several owners of the lands necessary to be acquired, for the purchase of the fee simple, of all the lands described in said survey which cannot be acquired by gift. And it is further made the duty of the common council and the proper city officers, to provide for the payment of the amounts necessary for such purpose and which shall be agreed upon by the said board of public works out of the fund hereinafter to be provided. It is hereby made the duty of the said board of public works within sixty days after the filing of said survey and plat, to report to the common council a list of all the lands set off in said survey and plat, which they have been unable to acquire by gift, and of all lands for which they have entered into negotiations with the owners to be acquired by purchase, together with the various sums and amounts for which the tracts and parcels of land can be acquired. And the common council may, by resolution, authorize the board of public works to purchase any of such lands at the prices proposed, or may reject any or all of the proposals as they may deem proper. And the common council shall thereupon proceed to acquire the several parcels described in the report of the said board of public works by condemnation which have not been acquired by gift or the proposals for the purchase which have not been accepted, and shall proceed in that behalf as provided in the charter of said city for the condemnation and taking of lands for streets and other public use, and without petition therefor. All provisions of the charter of the city of Milwaukee and the several acts amendatory thereof, in relation to the condemnation of lands for highway and public purposes and the assessment of benefits and damages arising therefrom and the time for appealing and the manner of appeal of any person who shall feel aggrieved on account of such assessment, shall apply to the proceedings for the taking or condemnation of the lands which shall be taken by proceedings for condemnation under and by virtue of the provisions of this act. The damages in all cases shall be paid out of the fund herein provided to be provided as aforesaid. And it is further provided that whenever the common council shall have confirmed the assessment of benefits and damages in said condemnation proceedings, and shall have advertised for six days in the official newspaper of said city that the amount awarded to the owners of said lands, respectively, has been provided in the hands of the city treasurer, and is ready to be paid over to such several owners, the city of Milwaukee shall have full power and authority to enter upon and appropriate the property so taken and condemned and the same shall thereafter be subject to the provisions of this act, and to all the laws and ordinances of the city of Milwaukee applicable thereto. And it is further provided that if any person shall appeal from said assessment of benefits and damages in the manner provided by said charter, that such appeal shall not prevent the city of Milwaukee from entering upon possession of said lands as hereinbefore provided and the owners of said lands so appealing may receive and accept the amount so awarded to them without any prejudice whatever to said appeal, and if a greater sum than the amount awarded shall be recovered in any case, the same with costs shall be paid out of said fund hereinafter to be provided, and if a less sum be recovered the appellant shall pay the costs. In all other respects said proceedings shall be governed by the provisions of said charter relating to the taking of lands for public use.

SECTION 2. The said city of Milwaukee is authorized and empowered to use the lands so acquired for all public purposes of whatever kind and may construct, erect and maintain thereon and public bridge or bridges, viaducts, abutments, piers or other thing, and improve the same or any portion thereof, as a public street or walk, and construct therein any sewer, water main, and use the same for all other public purposes or uses, as the common council of said city of Milwaukee may from time to time prescribe.

May use lands for all public purposes.

May build a viaduct.

SECTION 3. The common council of the city of Milwaukee is hereby authorized to cause to be built with all reasonable despatch after procuring the right of way as hereinbefore provided, a suitable viaduct from the intersection of Eleventh avenue and Pierce street, in said city, and extending as nearly as practicable on the level across the Menomonee valley in a northerly direction to the intersection of Sixteenth and Fowler streets in the Sixteenth ward of the city of Milwaukee.

Viaduct, how to be constructed.

SECTION 4. Said viaduct shall be constructed in a substantial manner of iron (except the floor and floor beams). It shall rest upon iron columns of suitable size and dimensions set upon stone foundations and shall be of uniform width of not less than sixty feet and at least nineteen feet above and clear of railway tracks. Wherever necessary, draw-bridges shall be provided as well as suitable approaches at both termini of said viaduct and such intermediate points as may be necessary for safe and convenient access thereto. All abutments that may be needed shall be constructed of masonry in a solid manner.

Plans for same.

SECTION 5. The common council shall cause to be made a plan and detail specification for doing of said work, and the estimate of the cost thereof, and as soon thereafter as practicable, the city shall enter upon the construction of said viaduct, bridges, and approaches in conformity thereto. The city of Milwaukee is hereby authorized to enter into a negotiation with the Chicago, Milwaukee & St. Paul railway company for the payment of such a portion of the expense of the construction of said viaduct by the said railway company, as shall be agreed upon in consideration of any agreement which shall be made by said railway company in regard thereto, to vacate such portions of Muskego avenue as are occupied by the tracks and right of way of said railway company as shall be desired by said railway company and agreed upon by said city and railway company, after said viaduct shall be completed and the said railway company shall have paid its portion of the expense and cost of the same which may have been agreed upon.

Viaduct to be under control of city.

SECTION 6. The said viaduct and approaches thereto shall forever remain under the absolute control and management of the city of Milwaukee and no exclusive rights or franchises for purposes of horse railway communication, the lighting of streets, highways or the like, or any other exclusive franchises, privileges or immunities shall ever be granted over the same or any part thereof by said city, to any person or corporation whatever.

May issue bonds—proceeds thereof, how to be used.

SECTION 7. The mayor and common council of the city of Milwaukee are hereby authorized to issue the corporate bonds of said city to an amount not exceeding three hundred thousand dollars, to be issued as follows: fifty thousand dollars after the first of July, 1891; one hundred and fifty thousand dollars after the first of July, 1892; one hundred thousand dollars after the first of July, 1893. The proceeds of said bonds to be applied to the building of said viaduct and the procurement of the right of way and the payment of all damages that may be assessed or allowed to the owners of property which shall be purchased or condemned for the uses and purposes in this act provided; and such bonds shall be payable at such time or times as the common council by ordinance may see fit and determine, with interest not exceeding five per centum per annum. Said council may also levy such tax or taxes upon all the taxable property of the city of Milwaukee as may be found necessary from time to time to pay the balances of the expenses or cost of such construction, and right of way if such there should be. The provisions of chapter 465, of the laws of 1885, as to form of bonds, the issue and sale thereof, the levy of taxes creating a sinking fund, and all other details not inconsistent herewith, are made applicable to the bonds herein provided for, to be issued for the purposes named in this act. Provided, that the common council of said city upon the recommendation of the commissioners of public debt may elect and specify by ordinance what particular bonds issued hereunder shall expire and be retired in each year, not less than five per centum of the whole issue, and said common council is hereby authorized to so elect.

SECTION 8. In case the Chicago, Milwaukee & St. Paul Railway Company shall pay a just and fair proportion of the expenses of constructing the said viaduct, and of the right of way, which shall be agreed upon between the city of Milwaukee and the said railway company, the city of Milwaukee shall institute proceedings to vacate so much of Muskego avenue as shall be occupied by the tracks and right of way of the said railway company; and the said railway company shall be freed and discharged from any obligation to build or construct any viaduct, causeway or passage way, for public use over any part of Muskego avenue, although its tracks may be multiplied and extended, or additional territory in the future be occupied by the railway for its purposes. But nothing herein contained shall be construed so as to lessen or impair the right of the city of Milwaukee to require or compel the said railway company to construct causeways, bridges or viaducts over any other street in said city. And in case the Chicago, Milwaukee & St. Paul Railway and the city of Milwaukee shall fail, neglect or refuse to make and enter into the agreement above named, then and in such case the right and power of the city to require and compel the railway company to construct a bridge, causeway or viaduct over any part of Muskego avenue, shall in no wise be lessened, abridged or impaired.

C., M. & St. P. Ry. Co. to pay part of expense of constructing viaduct.

SECTION 9. Chapter 476, of the laws of 1887, and chapter 231, of the laws of 1889, and all other acts and parts of acts contravening the provisions of this act are hereby repealed.

Repeals chapter 476, laws of 1887, and chapter 231, laws of 1889.

SECTION 10. The board of public works shall have power and authority by and under the direction of the common council, to enter into contract or contracts for doing all the work of erecting and constructing viaduct and approaches herein provided for without any other appropriation for doing such work than is herein provided, and in advance of and prior to the issuance and disposal of the bonds herein authorized to be issued and disposed of during the year 1892. The common council shall, from time to time, during the progress of said work in the erection and construction of said building, appropriate out of the funds realized from the proceeds of the sale of the bonds, as herein provided, such sum

Board of public works may make contracts for building viaduct.

or sums as may become necessary and required for defraying the cost of the erection of said building, not exceeding in any one year the amount realized from the sale of said bonds.

Duty of comptroller.

SECTION 11. It shall be the duty of the comptroller to countersign any contract or contracts for doing the work of erecting and constructing the said viaduct and approaches herein provided for, which shall be made and entered into by the said board of public works, as aforesaid; provided, however, that the amount of money to be expended and the liability to be incurred by such contract or contracts shall not exceed the amount of bonds authorized to be issued for the purpose of such contract or contracts, and the amount of the fund to be realized from the sale of such bonds.

Certain sections of charter not to apply.

SECTION 12. The provisions of section 14 and 15, of chapter 5, of the charter of the city of Milwaukee, as revised and amended, and any other provision or provisions of said charter which are inconsistent with the provisions of this act, shall not apply to the contract or contracts to be made and entered into for the purposes and under the provisions of this act.

CHAPTER 311, LAWS OF 1893.

AN ACT to authorize cities operating under special charters granted by the legislature of this state and containing a population of three thousand or more inhabitants, to issue corporate bonds, for certain purposes.

Common council may issue corporate bonds.

SECTION 1. The common council of any city incorporated by and operating under a special charter granted by the legislature of this state, containing a population of three thousand inhabitants or more, as shown by the last state or national census, is hereby authorized to issue corporate bonds, payable in lawful money of the United States within twenty years from their issue, bearing interest payable annually or semi-annually at a rate not exceeding six per cent. per annum, for the following purposes:

City hall.

1. For the erection and construction of a city hall and the purchase of a site for the same.

Waterworks and sewers.

2. For the construction and extension of water works, or the purchase of the same, and for constructing sewers, and for the improvement and maintenance of the same.

School buildings.

3. For the erection, construction and completion of school buildings, and the purchase of school sites.

Engine houses and equipments.

4. For the purchase of sites for engine houses, for fire engines and other equipments of the fire department, and for the construction of engine houses.

Police station.

5. For the purchase of sites for police stations, and for the construction of buildings thereon for the use of the police department.

Viaducts and bridges.

6. For the construction of viaducts, bridges, and for repairs of the same.

7. For the erection and construction of library and museum buildings, and the purchase of sites for the same.

Library and museum buildings.

8. For the establishment of public baths and hospitals, and the purchase of sites for the same.

Public bath and hospitals.

9. For the purchase of lands for public parks and improvements thereof, and for the payment of purchase money and interest thereon which may be or become due for park lands already acquired or contracted for.

Public parks.

10. For permanently improving streets in such city and for creating a fund out of which to advance the cost of repairs to sidewalks, in anticipation of the collection of special assessments for such cost of repairs by the treasurer of such city.

Improving streets.

11. For the construction or purchase of electric or gas light plants for lighting streets and public buildings.

Electric and gas light plants.

12. For refunding existing indebtedness.

Refunding Indebtness.

SECTION 2. No bonds shall be issued under the provisions of this act, and no contract shall be entered into or obligation incurred by any such city in contemplation of the issue of such bonds in the future, unless such contract or obligation and the issue of such bonds for the payment of the same shall have been authorized by ordinance adopted by a vote in favor of the same of at least three-fourths of all the members of the common council elect, said vote to be at a regular meeting of such common council, not less than one week after the proposed ordinance shall have been published in the official paper of such city; and provided, that no such bonds shall be issued so that the amount thereof, together with all the other indebtedness of such city, shall exceed five per cent. of the assessed valuation of such city at the last assessment for state and county taxes previous to the incurring of such indebtedness.

Ordinance authorizing bonds to be adopted by three-fourths vote.

Ordinance to be published.

Limitation of indebtedness.

SECTION 3. Bonds issued under the authority of this act shall be executed and disposed of in the manner provided by the charter of the city issuing the same, and where the charter shall fail to provide such manner, the common council of the city authorizing the issue of such bonds shall, by ordinance, provide the manner in which the same shall be executed and disposed of. In all cases, however, all such bonds shall bear an appropriate name, indicating the purpose of their issue, and shall be consecutively numbered, and shall have interest coupons attached, and shall show on their face the amount of indebtedness of the city issuing the same, the annual amount of the assessment of the taxable property therein for the five years next preceding the issue, and the average amount thereof, and shall not be sold for less than their par value and accrued interest.

Bonds, execution and disposal of.

Bonds, what to show.

SECTION 4. The common council of any city included in this act is hereby empowered to provide for the purchase of the real and personal property, and for the construction of the buildings mentioned in the first section of this act, and to determine the amount of the appropriation necessary therefor, and for the purpose of entering into any contract or contracts for such purchase or construction, the amount of bonds issued or to be issued for

Powers of common council.

that purpose shall be treated as cash on hand; but no such power shall be exercised, or contract entered with or obligation incurred by the common council of any such city except by ordinance adopted as prescribed in section 2, of this act.

Tax to pay bonds, how to be levied. Section 5. The common council of any city, having issued bonds authorized by this act, shall annually levy a tax upon all the taxable property within such city, sufficient to pay the annual interest thereon, and to provide a sinking fund each year equal to five per cent. on the principal of said bonds for the payment of said bonds.

The foregoing law *held* valid.

Johnson vs. Milwaukee, 88 Wis., 383.

City bonds conditioned for the payment of the principal sum at a specified time, "together with interest thereon at ten per cent. per annum, payable annually on presentation of the annexed warrants," continue to draw interest at the same rate after default in payment of the principal, such rate being higher than that fixed by law in the absence of special contract.

Pruyn vs. Milwaukee, 18 Wis., 386.

CHAPTER XVIII.

ASSESSMENT AND COLLECTION OF TAXES.

Property subject to taxation. Section 1. All property in said city, real, personal, or mixed, shall be subject to taxation for all purposes authorized by law, excepting only such property as is or shall be exempted from taxation by general laws exempting from taxation throughout the state particular classes of property or property of particular classes of corporations or persons; and the same shall be assesed in the **Powers of city assessors.** manner hereinafter provided; and the assessors appointed under this act shall have and possess the same powers that are, or may be, conferred upon township assessors, except so far as they may be altered by this act; and the common council may prescribe the form of assessment roll, or more fully define the duties of assessors, and make such rules and regulations in relation to revising, altering or adding to such rolls, as they may from time to time deem advisable; provided, that the same shall not be inconsistent with the provisions of this act.

The "accumulated profits" of a bank, which have not been divided among the stockholders, but have been retained for banking purposes, are not a part of its capital stock in such a sense as to be exempt from the general rules of taxation applicable to other taxable property.

State Bank vs. Milwaukee, 18 Wis., 295.

A court of equity has no jurisdiction to restrain the collection of taxes illegally or improperly assessed upon personal property, since the party injured has an ample remedy at law.

Van Cott vs. Supervisors, 18 Wis., 259.

An excessive valuation of property intentionally made, for the purpose of compelling the owner to pay more than his just proportion of the taxes, is a sufficient ground for declaring the assessment void.

Mil. Iron Co. vs. Hubbard, 29 Wis., 51.

The intentional omission from the assessment roll of valuable property which should have been assessed vitiates the whole tax levied upon such roll.

Weeks vs. Milwaukee, 10 Wis., 186.

G. B. & M. Canal Co. vs. Outagamie Co., 76 Wis., 587.

Smith vs. Smith, 19 Wis., 649.

Hersey vs. Supervisors, 16 Wis., 198.

The articles of incorporation of a steamship company, provided its principal office should be in the town of Lake. It had an office there where were held the meetings of stockholders and directors, both annual and special, but all its other and general business was transacted at the office in Milwaukee of its president and secretary. *Held*, that for the purposes of taxation its "principal office and place of business" was in Milwaukee.

Mil. Steamship Co. vs. Milwaukee, 83 Wis., 590.

SECTION 2. The mayor shall appoint and submit to the common council at its first regular meeting in December of every third year for its confirmation, a tax commissioner, whose term of office shall commence on the first day of January ensuing such meeting and who shall at the time of his appointment, be a resident freeholder in said city of Milwaukee. Such commissioner shall take and subscribe an oath of office and shall execute and deliver to the city of Milwaukee a bond in the penal sum of five thousand dollars with, at least, two sureties for the faithful performance of his official duties, which bond shall be approved by the comptroller as to its sufficiency, and by the city attorney as to its form and execution. The present tax commissioner shall remain in office until the expiration of three years from the first Monday of December, 1884. The said tax commissioner may appoint a deputy tax commissioner who is hereby authorized to do all acts required by law of the tax commissioner, but said tax commissioner shall be responsible to the city and to any person interested for

Tax commissioner, how appointed.

Shall give bond.

May appoint deputy.

all acts of his said deputy. The said tax commissioner shall receive in addition to his salary now fixed by law in full payment of his deputy and all clerk hire in his said office the sum of twenty-two hundred dollars per annum.

As amended by Section 46, Chapter 144, Laws of 1875, further amended by Section 2, Chapter 291, Laws of 1885.

See State ex rel. Milwaukee Street Railway Co. vs. Anderson, 63 N. W. 746.

CHAPTER 191, LAWS OF 1889.

May fix salary of deputy tax commissioner, and wages for clerk hire.

SECTION 1. The common council shall hereafter have full power to fix, by resolution or ordinance, the salary of the deputy tax commissioner, and to increase from time to time, the compensation for all clerk hire in the tax commissioner's office, in proportion to the increase of the clerical work therein.

SECTION 2. All acts and parts of acts conflicting with the provisions of this act are hereby repealed.

Tax commissioner to keep record of real estate subject to taxation.

SECTION 3. Said tax commissioner shall have an office, which shall be kept open during the usual business hours of each business day during the term of his office; and shall, in suitable books provided for the purpose, keep a record of all lots, blocks, fractional lots, or parcels of land contained in said city, with the assessed value of each in separate columns, together with the assessed value of the improvements theron, and the name of the owner of each, and the street and number of his residence as far as possible, during each and every year of the term of his office; and shall also keep a record of the names of

Names of persons liable for personal taxes.

all persons liable to assessment for personal property during each year of the term of his office, with the amount assessed to each person; and as far as possible shall cause to be entered upon said record in a suitable column, opposite the name of such person so assessed, an accurate description of the class of such personal property, whether

Character of personal property.

bonds, stocks, mortgages or money, notes, accounts, choses in action of any kind, or merchandise, manufacturers' stock, capital invested in business, household goods, vessels, pianos, horses and carriages, sewing machines, watches, etc., and any and all other personal property, taxable under the laws of Wisconsin.

Record of vessels.

SECTION 4. He shall also keep a record of all vessels registered in the books of the custom house at the port of Milwaukee, with the names of the owners residing in Milwaukee, and the amount of the interest held by each said owner, together with all other information in relation thereto which may be serviceable in making an assessment of the vessel property owned in whole or in part by any resident of the city of Milwaukee.

SECTION 5.   Said tax commissioner shall also procure and keep on file in his office all published plats of all lots, blocks, additions, divisions and subdivisions of lots or lands which have been duly authorized by the common council, and all other matters or information which may be valuable in making an assessment of the real and personal property in the said city of Milwaukee. He shall also cause to be copied in a book provided for that purpose, all complaints made in writing at any time in said office of the said tax commissioner, of excessive or erroneous assessments, either of real or personal estate, which said complaints shall be considered and disposed of by the board of assessors at their first meeting thereafter, in the order of their entry, unless otherwise ordered by said board. *Shall keep plats of lots, blocks, etc.* *Shall keep record of complaints.*

SECTION 6.   The mayor, with the concurrence of the common council, shall, on the first Monday of January in every second year, appoint an assessor for each ward in said city of Milwaukee, whose term of office shall commence on the first day of February following, who shall have been recommended to him by the tax commissioner, and who shall be a resident of the ward for which he is appointed, at the time of his appointment, and who shall continue to reside in such ward during the term for which said appointment is made.   Said assessors shall each take the oath of office provided by law to be taken and subscribed by ward or town assessors; and said ward assessors, with said tax commissioner, shall constitute the board of assessors, of which board said tax commissioner shall be ex-officio the president.   The present assessors shall remain in office until the first day of February, 1887, unless sooner removed according to law. *Ward assessors, when and how appointed.*

As amended by Section 3, Chapter 391, Laws of 1885.

The appointment of assessors in the manner above provided for, instead of their being elected by the people, is legal, and not in conflict with Sec. 1. Art. VIII, of the constitution.

State ex rel. vs. Anderson, 63 N. W. 746.

CHAPTER 328, LAWS OF 1891.

AN ACT amending the charter of the city of Milwaukee, and providing for the appointment of assistant assessors therein.

Council may provide for assistant assessors.

SECTION 1. It shall be lawful for the common council of the city of Milwaukee, to provide by resolution or ordinance, either for extra compensation, or assistants to those assessors, whose wards or districts have been enlarged and whose labor has been increased by annexation of additional territory to the city. Such assistants, if needed, shall be appointed in the same manner as assessors, and shall be residents of the respective wards for which they are appointed. They shall enter upon their duties under the direction of the tax commissioner, for such time and at such compensation as the common council shall determine. They shall take the oath required of city officers and shall have the same authority under the law as regular assessors. Where an assessor and an assistant assessor, shall be appointed for any ward, the tax commissioner shall designate the property and terrritory to be assessed by each.

Duties and compensation.

Present incumbents.

SECTION 7. The tax commissioner and ward assessors now in office shall continue in office until the expiration of the respective terms for which they were appointed, and the first appointments by the mayor under sections two and six of this chapter, shall be made at the expiration of the terms of the present commissioner and assessors respectively, unless a vacancy shall sooner occur.

Ward assessors, how removed from office.

SECTION 8. The tax commissioner of the said city shall have power, with the written approval of the mayor, to remove from office any assessor in the said city who shall, in his opinion, be incompetent, or neglect to perform the duties of his office. The mayor and common council shall have power to make appointments to fill the vacancy or vacancies caused by such removal, or occurring in any other manner, and such appointments shall be made in all respects in the same manner as provided in section six of this chapter for original appointments to said office, and the assessors so appointed to fill vacancies shall hold their office for the unexpired term.

Duties of assessors.

SECTION 9. Said assessors shall, as soon after their appointment as practicable, under the direction of said tax commissioner, proceed to examine and determine the valuation of all taxable real and personal estate within their several wards. Schedules or rolls of all the taxable real estate in each said ward, and also a list of the names of all persons assessed for personal property in each ward, shall be furnished by the said tax commissioner to the said assessors respectively, to aid them in the performance of their duties, and upon which they shall enter their valuation; and said assessment rolls shall be fully completed and filed in the office of the said tax commissioner within the time provided by law for the completion of the same.

Completion of assessment rolls.

SECTION 10. The ward assessors, in the listing, assessment and valuation of real and personal property liable to taxation in their several wards, and in the review, equalization and correction of their assessments, shall proceed in the manner prescribed by the general laws of this state, except as otherwise provided in this act. Where there are buildings upon any lot or parcel of land, the value of the same shall be set forth in a separate column. The assessors may, if they deem it advisable, assess any lot or tract of land in such parcels or such subdivisions as they may deem proper, but it shall not be necessary to enter the name of the owner opposite to any tract or parcel of land.

Assessment of buildings, and subdivisions of land.

SECTION 11. On the receipt of the rolls of the several ward assessors, with their valuation and assessments of real and personal property, from all the wards, the tax commissioner shall give notice by publication in the official papers of said city for ten days, that on a certain day therein named for each ward, the assessment roll for said ward will be open for the examination of the taxable inhabitants thereof; and the tax commissioner and ward assessors shall make all necessary additions to such roll, and correct the same by changes in valuation or description, so as to make the roll as perfect as possible. Any act done by a majority of the board of assessors, shall have the same force and effect as if done by the tax commissioner and all the assessors appointed under this act. After the corrections are made, the tax commissioner shall submit the corrected assessment rolls to the board of review.

Tax commissioner to publish notice, etc.

Correction of roll.

SECTION 12. The mayor, city clerk, tax commissioner and ward assessors shall constitute the board of review for said city. Said board shall meet annually, at the time fixed by the laws of the state, and proceed, as such board, to review, examine, and correct such assessment

Board of review.

rolls, and in so doing shall have and exercise all the powers and perform all the duties of a board of review, as the same are, or may be prescribed by the general laws of this state, except as may be otherwise provided in this act. Notice of the time and place of the meeting of such board of review, signed by the city clerk, shall be published for ten days in the official papers of the city, prior to the day of such meeting. The concurrence of a majority of the board shall be sufficient to decide any question to be passed upon by the board of review.

Notice of time and place of meeting, how given.

The members of the board of review act judicially, and they are not liable in a civil action for their acts as such members.

Steele vs. Dunham, 26 Wis., 393.

State ex rel. Mil. St. Ry. vs. Anderson, 63 N. W., 746.

Rolls to be delivered to city clerk.

SECTION 13. After the rolls have been examined, corrected and completed by the board of review, and within the time prescribed by law, the assessor shall annually deliver the same as completed, duly verified by their respective oaths annexed thereto, as required by law, together with the sworn statements and valuations of personal property, to the city clerk, who shall file and preserve such statements and valuations in his office.

Duty of the city clerk.

SECTION 14. The city clerk upon receiving such assessment rolls, shall examine and perfect the same, and make out therefrom a complete tax roll, in the manner and form as provided by law. Such tax roll may be bound in one or more volumes, but shall be consecutively paged, and such volumes, if more than one, shall be consecutively numbered, and shall be referred to by their numbers in a warrant attached to such tax roll as provided in the next section. The common council shall thereupon, by resolution, levy such sum or sums of money, or taxes, as may be sufficient for the several purposes for which taxes are by law authorized to be levied in said city, not exceeding, however, the amounts authorized by law, particularly specifying in such resolution the purposes for which the same are levied and if not for general city purposes, the ward or district of the city in or upon which the same are levied.

As amended by Section 39, Chapter 144, Laws of 1875, and further amended by Section 49, Chapter 324, Laws of 1882.

The legislature cannot create a public debt, or levy a tax, or authorize a municipal corporation to do so, in order to raise funds for a merely *private* purpose. The objects for which money is to be raised by taxation must be public, and such as subserve the common interest and well-being of the community required to contribute.

Brodhead vs. Milwaukee, 19 Wis., 658.

SECTION 15.   As soon as said sums, or taxes, shall be levied, the common council shall cause the same to be apportioned and extended upon said tax roll, upon a uniform percentage, by setting opposite to the description of each lot, tract, or parcel of land, and to the name of each person named in said roll, in proper columns, such proportionate share of the sums, or taxes, so levied, as may be chargeable upon such lot, tract, or parcel of land, or against such person.   To such tax roll shall be appended a warrant signed by the mayor and clerk, and sealed with the corporate seal of said city, directed to the city treasurer, requiring and commanding him to collect the taxes and assessments in said tax roll specified, in the manner prescribed by this act, and in case said taxes and assessments shall not be paid within such time as in said warrant shall be specified, that then he shall proceed to sell the several lots or parcels of land, or those parts thereof upon which said taxes or assessments shall remain unpaid, and to make due return to the common council, within such time as shall be fixed in said warrant.   Such warrant shall be signed, and such tax roll and warrant shall be delivered to the city treasurer on the second Monday of December in each year.

Apportionment of taxes.

Warrant to city treasurer.

As amended by Section 40, Chapter 144, Laws of 1875.

SECTION 16.   Such tax roll, before being delivered to the treasurer, shall be compared by the clerk with the assessment rolls on file in his office, as corrected; and said clerk shall cause the several columns of valuations of property, and of taxes and assessments thereon, in said roll, to be footed up and the sum of each column to be set down at the foot thereof, and the sum totals of each ward to be set down at the foot of the last columns of the roll for each ward, and a summary of the totals for the several wards and for the whole city to be set down at the end of said tax roll, showing separately the totals of valuations and of taxes and assessments upon real estate and personal property respectively for the whole city and for each ward thereof, and to said tax roll he shall append

Compared and certified copy of tax roll.

his certificate that the same has been so compared by him and that the said assessment rolls and the whole thereof have been copied into such tax roll; and the said tax roll, when so certified, shall be prima facie evidence in any court that the lands and persons therein named were subject to taxation, and that the assessment was just and equal.

As amended by Section 48, Chapter 324, Laws of 1882.

Causes for remission of taxes. SECTION 17. After the assessment roll is completed, the rate of taxation is fixed, the taxes are extended and the tax roll is placed in the hands of the city treasurer for collection, it shall not be lawful for the common council to remit, annul, or cancel any tax charged against any real or personal property, except in the following specified cases:

Clerical error in description, transfer or extension. 1st. When a clerical error has been made in the description or transfer of the property from the original assessment books to the tax roll, or in the extension of the tax.

Clerical error as to special taxes. 2d. When a clerical error has been made whereby any property in the city becomes wrongly charged or assessed with certificates of board of public works, or with special taxes for water pipe, sewers, street work and all other work or improvements.

Mistake in improvements. 3d. When improvements, by the erection of buildings, have been assessed on lots or lands where none had been made at the time fixed by law for making the assessments.

Exempt. 4th. When the tax is manifestly illegal and void by reason of the exemption of the property from taxation by law.

Double assessment. 5th. When a person has been assessed the same year for the same personal property in more than one ward.

Same. 6th. When the same personal property has been assessed the same year more than once in the city.

Tax levied on property not in existence. 7th. When the tax is levied for, upon or on account of specific tangible personal property, or buildings, not in fact in existence, on the first day of May in the year of such levy.

As amended by Section 41, Chapter 144, Laws of 1875, and further amended by Section 50, Chapter 324, Laws of 1882 and Chapter 190, Laws of 1891.

SECTION 18. All taxes and assessments, general or special, levied under this act, shall be and remain a lien upon the lands and tenements upon which they may be assessed, from the time of the filing of such assessment rolls in the office of the city clerk, and on all personal property of any person or body politic assessed for personal taxes, from the delivery of the warrant for the collection thereof, until such tax shall be paid; and no sale or transfer of such real or personal estate shall affect such lien; provided, that as between the grantor and grantee of any land or lot, when there is no express agreement as to which shall pay the taxes or assessments that may be assessed or become chargeable thereon before the conveyance, if such land is conveyed even with or prior to the date of the warrant authorizing the collection of such taxes or assessments, then the grantee shall pay the same; but if conveyed after that date, the grantor shall pay them. Any personal property belonging to the person taxed, may be taken and sold for the payment of taxes upon personal property.

Taxes and assessments a lien on all real and personal property.

Number of this Section changed to " 18 " by Section 42, Chapter 144, Laws of 1875.

SECTION 19. In all cases where, by the provisions of this act, any special charge or assessment is made a lien upon land, the amount of such charge or assessment shall be carried out on the tax roll in a separate column or columns, opposite the lot or tract upon which the same may be a lien; and the treasurer may collect and sell, and do all other acts in relation thereto, in the same manner as if the amount of such lien was a general tax.

How carried out.

SECTION 20. On the receipt of such tax roll, the treasurer shall give one week's notice thereof in the official papers. Such notice shall specify that the taxes on personal property must be paid within twenty days from the first publication of said notice, and the taxes and assessments on real estate before the last day of December following, and that all tracts or parcels of land specified in said tax roll, upon which the taxes and assessments shall not be paid by that day, will be sold at a certain time and place to be therein specified; and the publication of such notice shall be deemed a demand; and neglect to pay the taxes and assessments within the time specified, shall be deemed a refusal to pay the same.

Treasurer to give notice in official papers.

Notice to specify, etc.

Treasurer to enforce collection of personal taxes.

SECTION 21. On the expiration of the twenty days mentioned in the preceding section, the treasurer shall proceed to enforce the collection of the personal taxes in the manner provided by law for the collection of personal taxes by town treasurers, and if any such personal taxes shall not be paid or collected in consequence of the neglect or delay of the treasurer, the common council may sue for and recover the amount thereof from the said treasurer and his sureties. In case the taxes on personal property shall not be paid by the third Monday of January next following the expiration of said twenty days, the treasurer shall, on or before the first day of March next following, issue a warrant directed to the chief of police of said city, requiring and commanding him, within a certain time in such warrant to be specified, to proceed and collect such taxes on personal property as shall then remain unpaid, and the additional sum of one per cent. thereof per month, from the first day of February, to be added to such taxes as then remain delinquent, on the first day of each month, commencing with the first day of March, and continuing until the day of payment. And the chief of police receiving such warrant for the purpose of collecting such unpaid taxes and interest, shall have all the powers of levying, distraining and selling property, and all other remedies and powers that are given by law to town treasurers for the collection of taxes on personal property, and shall be subject to all the liabilities of such town treasurers, and shall be entitled to demand and collect a commission or percentage of five per cent. on all sums collected by him, which percentage shall be added by him to said taxes and monthly additions of one per cent. and collected with the same and in addition thereto, as compensation for his services, and in case of levy, distress or sale of property by said chief of police in virtue of such warrant, he shall be entitled, in addition to such commission of five per cent., to collect the same costs and fees allowed by law to constables on execution, and all such fees and commissions or percentages shall be paid into the city treasury.

As amended by Section 1, Chapter 139, Laws of 1878, and further amended by Section 51, Chapter 324, Laws of 1882.

Other unpaid taxes.

SECTION 22. The warrant of the city treasurer to the chief of police, for the collection of taxes on personal property, shall include, in addition to the unpaid taxes on personal property for the current municipal year, all unpaid taxes on personal property for the next preceding three years. And the chief of police of said city shall have the power, and it shall be his duty to collect the same in like manner as is herein provided for the collection of the taxes on personal property for the current year.

SECTION 23. Before the treasurer of the city shall issue his warrant to the chief of police for the collection of unpaid personal taxes, the chief of police shall give a bond to the said city in such penal sum not less than twenty thousand dollars, as the common council may prescribe, with at least three sureties, conditioned for the faithful execution of such warrant, conditioned for the faithful execution of such warrant, and for the payment to the city treasurer, monthly, of all personal taxes by him collected or received under or by virtue of the said warrant in pursuance of law. Such bond shall be executed, acknowledged, approved and recorded as provided and required by section one of chapter three of this act. The chief of police at the end of each and every month from the time of receiving such warrant, shall report to the treasurer a statement in detail of all the personal taxes collected by him during such month, and shall pay over to the treasurer at the same time the whole amount so collected and take his receipt in duplicate therefor, one of which duplicate receipts he shall immediately file with the city comptroller. *Chief of police to give bond.* *To pay over all collections monthly.*

SECTION 24. On the day and at the place designated in the treasurer's notice, he shall commence by public auction the sale of all tracts and lots, or parts thereof, upon which the taxes or assessments shall remain unpaid, and shall continue such sale from day to day until the whole are disposed of. The sale shall be the smallest undivided portion of the lot or tract, which any person will take and pay the taxes and charges on the whole lot or tract. On receiving the amount of such taxes and charges, the treasurer shall issue to the purchaser, his heirs or assigns, a certificate of such sale, containing the name of the purchaser, a description of the premises sold, the amount paid therefor, the rate of interest said certificate may bear, and the time when the right to redeem the same will expire. The treasurer shall keep a record *Treasurer's sales for delinquent taxes.* *Record to be kept.*

of the lots or tracts sold, the names of the purchasers, the dates and amounts of sales, the time, by whom, and for what sum any lot or tract sold, or any part thereof, was redeemed, and the time, and to whom, the same was conveyed, if not redeemed.

Forfeiture for neglect to pay for lands so purchased.

SECTION 25. In case any purchaser at such sale shall neglect or refuse to pay the amount for which any lot or tract was sold, at such time as the treasurer shall designate, he shall, on the day following, offer said lot or tract again for sale, and any person bidding off, at any such sale, any lot or tract of land, and refusing to pay for the same within the time designated, shall forfeit and pay to the city the sum of five dollars for each lot so purchased and not paid for, to be sued for and collected as other penalties are, under this act.

Time for redemption.

SECTION 26. Any lot or tract of land so sold, or any undivided interest therein, may be redeemed by the owner thereof, or by any person interested therein, within three years from the day of sale, and at any time prior to the recording of a deed thereof by the treasurer to the purchaser, by the payment to the treasurer of the amount for which the same was sold, together with the interest

Rate of interest.

thereon, at the rate of 25 per cent. per annum, and the legal charges thereon; and the city treasurer shall receive such redemption money on the same being tendered to him, at any time prior to the recording of the tax deed.

Infants and lunatics.

If the estate of an infant or lunatic be sold, the same may be redeemed upon the like terms at any time within one year after such disability shall be removed.

As amended by Section 52, Chapter 324, Laws of 1882.

Redemption laws are liberally construed in favor of the owner of the real estate.

Jones vs. Collins, 16 Wis., 594.

The tender of the amount to the officer must be unconditionally made.

Woodbury vs. Shackleford, 19 Wis., 55.

Tax deeds—when and how given.

SECTION 27. Any tract or lot of land sold in pursuance of this act, or any part thereof, which shall not be redeemed within three years from the day of sale, shall be conveyed by the treasurer to the purchaser, or his assigns, as herein provided; and the assignee of any tax certificate by endorsement thereon, on any premises sold for taxes by virtue of this act, shall be entitled to

receive a deed of such premises in his own name, and
with the same effect as though he had been the original
purchaser; provided, that it shall not be lawful for the
treasurer of the city of Milwaukee to issue tax deeds for
taxes unpaid on any lot, or part of lot or parcel of land
in said city of Milwaukee, unless three months' previous
notice, in writing, of the application for such deed, shall
have been served by the sheriff of Milwaukee county,
upon the occupant or occupants thereof, if the same be
occupied, and upon the owner or owners thereof, if known,
and the proof of such service, by affidavit, shall be first
furnished to and filed in the office of said city treasurer.
Such service may be made personally, or by mailing such
notice, with the postage prepaid, to each person required
to be served therewith, directed to such person, at his
place of residence, unless it appears that such residence
is not known to the party applying for such tax deed,
and cannot with reasonable diligence, be ascertained by
him.   Like affidavit of service, in either case, shall be
made and filed, as is now required by law of the service
of summons in civil actions, in this state, and the said
sheriff shall be entitled to the same fees for making such
service, that are allowed by law for the service of summons
in civil actions.   No other notice of application for a tax
deed shall be necessary in any case than that required
in this section, and if the treasurer shall issue any deed
for taxes without the foregoing provisions of this section
having been complied with, he shall be deemed guilty
of a misdemeanor, and upon conviction thereof, shall
be punished by fine of not less than five hundred nor
more than one thousand dollars, and by imprisonment
in the county jail for a term of not less than six months
nor more than one year, and his office shall be deemed
vacated.

As amended by Section 53, Chapter 324, Laws of 1882; also
amended by Section 1, Chapter 181, Laws of 1881.

Chapter 113, laws of 1867, which prohibits the issue of a tax
deed, unless a specified notice has been served on the owner or
occupant of the land at least three months previously, is invalid as
to cases in which tax deeds were due *before* its passage. Such
chapter applies to deeds issued by both *city* and *county* officers.

State ex rel. Knox vs. Hundhausen, 23 Wis., 508.

The charter of the city of Milwaukee, Ch. 184 of the laws of
1874, is a mere consolidation and revision of the various acts then
in force, defining the corporate powers of the city, including the

charter of 1852 and subsequent amendments. The words "this act" in the above section must have the same signification that they had in the charter of 1852; and the provisions of the charter of 1852, so far as they are re-enacted in the consolidated charter of 1874, are. but a continuation of the provisions of the charter of 1852.

Scheftels vs. Tabert, 46 Wis., 439.

Form of tax deed.   SECTION 28.   All deeds executed by the city treasurer on account of sales for taxes or assessments under this act, shall be made in substantially the same form prescribed by law for deeds by the county clerk on account of sales for unpaid taxes; and such deeds shall have the same force and effect as evidence that is or may be given by law to such deeds executed by the county clerk.

Struck off to city in absence of other bid.   SECTION 29.   If, at any sale of real or personal estate for taxes or assessments, no bid shall be made for any parcel of land, or for any goods and chattels, the same shall be struck off to the city, and thereupon the city shall receive in its corporate name a certificate of the sale thereof, and shall be vested with the same rights as other purchasers are.   If the city shall be purchaser of any personal property by virtue of this chapter, the treasurer shall have the power to sell the same at public sale, and **City may re-sell.** in case the city shall become the purchaser of any real estate at any tax sale, the treasurer is authorized to sell the certificates issued therefor for the amount of such sale and interest at twenty-five per cent. per annum, and to indorse and transfer such certificates to the purchasers.

Where the lot owner does not pay special assessment certificates issued against his lot, and no bid is made when the lot is offered for sale by the city, it is proper for the latter to buy it in, to issue a certificate of sale therefor in its corporate name, which vests in the city the same right at law as any other purchaser would have had; and thereupon, the city treasurer is authorized to sell the certificate issued therefor for the amount of such sale and interest at twenty five per cent. per annum, and to indorse and transfer such certificate to the purchaser.

Hoyt vs. Fass, 64 Wis., 273.

In the sale and conveyance of land for taxes, municipal corporations have only the powers *expressly* conferred. Under the charter of 1852, the city of Milwaukee was not authorized to purchase land at a tax sale, and such a sale to the city is void.

Knox vs. Peterson, 21 Wis., 249.

A certificate issued on a sale of land for non-payment of an assessment for benefits for a street improvement, is a "tax certificate."

Dalrymple vs. Milwaukee, 53 Wis., 178.

SECTION 30.   Whenever any person shall bid off any lot offered for sale for taxes, which lot shall have been bid off in the name of the city for the taxes of any previous year or years, and the certificate or certificates of such previous sale or sales thereof shall at the time of such subsequent sale remain the property of the city, such person shall, before being entitled to his certificate of such sale, purchase of the city its certificate or certificates by paying the amount of principal, interest and charges thereon, and receive from the treasurer an assignment thereof; provided, that any certificate of sale for the amount of any street commissioner's certificate or board of public works' certificate, or other special tax or assess- ment, held by the city of Milwaukee in trust for the owner of such certificate or of such special tax or assess- ment. or any certificate of sale for general, city or ward taxes held by said city, may be assigned, sold and trans- ferred by the city treasurer, although said city may hold in trust, in whole or in part, certificates for the sale of lots for the amount of street commissioners' certificates or other special certificates or special taxes or assessments, issued in any prior year, and no liability shall attach to the city or said treasurer by reason thereof; but any such sale, assignment and transfer shall only be made upon payment of all previous general, city and ward taxes. The city treasurer shall report to the comptroller on the first day of each month a detailed statement of all his sales and transfers of tax certificates and of all moneys received by him upon redemptions from tax sales during the preceeding month, in cases where the certificates of sale were held by him as such treasurer, giving in all cases the dates of such sales and transfers, and of such redemptions respectively, and the amounts received by him therefor in every case.

As amended by Section 54, Chapter 324, Laws of 1882.

It is apparent from the whole theory of our charter that the certificate of sale for the amount of the board of public works' certificates so taken in the name of the city, is held in trust by it for the owners of such certificates.

Hoyt vs. Fass, 64 Wis., 273.

In an action to set aside a street commissioners' certificate, and to restrain the city and its treasurer from issuing a tax deed upon the same, *held*, under the special circumstances of the case, that the city and its treasurer had no interest in the result, and were bound by the judgment rendered in another action only to abstain from issuing a deed to the other defendant, or person claiming under him after commencement of the action.

Smith vs. Milwaukee, 18 Wis., 388.

Omitted lands to be assessed for back taxes.

SECTION 31. If it shall appear to the assessors that any lot or parcel of land was omitted in the assessment roll of either or both of the two preceeding years, and that the same was then liable to taxation, they shall, in addition to the assessment for that year, assess the lot or tract so omitted, for such year or years in which it shall have been so omitted, at the just value thereof, noting the year when such omission occurred, and such assessment shall have the same force and effect as it would have had if made in the year when the same was omitted. And the common council shall. in addition to the taxes for the current year, levy such taxes upon such lot or tract as the same would have been chargeable with had not the same been so omitted. and such taxes shall be collected as other taxes or assessments are for the current year. All land shall be subject to taxes that may have been omitted, in whosoever hands they may have come.

Taxes set aside for informality may be relevied.

Should the tax or the assessment upon any parcel of land be set aside or declared void by reason of any defect or informality in the assessing, levying, selling or conveying the same but not affecting the equity or justice of the tax itself, the common council shall cause the tax or assessment so set aside or declared void to be re-levied in such manner as they shall by ordinance direct; provided, that if the defect was in the assessment, the same shall be again assessed at such time as the common council may direct. and the said tax or assessment so re-assessed or re-levied shall be and continue a lien upon said lot or tract, and shall be collected as other taxes and assessments are collected under this act.

As amended by Section 55, Chapter 324, Laws of 1882.

Chapter 395, laws of 1862, and Ch. 115, laws of 1863, providing for re-assessment of both real and personal property for the year 1857 in Milwaukee, *held*, valid enactments.

Cross vs. Milwaukee, 19 Wis., 535.

Treasurer to receive redemption moneys and cancel certificates.

SECTION 32. The treasurer shall receive all moneys that may be legally tendered him for the redemption of lands sold for taxes, and he shall keep an account thereof, and pay the same over on demand to the persons entitled to receive the same. He shall cancel all certificates so redeemed, and preserve the same in his office; and at the expiration of his term of office, he shall deliver over to his successor all redemption moneys in his hands, with a statement of the amounts so received.

SECTION 33.   When there shall be a sale by the county treasurer and by the city treasurer, of any piece or parcel of land for taxes, in the same year, the purchaser of such piece or parcel, who may be first in point of time, may redeem the same from the subsequent purchaser; and in case he shall not redeem, the right of the last purchaser shall be held paramount in case of the execution of any tax deed therefor.   If the first purchaser in point of time shall redeem, it shall be the duty of the proper officer to make an entry in the sales book of the character in which such person may have redeemed; and thereupon the person so redeeming shall be substituted to all the rights of the holder of the certificate so redeemed, as aforesaid.

First purchaser to have preference.

SECTION 34.   No person shall be permitted to institute any action or proceeding to set aside any assessment or special tax hereafter levied or assessed upon any lot or tract of land, or to set aside any deed executed in consequence of the non-payment of such taxes and of the premises therefor, unless such person shall first pay or tender to the proper party, or deposit for his use with the treasurer, the amount of all state, county and city taxes that may remain unpaid on such lot or tract, together with the interest and charges thereon.

Instituting actions to set aside assessments and taxes.

Where a tax payer attempts, by a proceeding in equity, to stop the officers of the law from collecting a tax charged against his property, his complaint must demonstrate that his property is not legally or equitably chargeable therewith.

Kaehler vs. Dobberpuhl, 56 Wis., 480.
Fifield vs. Marinette Co., 62 Wis., 532.

SECTION 35.   All the directions hereby given for the assessing of land and the levying and collection of taxes and assessments, shall be deemed only directory, and no error or informality in the proceedings of any of the officers entrusted with the same, not affecting the substantial justice of the tax itself, shall vitiate or in any way affect the validity of the tax or assessment.

Informality shall not affect validity of tax.

When the common council acquires jurisdiction in the ways prescribed by Sec. 5, of Ch. IV, any subsequent omission of any step directed in the charter would have been deemed only directory.

> Gilman vs. Milwaukee, 61 Wis., 588.
>
> This section considered in Cramer vs. Stone, 38 Wis., 259.

The mere failure of the assessor to verify the assessment roll, as required by law, does not necessarily render the tax apportioned upon such assessment unequal or unjust.

> Fifield vs. Marinette Co., 62 Wis., 532.

In an equitable action, any irregularity in the proceedings which does not prejudice the plaintiff, or affect the substantial justice of the tax, is not a sufficient ground for avoiding the assessment.

> Wright vs. Forristal, 65 Wis., 341.

A complaint showed that a contract for laying a pavement was not let within the time required by law, and that no "plan" or "profile" of the work was filed before letting the contract, but states no facts showing injury to plaintiff by such omissions. *Held*, on demurrer, there was no ground for interference of equity to restrain sale of plaintiff's lots for non-payment of special tax assessed.

> Warner vs. Knox, 50 Wis., 429.

Defects in proceedings which affect the substantial justice of an assessment cannot be aided by the provisions of this section.

> Liebermann vs. Milwaukee, 89 Wis., 336.

Fees for certificates, redemptions, etc.

SECTION 36. The city treasurer shall collect the following fees, which he shall account for and pay into the city treasury for the use of the city, to-wit: for each certificate by him issued on sale of lands for non-payment of taxes or assessments, twenty-five cents, to be added to the amount of such tax or assessment, and included in such certificate; for each lot redeemed, for which he shall issue a certificate, twenty-five cents, and five cents for each additional lot embraced in such certificate, to be paid by the person redeeming; for each tax deed executed

For tax deed.

by him, one dollar, and five cents for each additional lot or tract embraced in the same deed, to be paid by the person receiving the same. It shall also be his duty to pay into the city treasury, for the use of said city, the

Collection fees.

full amount of the percentage or collection fees received by him upon all state, county, and school taxes levied upon personal property and real estate in the city of Milwaukee, and collected by said treasurer as required by law to that effect. In case of a distress and sale by him of goods and chattels for the payment of any tax,

said treasurer shall be entitled to such fees as are allowed
to sheriffs on sales of goods under execution.

COUNTY AND STATE TAXES.

SECTION 37. The city clerk shall annually make a
duplicate tax roll embracing a list of all real property in
the city subject to taxation, and also a list of all persons
in the city having personal property subject to taxation,
and being a copy of the tax roll made by him as provided
by section fourteen of this chapter, and upon receiving
the certificate of the county clerk of the amount of state,
county and school taxes respectively to be collected in
said city for the current year, he shall calculate, carry
out and extend the same upon such duplicate roll in the
manner provided by law, and shall deliver such tax roll
with his warrant thereto attached in due form as provided by law, to the city treasurer for the collection of the
state, county and school taxes therein entered and contained.

City clerk to make list of real and personal property subject to taxation.

SECTION 38. The treasurer of the city, in giving
bonds, collecting such state, county and school taxes,
and making his return to the county treasurer, and in all
other things relating to such taxes, shall conform to and
be governed by the general laws of the state, except that
the return to the county treasurer shall be for the city and
not for the wards.

City treasurer to comply with state laws.

CHAPTER 301, LAWS OF 1889.

AN ACT to amend the charter of the city of Milwaukee, and to
authorize said city to raise a special tax in the Bay View sewerage
district.

SECTION 1. The common council of the city of Milwaukee is
hereby authorized to levy and raise by taxation upon all the
taxable property, real and personal, within the Bay View sewerage
district of said city, in addition to the amount authorized to be
raised for a sewerage fund in said district, and in the addition to
the amount of money authorized to be raised by taxation for all
purposes within said district now limited by law for each of the
years 1889 and 1890, a sum of money not exceeding one mill on
the dollar in each of said years, upon all the taxable property
within said district, for the purpose of continuing and completing
the sewers contemplated by the plans for sewers in said Bay View
sewerage district of said city, now on file in the offices of the
proper city officers of said city, and for the purpose of continuing

the construction of such sewers as shall or may be included in any amendments to or changes of the said plans during the years 1889 and 1890.

CHAPTER 278, LAWS OF 1880.

AN ACT pertaining to and amendatory of chapter one hundred and eighty-four of the laws of 1874, entitled "an act to revise, consolidate and amend the charter of the city of Milwaukee, approved February 20, 1852, and the several àcts amendatory thereof, approved March 10, 1874."

SECTION 1. Certificates of the sale of lands for non-payment of taxes or assessments, and charges, hereafter to be issued by the treasurer of the city of Milwaukee, under the act to which this act is amendatory, shall be in the following or equivalent form:

STATE OF WISCONSIN, } ss.
Milwaukee City and County. }

I, ———, treasurer of the city of Milwaukee in said state, do hereby certify that on this ——— day of ———, A. D. 18—, I sold at public auction, pursuant to law (here describe the land sold), unto ———, for the sum of ——— dollars and ———cents, being the amount due for city taxes, assessments and charges, on said ———.

This certificate bears interest at the rate of twenty-five per cent. per annum, and if the land so sold is not redeemed according to law, the owner of this certificate will be entitled to a conveyance of so much of said land as shall remain unredeemed.

This certificate is transferable by indorsement.

———————,
City Treasurer.

SECTION 2. All certificates of the sale of lands for non-payment of taxes or assessments and charges heretofore issued by the treasurer of the city of Milwaukee, under the act to which this act is amendatory, substantially in the form prescribed in the preceding section, shall be and are hereby declared to be and to have been valid and legal and no additional matter contained in such certificates shall in any way affect or invalidate the same.

CHAPTER XIX.

DISQUALIFICATIONS, IMPEACHMENTS, ETC.

SECTION 1. No member of the common council shall hold any other city office, and if any member of the common council, shall, while a member, accept any other elective public office, he shall be deemed to have vacated his office as a member of the common council.

As amended by Section 43, Chapter 144, Laws of 1875, and further amended by Section 1, Chapter 55, Laws of 1887.

SECTION 2.   No member of the common council shall **Ineligible to vote.**
vote upon any question, matter or resolution in which he
may be directly or indirectly interested.

SECTION 3.   No member of the common council shall **Debarred from jobs or contracts.**
be a party to or interested in any job or contract with
the city, or with any of the wards, and any contract in
which any such member may be so interested shall be
null and void, and in case any money shall have been
paid on any such contract, the common council may sue
for and recover the amount so paid, from the parties to
such contract, and from the member of the council interested in the same.

SECTION 4.   No person interested directly, or indi- **Principals and sureties in contracts ineligible to office.**
rectly, as principal or surety, in any contract or agree-
ment written or verbal, to which the said city shall be
a party in interest,—or to which any officer or board
under this act shall officially be a party,—for the
construction of any sewer, pavement or building, or the
performance of any public work whatever, or involving
the expenditure, receipt or disposition of money or property of the said city, or of any ward, or by any officer or
board under this act, shall be eligible to any office
or appointment in said city that will in any manner give
him official cognizance or authority over the subject
matter of such interest; and if any person thus interested **Office held vacant.**
shall be elected or appointed to office, his election or
appointment shall be void, and such office shall be
deemed vacant.

SECTION 5.   If any member of the common council, **No member of council to be interested in contract with city.**
or other officer of the corporation, after his election or
appointment, or while in office, shall become or cause
himself to become interested, directly or indirectly, in
any contract or agreement, whether written or verbal, to
which the corporation or any ward shall be a party in
interest, or to which any officer or board under this act
shall officially be a party, or in any question, subject or
proceeding pending before the common council or on
which such officer may be called to act officially, with
intent to gain directly or indirectly, any benefit, profit, or
pecuniary advantage, or if an attorney of any court of
record shall, while a member of the common council,
prosecute or be interested in the prosecution of any action
against said city of Milwaukee, or any of its officers, he

Penalty.

shall be removed from his office, and the same shall be declared vacant by the common council; and he shall be deemed guilty of felony, and on conviction thereof shall be punished by imprisonment in the state prison for not more than one year, or by a fine of not more than five thousand dollars nor less than five hundred dollars, or by both such fine and imprisonment, in the discretion of the court; provided, however, that the provisions of this section shall not be considered as applying to purchases in open market, nor to the performance of any work for the city, the cost of which shall not exceed the sum of two hundred dollars.

As amended by Section 44, Chapter 144, Laws of 1875.

Penalty for member of common council accepting consideration for any vote or omission to vote or using his influence corruptly.

Penalty for offering bribe to member of council.

SECTION 6. If any member of the common council, or other officer or agent of the city government, shall, directly or indirectly, accept or agree to accept or receive any money, goods or chattels, or any bank note, bank bill, bond, promissory note, due bill, bill of exchange, draft, order or certificate, or any security for the payment of money or goods or chattels, or any deed of writing containing a conveyance of land or conveying or transferring an interest in real estate, or any valuable contract in force or any other property or reward whatever, in consideration that such member of the common council, or other officer or agent, will vote affirmatively or negatively, or that he will not vote, or that he will use his interest and influence, on any question, ordinance, resolution, contract, or other matter or proceeding, pending before the common council, or on which such officer or agent may be called upon to decide or act in any particular manner, such member of the common council, officer, or agent, shall be removed from office and his office declared vacant by the common council; and both he and the person or persons offering or paying such consideration, directly or indirectly, shall be deemed guilty of felony, and on conviction thereof, shall be punished by imprisonment in the state prison for not more than three years nor less than one year, or by fine not exceeding five thousand dollars nor less than five hundred dollars, or by both such fine and imprisonment at the discretion of the court.

Dismissal of appointed officers.

SECTION 7. A majority of all the members elect of the common council shall have power to dismiss from office, for malfeasance in office in said city, any person elected or appointed to office in said city, except justices of the peace. And the common council shall provide by ordinance the manner of hearing and disposing of complaints against such officers.

SECTION 8. Whenever any charges of official miscon- Investigation of charges against members of council or city officers. duct shall be preferred against any member of the common council of the city of Milwaukee, or any officer of said city, the common council shall appoint a committee to investigate such charges; and it shall be the duty of the committee as soon as practicable after their appointment, to investigate the matter of any charges which may have been so preferred, and report the results of their investigation to the said common council; and in case such committee shall deem it necessary or proper for the purposes of their investigation, they may examine witnesses on oath in relation to any such charges; and the several members of such committee are hereby authorized and empowered to administer oaths to witnesses to be examined for the purposes of such examination.

NOTE.—Only two proceedings in the nature of impeachment have been had under the above provision, viz; that against Garrett Dunck, the report of which will be found in the council proceedings for 1891-92, and that against Dr. Walter Kempster, now pending in the circuit court, being removed there on *certiorari*.

SECTION 9. Subpœnas may be issued for the purpose Witnesses may be subpœnaed. of procuring the attendance of witnesses before any committtee appointed pursuant to the preceding section. Each subpœna shall state when and where, and before whom, the witness is required to appear and testify, and may require such attendance forthwith, or on a future day named, and the production of books, records, documents and papers therein to be designated. All such subpœnas shall be signed by the city clerk of said city, and shall be issued under the seal of said city, and may be served in the same manner, and shall have the same force and effect as subpœnas issued out of the circuit court. Any willful or corrupt false swearing, by any False swearing, how punished. witness or person giving testimony before such committee, or any member thereof, or making deposition to any material fact relating to the matter under investigation before such committee, shall be deemed guilty of perjury, and shall be punished as such, in the manner provided by law. The provisions of law in respect to the attachment

**Compelling attend-
ance of witnesses.**

of witnesses subpœnaed before justices of the peace, and compelling the attendance of such witnesses to appear and testify before them, are hereby applied to the case of witnesses subpœnaed before such committee, and such committee may exercise the powers of arrest, fine and imprisonment for contempt, vested in the court in such cases.   Writs of attachment and commitment for contempt, shall be signed by the chairman of such committee.

**Removal from
office for making
false certificates.**

SECTION 10. If any member of the common council or other officer or agent of the city government, or any person employed, appointed or confirmed by the common council, or appointed by any department of the city government, shall knowingly certify that any work has been done for said city, or any contract with said city has been completed in compliance with the terms thereof, when in fact such work had not been done, or said contract had not been completed, such member of the common council, officer or agent, shall be removed from office, and his office declared vacant, and no such officer, agent or employe, shall again be elected, appointed or employed by, or for the city of Milwaukee, to any office, place, or position whatever.

Section 45, Chapter 144, Laws of 1875.

CHAPTER XX.

MISCELLANEOUS.

**Liability for dam-
ages to persons
or property.**

SECTION 1. Whenever any injury shall happen to persons or property in the said city of Milwaukee, by reason of any defect or incumbrance of any street, sidewalk, alley or public ground, or from any other cause, for which the said city would be liable, and such defect, incumbrance, or other cause of such injury shall arise from, or be produced by the wrong, default or negligence of any person or corporation, such person or corporation so guilty of such wrong, default or negligence, shall be primarily liable for all damages for such injury; and the said city shall not be liable therefor until after all legal remedies shall have been exhausted to collect such damages from such person or corporation.

The provision of this section holding the person or corporation guilty of wrong doing primarily liable, applies only when the default or negligence of such person or corporation was the *sole* cause of the injury.

> Papworth vs. Milwaukee, 64 Wis., 389.

Chapter 471, laws of 1889, *held* to apply to injuries happening in a city, though not in terms an amendment of the charter thereof.

> Raymond vs. Sheboygan, 76 Wis., 335.

(Chapter 332, laws of 1878, and Chapter 261, laws of 1882.) The remedy given by these acts is exclusive, and the filing of a proper statement or petition in the office of the city clerk is essential. These laws *held* amendatory of the charter of Milwaukee.

> Thompson vs. Milwaukee, 69 Wis., 492.

The lot owner has a right to deposit excavated earth on the half of the street adjoining, provided the street is not improperly obstructed thereby, and that it is guarded by due precaution against accident; and further, that it be removed within a reasonable time.

> Hundhausen vs. Bond, 36 Wis., 29.
>
> See generally, Johnson vs. Milwaukee, 46 Wis., 568.
>
> Whitney vs. Milwaukee, 57 Wis., 639.

A complaint which shows that no action against the party primarily liable was commenced until five and a half years after the injury, and states no facts to explain the delay, or to show whether the city, if held liable, would be injured by such delay, fails to state a cause of action against the city.

> McFarlane vs. Milwaukee, 51 Wis., 691.

Ordinarily a city is liable for a nuisance where a private person would be. If it causes earth to be left or placed in a street unnecessarily, so as to obstruct the flow of water in the gutters, it will be liable to an adjoining lot owner who is injured by the overflow of water caused by such obstruction.

> Harper vs. Milwaukee, 30 Wis., 365.

A person was injured by falling on ice formed on a sidewalk by reason of water pumped upon a street by a city fire-engine. Held, that the city was not liable, it not appearing the engine was not used for a lawful purpose.

> Cook vs. Milwaukee, 27 Wis., 191.

If ice or snow is permitted to accumulate upon a sidewalk in such a rounded or uneven form that one using due care cannot walk over it without danger of falling, the municipality is liable to the person injured thereby. Otherwise, if the injury results from mere slipperiness, arising from the smooth surface of the ice or snow accumulated upon it.

> Cook vs. Milwaukee, 24 Wis., 270.
>
> Perkins vs. Fond du Lac, 34 Wis., 435.
>
> See, also, Kittredge vs. Milwaukee, 26 Wis., 46, and Lane vs. Madison, 86 Wisconsin, 453, and note in 47 Am. and Eng. Corp. Cases, 36.

A municipal corporation making improvements for the public good, is not answerable for consequential damages produced thereby to property in the vicinity of such improvement, no part of which is taken or used therefor.

Alexander vs. Milwaukee, 16 Wis., 264.

The provisions of this section *held* valid, but not applicable when the defective condition is caused by the negligence of persons making *public* improvements *under a contract with the city*.

Hincks vs. Milwaukee, 46 Wis., 559.

In general, the question as to whether or not a particular condition of a street or sidewalk amounts to a defect for which the municipality will be held liable, is a question of fact for the jury.

McMaugh vs. Milwaukee, 32 Wis., 200.

Also whether the defective condition has existed long enough to charge the city with notice.

Sheel vs. Appleton, 49 Wis., 125.

Every municipality is bound at its peril to keep its highways in sufficient repair, or to take precautionary measures to protect the public against damages from insufficient highways.

Prideaux vs. Mineral Point, 43 Wis., 513.

When city primarily liable.

SECTION 2. Whenever any injury shall happen to person or property in the said city of Milwaukee, at any place in said city where work of any kind or nature is being done in or on any street or sidewalk by any person or party under contract with said city, or with the board of public works, in the name of the city, in consequence of any neglect or default of such person or party in doing such work or improperly fencing or otherwise guarding such street or sidewalk to prevent accident while such work is going on, such person or party doing such work and guilty of such neglect or default shall be primarily liable for all damages for such injury, and the said city shall not be liable therefor until after all legal remedies shall have been exhausted to collect such damages from such person or party so primarily liable.

As amended by Section 56, Chapter 324, Laws of 1882.

The provisions of this section, before its amendment in 1882, *held* invalid, as granting to the city of Milwaukee a special immunity against a general rule of law, to which all other municipal corporations are left subject.

Hincks vs. Milwaukee, 46 Wis., 559.

Under this section, the injury must be incurred at the place where the work is being done, in order to render the city liable. "We are inclined to think that the object of the law is to restrict the *statutory* liability of the city for injuries to person and property of travelers in the streets."

Harper vs. Milwaukee, 30 Wis., 376 *op.*

SECTION 3. No penalty or judgment recovered in favor of the city shall be remitted or discharged without payment, and no resolution for a stay of prosecution for a violation of a city ordinance shall be passed, except by an affirmative vote, in either case, of two-thirds of all the members elect of the common council. Two-thirds vote necessary to remit, etc.

SECTION 4. No person shall be an incompetent judge, justice, witness, or juror, by reason of his being an inhabitant or freeholder in the city of Milwaukee, in any proceeding or action in which the city shall be a party in interest. Competency.

SECTION 5. All ordinances, regulations, or resolutions now in force in the city of Milwaukee, and not inconsistent with this act, shall remain in force under this act until altered, modified or repealed by the common council after this act shall take effect. Remaining in force.

SECTION 6. All actions, rights, fines, penalties and forfeitures, in suit or otherwise, which have accumulated under the several acts consolidated herein, shall be vested in and prosecuted by the corporation hereby created. Vested actions, etc.

SECTION 7. If any election by the people or common council shall, for any cause, not be held at the time or in the manner herein prescribed, or if the council shall fail to organize as herein provided, it shall not be considered reason for arresting, suspending or absolving said corporation, but such election or organization may be had on any subsequent day, by order of the common council; and if any of the duties enjoined by this act, or the ordinances or by-laws of the city, to be done by any officer at any specified time, are not then done or performed, the common council may appoint another time at which the said acts may be done and performed. Accidental failure, not to suspend corporation.

SECTION 8. When any suit or action shall be commenced against said city, the service of process therein may be made by leaving a copy of the process by the proper officer with the mayor, and it shall be the duty of the mayor, forthwith to inform the common council thereof, or to take such other proceedings as by the Service of process in city cases, how made.

ordinances or resolutions of said council may be in such case provided.   When, in any suit, the city shall take an appeal from the order or judgment of any court in the state, to a higher court, it shall not be required to furnish an appeal bond.

Real and personal property of city exempt from execution.   SECTION 9.   All property, real and personal, now or at any time hereafter belonging to said city, or to either of the wards thereof, shall be exempt from levy and sale, under or by virtue of any execution; provided, that any such property, real or personal, shall be subject to levy and sale by virtue of any execution issued on a judgment for the purchase money thereof.   Nor shall any real or personal property of any inhabitant of said city, or of any individual or corporation, be levied on and sold by virtue of any execution issued to satisfy or collect any debt, obligation or contract of said city.

Real, personal and mixed property vested in city.   SECTION 10.   All property, real, personal, or mixed, belonging to the city of Milwaukee, is hereby vested in the corporation created by this act.   The officers of said corporation, now in office, shall respectively continue in the same until superseded in accordance with the provisions thereof, but shall be governed by this act, which shall take effect and be in force from and after its passage and publication; provided, that the common council of said city, as now constituted and organized, being a board of aldermen and a board of councilors, separate and distinct from each other, shall until the organization of the new common council, under this act, on the third Tuesday of April, A. D. 1874, have and exercise the duties, powers and functions of the common council of **Powers of old council continued.** said city, as defined by this act, but in the manner and under the forms and course of procedure prescribed by the act, under which said existing common council was organized; and the mayor shall continue to act as the presiding officer of such common council; and provided further, that until the board of health created by this act shall be appointed and organized, the now existing board **Board of health continued.** of health shall continue in office with the duties and powers conferred upon them by the laws creating and regulating such board; and provided further, that until **Salaries to remain unchanged.** the third Tuesday in April, 1874, the salaries and allowances to officers in said city shall continue as they now are, unchanged by anything in this act contained; and further provided, that chapter ten of this act, except the first section thereof, shall only take effect and become operative on the first day of January, A. D. 1875, or at the time, either before or after that date, when, in accordance with the provisions of said section one, the powers, duties and functions of the board of water commissioners of the city of Milwaukee, and of their officers, agents, employes and servants shall cease and determine.

SECTION 11.   The said city may lease, purchase and hold real or personal estate sufficient for the convenience of the inhabitants thereof; and may sell and convey the same; and the same shall be free from taxation.

City may acquire real and personal property.

> The city may lease lands for temporary use as a public street.
> Gilman vs. Milwaukee, 31 Wis., 563.

> But it has no power to purchase an easement for street purposes.
> Trester vs. Sheboygan, 87 Wis., 496.

SECTION 12.   Real estate exempted from taxation by the laws of the state shall be subject to special taxes, as other real estate under this act.

SECTION 13.   The justices of the peace elected in the said city shall not have jurisdiction to hear complaints or conduct examinations or trials in criminal cases within the city; but they may issue warrants in criminal cases, returnable before the municipal court, but no fees shall be received therefor by them.

> As amended by Section 57, Chapter 324, Laws of 1882.

SECTION 14.   No general law of this state, contravening the provisions of this act, shall be considered as repealing, amending, or modifying the same, except such purpose be expressly set forth in such law.

> Where it is clear that the legislature intended an act to apply to the city of Milwaukee, as well as to other towns and cities, such intention must prevail.
> Brighman vs. Kirner, 22 Wis., 53.
> Raymond vs. Sheboygan, 76 Wis., 335.

SECTION 15.   The common council of the city of Milwaukee are hereby authorized to cause this act, together with any other acts or parts of acts of the legislature of Wisconsin relating to it, affecting said city, and also any of the ordinances, by-laws, rules and regulations of said city or any of its departments, and any other acts, resolutions, contracts or other documents relating to or affecting said city, to be printed and published in book form, and such book shall be deemed prima facie evidence of the contents and passage, and shall be a sufficient publication of all such acts, ordinances, by-laws, rules, resolutions and regulations, printed copies of the ordinances, by-laws, resolutions and regulations of the city of Milwaukee in any newspaper, book, pamphlet or other form purporting to be published by authority of the common council of said city shall be admitted in all courts of this state as presumptive evidence of such ordinances, laws, resolutions and regulations, and of the due passage, publication and recording thereof.

As amended by Chapter 30, Laws of 1889.

Old liabilities not to be disturbed.

SECTION 16. This act shall not invalidate any legal act done by the common council of the city of Milwaukee, or by its officers, nor divest their successors under this act of any rights of property or otherwise, or of any liability which may have accrued to, or been created by said corporation prior to the passage of this act.

Enumeration of laws repealed by the passage of this act.

SECTION 17. Chapter fifty-six of the session laws of this state for 1852, entitled "an act to consolidate and amend the act to incorporate the city of Milwaukee and the several acts amendatory thereof," approved February 20, 1852; the several acts amendatory of said chapter fifty-six or relating to said city of Milwaukee, particularly mentioned and described as follows, to-wit: chapter three hundred and eighty-five of the session laws of the year 1852; chapters twenty-six and one hundred and seventy of the session laws of the year 1853; chapters seventy-three, one hundred and ninety-six, two hundred and forty-seven, and three hundred and seventy-two of the session laws of the year 1855; chapters one hundred and fifty-six and three hundred and thirty-eight of the session laws of the year 1856; chapter three hundred and forty-four of the session laws of the year 1857; chapters one hundred and seventeen and two hundred and thirty-three of the session laws of the year 1858; chapters one hundred and seventy-two and one hundred and ninety of the session laws of the year 1859; chapter three hundred and fifty-six of the session laws of the year 1860; chapters two hundred and ninety, two hundred and ninety-one and two hundred and ninety-two of the

session laws of the year 1861; chapters one hundred and
forty-two, three hundred and eight, three hundred
and nine, three hundred and ten and three hundred and
forty-seven of the session laws of the year 1862; chapter
two hundred and thirty-nine of the session laws of the
year 1863; chapters two hundred and eighty-three and
five hundred and thirteen of the session laws of the year
1865; chapter two hundred and sixty-eight of the session
laws of the year 1866; chapters two hundred and fifty-
two, three hundred and ninety-four, five hundred and
five, five hundred and forty-four, five hundred and ninety-
five and six hundred and eight of the session laws of 1867;
chapters one hundred and forty-six, three hundred and
thirty-three, three hundred and forty and three hundred
and eighty-six of the session laws of the year 1868;
chapters two hundred and ninety-nine, three hundred and
twenty-four, three hundred and ninety-nine, four hundred
and one, four hundred and twenty-seven, four hundred and
twenty-four, three hundred and ninety-nine, and four
hundred and thirty-two of the session laws of the year
1869; chapters two hundred and forty-five, two hundred
and seventy-four and four hundred and one of the session
laws of the year 1870; chapters seven, one hundred and
eight, three hundred and sixty, four hundred and fourteen, four hundred and thirty-eight, four hundred and .
ninety-two and four hundred and twenty-one, except
section four thereof, of the session laws of the year 1871;
chapters forty-five and sixty-one of the session laws of
the year 1872, and sections one, two, three, four, five, six,
seven, eight, nine, ten, eleven, twelve, thirteen, fourteen,
fifteen, twenty-two, twenty-three, twenty-four, thirty-two
and thirty-three of chapter one hundred and twenty-nine
of the session laws of the year 1873; these and all other
acts and parts of acts, inconsistent with or superseded by
this act, are hereby repealed; but such repeals shall not
in any manner affect, injure or invalidate any contracts,
acts, suits, proceedings, claims or demands that may have
been entered into, performed or commenced, or that may
exist under or by virtue or in pursuance of the said acts,
or any of them; but the same shall remain in full force
and effect, and be in force and carried out as fully and
effectually as if this act had not been passed, but in
conformity with the provisions of this act so far as the
same may be applicable.

Our courts will take judicial notice of the charter of the city of Milwaukee, and the acts amendatory thereof, as being public acts.

Terry vs. Milwaukee, 15 Wis., 543.

Alexander vs. Milwaukee, 16 Wis., 264.

CHAPTER 459, LAWS OF 1887.

Mayor may appoint inspectors of buildings; term of office four years; to give bond; salary of inspectors.

SECTION 1. The mayor of the city of Milwaukee shall, at the time of the first meeting of the common council of said city in the month of May, once in every four years, commencing with the year 1887, appoint an inspector of buildings, who shall reside in the city of Milwaukee, and who shall be an experienced architect or builder. Such appointment shall be made by sending the name of the person so appointed by the mayor, either for a full term or to fill any vacancy in any unexpired term, to the common council of said city, and no appointment shall be valid until confirmed by the said common council. In case the said council shall neglect or refuse to confirm any such appointment, the mayor shall make another appointment, until the same shall have been so confirmed. The said inspector of buildings shall hold office, unless sooner removed, for the term of four years from the first day of June in the year in which he shall have been appointed, except when appointed to fill a vacancy in said term; in which latter case, he shall hold office for the unexpired term of his predecessor. In all cases the inspector of buildings shall hold office until the appointment, confirmation and qualification of his successor. Before entering upon the duties of his office, the person appointed inspector, whether for a full term or to fill a vacancy in any unexpired term, shall file with the city clerk of said city, within ten days after receiving notice of the confirmation of his appointment by the common council, a bond in the sum of five thousand dollars, with at least two sureties, conditioned for the faithful performance of the duties of his office. Such bond shall be approved by the comptroller of the city of Milwaukee as to the sufficiency of the sureties therein, and by the city attorney of the city of Milwaukee, as to the form and execution thereof; and the said person so appointed shall at the time of the filing of said bond, file also with the clerk of said city his oath in writing, to be executed in the form and manner as are the oaths of other public officers of said city. The mayor of the city of Milwaukee shall have power to remove such inspector at any time, in case he shall neglect to perform the duties of his office, or shall for any reason be incompetent to perform the same. The inspector of buildings so appointed shall receive an annual salary of fifteen hundred dollars, which shall be paid to him out of the treasury of the city of Milwaukee in monthly installments, the same as the salaries of the other officers of the said city are now paid. In case of the failure or neglect of the city of Milwaukee or the common council thereof to provide said inspector of buildings with a suitable office, then and in such case he shall receive the sum of three hundred dollars per annum, to be paid to him monthly, at the time when his salary is herein directed to be paid to him, and he shall continue to receive said sum so long as said common council shall

Mayor may remove.

fail or neglect to provide him with such office. His office shall be held at all times in the city of Milwaukee and shall be open during the business hours of each day for public business, The said inspector of buildings shall have authority to incur liability on the part of and against the city of Milwaukee not to exceed the sum of five hundred dollars in any one year.

From the liability so incurred he may hold inquests, employ clerks and stenographers, and defray other incidental expenses necessary to carry into effect the purposes of this act; and the bills for expenses within said amount shall be audited by the city comptroller of said city, and paid by the city treasurer, as are other claims against the city of Milwaukee.

SECTION 2. The duties of the inspector of buildings shall be to inspect all buildings within the city of Milwaukee, and especially those now being built or repaired, and such as may hereafter be built or repaired, and to ascertain, by or without the aid of a jury, whether said buildings have been built or repaired, or are being built or repaired as required by law, and the ordinances of the city of Milwaukee. It shall also be the duty of such inspector, when he shall deem it necessary, to examine into and ascertain, by or without the aid of a jury, the cause of all fires happening to any building in said city, and of all accidents caused by the breaking or falling down of any building in said city, and also to ascertain, by or without the aid of a jury, what buildings in said city are unsafe and dangerous to be occupied, arising either from the condition of the building or the manner in which it is used. It shall also be the duty of said inspector, by or without the aid of a jury, to find out all cases of the violation of any of the laws of the state, or any ordinance of the city of Milwaukee, relating to the construction, repairing or moving of any building in said city.

Duties of inspector.

SECTION 3. Such inspectors of buildings shall have authority and power to hold inquests, either with or without the aid of a jury, to be summoned by such inspector in the manner now provided by law for coroners juries. Whenever such inspector shall think the interests of the public require an inquest to be held, he shall proceed to hold the same, and shall have the authority to administer oaths, summon juries, if such inquest is before a jury, in the same form and manner as is now provided by law for the coroners of the several counties within this state. The expenses of said inquest shall be paid from the said sum of five hundred dollars hereinbefore provided for. The said inspector of buildings shall keep a record of all proceedings had in any inquest held under the provisions of this act; and it shall be the duty of the chief of police of said city to cause to be served all subpoenas, demands and warrants issued by said inspector, and attend or cause a policeman to attend any inquest held by said inspector when notified so to do. Such inspector shall have all the power and authority of a court commissioner of the circuit court for the purpose of administering oaths, compelling witnesses to answer questions, issuing subpoenas and enforcing obedience to the same, preserving order during the holding of an inquest, and punishing for contempt any violation of such order, or refusal to answer any question pertinent to the subject matter of the inquest. No

May hold inquests; to keep a record of all proceedings held by him; may administer oaths to witnesses.

one shall be excused from answerwing any question pertinent to the subject matter of the inquest on the ground that his answer may tend to criminate himself; but no such answer shall be used against such witness in any matter or proceeding whatever.

May demand and have admission to buildings for purpose of inspection; when admission refused may apply to judge of circuit court of Milwaukee county for writ of assistance.

SECTION 4. Such inspector of buildings may demand and shall have admission to any building within the city of Milwaukee at any time, except any building used exclusively as a place of residence of not exceeding two private families, for the purpose of inspecting the same, ard in the performance of the duties of his office; and if such admission be refused and he be unable to obtain such admission for any reason, after properly demanding the same at a reasonable time, he may apply to the judge of the circuit court of Milwaukee county for a writ of assistance, and if the judge of said court shall be satisfied that it is proper and necessary for such inspector to gain admission to such building and is unable to do so, he may issue a writ of assistance to the sheriff of Milwaukee county, commanding said sheriff to enter in and upon said building with said inspector, with such force as may be necessary to enable such inspector to perform his duties. The board of public works of the city of Milwaukee shall issue no permit to any one to use any street for the deposit of material for the construction or repair of any building in said city, unless such person shall first file with said board his written consent, authorizing said inspector of buildings, upon reasonable notice and demand, to enter into and upon and inspect said buildings and repairs.

May apply for order restraining construction of building—when.

SECTION 5. When in the opinion of the inspector of buildings the erection or construction of any building within the city limits of said city, or the making of alterations or repairs upon any buildings within the limits of said city, are being done in a reckless, careless or unsafe manner, or in violation of the provisions of any law or of any ordinances of the city relating thereto, he may make application upon his verified complaint to any court of record of civil jurisdiction in the county of Milwaukee for an order restraining the person or persons constructing, erecting or repairing such building or buildings, and upon such application the court may issue such order restraining such person or persons from erecting, constructing or repairing such building or buildings until sufficient cause shall be shown for the dissolution of such restraining order. Such restraining order may be dissolved upon sufficient cause being shown, or upon the certificate in writing of the said inspector of buildings that the person or persons restrained therein and thereby have agreed to construct or erect such buildings, or make such alterations or repairs according to law and in conformity with the directions of the said inspector of buildings. No costs shall be taxed against the city of Milwaukee in any event upon the dissolution of any such restraining order.

"Inquest" defined.

SECTION 6. The word " inquest " as used in this act, shall be construed to mean an examination and inquiry by said inspector into those matters into which he is required by law to inquire, in order to perform the duties imposed upon him by this act.

SECTION 7. This act is amendatory of the charter of the city of Milwaukee, being chapter 184, of the laws of 1874, and the various laws amendatory thereof; and any of the provisions thereof which are inconsistent with the provisions of this act, or not in harmony with its provisions are declared to be modified, amended, superseded or repealed by this act, as the intention herein may require.

Amendatory of charter.

CHAPTER 375, LAWS OF 1885, AS AMENDED BY CHAPTER 304, LAWS OF 1889.

AN ACT to protect life and property from destruction by fire.

SECTION 1. Every inn, hotel, boarding-house, or tenement building in this state, more than two stories in height, and containing sleeping apartments, offices, theaters or assembly halls above the ground floor, designed for occupancy by twenty-five or more persons, shall be provided with not less than two fire-proof stairs or ladders outside; said stairs or ladders to be located on different sides of said inn, hotel, boarding-house or tenement building, in each case connecting the cornice with the top of the first story of any such inn, hotel, boarding-house or tenement building, with a platform, balcony, piazza or other safe and convenient resting place on a level with the floor of each story so connected. Such stairways or ladders herein named shall, in every case be convenient of access from the interior of any such building, commodious in construction and of sufficient strength and firmness to render the same amply safe and reliable for the purpose of ascent and descent in case of danger from fire. But this act shall not be construed so as to apply to private dwellings.

Fire escapes. Boarding houses and tenement buildings required to have—how constructed.

SECTION 2. The inside walls or casings of every elevator for the conveyance of passengers to and from the upper stories of any such building, as is described in the preceding section of this act, shall be constructed of fire-proof material throughout.

Elevator, how to be constructed.

SECTION 3. In all inns, hotels or other buildings hereinbefore described, not less than one efficient and faithful watchman shall be on service from ten o'clock P. M., until five o'clock A. M., during each and every night that said inn, hotel or other building described is occupied, and every said watchman shall be required to establish the fact of his fidelity on every occasion when on duty, by the most efficient methods in use for that purpose.

Watchmen shall be on duty.

SECTION 4. In every inn, hotel or other building hereinbefore described, there shall be posted in every room, in legible print, a brief and accurate statement of all means of safety and escape in case of fire.

Statement to be posted.

SECTION 5. Any owner, landlord or other person in charge of any building hereinbefore described, and coming within the provisions of this act, who shall omit to comply with the provisions of this act, or who shall knowingly permit any violation of the provisions of this act, shall be held guilty of a misdemeanor in permitting the violation of any provisions of this act, and for such

Penalty for non-compliance.

misdemeanor may be punished by fine not exceeding one thousand dollars, or by imprisonment not exceeding ninety days on each conviction thereof.

CHAPTER 342, LAWS OF 1887.

May employ veterinary.

SECTION 1. The city of Milwaukee shall be authorized, and is hereby authorized to employ a veterinary surgeon in its fire department, who may be required to render service in respect to all horses used by the city.

Chief engineer to nominate.

SECTION 2. On or before the first Monday in July, 1887, the chief engineer of the fire department may nominate, with the approval of the board of fire and police commissioners, he may appoint a qualified and suitable person to be the veterinary surgeon of the fire department, who shall take the official oath required of officers of the city and shall hold his position at the pleasure of the chief. In case of a vacancy in the office at any time it shall be filled by appointment in the same way.

To be subject to all the rules of the department.

SECTION 3. The veterinary surgeon so appointed and his successors in office, shall be subject to all the rules of the department which are applicable to such an officer, and shall also be subject always to the special control and direction of the chief. The salary of the veterinary surgeon is hereby fixed at six hundred dollars per year, and shall be paid in monthly installments, at the same time and in the same manner as other salaries in the fire department are paid.

Services the surgeon shall render.

SECTION 4. The veterinary surgeon shall render such services and perform such duties as shall be required by the rules of the fire department, and also such as may be required by the chief at any time. Especially the veterinary surgeon will be required to make careful examinations of horses offered for purchase by the city for the use of the fire department when required by the chief (or by) any officer of the city or any board having authority to purchase such horses, and no horses shall be purchased for such use without a certificate by the veterinary surgeon that, in his opinion, the horse is fit for the service intended; and no bill or resolution for the payment for any horse purchased for such use shall be countersigned by the comptroller unless it is accompanied by such a certificate of the veterinary surgeon. It shall be the duty of the veterinary surgeon, at least once in each month, to visit the quarters of each company belonging to the fire department, and to inspect carefully and thoroughly the stables and horses, and the forage and feed provided, and to make prompt report in writing to the chief of any deficiency found or anything needing correction, or improvement, either in the horses or the stables, or the forage or feed provided. It shall be the duty of the veterinary surgeon to make a prompt written report to the chief immediately upon discovering that any horse in use in the department is not fit for further service therein, and upon the approval by the chief of any such report the horse or horses named therein may be sold or otherwise disposed of by the proper officer or officers of the city.

Comptroller not to countersign without certificate of surgeon.

SECTION 5. The veterinary surgeon of the fire department may also be required by the chief to inspect and make written report as to horses owned by the city or offered for purchase by the city for use elswhere than in the fire department, and also to render medical or other service in relation to horses owned or in use by the city elsewhere than in the fire department, and it ss hereby made the duty of the chief of the fire department, to communicate the opinion or certificate of such surgeon as to any such horses inspected by him to the officer or board having charge of or authorized to purchase such horses, and no horse shall be purchased for the city without the certificate of such surgeon that in his opinion the horse is fit for the service intended. No compensation beyond the salary fixed by this act shall be allowed or paid to such surgeon for any services which he shall perform under this act.

Shall inspect horses owned by city.

SECTION 6. This act is to be taken as an amendment to the charter of the city of Milwaukee, and any provisions thereof, which are inconsistent herewith, are declared to be hereby modified, amended, superseded or repealed, as the intention herein declared may require.

Amendment.

CHAPTER 261, LAWS OF 1882.

AN ACT to amend chapter 332 of the laws of 1878, entitled an act to protect laborers and material men in the city of Milwaukee.

SECTION 1. Any person, corporation or party that shall hereafter furnish supplies or materials for the use of the contractor or contractors or of his or their assigns, in the performance of any contract made with the board of public works of the city of Milwaukee, in the name of said city, or that shall do any labor for such contractor or contractors or for his or their assigns in the performance of any such contracts, shall have a lien for the amount due and unpaid by such contractor or contractors or by his or their assigns, to the person, corporation or party furnishing such supplies or materials or doing such labor in the performance of such contract, upon any certificates of said board and upon any city orders of said city, to be issued and delivered to such contractor or contractors, or to his or their assigns under such contract; provided, that any persons, corporation or party claiming a lien shall, within twenty days after the date of the last charge for such supplies or materials furnished or labor done, file in the office of the city clerk of said city and in the office of the board of public works of said city notices in writing of such claim (one notice in each office), which notice shall set forth the nature and particulars of the demand, the date and amount of each charge therefor, the name of the person or party indebted, and the amount that is justly due and owing to the claimant from the contractor or contractors or from his or their assigns for supplies or materials furnished or labor done in performance of a contract stating the general nature of the contract and its date, each of which notices shall be verified by the affidavit of the claimant; and provided, further, that within twenty days after the filing of such notice the claimant shall begin an action against the person or party named in such notice for the

Protection of laborers and material men.

Persons claiming lien to file same in twenty days.

recovery of the amount of such claim, and for the enforcement of
such lien in some court in Milwaukee county having jurisdiction
of the matter, in which action the city of Milwaukee shall be
made a party defendant and shall be served with process and may
appear and defend as in other actions, but said city shall in no
case be liable to any judgment for costs and charges in such action.
In case of the filing of the notices as herein directed, claiming
lien on any certificates or city orders or both, it shall be the duty
of the respective officers having charge and custody of the same
to retain them twenty days, and in case an action is begun within
that time as herein provided, then to retain the same until the
determination of such action in court.

In relation to work done by contract. SECTION 2. No contractor under any such contract as is mentioned in the preceding section, and no assignee of any such
contractor shall receive, either in certificates of the board of
public works or in city orders, any amount exceeding seventy-
five per centum of the amount named and provided in the contract
until after the expiration of twenty days from the completion of
the work contracted for, or other termination of the contract; and
if any person, corporation or party shall file notices of claim of
lien, as provided in the preceding section, against such contractor
or contractors, or his or their assigns, all certificates and all city
orders not then delivered shall be held and retained by the respective officers in whose charge or custody they are, until twenty
days after the filing of such notices, and if within such last period
of twenty days an action shall be brought as provided in the
preceding section, such certificates and such city orders shall be
retained until the determination of such action in court.

CHAPTER 7, LAWS OF 1878, AS AMENDED BY CHAPTER 152, LAWS OF 1879.

AN ACT to establish and maintain a public library in the city of
Milwaukee.

Authority of city. SECTION 1. The city of Milwaukee is hereby authorized to
establish and maintain a public library therein, for the free use of
the inhabitants thereof, and to receive, hold and manage any
devise, bequest or donation for the establishment, increase and
maintenance of such library, under such regulations as are herein
contained or as may hereafter be adopted, as provided in this act.

Library, part of educational department. SECTION 2. The public library, established under this act, shall
be considered a branch of the educational department of the city
of Milwaukee, and shall be under the general management, control
and supervision of a board, consisting of nine members, who shall
be styled " The Board of Trustees of the public library of the city
of Milwaukee."

Management and style of board of trustees. SECTION 3. The president of the school board and the
superintendent of public schools of said city, shall be ex-officio
members of said board of trustees. William Frankfurth, Gustave
C. Trumpff, Matthew Keenan and John Johnston, residents and
Trustees. tax-payers of the city of Milwaukee, and three members of the
common council of said city, to be appointed as hereinbefore

provided, together with said president of the school board and said superintendent of public schools, shall be and are hereby constituted the first board of trustees. The four trustees above designated by name shall serve for one, two, three and four years from the date of the organization of said board, so that the term of one of them shall expire each year. The respective terms of these four trustees shall be determined by lot at the first meeting of said board after the passage of this act, and their places shall be filled whenever a vacancy shall occur, by election by the board, from among the citizens at large; and annually, upon the expiration of the term of any such designated trustee, the board shall at their annual meeting, elect from among the citizens and taxpayers of said city, his successor, to serve for the term of four years. The first three members from the common council shall be appointed by the mayor of said city at the first meeting of the common council held for organization after the charter election in 1878, from the members of the common council, to-wit: One from the three year class of aldermen, one from the two year class of aldermen, and one from the one year class of aldermen, who shall serve as such trustees during their respective term as such aldermen. And annually on the third Tuesday in April thereafter, at the expiration of the term of any such trustee, the mayor shall appoint his successor for the term of three years from the aldermen then having three years to serve. In case any person so appointed trustee shall vacate the office of alderman before the expiration of his term, he shall at the same time cease to be a member of said board of trustees, and the mayor shall appoint some other alderman of his class in his place, for the balance of his term. None of said trustees shall receive any compensation from the city treasury or otherwise, for their services as such trustees. And no member of said board of trustees shall become, or cause himself to become interested, directly or indirectly, in any contract or job for the purchase of books, pamphlets or other matter pertaining to the library, or of fuel, furniture, stationery, or things necessary for the increase and maintenance of the library.

Terms of office of trustees.

Mayor to appoint.

Vacancies.

Trustees not to receive compensation nor become interested in contracts, etc.

See Section 1, Chapter 521, Laws of 1887, Page 196.

SECTION 4. The first annual meeting of the board of trustees shall be held on the sixth day of May, 1878, at which meeting the board shall organize, by the choice of one of their number as president, to serve for one year, and until his successor shall be chosen. And it shall be the duty of the city clerk of said city, as soon as practicable, after the appointment of the three trustees to be selected from the common council, to give at least three days' notice, in writing, of such meeting of organization, to be held at the office of said city clerk, on the sixth day of May, 1878, to every member of said board. And all subsequent annual meetings of said board shall be held on the second Monday of May in each year, at which a president shall be chosen from their number, to serve for one year, and until his successor shall be chosen.

Annual meeting.

Duty of city clerk.

President to be chosen.

SECTION 5. The board of trustees shall have general care, control and supervision of the public library, its appurtenances, fixtures and furniture, and of the selection and purchase of books,

Powers of trustees.

pamphlets, maps, and other matter appertaining to a public library; and also of the disbursement of all moneys appropriated for and belonging to the library fund, in the manner hereinafter provided. And said board shall adopt, and at their discretion modify, amend or repeal by-laws, rules and regulations for the management, care and use of the public library, and fix and enforce penalties for their violation, and generally shall adopt such measures as shall promote the public utility of the library; provided that such by-laws, rules and regulations, shall not conflict with the provisions of this act.

Proviso.

Meetings of board of trustees.

Librarian to be appointed.

SECTION 6. The board of trustees shall, at their first meeting, on the sixth day of May, 1878, or thereafter as soon as practicable, and every five years thereafter, at an annual meeting, elect by ballot a person of suitable learning, ability and experience, for librarian, who shall also act and be ex-officio secretary of said board of trustees, who shall hold his office for five years from the time of said first annual meeting, unless previously removed, and who shall receive such compensation as may be hereafter fixed by the said board of trustees. And said board of trustees shall also appoint such assistants and employes for said library as they may deem necessary and expedient, and shall fix their compensation. All vacancies in office of librarian, assistants and other employes, shall be filled by said board of trustees, and the person so elected or appointed, shall hold for the unexpired term.

Vacancies, how filled.

As amended by Section 1, Chapter 152, Laws of 1879.

Removals authorized.

SECTION 7. The librarian elected under this act, may be removed from office for misdemeanor, incompetency, or inattention to the duties of his office, by a vote of two-thirds of the board of trustees; the assistants and other employes may be removed by the board for incompetency, or for any other cause.

Duties of trustees.

SECTION 8. It shall be the duty of the board of trustees, within ten days after the appointment of the librarian and other salaried employes, to report and file with the city comptroller a duly certified list of the persons so appointed, with the salary allowed to each, and the time or times fixed for the payment thereof, and they shall also furnish such comptroller with a list of all accounts and bills which may be allowed by said board of trustees, stating the character of the materials or services for which the same were rendered, immediately after the meeting of said board at which said allowance shall be made. And said board of trustees shall also, on or before the first day of October in each year, make to the common council a report, made up to and including the thirty-first day of August of the said year, containing a statement of the condition of the library, the number of books added thereto, the number of books circulated, and the number of books not returned, or lost, together with such information, or suggestions, as they may deem important; and this report shall also contain an account of the moneys credited to the library fund, and expended on account of the same during the preceding year.

As amended by Section 2, Chapter 152, Laws of 1879.

SECTION 9. The common council shall levy and collect annu- **Common council to levy tax.** ally, upon all taxable property of the said city, at the same time and in the same manner as other city taxes are levied and collected by law, a special tax, not exceeding one-fifth of a mill upon each dollar of the assessed value of said taxable property, the amount of which shall be determined by said board of trustees, and certified to the common council, and to the city comptroller, at the time of making their annual report to said council, and the entire amount of said special tax shall be paid into, and held in, the city treasury, as a seperate and distinct fund, to be known as the "Library Fund," and shall not be used or appropriated, directly or indirectly, for any purpose than for the maintenance and increase of the public library, the payment of the salaries of the librarian, assistants and other employes of the library, the purchase of books, supplies and fuel, and the incidental repairs of the library room and furniture.

As amended by Section 3, Chapter 152, Laws of 1879.

SECTION 10. The board of trustees shall erect, purchase, hire **Erection and leasing of buildings.** or lease buildings, lots, rooms and furniture for the use and accommodation of said public library, and shall improve, enlarge and repair such library buildings, rooms and furniture; but no lot or building shall be purchased, or erected or enlarged for the purpose herein mentioned, without an ordinance or resolution of the common council of said city, and deeds of conveyance and leases shall run to the city of Milwaukee.

As amended by Section 5, Chapter 152, Laws of 1879.

SECTION 11. All moneys received by or raised in the city of **City treasurer to be custodian of library funds.** Milwaukee for library purposes shall be paid over to the city treasurer, to be disbursed by him on the orders of the president and secretary of the board of trustees, countersigned by the city comptroller. Such orders shall be made payable to the order of the persons in whose favor they shall have been issued, and shall be the only vouchers of the city treasurer for the payments from the library fund. The said board of trustees shall provide for the purchase of books, supplies, fuel and other matters necessary for the maintenance of the library. Provided, however, that it shall **Proviso.** not be lawful for said board of trustees to expend, or contract a liability for any sum in excess of the amount levied in any one year for the library fund, on account of such fund.

SECTION 12. In case the Young Men's Association of the city **City to accept gifts.** of Milwaukee shall donate and transfer to the city of Milwaukee, its library, fixtures, furniture and other property for the purposes of free public library, it shall be lawful for said city to accept such donation and transfer, and the board of trustees herein created shall assume the charge and control of said property. It shall, also, be lawful for said city to receive money, books and other property by devise, bequest or gift from any person or corporation for library purposes, and to employ or invest the same for the use and benefit of the public library, so far as practicable, in conformity with the conditions and terms of such devise, bequest or gift.

Duty of mayor.

SECTION 13. In case said Young Men's Association shall make the transfer and donation mentioned in the preceding section, and said city shall accept the same before the date of the annual meeting, in May, 1878, as provided in this act, then immediately upon such transfer and acceptance, it shall be the duty of the mayor to appoint three aldermen, who, together with the trustees hereinbefore designated by name, and the president of the school board of the said city, and the superintendent of public schools, shall constitute a temporary board of trustees, who, until the time of such annual meeting, shall be clothed with all the powers and responsibilities hereinbefore provided, and shall assume the charge, control and management of the property thus donated and accepted, and shall hold and manage the same as provided in this act.

SECTION 4, CHAPTER 152, LAWS OF 1879.

Control of donations.

(All moneys, books and other property received by the city of Milwaukee by devise, bequest or gift, from any person or corporation, for public library purposes, shall, unless otherwise directed by the donors, be under the management and control of said board of trustees; and all moneys derived from fines and penalties for violations of the rules of the library, or from any other source in the course of the administration of the library, including all moneys which may be paid to the city upon any policy or policies of insurance, or other obligation or liability, for or on account of loss or damage to any property pertaining to the library, shall belong to the "library fund" in the city treasury, to be disbursed on the orders of the said board of trustees, countersigned by the city comptroller, for library purposes, in addition to the amount levied and raised by taxation for such fund).

CHAPTER 328, LAWS OF 1882.

AN ACT to authorize the city of Milwaukee to establish and maintain a public museum in said city.

City may accept.

SECTION 1. The city of Milwaukee is hereby authorized to receive and accept from "the Natural History Society of Wisconsin,"— a corporation located in the said city of Milwaukee—a donation of its collection of objects in natural history and ethnology, or of the greater part thereof, upon such conditions as may be agreed upon by and between said city and said society, subject, however, to the provisions of this act.

Public museum.

SECTION 2. In case of such donation and acceptance, said city of Milwaukee is hereby authorized and empowered to establish and maintain in said city a free public museum, exhibition of objects in natural history and ethnology, and for that purpose to receive, hold and manage the collection so donated, and any devise, bequest or donation that may be made to said city for the increase and maintenance of such museum under such regulations and conditions as are herein contained, or may be agreed upon by and between the donors and said city, or as may be hereafter adopted as provided in this act.

SECTION 3. The museum established and maintained under this act shall be under the general management, control and supervision of a board of nine trustees, who shall be styled "the board of trustees of the public museum of the city of Milwaukee." Said board of trustees shall consist of the president of the school board and the superintendent of schools of said city, ex-officio, of three members of the common council of said city, designated and appointed by the mayor thereof, and of four residents and tax-payers of said city, to be appointed by the mayor as herein provided. The first appointments of trustees by the mayor under this act shall be made within ten days after the formal acceptance by the common council of said city of a donation by said natural history society as authorized in the first section of this act. Of the first three trustees appointed from the members of the common council of said city, one shall be appointed from the three year class, one from the two year class and one from the one year class of aldermen, and they shall serve as such trustees during their respective terms as such aldermen. And anually on the third Tuesday of April thereafter, at the expiration of the term of any such trustee, the mayor shall appoint his successor for three years, from the aldermen then having three years to serve. In case any such trustee shall vacate the office of alderman before the expiration of his term, he shall at the same time cease to be a trustee under this act, and the mayor shall appoint some other member of the common council of his class in his place for the balance of his term. In the appointment of the four remaining trustees, and their successors, the mayor shall prefer such persons as may be recommended for such appointment by said natural history society. Such four trustees first appointed shall, at the first meeting of the board after their appointment, determine by lot their term of service, so that one of their number shall serve for one year, one for two years, one for three years and one for four years, from the third Tuesday of May next after the organization of such board. And all vacancies shall be filled by like appointment of the mayor for the remainder of the term, and annually on the third Tuesday of April a trustee shall be appointed by said mayor in like manner for the term of four years, in place of the trustee whose term shall expire the following May. None of said trustees shall receive any compensation from the city treasury or otherwise, for their services as such trustees. And no member of said board of trustees shall become, or cause himself to become interested, directly or indirectly, in any contract or job for the purchase of any matter pertaining to the museum, or of fuel, furniture, stationery or things necessary for the increase and maintenance of the museum. Said trustees shall take the official oath and be subject to the restrictions, disabilities, liabilities, punishments and limitations prescribed by the law as to aldermen in the said city of Milwaukee.

See Section 2, Chapter 521, Laws of 1887, *infra.*

SECTION 4. The first meeting of said board of trustees for the purpose of organizing shall be held on the third Tuesday of the month next following their appointment and the city clerk shall ive at least one week's previous notice of the time and place of

Board of trustees, duties, terms, etc.

Meetings of board.

such meeting to each member of such board, in writing. At such first meeting said board shall organize by the choice of one of their number as president to serve until the third Tuesday of May next following and until his successor shall be chosen. The annual meeting of said board shall be held on the third Tuesday of May in each year, and at such meeting a president shall be chosen from their number to serve for one year and until his successor shall be chosen.

Duties of board.

SECTION 5. The board of trustees shall have general care, control and supervision of the public museum, its appurtenances, fixtures and furniture, and of the selection, arrangement and disposition of the specimens and objects appertaining to said museum, and also of the disbursements of all the moneys appropriated for and belonging to the museum fund, in the manner hereafter provided. And the said board shall adopt, and at their discretion modify, amend or repeal by-laws, rules and regulations for the management, care and use of the public museum, and fix and enforce penalties for their violation, and generally shall adopt such measures as shall promote the public utility of the museum; provided, that such by-laws, rules and regulations shall not conflict with the provisions of this act.

Secretary of board —term.

SECTION 6 The board of trustees shall at their first meeting, or thereafter as soon as practicable and every five years thereafter, at an annual meeting, elect by ballot a person of suitable scientific attainments, ability and experience for custodian, who shall so act and be ex-officio secretary of said board of trustees. The custodian first appointed shall hold his office for five years from the time of the first annual meeting, unless previously removed, and thereafter the term of appointment shall be for the term of five years, and the compensation of the custodian shall be fixed by said board of trustees. Said board of trustees shall also appoint such assistants and employes for said museum as they may deem necessary and expedient, and shall fix their compensation. All vacancies in the office of the custodian, assistants and other employes shall be filled by said board of trustees, and the persons so elected or appointed shall hold for the unexpired term.

See Chapter 433, Laws of 1887, *infra.*

May be removed.

SECTION 7. The custodian elected under this act may be removed from office for misdemeanor, incompetency or inattention to the duties of his office, by a vote of two-thirds of the board of trustees; the assistants and other employes may be removed by the board for incompetency or for any other cause.

Further duties of board of trustees.

SECTION 8. It shall be the duty of the board of trustees, within ten days after the appointment of the custodian and other salaried employes, to report and file with the city comptroller a duly certified list of the persons so appointed, with the salary allowed to each, and the time or times fixed for the payment thereof, and they shall also furnish such comptroller with a list of all accounts and bills which may be allowed by said board of trustees, stating the character of the materials or services for which the same are rendered immediately after the meeting of said board at which such allowance shall be made. And said board of trustees shall also, on or before the first day of October in each year, make to the common council a report, made up to and including the 31st day of August of the said year, containing a statement of the condition of the museum, and of the additions thereto during the year, together with such information and suggestions as they may deem important, and such report shall also contain an account of the moneys credited to the museum fund, and expended on account of the same during the year.

SECTION 9. From and after the organization of the board of trustees under this act, the common council of said city shall levy and collect annually upon all the taxable property of the said city, at the same time and in the same manner as other city taxes are levied and collected by law, a special tax not exceeding one-tenth of a mill upon each dollar of the assessed value of said taxable property, the amount of which shall be determined by said board of trustees, and certified to the common council at the time of making their annual report to said council, and the entire amount of said special tax shall be paid into, and held in, the city treasury, as a separate and distinct fund, to be known as the museum fund, and shall not be used or appropriated directly or indirectly in any other purpose than for the maintenance and for the increase of the public museum, the payment of the salaries of the custodian, assistants and other employes of the museum, the purchase of furniture, fixtures, supplies and fuel, and the incidental expenses of the museum. *Tax to be levied.*

SECTION 10. The board of trustees shall erect, purchase, hire or lease buildings, lots, rooms and furniture, for the use and accommodation of said public museum, and shall improve, enlarge and repair such buildings, rooms and furniture; but no lot or building shall be purchased, erected or enlarged for the purpose herein mentioned, without an ordinance or resolution of the common council of said city, and deeds of conveyance and leases shall run to the city of Milwaukee. *Grounds for museum.*

SECTION 11. All moneys received by or raised in the city of Milwaukee for museum purposes shall be paid over to the city treasurer to be disbursed by him on the orders of the president and secretary of the said board of trustees, countersigned by the city comptroller. Such orders shall be made payable to the order of the persons in whose favor they shall have been issued, and shall be the only voucher of the city treasurer for the payments from the museum fund. The said board of trustees shall provide for the purchase of specimens, supplies, fuel and other matters necessary or useful for the maintenance of the museum; provided, however, that it shall not be lawful for said board of trustees to expend or contract a liability for any sum in excess of the amount levied in any one year, for the museum fund, on account of such fund. *Moneys to be paid over to city treasurer.*

SECTION 12. All moneys, books, specimens and other property received by the city of Milwaukee by devise, bequest or gift, from any person or corporation, for public museum purposes, shall, unless otherwise directed by the donors, be under the management *Gifts to be under control of board.*

and control of said board of trustees; and all moneys derived from fines and penalties for violation of the rules of the museum, or from any other source in the course of the administration of the museum, including all moneys which may be paid to the city upon any policy or policies of insurance, or other obligation or liability, for or on account of loss or damage to any property pertaining to the museum, shall belong to the museum fund in the city treasury, to be disbursed on the orders of the said board of trustees, conntersigned by the city comptroller, for museum purposes in addition to the amount levied and raised by taxation for such fund.

Section 13. This act shall take effect and be in force from and after its passage and publication.

CHAPTER 41, LAWS OF 1895.

AN ACT relating to the building of public libraries and museums.

Building to be erected under direction of trustees.

Section 1. In all cities in this state, wherein their exists boards known as "a board of public works," "a board of trustees of the public library," and "a board of trustees of the public museum," and wherein authority shall have heretofore been granted to erect and construct a building or buildings for a public library and public museum, the work of such erection and construction shall be done by the board of public works, under the direction and supervision of the board of trustees of the public library and the board of trustees of the public museum, acting together as a joint board. The board of public works being hereby authorized to enter into a contract or contracts for doing all work of erecting and constructing such building; but no contract shall be let authorizing the expenditure of a greater sum of money than heretofore appropriated or authorized by law, or shall be hereafter appropriated or authorized by the common council of such city.

CHAPTER 521, LAWS OF 1887.

AN ACT to amend Chapter 328, of the Laws of 1882, authorizing the city of Milwaukee to establish and maintain a public museum, and Chapter 7, of the Laws of 1878, to establish a public library in the city of Milwaukee.

Appointments of trustees of public library, Milwaukee.

Section 1. Hereafter all appointments of members from the common council of the board of trustees of the public library of the city of Milwaukee, made by the mayor on the third Tuesday in April, shall be made from aldermen having two years to serve, and in case any person so appointed shall vacate his office of alderman before the expiration of his term, he shall thereupon cease to be a member of said board of trustees, and the mayor shall appoint some other aldermau of his class in his place, to be such trustee for the remainder of his term. Each alderman appointed shall serve as such trustee during his term as alderman.

Mayor to appoint.

It shall be the duty of the mayor, on the third Tuesday in April in each year, to appoint a sufficient number of aldermen having two years to serve as aldermen, to be members of such board of trustees, to keep the number of members of such board from the common council always three. All provisions of chapter 7, of the laws of 1878, which in any way conflict with the foregoing provisions of this section are hereby amended accordingly.

SECTION 2. Hereafter all appointments of members from the common council of the board of trustees of the public museum of the city of Milwaukee, made by the mayor of said city on the third Tuesday in April, shall be made from aldermen having two years to serve, and in case any person so appointed shall vacate his office of alderman before the expiration of his term, he shall thereupon cease to be a member of said board of trustees, and the mayor shall appoint some other alderman of his class in his place to be such trustee for the remainder of his term. Each alderman appointed shall serve as such trustee during his term as alderman. It shall be the duty of the mayor on the third Tuesday in April in each year to appoint a sufficient number of aldermen having two years to serve to be members of such board of trustees of the public museum to keep the number of members of such board from the common council, always three. All provisions of chapter 328, of the laws of 1882, which in any way conflict with the provisions of this section, are hereby amended accordingly.

Trustees of public museum, when appointed.

CHAPTER 433, LAWS OF 1887.

AN ACT to amend chapter 328, of the laws of 1882, entitled, an act to authorize the city of Milwaukee to establish and maintain a public museum in said city.

SECTION 1. The board of trustees of the Milwaukee public museum are hereby authorized to appoint an acting custodian whenever the proper service of the museum shall require it, and for such time and on such terms as they may deem proper. Such acting custodian shall be ex-officio the acting secretary of said board of trustees, and his acts as such shall receive full credit. Said board of trustees are also authorized to appoint from time to time honorary curators, who shall perform such duties and have such special privileges as may be provided in the by-laws of the museum, but shall receive no pecuniary compensation. Such appointments shall be made of persons who have manifested a special interest in the museum or some particular department thereof.

Trustees of Milwaukee public museum authorized to appoint a custodian and curators.

SECTION 2. This act shall be in force from and after its passage and publication.

CHAPTER 329, LAWS OF 1882.

AN ACT relating to the Natural History Society of the city of Milwaukee.

SECTION 1. The board of directors of the Natural History Society of the city of Milwaukee is hereby authorized and empowered, in the name of said association or society, to assign, transfer and convey to the city of Milwaukee, all and singular,

Relating to Natural History Society.

the natural historical collections of every kind constituting the museum belonging to said Natural History Society, in trust to be kept, supported and maintained by said city, as a free museum for the benefit and use of all citizens of said city; provided, the said city shall accept the trust and assume the care and maintenance of such museum.

CHAPTER 237, LAWS OF 1885.

AN ACT to amend chapter 319, of the laws of 1881, entitled "an act to provide for the recording of lands taken for streets and other purposes by city or village corporations."

Records of streets, etc.

SECTION 1. In every application made to any court of record, county board of supervisors, common council of any city, or the authorities of any village, for the laying out, widening of any street, alleys, water channels, parks or other public places, or for the vacation of any streets, alleys, water channels, parks or other public places, the applicant or applicants shall at the time of the filing of such application with the proper officer, or prior thereto, file in the office of the register of deeds of each county where the lands or any part thereof, are situated, a notice of the pendency of such application, containing the name of the applicant or applicants, the object of such application, and map and description of the lands to be taken or vacated. In case of a failure to comply with the foregoing provisions, all proceedings based upon such application shall be void. A certified copy of every final order, judgment or decree of a court of record, every final resolution or order of a county board of supervisors, common council of any city, or the authorities of any village giving a full and accurate description of all the lands so taken or vacated, accompanied with a map showing the location of such lands based upon such application, shall be recorded in the office of the register of deeds of the county in which such lands are situated, and such final order, judgment, decree or resolution, shall have no force or effect, nor shall it be notice to any subsequent purchaser or incumbrancer until it is so recorded.

SECTION 2. Where no application is made as mentioned in the preceding section, and a resolution or order shall be adopted without application, by a county board of supervisors, common council of any city, or the authorities of any village, whereby any lands shall be taken or vacated for the purposes specified in section 1, of this act, a certified copy of such resolution or order shall be recorded in the office of the register of deeds of the county in which such lands are situated, and such resolution or order shall have no force or effect, nor shall it be notice to any subsequent purchaser or incumbrancer until it is so recorded.

SECTION ?. Section 2, of said chapter 319, is hereby repealed.

CHAPTER 206, LAWS OF 1887.

AN ACT to legalize certain proceedings of the officers and common council of the city of Milwaukee.

Legalizing certain proceeding of the common council of Milwaukee.

SECTION 1. All the proceedings instituted in the common council of the city of Milwaukee since the eleventh day of April, 1885, for the opening or vacation of public streets, alleys, squares

aud other public places, so far as such proceedings are affected by
a failure to comply with the provisions of chapter 237, of the laws
of 1885, are hereby declared to have full force and effect in law
the same as if such act had never been passed; and all of said
proceedings so far as they are affected by a failure to comply with
the provisions of said chapter 237, are hereby legalized; and no
court of record within this state shall hereafter declare any of said
proceedings void in consequence of a non-compliance with any of
the conditions and provisions of said chapter 237.

CHAPTER 462.

AN ACT to provide for the laying out and establishing a state
road from the city of Milwaukee to Port Washington, in the
counties of Milwaukee and Ozaukee.

SECTION 1. John W. Bussey, H. G. H. Reed and Dr. F. W. Williams, of the county of Milwaukee, are hereby appointed commissioners to lay out and establish a state road from the city of Milwaukee, in the county of Milwaukee, to the village of Port Washington, in the county of Ozaukee, to-wit: A road not less than four rods nor more than one hundred feet wide, beginning on the north line of the city of Milwaukee at the northern terminus of Humboldt avenue, on the north and south half section or quarter line of sections nine and sixteen, in town seven, range twenty-two, and running thence north on said quarter line through sections four and nine in town seven, and through sections thirty-three in town eight, range twenty-two, on the north and south quarter line through said section thirty-three to a point eighty rods north of the east and west quarter line through said section thirty-three (passing Milwaukee river at or above the locality of the late Humboldt bridge), and thence to the village of Port Washington. In so laying out and establishing said road, said commissioners may connect with and adopt as part of said road, any such part of any existing public road or highway as they may deem desirable; provided, that no expense shall be incurred by reason of this act by the county of Ozaukee, until a majority of the county board have consented to the same at some regular or special meeting of said board. *(Appointing commissioners to lay out and establish state road.)*

SECTION 2. Otherwise than provided in this act said road shall be laid out, established, opened and maintained as provided by the general laws of this state in case of state roads; provided that said commissioners shall receive no compensation for services rendered in pursuance of this act. *(Commissioners to receive no compensation.)*

SECTION 3. If it shall be necessary, or in the opinion of a majority of said commissioners, advisable to build as part of said state road, any bridge or bridges over any stream which the route of said road shall cross, whether upon a former highway or otherwise, said commissioners shall cause to be made full working plans of any such bridge, including the necessary abutments or other supports, and shall place the same open to inspection at a time and place mentioned in the notice hereinafter provided to be given. *(Commissioners may build bridges over streams.)*

Commissioners shall publish notice calling for sealed proposals.

SECTION 4. Said commissioners shall publish for two weeks, once in each week, a notice in one newspaper or more of general circulation and printed in the county where said bridge is to be built, calling for sealed proposals to be made to them for furnishing the materials and doing the work of building such bridge according to such plans, which notice shall also state the place where, and the time when such plans will be so open for inspection, which time shall not be less than four hours in each day of five consecutive days, and shall also state the time and place when and where such proposals will be received and the time and place when and where said proposals will be opened and considered and a contract for the building of such bridge will be let.

Contract to be awarded to lowest bidder.

SECTION 5. At the time named in said notice for the opening of such proposals, said commissioners or a majority of them, shall proceed to examine and consider the same, and to award a contract to the lowest bidder for furnishing the materials for and building such bridge, or may reject all proposals made and proceed to call for new proposals in the same manner as hereinbefore provided for a call for first proposals, if they deem it advisable.

Cost of bridge shall not exceed $10,000.

SECTION 6. When such proposals shall be accepted by said commissioners or a majority of them, they shall proceed to make a contract with such lowest bidder for furnishing such materials and completing the building of such bridge; provided, the cost of building said bridge shall not exceed ten thousand dollars.

Bond required from each bidder.

SECTION 7. Said commissioners shall require a bond with two sufficient sureties from each bidder to accompany his proposal, conditioned in a penal sum of not less than double the sum it is proposed to furnish said materials and build said bridge for. If on opening said proposal, the sureties shall not be satisfactory, the commissioners may reject the proposal or require satisfactory sureties before considering such proposal.

Monthly estimates may be made by commissioners.

SECTION 8. As the work of such bridge progresses, monthly estimates of the amount and value of materials furnished and work done may be made by said commissioners, or a majority of them, and after deducting and reserving fifteen per cent. thereof until the completion of the contract, they may deliver a certificate of the amount due thereon after such deduction to such contractor; and they shall at the same time execute and deliver a duplicate of such certificate to the county clerk to be filed in his office, and when such bridge is completed satisfactorily to said commissioners under said contract, they shall issue and deliver to such contractor a certificate of the entire amount remaining due him in full of his contract, and they shall at the same time file a duplicate of said final certificate with the county clerk.

Contractor entitled to amount due him.

SECTION 9. Upon receiving such certificates, or any of them, such contractor shall be entitled to and shall be paid the amount thereby certified to be due him, out of the treasury of the county in which such bridge shall be, from any funds not otherwise appropriated; and it is hereby declared to be the duty of the county board of such county to cause such payment to be made forthwith, and if there shall be no funds available for such purpose, then it is hereby made the duty of the county board of such county to levy a tax upon all the taxable property of said county, sufficient to raise the amount due on said certificates, and cause the same to be collected with the tax of that year.

SECTION 10. Said commissioners shall not be individually responsible on account of anything by them done, or any contract entered into by them as such commissioners in attempting to carry out the provisions of this act.

Commissioners not individually responsible.

SECTION 11. Said commissioners are hereby given the term of five years from the date of the passage of this act, for the laying out and establishing this road and building such bridges.

Term of commissioners five years.

SECTION 12. This act shall take effect and be in force from and after its passage and publication.

CHAPTER 476. LAWS OF 1887.

AN ACT to provide for the laying of a highway and the building of a viaduct across the Menomonee river.

SECTION 1. The common council of the city of Milwaukee is hereby authorized to cause to be built with all reasonable dispatch a suitable viaduct from a convenient point at or near the intersection of Eleventh avenue with Pierce street, and extending as nearly as practicable on a level across the Menomonee valley in a northerly direction towards the intersection of Sixteenth and Fowler streets, in the Fourth ward of the city of Milwaukee, or such other northern terminal point as may be found available for this purpose.

City of Milwaukee authorized to build viaduct.

SECTION 2. Said viaduct shall be constructed in a substantial manner of iron (except the floor and floor beams). It shall rest upon iron columns of suitable size and dimensions set upon stone foundations, and shall be of a uniform width of no less than sixty feet, and at least nineteen feet above and clear of railway tracks. Wherever necessary, draw-bridges shall be provided, as well as suitable approaches, at both termini of said viaduct and such intermediate points as may be necessary for safe and convenient access thereto. All abutments that may be needed shall be constructed of masonry in solid manner.

How constructed.

SECTION 3. All provisions of the charter of the city of Milwaukee, and the several acts amendatory thereof, in relation to public work or improvements in said city, and the condemnation of lands for highways and public purposes, and the assessment of damages and benefits arising therefrom, which are not inconsistent with the provisions of this act, shall apply to the work hereby authorized, and all official acts incidental thereto.

Provisions of charter, to apply.

SECTION 4. The said common council, within two months from the passage and publication of this act, shall cause to be made a plan and detailed specifications for doing said work, and an estimate of the cost of such improvement, and as soon thereafter as practicable, the city shall enter upon the construction of

C., M. & St. P. R'y Co. to build portion of viaduct.

the north half of the said viaduct, bridges and approaches in conformity thereto. The common council shall also furnish a duplicate of said plan and specifications to the Chicago, Milwaukee and St. Paul Railway Company, whose duty it shall be and who are hereby directed and required simultaneously with the building of the north half on part of the city of Milwaukee, to build the south half of said viaduct and the approaches thereto in accordance with such plan and specifications, so that the whole of said work and all necessary abutments, bridges and approaches, be completed with reasonable dispatch.

Duty of railway company either to accept or reject provisions of this act. SECTION 5. It shall be the duty of the Chicago, Milwaukee & St. Paul Railway company, within sixty days from and after the passage and publication of this act, to file with the city clerk of the city of Milwaukee its written declaration whether it will or will not accept of the provisions of this act, and comply with the terms thereof; and if unwilling to participate in said public improvement upon the terms herein prescribed, it shall communicate the particular reasons and points of objection; and thereupon the common council of said city may, in its discretion, appoint a committee of conference, and may consent to a change and modification of the particular terms and details of construction or division of said work, as may seem to be just and equitable; and may also by resolution or ordinance extend the time, in any particular that may be found to be essential, for entering upon such improvement, or completing the same, as the circumstances of the case may require, anything to the contrary herein contained notwithstanding.

Viaduct to remain under absolute control of city. SECTION 6. The said viaduct and approaches thereto shall forever remain under the absolute control and management of the city of Milwaukee, and no exclusive rights or franchises, for purposes of horse-railway communication, the lighting of streets, highways or the like, or any other exclusive franchises, privileges or immunities shall ever be granted over the same on part of said city to any person or corporation whatsoever.

SECTION 7. The mayor and common council of the city of Milwaukee are hereby authorized to issue the corporate bonds of said city to an amount not exceeding two hundred and fifty thousand dollars, to be applied to the building of the north half of said public improvement, in such denominations, and payable at such time or times, with interest, as the common council by ordinance may see fit and determine. Said council may also levy such tax or taxes as may be found necessary to cover the balance of the expenses or cost of such construction, if any such there should be. The provisions of chapter 465, general laws of 1885, as to form of bonds, the issue and sale thereof, the levy of taxes, creating a sinking fund, and other details not inconsistent herewith, are made applicable to the bonds intended to be issued for viaduct purposes under this act.

SECTION 8. Said viaduct and appurtenances shall be thereafter maintained by the city of Milwaukee and the Chicago, Milwaukee and St. Paul Railway Company, in the same proportions hereinbefore fixed for the original construction thereof, but no further or additional claims shall be hereafter made upon said railway company in that behalf, although its tracks may be multiplied and extended, or additional territory in the future secured by them or occupied for railway purposes; it being the intention of the legislature to liquidate hereby finally the rate and proportion in which the city and railway company shall participate in the expense of this common improvement, due regard being had not only to the present condition of things but to the future.

CHAPTER 91, LAWS OF 1885.

AN ACT to authorize the Milwaukee and Rock River Canal Company to grant and convey its property and franchises to the city of Milwaukee.

SECTION 1. The Milwaukee and Rock River Canal Company, incorporated by and under an act of the legislature of the territory of Wisconsin, approved January 5th, 1838, is hereby authorized and empowered to grant, convey and make over to the city of Milwaukee, upon such terms as shall be agreed upon between said company and said city, the lands, waters, locks, dams, dykes, canal and other works, devices and property, in the county of Milwaukee, belonging to or in the possession of said company, or any part or portion of the same, and also all rights, privileges and easements which the said company has in any manner acquired in, over and upon the Milwaukee river, the waters, bed and shores thereof, and lands under and adjacent to said river, and the canal of said company, connected therewith, and the said city of Milwaukee is hereby authorized to receive such grant and conveyance from said company, and to take possession of, and hold, maintain, use and enjoy the said property, works, rights, privileges and easements as fully, and to and for, the same purposes and extent as the said canal company has heretofore held, maintained, used and enjoyed the same, and to and for such other uses and purposes as the general interest and welfare of said city and its inhabitants shall, in the judgment of its common council, require.

Respecting franchises to be conveyed to city of Milwaukee.

CHAPTER 419.

AN ACT to amend section 2467, of the revised statutes, as amended by chapter 31, of the laws of 1879 relating to change of place of trial in certain cases.

SECTION 1. Section 2467, of the revised statutes of 1878, as amended by chapter 31, of the laws of Wisconsin of 1879, is hereby amended by adding at the end thereof the following: Provided, however, that whenever the city or county of Milwaukee shall be a party in any action or proceeding, pending in either the circuit or county court of Milwaukee county, and an application shall be made in the manner provided by law for a change of the place of trial of such action, on account of the prejudice or disqualification of both of the judges of said courts, or whenever such action or proceeding shall have been removed from either of said courts to the other upon the motion of the judge thereof, for any reason provided by law authorizing him so to do, and an appli-

Amending section 2467, R. S., change of place of trial—Milwaukee county.

May request judge of adjoining circuit to hold court

cation shall have been made thereafter to remove such action or proceeding from the court to which such judge has removed the same, then and in each such case such court shall, in lieu of awarding a change of venue therein to another circuit or county court, make an order requesting a circuit judge of an adjoining circuit to hold the court wherein such action is pending for the the trial of such action, and cause a certified copy of such order to be forthwith delivered or forwarded by mail or telegraph, prepaid, to such judge, whose duty it shall be, immediately upon the receipt thereof, to appoint, in writing, a reasonable time thereafter, and give notice thereof in one of the modes aforesaid to the judge of the court making such order, when he will hold such court for the trial of such action or proceeding and to hold and attend the same at the time aforesaid by him appointed for the purpose.

Expense to be paid by county.

The expenses of the judge requested to hold and holding the court as aforesaid shall be paid by the county in which the action shall, on the occasion of holding such court be pending.

SECTION 2. All acts and parts of acts in conflict with this act are hereby repealed.

CHAPTER 447, LAWS OF 1887, AS AMENDED BY CHAPTER 25, LAWS OF 1889.

AN ACT to authorized the city of Milwaukee to issue bonds, known as "Milwaukee river dam bonds."

City of Milwaukee authorized to issue bonds for construction of dam across Milwaukee river.

SECTION 1. The common council of the city of Milwaukee is hereby authorized to provide by ordinance for the issue of corporate bonds of said city, and to issue such corporate bonds to the amount of not to exceed fifty thousand dollars payable in not more than twenty years, bearing interest not exceeding five per cent. per annum, which bonds shall be called "Milwaukee river dam bonds," and shall be used exclusively to provide means for the construction and erection of a dam across the Milwaukee river in said city at a point between Racine street and the northern city limits of said city of Milwaukee. Provided, said dam when so constructed as provided by this act, shall not be raised above the original height of the present dam.

As amended by Chapter 25, Laws of 1889.

How signed, etc.

SECTION 2. The bonds hereby authorized to be issued, shall be signed by the mayor and clerk of said city, and sealed with the corporate seal, countersigned by the comptroller and attested by the commissioners of the public debt, and shall in terms be made payable in lawful money of the United States, in the city of Milwaukee or in the city of New York, and such bonds shall each be for the principal sum of one thousand dollars, or five hundred dollars, or one hundred dollars, or registered bonds to the amount of ten thousand dollars each, and shall have coupons or interest warrants attached thereto for the semi-annual payment of the interest thereon which bonds and coupons shall be numbered in the manner designated by the comptroller of said city.

SECTION 3. All bonds to be issued under the provisions of this act shall be delivered to the commissioners of the public debt, appointed under chapter 87, of the general laws of 1861, and the office of commissioners of public debt shall continue, and such commissioners shall be appointed from time to time, in pursuance of the provisions of this act, while any of the bonds issued under this act or under that act, shall remain outstanding, and all of the provisions of sections 2, 6, 7, 8, 9, 10, 11 and 17, of that act, so far as the same may be applicable and not inconsistent with this act, shall apply to all bonds to be issued under this act and are hereby incorporated into this act as a part thereof, it being the true intent and meaning of this act to provide for the bonds hereby authorized in the same manner as the bonds authorized by that act are provided for in the sections thereof last mentioned.

SECTION 4. The bonds provided for in this act shall be executed and issued from time to time, at such times and in such amounts as may be determined by the common council of the city of Milwaukee, and shall be sold and disposed of by the commissioners of the public debt, and the proceeds thereof paid from time to time, into the treasury of said city; and said proceeds shall constitute a separate and distinct fund in the treasury and be paid out and applied exclusively for the purposes stated in the first section of this act.

SECTION 5. A tax upon all the taxable property, real and personal, in said city, shall be annually levied by the common council, sufficient to pay the annual interest on all bonds issued under the provisions of this act and outstanding, and for twenty years before the principal of the bonds hereby authorized shall become due, a tax equal to five per cent. of the principal of the bonds actually issued, shall be annually levied by the common council for a sinking fund to pay the principal of such bonds.

SECTION 6. As soon as a sinking fund shall be actually collected for the said bonds, the commissioners of the public debt shall proceed, annually, in the cancellation of the bonds in the manner provided for in sections 10, and 11, of chapter 87, of the general laws of 1861, in regard to bonds issued under that act.

SECTION 7. The commissioners of the public debt shall from time to time, or when requested by the common council, report to the common council of said city, the sale or other disposition of all bonds authorized under this act.

SECTION 8. All bonds paid or otherwise retired shall be marked "cancelled" by the commissioners of the public debt, and by them returned to the common council of the said city, who shall forthwith publicly cancel the same.

SECTION 9. The commissioners of the public debt are hereby prohibited from selling or otherwise disposing of any of the bonds authorized by this act to be issued at a less rate than par, that is to say, for less than the principal of such bonds with accrued interest.

CHAPTER 450, LAWS OF 1887.

AN ACT to declare parts of certain avenues in the city of Milwaukee, boulevards, or pleasure ways, and to regulate the use of the same.

Declaring certain avenues boulevards.

SECTION 1. Prospect avenue from Juneau avenue, north to Irving Place, in the First ward, and Grand avenue from Eighth street west to the city limits or Western avenue, in the Fourth and Sixteenth wards of the city of Milwaukee, are hereby constituted and declared to be boulevards or pleasure ways.

What may pass or enter upon boulevards.

SECTION 2. No cart, dray, wagon, truck, sleigh or other vehicle, carrying goods, merchandise, timber, stone, building material, wood, manure, dirt or other articles, or solely employed and used for carrying goods, merchandise, timber, stone, building material, wood, manure, dirt or other articles, either loaded or unloaded, shall pass or enter upon any part of said avenues, designated in section 1, as boulevards or pleasure ways. Provided, however, that in so far as the foregoing of this section applies to and concerns said Grand avenue in said Fourth and Sixteenth wards the same shall go into effect and be in force when Clybourn street from Twentieth street to Western avenue in said wards, and State street from the west end and termination of the pavement thereon to said Western avenue in the Second ward of said city of Milwaukee, shall have been graded to the established permanent grade; the gutters paved, the roadway graveled or paved and put in condition for travel and use, and when said streets shall have been accepted by the board of public works and declared open for travel with said improvements thereon and notice thereof given by publication in at least three newspapers in said city to be designated by said board of public works; and provided, further, that nothing in this act shall be construed to prohibit the ordinary use of any and all parts of said boulevards or pleasure ways for the purpose of obtaining orders for and of carrying supplies or any other necessary thing to or from any place or residence fronting on either of said avenues.

Cattle, swine, sheep, etc., not allowed upon.

SECTION 3. No cattle, swine, sheep, goats, geese, or fowls shall be allowed to run at large, or be led or driven upon any part of said avenues, designated in section 1, as boulevards or pleasure ways.

Obstructions not to be placed or used upon, without permission.

SECTION 4. No person shall move any building along, across or upon any part of said avenues, designated in section 1, as boulevards or pleasure ways, nor use or occupy any portion thereof for the purpose of erecting or repairing any building, nor encumber or obstruct, or cause to be encumbered or obstructed any part thereof, by placing therein or thereon any building material or any article, or any thing whatsoever, nor dig down to expose, tear up, disconnect or connect with any of the sewers, water pipes or gas pipes in or under any portion thereof without having first obtained in each case the written permission of the board of public works of said city. The common council of said city shall have authority by ordinances or resolutions to regulate the conditions or terms, and prescribe the time under and for which such permits shall be granted and also to regulate the amount of fee to be paid upon application for a permit under this section.

Section 5. Any person or persons who shall violate any of the **Penalty.** provisions of this act shall be subject to prosecution and trial before any court having jurisdiction thereof, and upon conviction shall be fined not less than ten dollars nor more than one hundred dollars for each offense.

CHAPTER 426, LAWS OF 1891.

AN ACT to amend section 1, Chapter 450, laws of 1887, entitled an Act to declare parts of certain avenues in the city of Milwaukee, boulevards or pleasure ways, and to regulate the use of the same.

Section 1. Chapter 184, of the laws of 1874, entitled, "An act **Certain avenues** to revise, consolidate and amend the charter of the city of Milwau- **declared boule-** kee, approved February 20th, 1852, and the several acts amendatory **vards.** thereof," is hereby amended, together with the several acts amendatory thereof, by adding thereto a new section, which shall read as follows: Prospect avenue from Juneau avenue, north to La Fayette place, in the First ward, and Grand avenue from Eighth street, west to the city limits or Western avenue, in the Fourth and Sixteenth wards of the city of Milwaukee, are hereby constituted and declared to be boulevards or pleasure ways.

CHAPTER 113, LAWS OF 1893.

AN ACT to declare a part of a certain avenue in the city of Milwaukee, a boulevard or pleasure way, and to regulate the use of the same.

Section 1. Grand avenue, from Eleventh street west to the **Grand avenue de-** city limits or Western avenue, in the Fourth and Sixteenth wards, **clared a boule-** of the city of Milwaukee, is hereby constituted and declared to be **vard.** a boulevard or pleasure way.

Section 2. No cart, dray, wagon, truck, sleigh or other vehicle **What may not enter** carrying goods, merchandise, timber, stone, building material, **or pass upon.** wood, manure, dirt or other articles, or solely employed and used for carrying goods, merchandise, timber, stone, building material, wood, manure, dirt or other articles, either loaded or unloaded, shall pass or enter upon any part of said avenue, designated in Section 1, as a boulevard or pleasure way. Provided, that nothing in this act shall be construed to prohibit the ordinary use of any and all parts of said boulevard or pleasure way for the purpose of obtaining orders for, and of carrying supplies or any other necessary thing to or from any place or residence fronting on said avenue.

Section 3. No cattle, swine, sheep, goats, geese, or fowls, **Cattle, swine,** shall be allowed to run at large or be led or driven upon any part **sheep, etc., not** of said avenue, designated in section one, as a boulevard or **allowed upon.** pleasure way.

Obstructions not to be placed upon without permission.

SECTION 4. No person shall move any building along, across or upon any part of said avenue, designated in section 1, as a boulevard or pleasure way, nor use or occupy any portion thereof for the purpose of erecting or repairing any building, nor encumber or obstruct, or cause to be encumbered or obstructed, any part thereof, by placing therein or thereon any building material or any article, or anything whatsoever, nor dig down to expose, tear up, disconnect or connect with any of the sewers, water pipes or gas pipes in or under any portion thereof, without having first obtained in each case the written permission of the board of public works of said city. The common council of said city shall have authority by ordinance or resolutions to regulate the conditions or terms, and prescribe the time under and for which such permits shall be granted, and also to regulate the amount of the fee to be paid upon application for a permit under this section.

Penalty.

SECTION 5. Any person or persons, who shall violate any of the provisions of this act, shall be subject to prosecution and trial before any court having jurisdiction thereof, and upon conviction shall be fined not less than ten dollars, nor more than one hundred dollars for each offense.

CHAPTER 167, LAWS OF 1895.

AN ACT authorizing cities of the first and second class to set aside certain streets therein as boulevards or pleasure ways and to regulate the use of the same.

Cities may designate boulevards.

SECTION 1. Any city within this state of the first or second class as defined by chapter 40a of Sanborn & Berryman's annotated statutes of this state and the acts amendatory thereof, whether operating under said chapter or under special charter is hereby authorized to set aside certain streets therein in the manner hereinafter designated to be known as boulevards or pleasure ways and may regulate the use of the same.

Common council may declare what streets shall be boulevards.

SECTION 2. Any of the cities defined in section one, of this act, having a board of park commissioner or commissioners of public parks may, by a majority vote of the common council of such city, upon recommendation of said park commissioners or commissioners of public parks designate any street within such city and declare the same to be a boulevard or pleasure way and may provide for the use thereof and designate what character of vehicles may travel thereon; provided, that no such city shall be authorized to prohibit the ordinary use of any or all parts of such boulevard or pleasure way for the purpose of obtaining orders for, and the carrying of supplies or any other necessary things to or from any place or residence fronting on said boulevard.

Certain cities may declare boulevards, how.

SECTION 3. Any of the cities designated in section 1, of this act, which have no board of park commissioners or commissioners of public parks may, upon recommendation of the mayor and a majority of such common council, adopt and prescribe rules and designate and declare certain streets to be boulevards or pleasure ways and regulate the use of the same in the same manner and with the same effect as if such cities had a board of park commissioners or commissioners of public parks.

SECTION 4. Any such city by its common council may prescribe penalties for the violation of any rule or regulation it may prescribe for the use of any such boulevard or pleasure way.

Council may prescribe penalty.

CHAPTER 197, LAWS OF 1893.

AN ACT to grant to the city of Milwaukee a certain portion of submerged land, lying along and adjacent to the shore of Lake Michigan, on the eastern frontage of the city of Milwaukee, for public park and boulevard purposes.

SECTION 1. The right, title and interest of the State of Wisconsin in and to a strip of submerged land, three hundred feet in width, along and adjacent to the shore of Lake Michigan, constituting the bed of said lake, being on the eastern frontage of the city of Milwaukee, having for its westerly boundary the easterly face of the breakwater constructed by the Chicago and Northwestern Railway Company, for its south boundary the south line of Mason street, in the Seventh ward in the city of Milwaukee, extended, and for its north boundary the extension of the east and west quarter section line, running through section twenty-one, in town seven north, range twenty-two east, in the Eighteenth ward of said city of Milwaukee, are hereby granted and ceded to the said city of Milwaukee, to be held and used by said city forever as part of its system of public parks and boulevards, and to be managed, controlled and improved by the board of park commissioners as provided in chapter 488, of the laws of 1889, and chapter 179, of the laws of 1891, of Wisconsin; provided, that said land hereby ceded and granted shall not be leased or sold by said city of Milwaukee, nor used by it for any other purpose than as a public park and boulevard; and provided further, that said city shall construct over any railroad track or tracks, intersected by any bridge or driveway to said park on above described strip of land, good and sufficient viaducts or bridges, at least twenty-two feet high in the clear above said track or tracks, and suffer or permit no grade crossings thereover; and provided further, that said strip of land hereby granted shall in part be filled in and improved so as to be made a public park or boulevard within five years from the date of the passage and publication of this act.

Certain submerged land in Lake Michigan ceded to City of Milwaukee.

For what to be used.

Viaducts to be built.

SECTION 2. Nothing in this act contained shall be construed to divest or otherwise affect the riparian rights and privileges of the several owners of the lots abutting on Lake Michigan, but all such riparian rights and privileges shall remain vested in such abutting or upland owners, subject only to the use of the land hereby granted to said city of Milwaukee, for the purpose of its system of public parks and boulevards, and any land which may be between the right of way of the Chicago and Northwestern Railway Company, as described in the several conveyances thereof to said company, and said easterly face of said railroad breakwater

Riparian rights not to be divested.

shall not be used by said railway company for any purpose whatsoever, except that of a slope or embankment to protect the road-
bed or tracks on said right of way.

CHAPTER 206, LAWS OF 1893.

AN ACT to grant to the city of Milwaukee a certain portion of
submurged land lying and adjacent to the shore of Lake Michigan, on the eastern frontage of the city of Milwaukee, northeasterly from the easterly line of section twenty-one, to the
northerly line of section fifteen, in the Eighteenth ward of the
city of Milwaukee, for public park and boulevard purposes.

Grants certain sub-merged lands in Lake Michigan to city of Milwaukee.   SECTION 1.   All the right, title and inteiest of the state of
Wisconsin in and to the following land along and adjacent to the
shore of Lake Michigan, and partly submerged, constituting the
bed of Lake Michigan, being on the southern and eastern frontage,
in the Eighteenth ward of the city of Milwaukee, described as
follows, to-wit: A strip of land three hundred feet in width,
having for its westerly boundary the extended center line of lot
fifteen, in block nine, of Glidden and Lockwood's addition, in
the Eighteenth ward of the city of Milwaukee, and lying southerly,
southeasterly and easterly of a line commencing at a point in the
said center line of said lot fifteen, four hundred feet south of
the north line of said lot, running thence northeasterly parallel to
the southerly line of La Fayette place, until the same intersects the
low water mark; thence along the present low water mark
of the shore of Lake Michigan to the north line of
section fifteen, extended to the shore of Lake Michigan in the
Eighteenth ward of the city of Milwaukee, are hereby granted in
To be used for public parks, etc.   fee to the said city of Milwaukee, to be held and used by said city
as a part of its system of public parks and boulevards; provided,
that said land hereby granted shall not be leased or sold by said
city of Milwaukee, nor used for any other purposes than as a public
park and boulevard; and provided further, that at least part of said
land hereby granted shall be filled in and improved, so as to be
made a public park or boulevard within five years from the date of
the passage and publication of this act.

Riparian rights not to be divested.   SECTION 2.   Nothing in this act contained shall be construed
to divert or otherwise affect the riparian rights and privileges of
the several owners of the lots abutting on Lake Michigan. All
such riparian rights and privileges shall remain vested in such
upland owners subject only to the use of the land hereby granted
to said city of Milwaukee for the purpose of its system of public
parks and boulevards.

CHAPTER 255, LAWS OF 1893.

AN ACT to authorize and direct the state board of health to
investigate and recommend a proper system of sewerage of the
Menomonee and Kinnickinnic valleys, in the county of Milwaukee; and to report thereon at the next session of the
legislature.

State board of health to recom-mend system of sewerage.   SECTION 1.   The state board of health is hereby authorized and
directed to investigate, consider and report at the next session of
the legislature upon a general system of sewerage for the relief

of the valleys of the Menomonee and Kinnickinnic rivers, and so
much of the territory as is tributary thereto, as in the opinion of
said board may be deemed advisable for the public health for the
city of Milwaukee, and town or towns, village or villages adjacent
thereto and within the proposed territory, or so much of said city,
town or towns, village or villages, as may in the opinion of said
board be best relieved by the use of such system; provided, the
board of supervisors of the County of Milwaukee shall
appropriate the money to pay the expense thereof, as hereinafter **Expense, how paid.**
provided.

SECTION 2. It shall be the duty of said board of health, to **Territory embraced**
designate the city, town or towns, village or villages, the whole **in system to be**
or parts thereof, which shall be tributary to and embraced in the **designated.**
territory and system so to be reported, and to describe the same in
their report with plans, specifications and maps, as they shall also
show by suitable plans, specifications and maps, such trunk line
or lines, and main branches thereto, as it shall recommend to be
constructed.

SECTION 3. The said board of health shall further consider, **Methods of using**
report and define the methods by which said city, town or towns, **system to be**
village or villages, or parts of said city, town or towns, village or **defined.**
villages, may utilize said trunk line and main branches as an
outlet of a system of sewerage for said city, town or towns,
village or villages, or such parts thereof as said board shall recommend, and show the same by such plans and maps.

SECTION 4. The said board of health shall cause such surveys **Surveys and levels**
and levels to be made as will enable said board to determine **to be made.**
approximately the location and grades of said trunk line and
main branches, and also such surveys and levels of the territory
which the said board shall determine should be tributary to such
trunk line or lines and main branches as will enable said board to
determine the method by which the said city, town and villages,
or parts thereof may respectively utilize such system, and report
thereon.

SECTION 5. Said board of health shall also recommend and **Capacity of trunk**
define the size and capacity of the trunk line or lines and main **lines, etc., to be**
branches, and the materials of which they should be constructed, **defined.**
the manner of construction, and such other particulars as will
enable the board to determine the probable expense thereof.

SECTION 6. The said board of health is hereby authorized to **Certain conditional**
enter into a conditional contract with the board of the national **contracts for use**
home for disabled volunteer soldiers, near Milwaukee, for the **of system may be**
use of such system of sewerage by said home, with the board of **made.**
supervisors of Milwaukee county for the use of said system of
sewerage by the County Hospital, by the Milwaukee County
Hospital for the chronic insane, and by the almshouse, either or
any of them, and with the board of trustees of the Milwaukee
Hospital for insane for the use of said system, and said board of supervisors of Milwaukee county, and said trustees of said Milwaukee
Hospital for insane are hereby authorized and empowered to enter'
into a like conditional contract with the said state board of

health, upon such terms as may be agreed upon, which contracts shall be subject to the ratification and approval of the legislature of the state of Wisconsin; and the said state board of health shall report to the next legislature the terms of any such contract as may be embraced in this section, together with their recommendation thereon.

Territory benefited to be described; taxes, etc.

SECTION 7. It shall be the duty of said board of health to describe the territory which in their judgment will be benefited by such system of sewerage, and which should be assessed for the purpose of raising a fund to pay for the expenses hereinafter mentioned, and for the cost of the construction of said system of sewerage, and also to recommend the manner and method of the assessment of the taxes and the collection thereof for that purpose, and in determining the method of assessment, the board may consider the special and peculiar benefits which any property may receive on account of any peculiar uses or business to which such property may be devoted, requiring the use of such sewer. And said board of health shall also recommend, if they deem advisable, the terms and conditions upon which the county of Milwaukee and the State of Wisconsin shall use such system of sewerage for the benefit of the institutions above mentioned, and what proportion, in their judgment, the county of Milwaukee and the State of Wisconsin should pay towards the construction of said sewerage system for the use thereof by the said institutions respectively.

May employ assistants.

SECTION 8. The said state board of health is authorized to employ such assistance as they shall deem advisable to enable them to perform the duties under this act.

Appropriation.

SECTION 9. The county board of supervisors of Milwaukee county is hereby authorized to levy and appropriate out of any funds not otherwise appropriated, the sum of not exceeding ten thousand dollars, for the purpose of carrying out the provisions of this act, which sum shall be deemed a part of the expense of the construction of such sewer system, and the same shall be repaid to the said county of Milwaukee, with interest thereon at the rate per cent. per annum received by said county on its deposits, out of the funds to be hereafter raised for the construction of such sewer system.

Account of expenses, etc.

SECTION 10. The said board of health shall keep an itemized account of the expenses incurred by them under this act, and shall from time to time, report the same to the said board of supervisors of Milwaukee county, and upon the approval of the same by said board of supervisors, said board of supervisors shall cause the amount thereof to be paid said state board of health, not exceeding in all, however, the sum of ten thousand dollars.

CHAPTER 238, LAWS OF 1895.

AN ACT to provide for the classification of cities incorporated under special charters granted by the legislature of this state.

Division of cities into classes.

SECTION 1. For the exercise of corporate power and other appropriate purposes, all cities incorporated under special charters, granted by the legislature of this state, shall be divided into classes as follows: Cities containing a population of one hundred and fifty thousand or over shall constitute the first class of cities incorporated under special charters; cities containing a population of forty thousand or over, and under one hundred and fifty thousand, shall constitute the second class of cities incorporated under special charters; cities containing ten thousand or over, and under forty thousand, shall constitute the third class of cities incorporated under special charters; cities containing less than ten thousand shall constitute the fourth class of cities incorporated under special charters. The population as affecting the class to which any city shall belong under this act shall be determined by the last national or state census.

POLICE COURT.

CHAPTER 6, LAWS OF 1895.

AN ACT to establish a police court in the city of Milwaukee.

SECTION 1. There is hereby constituted and established in the city of Milwaukee, a court to be known and called the Police Court of the city of Milwaukee. It shall be a court of record, and have a clerk, and a seal with suitable device, to be procured under the direction of the judge thereof, at the expense of the city of Milwaukee. **Police court established.**

SECTION 2. On the first Tuesday of April, 1895, and on the same day of the same month, each six years thereafter, the qualified electors of said city of Milwaukee shall elect, the same as they elect their city officers, a suitable person to the office of judge of said police court, to be called "police justice," who must be a resident of said city and an attorney at law, admitted to practice in the circuit court of Milwaukee county. Such police justice shall hold his office for the term of six years, from the first Monday of May next succeeding his election, and until his successor shall have been elected and qualified, and who may be removed from office for cause in the manner provided by law for the removal of justices of the peace. The resignation of the police justice shall be made to the governor of the state. Whenever a vacancy shall occur in the office of such justice from any cause whatever, the governor shall appoint a police justice, and the person so appointed shall hold for the residue of the term. **Term of office; when judge to be elected.** **Vacancy, how filled.**

SECTION 3. Before entering upon the duties of his office, the police justice shall take and subscribe the oath of office prescribed in the constitution, which oath shall be filed in the office of the city clerk of the city of Milwaukee. **Shall take and subscribe the oath of office.**

SECTION 4. Said police court shall have exclusive jurisdiction to try and sentence all offenders against the ordinances of said city of Milwaukee, and it shall also have exclusive jurisdiction to try all misdemeanors arising in said city of Milwaukee and triable before a justice of the peace, and to issue warrants for the apprehension of persons charged with the commission of offenses in said city of Milwaukee and not triable before a justice of the **Jurisdiction.**

peace, and to examine such alleged offenders, and commit or hold them to bail, the same as a justice of the peace might otherwise do.

Jurisdiction defined.

SECTION 5. No justice of the peace or court commissioner in said city of Milwaukee shall exercise any jurisdiction in any criminal cases, but all such jurisdiction is vested in said police court, and all examinations, recognizances, and commitments for trial from said police court, and from the other justices of the peace of the county of Milwaukee, in criminal cases not triable before justices of the peace, shall be certified, returned, and made to the municipal court of the city and county of Milwaukee instead of the circuit court, at or before the time fixed for the appearance of the accused. All such cases shall thereafter be prosecuted and tried in said municipal court as provided by law in similar cases in the circuit court, and all the general provisions of law relating to criminal actions, proceedings and examinations before justices of the peace, shall apply to said police court so far as applicable.

Court to be held in Milwaukee.

Time.

SECTION 6. Said police court shall be held at the said city of Milwaukee, in some suitable place, to be provided and suitably furnished by said city, and it shall open for business every morning (Sundays and legal holidays excepted). In case of the absence, sickness, or temporary disability of said police justice he may, by an order in writing, to be filed in said court, appoint a justice of the peace of said city to discharge the duties of said police justice during such absence, sickness or disability, who shall have all the powers of said police justice while administering such office, and such justice of the peace shall receive for his services five dollars per day, to be paid by said city. Said police justice shall not voluntarily absent himself from the duties of his office more than thirty days in any one year, except from sickness.

Clerk of municipal court shall be ex-officio clerk of police court.

Duties of clerk defined.

SECTION 7. The clerk of the municipal court of the city and county of Milwaukee shall be ex-officio clerk of said police court. He, or one of his deputies, shall be present during the sessions of said police court, and shall keep and have the care and custody of all records, books, and papers of the court, perform all ministerial acts required of him by and under the direction of the police justice, and when the court is not in session shall have power to take bail for the appearance of any person under arrest before the court, subject to the revision of the court; he, or one of his deputies, may administer all necessary oaths, enter the judgments of the court, issue commitments and executions to enforce the same, and make up and keep the records of the court in all cases therein under the direction of the judge; he, or one of his deputies, shall issue all process under his hand and the seal of the court, and attest it in the name of the judge, signing it by his title of office, and shall tax costs; he, or one of his deputies, may issue warrants upon complaint filed in writing, and upon oath in all cases. The complaints, warrants, recognizances, commitments, attachments, venires, subpœnas, and other writs and papers in said court shall be in substance in the form hitherto used in the municipal court of the city and county of Milwaukee.

In city prosecutions, said clerk, or one of his deputies, shall enter upon the record of the court a statement of the offense charged, which shall stand as the complaint, unless the court shall direct a formal complaint to be made; and the defendant's plea shall be guilty or not guilty, and shall be entered as not guilty on failure to plead, which plea of not guilty shall put all matters in such case at issue. Said clerk shall also, under the direction of the common council of said city, procure and furnish all the necessary blanks, stationery, book and paper cases, desks, record books, office furniture, lights and fuel for the use of said police court and its clerks, at the expense of said city. Such clerk and his deputies, and the police officers attending said police court and serving its processes shall receive no fees, and all costs collected in said court shall be paid into the city treasury as herein stated, and credited to the general fund, except as hereinafter provided.

SECTION 8. After issue joined and before trial in all cases **Jury, how drawn.** cognizable before said police court the accused may demand a trial by a jury of not more than twelve nor less than six men, and shall designate the number at the time of the demand. The court shall then direct the clerk to proceed to draw in the presence of the jury commissioners of Milwaukee county, from the box containing the names of persons furnished by said jury commissioners to serve as petit jurors in the municipal court of the city and county of Milwaukee, twice the number of jurors demanded, and from the list so prepared by the clerk, the parties shall then alternately strike, the accused commencing, so many names as shall leave remaining the number demanded. A venire shall thereupon be issued, commanding the officer to summon those so remaining to appear before the court at such time as may be directed, to make a jury for the trial of said action, and the court may compel their attendance by attachment. Either party may challenge any juror for cause, and deficiencies occasioned thereby, or by any other cause shall be supplied by talesmen to be selected and summoned by the officer. If no jury shall be demanded, it shall be deemed a waiver of a jury trial. If either party declines to strike from the list the names which he is entitled to strike, the court shall appoint some disinterested person to strike the same for such party. Each juror shall receive for his services the same fees allowed by law to petit jurors in courts of record in said county, and the fees of such jurors shall be taxed as costs in said action. Witnesses and jurors shall attend before said court in all city and **Witnesses and** criminal prosecutions without any payment of fees in advance or a **jurors shall attend** tender thereof, upon the processes of the court duly served, and in **without pre-pay-** default thereof their attendance may be enforced by attachment. **ment of fees.** In case the jury after being kept a reasonable time should disagree, they shall be discharged, and thereupon the court shall adjourn the cause to a day certain, and issue a new venire as aforesaid.

SECTION 9. The sheriff of Milwaukee county shall be the **Sheriff of Milwau-** officer of said police court, and shall serve its processes and carry **kee county shall** into effect its orders and judgments, and the police officers of said **be officer of** city of Milwaukee may serve its processes in city prosecutions. **police court.**

Phonographic reporter to be appointed.

SECTION 10. Said police court is hereby authorized to appoint a phonographic reporter, skilled in the art of shorthand reporting, for such police court. The person so appointed shall be deemed an officer of the court, and before entering upon the duties of his office shall take and subscribe the constitutional oath of office and file the same duly certified in the office of the city clerk of said city of Milwaukee. Such reporter so appointed shall attend all the sessions of said police court, and shall report all preliminary examinations held before said court, and report any other trial or proceeding which may be had before said court when directed by said police justice so to do. Said reporter shall receive a salary

Salary, $900 per annum.

of nine hundred dollars per annum, payable monthly, at the end of each and every month by said city of Milwaukee. It shall be the duty of said reporter, at the request of any party, to transcribe

Duties defined.

in long hand the evidence of any proceeding or trial taken by him in said police court, or any part thereof, which transcript shall be duly certified by him to be correct, and for which he shall be entitled to receive from the party requesting the same, five cents per folio, when written out in full, and when at the request of the party it shall be written in narrative form, ten cents per folio.

Shall be furnished requisite stationery.

Said reporter shall be furnished all necessary stationery. Said court may in its discretion order a transcript of the evidence or proceedings, or any part thereof to be made and certified by the reporter, and filed with the clerk of the court, and the costs thereof, not exceeding five cents per folio, shall be paid upon certificate of said police justice, from the city treasury, in city prosecutions, and from the county treasury in all other criminal actions. It shall be the duty of such reporter to transcribe, free of charge and file as soon as ready be, the charge of the court to the jury, and the evidence taken upon preliminary examinations, and in cases where the accused is committed to the Industrial school for boys.

Fines and penalties to be accounted for.

SECTION 11. All fines and penalties imposed by said police court, and the costs and fees of a trial, shall be payable to the clerk of said court, and it shall be his duty to account for and pay over to the treasurer of said city of Milwaukee on the first Mondays of January, April, July and October, all fines,

Witness fees, etc.

penalties, collections and other fees, except witnesses' fees, collected, which may have come into his hands as such clerk up to the day of such payment, and shall also account for and pay over to said city treasurer on the first Mondays of January and July in each year, all witnesses' fees which may have come to his hands as such clerk up to the day of payment, which have not been paid to the persons entitled thereto, which witnesses' fees may thereafter be paid by said treasurer to such persons upon the certificate of said clerk, specifying the name of the person entitled thereto, the amount due him, and the title of the case in which he was a witness. The foregoing provisions shall not apply, however, to witness' fees of members of the police department of the city of Milwaukee, who may testify for the prosecution. It shall be the duty of the clerk to tax witness' fees for such members, but when collected, such witness' fees shall be paid by the clerk to the treasurer of the Policemen Relief Fund Association of the city of

Milwaukee, on the first Mondays of January, April, July and October of each year.

SECTION 12. All fines and penalties collected in criminal cases and paid into the treasury of said city, shall be accounted for and paid over to the treasurer of said county annually at the time of paying over state and county taxes. The county of Milwaukee shall also at the same time pay to the city of Milwaukee, one-half of the salaries of the police justice and the phonopraphic reporter of said court, and one-half of the expenses of blanks, stationery, book and paper cases, desks, record books, office furniture, lights, and fuel, used for said court and its clerks, and the other expenses of said court which may have been paid for by said city.

Fines and penalties to be paid over to city treasurer.

SECTION 13. In all cases brought before the police court, the court may, in its discretion, grant such continuances as may be necessary to the ends of public justice either with or without bail.

Continuances.

SECTION 14. The salary of said police justice shall be two thousand five hundred dollars, per annum, payable monthly, at the end of each and every month by the city of Milwaukee. The fees of the clerk, witnesses, jurors, sheriff, and other officers and the taxable costs of suit shall be the same as now in the municipal court of said city and county of Milwaukee in similar cases. In all cases before said police court, the costs shall be paid in criminal prosecutions in the name of the state, by the county of Milwaukee, and in city prosecutions by the city of Milwaukee, when not otherwise collected, upon the certificate of the clerk of said court.

Salary $2,500 per annum.

Costs, and how paid.

SECTION 15. All persons convicted in said police court who would otherwise be sentenced or committed to imprisonment in the county jail, shall be sentenced to imprisonment in the House of Correction in Milwaukee county, and the court may order the prisoner to be kept therein at hard labor during the term of his imprisonment, if he shall have the ability to labor.

Commitments to be to House of Correction.

SECTION 16. Every person convicted before said police court may appeal from the sentence or judgment against him to the municipal court of said city and county of Milwaukee, within the time and in the manner as is now provided by law for apppeals in criminal cases from justices of the peace of the county of Milwaukee. Said municipal court is empowered to hear, try and determine such appeals and all provisions of law relating to appeals in criminal cases from justices' courts, and the trial and determination thereof shall apply to appeals from said police court to the municipal court.

Appeals, how made.

SECTION 17. On the first Monday of May, 1895, all actions, causes, pleadings, processes, and proceedings, which may be pending in the municipal court of the city and county of Milwaukee in relation to any violations of the ordinances of said city, or of the laws of this state in cases of crimes and misdemeanors not indictable arising in said city, and in relation to the examination of persons charged with the commission of an offense in said city, and not triable before a justice of the peace, shall on that day be transferred, returnable and continued to and become actions, proceedings, and examinations in said police court, and such actions, proceedings, and examinations shall, on and after that date

Date when business of court begins.

be deemed and treated as pending in said police court for all
purposes, to the same extent, and with the same effect as if said
actions, proceedings and examinations had been originally
commenced and had in said police court, but until said first
Monday of May, 1895, the jurisdiction and procedure of said
municipal court shall continue unaffected by this act.

SECTION 18. All laws, and provisions of laws contravening the
provisions of this act are hereby repealed.

CHAPTER 35, LAWS OF 1853.

SECTION 2. The city of Milwaukee, in its corporate name,
may sue for and recover any and all fines, penalties, and forfeitures
under said city charter, and the acts amendatory thereof; or under
the ordinances, by-laws, or police or health regulations made in
pursuance thereof, any general law of the state to the contrary
notwithstanding; and such action shall be commenced by
complaint substantially in the following form:

STATE OF WISCONSIN,
  Milwaukee County,   } ss.
  City of Milwaukee

being duly sworn, complains on oath to
the police justice of the city of Milwaukee, that   did,
on the   day of   18 , violate the
       section of an ordinance, by-law, or resolution (describing
it by the title,) which said   is now in force, as this
complainant verily believes, and prays that said
may be arrested, and held to answer to the said city of Milwaukee
therefor.

Subscribed and sworn to before me, this   day of   18 .

It shall be sufficient to give the number of the section or
sections, and the title of the ordinances, by-law, regulations, or
resolution, or of the law violated, in such complaint. And said
complaint may be sworn to before any officer authorized to administer oaths in the courts of this state. Upon the filing of such
complaint in the office of the police justice, he shall issue a
warrant thereon, substantially as follows:

STATE OF WISCONSIN,   }
City and County of Milwaukee

To the sheriff, or any constable
of said county, or to the marshal of the city of Milwaukee,
Greeting:

Whereas,   has this day complained to me in
writing, on oath, that   did, on the   day of
       18 , violate the section or sections of an ordinance,
by-law, regulation, or law (describing it by its title), which said
              is now in force and effect, as said complainant verily
believes; therefore, in the name of the state of Wisconsin, you
are hereby commanded to arrest the body of the said
and him forthwith bring before the police justice of the said city,
to answer to the said city of Milwaukee, on the complain
aforesaid.

Given under my hand, this   day of   18 .

_____

Police Justice.

Upon the return of the warrant, the court may proceed summarily with the case, unless it be continued by consent, or for cause. If the cause be adjourned, the defendant, if required by the court so to do, shall recognize with surety for his appearance, in such sum as the court shall direct; or, in default thereof, may be put in charge of the officer who made the arrest; or be committed to the common jail of Milwaukee county. The complaint made aforesaid shall stand in lieu of a declaration, and the plea of not guilty shall put at issue all subject matter which pertains to the defense of the action.

SECTION 5. In city prosecutions the finding of the court or jury, shall be either guilty, or not guilty. If guilty, the court shall render judgment thereon against the defendant, for the fine, penalty, or forfeiture contained in the ordinance, by-law or resolution for the violation of which the person or persons shall have been adjudged guilty, and for the costs of suit; but if not guilty, the costs shall be taxed against the city. Upon conviction and the non-payment of such judgment, the court may forthwith issue an execution, and shall determine and enter upon the docket the length of time the defendant shall be imprisoned, which, in no case, shall exceed six months, and also insert such time in the commitment or execution.

Such execution may be in the following form:

STATE OF WISCONSIN,   }
City and County of Milwaukee }

To the sheriff or any constable of the county of Milwaukee, the city marshal, and to the keeper of the common jail in said county:

Whereas, the city of Milwaukee, on the   day of   18 , recovered a judgment before the police court of said city, against   for the sum of   dollars, together with   dollars costs of suit, for the violation of, (here insert the number of section and the title of the ordinance, as set forth in the complaint). These are, therefor, in the name of the state of Wisconsin, to command you to levy distress on the goods and chattels of the said   (excepting such as the law exempts), and make sale thereof, according to law in such cases made and provided, to the amount of said sums, together with your fees, and twenty-five cents for this writ, and the same return to me in thirty days; and for want of such goods and chattels, whereon to levy, take the body of the said and him convey and deliver to the keeper of the common jail in Milwaukee county. And the said keeper is hereby commanded to receive and keep in custody, in said jail, the said for the term of   , unless said judgment, together with all costs and jail fees are sooner paid, or he be discharged by due course of law.

Given under my hand and seal this   day of   18 .
    [L. S.]   _____
                            Police Justice.

The form of commitment may be substantially the same as that of the execution, leaving out all that relates to levy and sale, and return of the writ.

Section 7. * * * And said common council may, by resolution, direct the police justice to discharge from the jail, any person confined for a judgment, unless said common council shall so direct in their resolution. Upon filing a certified copy of such resolution, attested by the clerk of the common council, the police justice shall order such defendant discharged from custody, and make an entry of such discharge upon his docket; an execution may issue or be renewed by indorsement from time to time before or after the return day thereof, and before or after the commitment of the defendant, until the judgment is satisfied or released; but after the defendant shall have been committed no execution shall be issued against the body of the defendant nor if previously issued shall authorize the taking of the body of the defendant thereon.

Section 2501, Rev. Stat. 1878 as amended by Sec. 3, Ch. 256, 1879, and Ch. 265, 1891.

The provisions of an act entitled "An Act to establish a code of procedure for the police court of the city of Milwaukee," approved March 17, 1853, so far as the same are applicable, shall apply to the municipal court, except the sixth section of said act, which is repealed.

SECTIONS 938, 939 AND 940, R. S.
LIABILITY OF CITY FOR INJURIES BY MOB.

938. Whenever any property, real or personal (except houses of ill-fame, when the owner has notice that the same are used as such), shall be destroyed or injured by, or in consequence of, any mob or riot, the city, or if not in a city, then the county in which such property is situated, shall be liable to the owner thereof for the damages so sustained by him. And in like manner, a remedy in law is hereby given against such city or county (as the case may be), for any bodily harm or injury sustained by persons, not in any way implicated in such unlawful assemblage or riot, and who have not by their own act or negligence contributed to the injury thus sustained; provided, that within six months after such destruction or injury, an action shall be commenced therefor, or the claim be presented to the proper authorities of such city or county in the manner prescribed by law.

(Secs. 1 and 5, Ch. 211, 1863, amended so as to exclude houses of ill-fame from the right to damages, inasmuch as they may be said to have invited destruction by violating law. The exception, however, does not embrace such property as the owner has no notice of the illegal use of. In New York the courts have held, under a similar statute to our present one, that the owner of such property is not debarred from recovery.)

939. No person shall be entitled to recover under the provisions of the preceding section, when such destruction or injury to his property was occasioned, or in any manner aided, sanctioned or permitted by him, or caused by his negligence, nor unless he shall have used all reasonable diligence to prevent the same, and shall have immediately notified the mayor of the city, or sheriff of the county, after being apprised of any threat or attempt to destroy or injure his property by any such mob or riot. Every mayor and sheriff receiving such notice shall take all legal means to protect the property threatened or attacked; and every such officer who shall refuse or neglect to do so shall be liable to the party aggrieved

for the damages sustained to his property by reason of such mob or riot, if such party shall elect to bring his action against such officer instead of against such city or county.

(Sec. 3, Ch. 211, 1863, verbally amended.)

940. Any city or county may settle with and pay the owner of any such property the damages so sustained; and any city or county which shall have paid any sum under the provisions of the two preceding sections, or upon such settlement, may recover the same, with all costs paid by it from any or all the persons engaged in such destruction or injury.

(Secs. 6 and 7, Ch. 211, 1863, amended to enable the municipality to recover the sum actually paid, without the necessity of proving against the wrong-doer that it was not cheated. Secs. 2 and 4 of Ch. 211 are omitted as entirely unnecessary, the law not being doubtful without them.)

SECTIONS 1339, 1339a, 1339b, 1339c.
LIABILITY OF CITY FOR INJURIES FROM DEFECTIVE HIGHWAYS.
Recovery for damages caused by defective road.

SECTION 1339. If any damage shall happen to any person, his team, carriage or other property, by reason of the insufficiency or want of repairs of any bridge, sluiceway or road in any town, city or village, the person sustaining such damage shall have a right to sue for and recover the same against any such town, city or village; but if such damage shall happen by reason of the insufficiency or want of repairs of a bridge, sluiceway or road, which any county shall have adopted as a county road, and is by law bound to keep in repair, such county shall be liable therefor, and the claim for damages shall be against the county. If such damages shall happen by reason of the insufficiency or want of repairs of a bridge erected or maintained at the expense of two or more towns, the action shall be brought against all the towns liable for the repairs of the same; and upon recovery of judgment, the damages and costs shall be paid by such towns, in the proportion in which they are liable for such repairs; and the court may, in its discretion, direct the judgment to be collected from, or issue execution against each town for its proportion only. No such action shall be maintained against any county, town, city or village, unless within ninety days after the happening of the event causing such damage, notice in writing, signed by the party, his agent or attorney, shall be given to the county clerk of the county, a supervisor of the town, one of the trustees of the village, or mayor, or city clerk of the city, against which damages are claimed, stating the place where such damage occurred, and describing generally the insufficiency or want of repair which occasioned it, and that satisfaction therefor is claimed of such county, town, city or village.

But no notice given under the provisions of this section shall be deemed invalid or insufficient, solely by reason of any inaccuracy or failure in stating the time or in describing the place and the insufficiency or want of repair; provided, it shall appear that there was no intention to mislead, and that the party entitled to notice was not in fact misled thereby.

Limitation as to recovery.

Section 1339*a*. (Ch. 454, 1885.) In any action brought against any county, town, city or village under the provisions of section 1339, of chapter 52, of the revised statutes, the amount recovered by any person for such damage or injury shall in no case exceed the sum of five thousand dollars.

Primary liability for damages—Parties.

Section 1339*b*. (Sec. 1, Ch. 471, 1889.) Whenever any injury has happened or shall happen to any person or property in any city or municipal corporation or towns by reason of any defect in any highway, street, alley or public ground, or for any other cause for which such city or municipal corporation or towns would be liable, and such defect, incumbrance or other cause of such injury shall be caused by, arise from, or be produced by the wrong, default or negligence of any person or corporation or towns, such person or corporation or towns so guilty of such wrong, default or negligence, shall be primarily liable for all damages arising from such injury; but such city or municipal corporation or towns may be sued in the same action with the one so primarily liable and be complained against as if primarily liable. If said city or municipal corporation or towns shall answer that it is not primarily liable, showing who is, and the verdict or finding shall be that it is liable, but not primarily, then the court shall enter judgment for the amount stated in the verdict or finding against all the defendants against whom the verdict shall be found or the finding shall be made; but the court shall stay execution against such city or municipal corporation or towns, until execution against those found to be primarily liable shall have been returned unsatisfied in whole or in part. When such execution shall have been so returned, then such judgment may be enforced against such city or municipal corporation or towns for whatever amount shall remain uncollected or unpaid thereon.

Amendment of Complaint.

Section 1339*c*. (Section 2, ch. 471, 1889). If any action shall be brought against any city or municipal corporation, as mentioned in the preceding section, and such city or municipal corporation shall answer that it is not primarily liable therefor, showing who is, and the person or corporation thus shown to be so primarily liable shall not have been made a party, the plaintiff may amend as provided by section 2834, of the revised statutes. And if any action shall be brought against any person or corporation, not making such city or municipal corporation a party, the plaintiff may amend in like manner by making such city or municipal corporation a party.

SECTION 4986, R. S.
RELATING TO CHARTER PROVISIONS.

In force in cities and villages.

Section 4986. All the laws contained in these revised statutes shall apply to and be in force in each and every city and village in the state so far as the same are applicable, and not inconsistent with the charter of any such city or village; but when the provisions of any such charters are at variance with the provisions of these revised statute, the provisions of such charters shall prevail, unless a different intention be plainly manifested.

INDEX.

Index to City Charter.

330   INDEX TO CITY CHARTER.

338   INDEX TO CITY CHARTER.

I

356   INDEX TO CITY CHARTER.

	Page.	Sec.	Chap.

N

Q

384   INDEX TO CITY CHARTER.

www.ingramcontent.com/pod-product-compliance
Lightning Source LLC
Chambersburg PA
CBHW030859270326
41929CB00008B/487